MW00358913

Psalms by the Day

This book is an absolute treasure – a life-time of godly scholarship, faithful preaching and pastoral wisdom all in one volume! Alec Motyer's fresh translation of each of the Psalms, the insightful notes, and the crisp, thought-provoking summary applications make these daily readings a wonderful way to engage freshly with these rich Biblical songs!

JONATHAN LAMB
CEO and minister-at-large, Keswick Ministries.
Vice President of IFES,
Former Director, Langham Preaching

This book is the dream combination: the Psalms presented as a daily devotional by the great Christian scholar, Alec Motyer. Learned, orthodox, practical and shot through with a love for the LORD and a desire to see his people grow closer to him, this volume is a true treasure. All Christians need to be immersed in the Psalms as here we find the Christian life laid out in all of its emotional dimensions. yet too often we struggle to see Christ therein. Everyone who picks up this book will find that they not only learn to read and understand the Psalms as Christian scripture, they may also find their prayer life changed in a profound and dramatic way.

CARL R. TRUEMAN
Paul Woolley Professor of Historical Theology and Church History,
Westminster Theological Seminary, Philadelphia, Pennsylvania

Psalms by the Day

A New Devotional Translation

Alec Motyer

CHRISTIAN
FOCUS

To
Timothy Dudley-Smith
Hymn-writer, Bishop, Cherished Friend
with affection and respect

Copyright © J. A. Motyer 2016

Hardback ISBN: 978-1-78191-716-9
epub ISBN: 978-1-78191-739-8
mobi ISBN: 978-1-78191-740-4

First published in 2016 and reprinted in 2017
by
Christian Focus Publications Ltd,
Geanies House, Fearn, Ross-shire
IV20 1TW, Scotland

www.christianfocus.com

The translation of the Psalms is © 2016 by the author, J. A. Motyer.
Unless otherwise stated, Scripture translations are the author's.

A CIP catalogue record for this book is available from the British Library.

Cover design by Paul Lewis

Printed and bound by Bookwell Digital, Finland

CONTENTS

Foreword

One of the first – and still perhaps the best – summaries of the Bible in just a few messages that I have heard was given by Alec Motyer about twenty-five years ago. I was a student, speaking to students at the same conference. But when I saw Motyer was speaking on this topic, I could not resist attending all his lectures. And the view of God's Word he gave me has been a lasting gift ever since.

In your hand you have three gifts. First, one of our finest scholars has used his knowledge and long experience as a linguist and a Christian to give us a fresh translation of all 150 Psalms. This in and of itself is a gift of no small value. The translation is fresh in a number of ways – the use of Yah and Yahweh, the word choice, even some modern idioms. But these translations have not been done – as they so often are – by those who are heavy in thinking of communications and light in understanding the text. Alec Motyer has tutored generations of pastors – me among them – in our understanding of God's Word. His Christ-centered reading of the Old Testament gives a fullness and a resonance to his reading of the Psalms which seems like the way our Lord taught us to read the Psalms. And the reading is reflected even in the translation itself. If you want to know more about the way he has approached translating the Psalms, take a moment and read the introduction. Embedded within the translation, you'll also find outlines which are suggestive for Bible study leaders and preachers in communicating the information.

Another gift that Dr Motyer has given us is in the notes. And let me be clear – in preparing to write this foreword – I read every word in the book, and the notes are themselves of great help to the Christian who would understand and appreciate the Psalms. Clear statements that would seem like hyperbole from others come with simple weight from Motyer's pen. For example, 'Psalm 51 is the Old Testament's central text on repentance.' In his notes he educates the reader on what was and was not done in Hebrew poetry. What causes some commentators to stumble in Psalm 105, he presents as an intentional emphasis by the author on our obedience. The 'Pause for Thought' about Hezekiah's tunnel on Psalms 123–125 is piercing! Plenty more perspective-giving notes await the reader.

In some of them, apparent problems are solved. In others, I've been shown better ways to conceive what the Psalmist is saying, sometimes suggesting new avenues for understanding the whole Psalm, and often making Christ clearer in the Psalm. Again and again he reads the

Psalms sensitively and persuasively as being centered on Jesus Christ. All together, even in the notes we have a rare combination of textual, grammatical knowledge of the Psalms with wide knowledge of the whole sweep of Scripture – Old and New, together with systematic theology, Christian experience, all with the warmth of a brother in Christ who knows himself to be more student than teacher, to have received more than he could ever give.

The 'Pause for Thoughts' devotions are a final gift that our author leaves us with. They act as a commentary for the reader who feels intimidated by the specific notes in the margins of the text. They summarize the main contribution the preceding Psalms make. And yet they are more than summary. They help to give us perspective on the significance or importance of what we've read, often in such a way that at least I have wanted to go back and re-read the preceding Psalm. Look at his thoughts on Psalm 37 for an example of this. Or those about hope in Psalms 61–63. Reflecting on Psalm 69, Motyer writes 'Our only escape from the Son of Man, our Judge, is to flee to the Son of Man, our Saviour.' His summary of the Psalms' teaching on the messianic king in his 'Pause for Thought' after Psalm 72 is a tiny, splendid, encouraging *tour-de-force*! Pithy and learned expressions abound. 'To abandon prayer is to embrace atheism' (p. 248).

In these concluding 'Pauses', Motyer's long Christian experience, his knowledge of the New Testament, as well as the Old, act together with the Psalm being considered to serve us. These thoughts are expository without being dry, devotional without being forced. His thoughts flow from an intelligent and careful reading of the Psalms immediately before him. And as we get to look over his shoulder, we learn to read the Psalms better for ourselves, and for those we may be called to teach.

Throughout this work, Motyer's writing gives us a delicious combination – richly full, concisely put. For generations now, Alec Motyer has been one of the best at combining the smallest of details with the grand sweep of the biblical narrative, and in ways which are not wrongly original or novel, but which are faithful and obvious in the text once we've noticed them. Here a master of systematic and biblical theology shows us the artificial nature of that very distinction. And he does it while taking us through the church's hymn-book, the Psalms, and all in seventy-three days! Read and profit.

MARK DEVER
Senior Pastor, Capitol Hill Baptist Church
and President, 9Marks.org,
Washington, DC

Introduction

Between You and Me: A Word of Explanation

The aim of this book is not to try to tell you what the Psalms mean, but to try to offer you a few helps towards discovering for yourself what they mean. Please use all the bits and bobs in this book to that end. I suppose the great stories in the Old Testament loomed largest in our Sunday School days (at least if you are of my age-group), but over the centuries – and I mean centuries – it is the psalms which have spoken loudest to the Christian church. Even in comparatively recent times they contributed hugely to our Sunday worship, much, much more than they are allowed to do today. But you and I can at least bring the Psalms and all their treasures back into our personal lives. Please, by means of this book, let me play a small part in your repossession of such wonderful richness.

1. The translation. It is on the whole not very helpful to play around with words like 'literal' and 'paraphrase'. What I have set out to do in offering my own translation of Psalms is to bring you as near as I can to the Hebrew of the original. Very often this extends to following the word order of the Hebrew – even where it is awkward in English – because word-order reflects emphasis.

2. Short lines. In part, the short lines in which the translation is set out match the way Hebrew poetry works, but I have used a short line presentation for a different reason – to try to encourage slower reading – in the hope of helping you to stop over individual thoughts, and to give them due weight!

3. I am dreadfully afraid in case my enthusiasm for analysis may prove a nuisance and hindrance to you. I was bitten by this delightful bug at a very early age, and, to me, analysis is the surest way into fruitful Bible study. But if you should find it a burden, just get on with reading. Hopefully, my occasional notes will open a door now and again for you.

4. If you find any day's allocation more than is manageable, why not spread it over two or more days?

5. Hebrew is an 'and' language. It does not on the whole go in for subordinate clauses, preferring to add a new clause introduced by the conjunction. This means that, in effect, the conjunction has a wide variety of significance. But I have tended simply to use 'and', leaving it to the reader's good sense (which is what the Hebrew is doing anyway!) to decide whether it means 'but' – or whatever.

6. Nouns and adjectives. Even where Hebrew has an adjective available ('holy' is a case in point) it often prefers to express the adjectival idea by means of the related noun – 'a mountain of holiness' instead of 'a holy mountain'. Since I am sure that this is a more emphatic way of expressing the same idea – and has been deliberately used in its context – I have preserved the genitive use of the noun rather than allowing it so relapse into being an adjective.

7. The divine Name 'Yahweh' will at first sound strange in your ears, being used to the established (but mistaken) English convention of representing the name as 'the Lord'. We who are of an older generation will remember the days when calling someone by their Christian name was a privilege granted, not to be presumed upon. It meant something to us when a senior friend said, 'Please call me by my Christian name'; the relationship had ripened into a new intimacy and privilege. So it was in Genesis 4:26 when people began to call their God by his personal name; so it was, even more, when the significance of that Name was revealed to Moses (Exod. 3:15). A totally false sense of reverence later said 'The Name is too holy for us to use,' and the custom was introduced of representing it as 'the Lord'. No, no. He has granted us the privilege, and we should learn (belatedly) to live in the benefit of it. Hebrew has two main nouns for 'God'. There is the plural *elohim,* God in the fullness of the divine attributes – for simplicity I translate this as 'God' – and the singular *el,* which I translate as 'transcendent God'. But there is only one 'Name'. 'God' is *what* he is; Yahweh is *who* he is.

I truly hope you will enjoy my book; I know you will enjoy the Psalms.

Day 1 Read Psalms 1–2

Psalm 1.
The Great Decision and its Fruits

A.1. Earthly distinctiveness: divine favour

1. Blessed[1] is the man
   who has determined[2] not to walk
   according to[3] the advice of wicked people,
   nor, according to the way of sinners,[4]
   to take his stand,
   nor in the seat of cynics[5] to sit.

B.1. Continuance: delight in God's law

2. To the contrary,[6]
   in Yahweh's teaching[7] is his pleasure,[8]
   and in his teaching he meditates by day and night.

C.1. Security: the flourishing tree

3. Consequently,
   he is like a tree,
   transplanted[9] beside channels of water,
   which yields its fruit in its season,
   and its leaf does not wither –
   and whatever he does, he prospers.[10]

C.2. Insecurity: the wind-blown chaff

4. Not so the wicked ones!
   To the contrary[11] –
   like chaff which the wind drives about!

1 Hebrew *ashrey* has three possible renderings according to context: 'under God's blessing' (as here); 'happy' in what one is doing or how one is placed (e.g. 1 Kings 10:8), 'doing what is morally justified/right, what is deserved' (e.g. Psalm 137: 8, 9).

2 The three verbs 'walk … stand … sit' are perfect tense, here perfects of fixed attitude or decision, expressing three aspects of life (e.g. Deuteronomy 6:17) – 'walk' is habitual 'life-style'; 'stand', to 'stand up and be counted'/ 'take a stand for'; 'sit', to be associated with such and such a company.

3 'According to' is, lit. 'in'; here 'in terms of'.

4 Both 'wicked' and 'sinner' are broad, general words. If we are to be more specific, 'wicked' possibly comes from a verb meaning 'to be loose' or 'lax'; 'sinners' means those who 'miss the target'. Compare the verb in its 'secular' use, Judges 20:16.

5 *letsiym*, those who have settled into a dismissive attitude of scoffing or 'rubbishing' all that is spiritual or 'serious'.

6 A very strong expression of an alternative: 'But indeed'.

7 'Teaching', *torah*, usually translated 'law'. 'Teaching' may be expressed as legislation, but its primary force is always 'instruction', as, e.g. Proverbs 4:1, what a careful father imparts to loved children.

8 Note the emphasis – not on outward obedience (as v. 1) – but on inward realities: 'pleasure', the delight of the will; 'meditates', directing and feeding the mind. Compare Joshua 1:8. Godliness starts on the inside.

B.2. No continuance: divine judgment

5.   Therefore, the wicked ones will not rise up[12] in the judgment,
     nor sinners in the assembly of the righteous[13] ones,

A.2. Eternal distinction and its explanation

6.   because Yahweh knows[14] the way[15] of righteous ones,
     and the way of the wicked ones will perish.[16]

Psalm 2.
The Anointed King of Kings

A.1. Kings opposing

1.   Why are the nations in turmoil,[17]
     and states[18] keep pondering empty schemes?
2.   The kings of the earth take up their stations,
     and the potentates[19] sit in conclave
     against Yahweh and against his anointed one:
3.   'Let us tear apart their restraints,
     and throw off from us their bondage.'

B.1. The LORD speaks

4.   He who sits enthroned[20] in heaven[21] laughs![22]
     The Sovereign One[23] mocks them!
5.   Then[24] he will speak to them in his exasperation,[25]
     and in his rage he will terrify them:
6.   'For my part,[26]
     I have installed my king
     On Zion, the hill of my holiness.'[27]

B.2. The Son speaks

7.   'I want to recount[28] Yahweh's statute.[29]
     He said to me:

9   Verb *shathal*, to transplant. Psalm 92:13–14 illustrates the meaning here: not the tree's natural position, not where it once was, but in a new place, chosen for fruitfulness; in Ps. 92, the position we have by grace.

10   Expressing a position of faith. It is, and always will be, well with the righteous (those right with God), e.g. Isaiah 3:10.

11   As in v. 2.

12   The verb 'to rise up' is used in the sense 'to have standing in law/ to maintain one's position when brought to trial'.

13   'Righteous', i.e. right with God, so also v. 6.

14   'To know' often has the meaning (as here) 'to be intimately aware of/ to maintain a caring relationship with'. Compare Exodus 2:25. The emphasis in the Hebrew would justify a rendering 'How well Yahweh knows!'

15   On 'way' see v. 1.

16   i.e. their characteristic habits of life will lead to perishing. Note how this psalm's first word is 'blessed' and its last word is 'perish' – the choice (and the warning) with which the Psalms begin.

17   Perfect and Imperfect tenses alternate: 'in turmoil' and 'sit' are perfect, giving the sense of fixed determination; 'pondering' and 'take up' are imperfects, expressing repeated actions, customary behaviour.

18   *le'umiym*, usually translated 'peoples'. The root verb is not used in the Bible, but cognate languages suggest 'to bring together/ make common cause'. 'States' is a reasonable rendering, in order to give the word a distinctive meaning.

"You are my son;[30]
I have myself begotten you today.

8. Ask from me,
and I will surely give nations as your inheritance,
and, as your holding, the very limits of the earth.

9. You will shepherd[31] them with an iron sceptre;
like a potter's vessel you will shatter them.'"

A.2. Kings submitting

10. Now then, kings, act prudently.
Accept correction, judges[32] of the earth.

11. Serve Yahweh with fear,
and exult with trembling.[33]

12. Kiss the son, lest he be exasperated,[34]
and you perish for[35] your way
when his anger burns even a little.
Blessed[36] are all who seek refuge in him!

19 *rozenim*, compare Judges 5:3; Isaiah 40:23. The verb is said to mean 'to be weighty, judicious'. The Scots/N. Irish coinage 'high-heid-yins' ('high-head-ones'), with its suggestion of position and pomposity, catches the thought exactly.

20 The verb 'to sit' frequently has the contextual meaning, as here, 'to sit enthroned'; e.g. Psalm 123:1 (NKJV 'to dwell').

21 'He who sits' and 'the Sovereign' are given the emphatic position in their sentences, thus underlining the reigning reality and power of Yahweh.

22 'Laughs' and 'mocks' are imperfects, either expressing 'goes on laughing' or, as a tense of emphasis, 'just laughs'. Hence the exclamation marks.

23 *Adonai*, which means 'lord' or 'master', always of Yahweh in his sovereignty.

24 The temporal 'then', at that point in time; when his laughter has run its course, and the time of forbearance is over.

25 *hebanas,* part of a wide vocabulary for 'anger'. Here *'aph*, a word also meaning 'nose' is the snort of anger.

26 Emphatic subject, 'I'.

27 Or 'my holy hill'. Hebrew can express an adjective by using the attached noun, but where an adjective exists, as in this case, 'holy', the noun-formation must surely be a technique of emphasis: the hill where my holiness is present and is its most significant feature.

28 The verb is cohortative in form, expressing (here) strong personal determination.

29 'Statute', from the verb 'to engrave'; something carved in the rock for permanency.

30 Compare 2 Samuel 7:14, the promise to the Davidic king. Psalm 2 may have been a 'coronation psalm', with this assertion of sonship (in an adoption sense) at its heart. It is, of course, literally true of Jesus: Acts 13:33; Hebrews 1:5; 5:5; compare John 1:18; and elsewhere.

31 The verb 'to shepherd' deprives the picture of an 'iron sceptre' of any thought of oppression or cruelty. Rather it implies firmness and strength. To his enemies, of course, it is different (compare Mark 1:24): the twinned images of 'iron sceptre' and 'shattered pot' contrast absolute power with total helplessness.

32 Not to be restricted to those who conduct courts of law. Nor, throughout the Old Testament, is 'judgment' to be equated with 'passing judgment/condemning'. e.g. Psalm 98:7–9 can depict the earth rejoicing when Yahweh comes to 'judge', because he comes to 'make authoritative decisions' which will 'put things to rights'. 'Judges', here, are the world's decision-makers.

Pause for Thought

Have you noticed that Psalm 2 ends where Psalm 1 begins, with blessing pronounced on the individual described in 1:1, and on all those described in 2:12? This has the effect of bracketing the two psalms together. They appear very different but, guided by this bracketing, we find them complementary. Psalm 1:1 describes the blessed way of life. This individual lives by distinctive directives ('advice'), distinctive principles ('takes his stand') and distinctive settled convictions ('sit'). Psalm 2:12 focuses on a special relationship, in this case with the anointed One, the Lord's Son: personal devotion ('kiss', compare, 1 Kings 19:18), and trustful reliance ('seek refuge'). Secondly, each psalm speaks in its own way of what Psalm 1:3 calls the transplanted life. Neither the individual of Psalm 1 nor the 'all' of Psalm 2:12 are where they once were; there has been a great change, the acquisition of a new position. In Psalm 1, new life comes from life-giving waters; in Psalm 2, an erstwhile 'king' has submitted to the Lord's King who reigns on Zion. Psalm 87 describes this as acquiring new citizenship (compare Philippians 3:20), and therefore new possibilities, resources and privileges. Thirdly, in each case, the newness of position and life has come about through heeding the Word of God. The Lord's Word came to the 'kings of the earth' (2:2) that their rebellion was hopeless because his King was already in office on Zion (2:6) – a word confirmed by the testimony of the Son that, by the Father's decree, it was his right to possess and rule the earth to its uttermost boundaries (2:8–9). In Psalm 1:2–3 the waters that refresh and renew the transplanted tree are consequent on delighting in and pondering the Lord's teaching. The heart of Psalm 2 is fulfilled in the reign of Jesus, the Lord's King, in the present (Heb. 12:22–24) and the eternal Zion (Rev. 22:10, 22–27; 22:1); the heart of Psalm 1 is fulfilled in the Lord's provision of the completed, inspired Scripture (2 Tim. 3:10–17); the heart of the spiritual life, Psalms teaches, lies in our devotion (2:12a) and constant resorting (2:12b) to the Lord Jesus, and in our assiduous attention to the Word of God (1:2).

---

33 'Fear ... trembling': the joy of salvation is ever aware of personal lack of merit, the greatness of divine mercy and the unabated holiness of God. Ponder 'it may be' (NIV, 'perhaps') in Zephaniah 2:3; compare Exodus 20:20.

34 See above v. 5.

35 The Hebrew has no preposition governing 'way'. It could be 'on your way': as you go blithely on (compare Matthew 5:25). 'For your way' means 'in retribution for your unchanged life-style'.

36 See Psalm 1:1.

Day 2   Read Psalms 3–7

Psalm 3.
Facing a New Day

A song[1] of David's when he fled from his son, Absalom.[2]

A.1. Problem

1. Yahweh, how[3] many my adversaries are!
   How many, those who are rising against me!
2. How many are saying to my soul,[4]
   'There is no salvation for him in God!' (*Selah*)[5]

B.1. Affirmation

3. And you,[6] Yahweh, are a shield around me,
   my glory,[7]
   and the One who lifts up my head!

C. Assurance

4. With my voice[8] to Yahweh I kept crying,
   and he did answer me,
   from Zion, the hill of his holiness.[9] (*Selah*)
5. As for me,
   I[10] lay down and slept;[11]
   I woke up,
   for it is Yahweh who keeps supporting me.[12]
6. I am not afraid of myriads of people
   who, all around, have taken their stand against me.

B.2. Prayer

7. Rise, Yahweh![13]
   Save me, my God!

1   *mizmor*, from the verb *zamar*, 'to make music', hence 'a musical composition', a 'song'. In flight for his life David still has a song in his heart! The psalm instructs us how to meet the troubled day. These 'titles' have, to our knowledge, always been an integral part of the text of the psalms, counting as verse 1 when verses were numbered. They should be treated as serious introductions to their psalms.

2   See 2 Samuel 15–17.

3   The exclamatory 'how' occurs only once but, in the manner of Hebrew verse, 'governs' the next two lines as well. The enmity is real and strong (line 1), active (line 2), triumphalist and confident (line 3).

4   'Soul', *nephesh*, is here an emphatic way of expressing 'me', the essential person, the person considered at the centre of his being and distinctiveness.

5   Found over seventy times in Psalms, but without clear meaning today. It seems to have been a direction how the psalm was to be used in worship.

6   Emphatic 'you', a deliberate turning to Yahweh, and concentration on him in the face of the enemy, step one in dealing with the troubled day.

7   David has at this moment lost all earthly 'glory' (compare 2 Samuel 15:30). His real glory remains: the surrounding presence of Yahweh.

8   'With my voice' describes spelling out our prayer in our own words, coming personally to Yahweh and telling him the whole tale as we know it.

A.2. Solution

For you will surely strike all my enemies on the cheek;
the teeth of the wicked you will surely break![14]

8. To Yahweh belongs salvation!
Upon your people[15] your blessing! (*Selah*)

Psalm 4.
Facing Another Night[16]

Belonging to the worship-leader[17]; set for strings;[18]
a song[19] of David's.

A.1. Assurance in praying to God

1. When I call out, answer me,
God of my righteousness.[20]
In adversity, you will surely have compassion[21] on me.
Grant me your grace,[22] and hear my prayer.

B.1. Detractors, undermining self-confidence

2. Sons of man,
how long is my glory to become ignominy?
How long will you love worthlessness,
seek[23] after deception? (*Selah*)

C. The sevenfold spirituality[24]

3. Know, then, that Yahweh has separated off for himself
the beloved one
(Yahweh will hear when I call out to him!).

4. Be agitated,
and stop sinning.
Speak in your heart in your bed,

9 See 2:6. Absalom has seized Mt Zion, but Yahweh has not abdicated from the 'real' Zion.

10 Emphatic 'I'. Imagine me, placed as I am, getting a good night's sleep!

11 Cohortative, here used as a form of emphasis: 'and how well I slept!'

12 The Lord my pillow! Note the emphasis on 'Yahweh'.

13 Compare Numbers 10:35. Is David seeing his tiny, fleeing company as the onward marching people of God – therefore able to repeat this ancient marching cry?

14 Perfects of future certainty. 'Strike the cheek' signifies rebuke; 'break the teeth' signifies disarming, rendering harmless (as in our expressing 'a toothless tiger').

15 Those rallying to David; all for whom he feels royal responsibility. His prayer runs beyond personal concern.

16 Another Psalm, probably, during the flight from Absalom. David is facing a second night under the stars! Allowing Absalom's forces another twenty-four hours to pursue and attack; therefore increased threat!

17 Lit. 'To the eminent one'. Applied to fifty-four psalms. Translated 'overseers' in 2 Chronicles 34:13. 1 Chronicles 6:31 records that David appointed worship-leaders. Presumably, at some stage before the psalms were brought into the present full collection, some 'worship-leader' assembled, from various sources, an earlier collection under his auspices.

18 *neginoth*, from the verb *nagan*, to strike, usually conjectured as striking a stringed instrument.

19 See Psalm 3 (heading).

and be silent.[25] (*Selah*)

5.   Sacrifice sacrifices of righteousness,
     and put your trust in Yahweh.

B.2 Detractors spreading despondency

6.   Many are saying:
     Who will let us see good?
     (Lift up on us the light of your face, Yahweh!)[26]

A.2. Peace through resting in Yahweh

7.   You have granted peace in my heart,
     more than the season their corn and new wine
     multiplied.[27]

8.   In peace
     I will lie down and sleep[28] at once.
     For it is only you, Yahweh,
     who makes me live in safety.

Psalm 5.
Starting a New Day:[29]
Prayer and Righteousness

Belonging to the worship-leader;[30] set for *nechiloth*;[31] a song of David's.

A.1. Looking to God: beginning with prayer

1.   My words[32] – give them a hearing, Yahweh.
     Discern[33] my meditation.

2.   Pay attention to the voice of my cry for help,
     my King and my God,
     for it is to you I keep praying.

3.   Yahweh, in the morning you will hear my voice;
     in the morning[34] I will set it out[35] to you,

20   i.e. 'my righteous God', the God who will never deviate from what is right; from his righteous principles and promises.

21   'Compassion'. The verb (*racham*) gives rise to the noun 'womb'. 'Compassion' is the tenderness of love, its emotional intensity; compare 1 Kings 3:26. The love of 'being in love'.

22   As ever in the Bible, from its first occurrence in Genesis 6:8, 'grace' is the sheer unmerited, undeserved goodness of God.

23   As often, with the sense 'devote your life and energies to' (as in following the 'no hoper' Absalom).

24   To whom are these verses addressed? In principle, to David's enemies, calling them to reformation; but, secondly, to David's own followers, instructing them how to act and react in their troubles and dangers; thirdly to us – in what spirit are we to face life's hazards? Seven commands. Grasp the truth that Yahweh looks after his own (verse 3); you can't help being afraid (4a), but don't let it become a sin (4b); enjoy regular private times (4c) and be quiet/silent before God (4d); make use of God's means of grace in the sprit in which they were intended to be used (5a); and always maintain an attitude of complete trust (5b).

25   Or 'keep quiet'. The notion of stopping talking is a good contrast with the detractors of verses 2 and 6.

26   For the second time (see verse 3), an 'arrow' prayer, compare Nehemiah 2:4.

27   i.e. more than any purely earthly, secular joy.

28   Acts 12:6.

and I will keep on the lookout.[36]

B.1. The fate of the wicked

4. For you are not a transcendent God[37] who takes pleasure
    in wickedness;
    an evil person will not be your guest;[38]
5. the arrogant[39] will not take their stand in front of your
    eyes;
    you hate all trouble-makers;[40]
6. you will destroy those who speak falsehood;
    the bloodthirsty[41] and deceitful man you abominate,
    Yahweh.

C. The balanced religious life

(a) With God

7. For my part,[42]
    in the abundance of your committed love[43]
    I will come into our house;[44]
    I will bow in worship towards the temple of your holiness
    in fear of you.

(b) Before the world

8. Yahweh,
    lead me in your righteousness
    on account of my foes;[45]
    make straight, before me, your way.

B.2. The fate of the rebellious

9. Because, in their mouth, there is no reliability;
    at centre they spell total ruin;[46]
    their throat[47] is an opened grave;

29 Psalm 5 offers no indication of time or place but it makes sense if it is viewed as belonging to the flight from Absalom: David facing another day of flight and danger.

30 See Psalm 4, heading

31 Unknown meaning: some say from *chalal*, to bore (holes), hence 'flutes', compare 1 Samuel 10:5.

32 It is very awkward to put 'my words' first like this, but it is what the Hebrew does. David thus stresses the importance of actually talking to God.

33 i.e. get right to the heart of what I am feeling and saying. Just as 'my words' stresses the importance of prayer, 'discern' requests closeness of hearing.

34 The repetition 'morning … morning' does not just mean 'every morning' (though that would be true), but emphasises the time: starting the day, first thing.

35 Verb *arak*, 'to set something out in proper order: sacrifice (Genesis 22:9), line of battle (1 Samuel 17:8), an ordered account (Isaiah 44:7)'.

36 Habakkuk 2:1. Watching for the answer from Yahweh.

37 The most commonly used noun for 'God' is the plural *elohim*, God in the fullness of divine attributes; here we have the singular noun *el*, God in his transcendent deity.

38 Verb *gur*: to be a resident alien, to take up temporary residence/seek asylum, to be an overnight guest.

39 *holelim*, boastful, in both senses of 'boast' – arrogant and hollow, senseless, unthinking, wild; without thought for safety (2 Kings 9:20).

with their tongue they implement what is slippery.
10. Declare them guilty,[48] O God!
    May they fall as a result of their plans![49]
    For[50] the abundance of their rebellions banish them,
    because they have revolted against you.

A.2. Receiving from God: joy, favour, protection

11. And[51] may all those who take refuge in you rejoice;
    for ever let them shout aloud,[52]
    and may you screen them,
    and may they exult in you,
    those who love your name!
12. Because you will yourself bless the righteous one,[53]
    Yahweh;
    like a body-shield,[54] with favour, you will encircle[55] him.

Psalm 6.
Deep Danger, Great Deliverance

Belonging to the worship-leader; set for strings; for the Eighth; a song of David's.[56]

A.1. The terrified soul[57]

1. Yahweh, let it not be in your exasperation[58] that you reprove me,
   and let it not be in your rage that you discipline me.
2. Grant me your grace, Yahweh,
   because I am withering away.
   Heal me, Yahweh,
   because my bones[59] are terrified,
3. and my soul itself is exceedingly terrified.
   And you, Yahweh – how long?[60]

40 *awen*, 'trouble/sorrow' (Genesis 35:18; Proverbs 22:8); idolatry (1 Samuel 15:23; Hosea 12:11); wickedness, general wrong in someone's life (Isaiah 1:13).

41 Lit. 'man of bloods', hence 'bloodthirsty' or blood-guilty. Basically someone with no respect for life. 'Deceitful', no respect for truth.

42 Emphatic pronoun, underlining personal resolve and commitment.

43 *chesedh*, used of the committed love the LORD has for his people. 'Compassion' (note 10 above) is emotional love; *chesedh*, ever-unchanging/committed love, is the love which says 'I will', love as a determination and commitment. 'Compassion' is heart love, being 'in love'; *chesedh* is the commitment of true love, a declaration of the will.

44 'House' and 'temple' do not require us to date this psalm after Solomon's building programme. Compare 1 Samuel 1:9, 24; 3:3, where the Tent at Shiloh is called the Lord's 'house' and 'temple'.

45 *shorer*, from an unknown verbal root with a possible meaning, 'to fix the eyes on', particularly, with hostility (Psalms 27:11; 54:5; 56:2; 59:10). The sense here is, 'keep me in the way of righteousness because I am always being watched'. The hostile watchers are described in verses 9–10.

46 Lit. 'their inside is total ruin', a typical Hebrew apposition – one thing totally identified with another. 'Inwardly, they are bad news.'

47 i.e. they 'devour' other people for their own satisfaction: insatiable, ruthless self-aggrandisement.

B.1. The first desire: the returning Yahweh

4. Oh do return, Yahweh!
   Oh do set my soul free!
   Save me, because of your committed love.[61]
5. For in death[62] there is no remembrance of you;
   in Sheol[63] who gives you thanks?

C. Sorrow upon sorrow

6. I am weary through my groaning;
   all night I flood[64] my bed –
   my couch with my tears I dissolve.[65]
7. Through vexation my eyesight fails[66] –
   grows old through all my adversaries.

B.2. The second desire: departing foes

8. Get away from me,
   all you trouble-makers,[67]
   because Yahweh has heard the voice[68] of my weeping.
9. Yahweh has heard my plea for grace.
   Yahweh himself accepts[69] my prayer.[70]

A.2. The terrified enemies

10. All my enemies
    will reap shame[71] and be terrified,
    turn back, reap shame – suddenly!

Psalm 7.
A Conscience Without Offence
(Acts 24:16)

A *shiggayon* of David which he sang to Yahweh because of the words of Cush, a Benjamite.[72]

48 The verb for the 'guilt offering' (Leviticus 5–6), the offering which required restitution manward as well as atonement Godward, i.e. dealing with every aspect of sin. So, here, 'let no aspect of their guiltiness go unnoticed and unpunished'.

49 Verse 10b calls for moral retribution, what their plans deserve; verse 11b looks for divine reaction to the offense caused to God.

50 i.e. 'In payment for'.

51 The Hebrew conjunction is versatile enough to cater for whatever connection the context suggests. If the intention is a contrast with verses 9–10, then 'But'. I have preferred to see verses 11–12 as continuing the descripton of divine, moral government.

52 This is what the verb means: 'to give a ringing cry'. Contextually, here, 'to shout aloud with joy'.

53 As regularly, 'the one who is "right with God"'.

54 The largest of shields, covering the whole body: 1 Samuel 17:7, 41; Psalm 91:4.

55 So, usually, but, possibly, 'you will crown him' – put a 'circlet' on him.

56 See heading of Psalm 5. *sheminith* is, lit. 'an 'eighth', and may be a musical direction whose significance has been lost. Some prefer 'an eight stringed (harp)'. The most interesting suggestion (Thirtle and Bullinger, *For the Chief Musician*, London, 1908, p.72), arising from a study of 1 Chronicles 15:21, is that it refers to the eighth company, leading the Ark, in David's carefully organized procession: therefore a Levitical choir which came to be called 'The Eighth'. The preposition 'for' (*al*) could mean, 'the responsibility of…'.

A.1. Prayer

1. Yahweh, my God
   in you I have taken refuge.
   Save me from all those pursuing me,
   and deliver me,
2. in case, like a lion, they savage me,
   tearing apart, and there is none to deliver.

B.1. Sin and penalty

3. Yahweh, my God,
   if I have done this,[73]
   if there is deviancy in my hand;
4. if I have paid back,
   to one at peace with me, evil,
   and despoiled those hostile to me without cause –
5. may an enemy pursue my soul,
   and overtake me,
   and may he trample to the ground my life,
   and in the dust make my glory dwell. (*Selah*)

C.1. The God of judgment

6. Rise, Yahweh, in your exasperation;[74]
   lift yourself up against the outbursts[75] of those hostile to
   me,
   and wake up on my behalf:
   it is judgment you have commanded.
7. The assembly of the states will surround you:
   over it,[76] on high, do return –
8. Yahweh will himself sit in judgment on the peoples.

C.2. Standing before the righteous God

Pass judgment on me, Yahweh,
in accord with my righteousness,[77]
and in accord with my integrity let it come upon me.

57 If we allocate this psalm also to the
time of David's flight from Absalom,
we see what a draining experience it
was for the king: with the unbidden
thought, had the LORD rejected him in
anger (verses 1–3), and the burden of
relentless enmity (verses 8–10)?

58 It is a natural logic to move from
experiencing deep trouble and shock
to the thought of an offended God.
In 2 Samuel (11 onwards) we see how
David's involvement with Bathsheba
and implication in the death of Uriah
inhibited him from dealing with
Amnon's rape of Tamar, and Absalom's
murder of Amnon, and ultimately
made it easy for the volatile (and
'spoiled') Absalom to rebel. David's
experience of terror had more than a
meager ground in his own sins and
errors. Well might he have entertained
the thought of divine wrath!

59 The 'bones' stand for the physical
'frame' in its stability and resilience.
The stress and pressure of David's
situation is such that he feels even his
body cannot take any more. 'Soul'
brings us into the realm of feeling:
David's mind and emotions, his life
itself, are all under dire threat.

60 Only divine intervention will save him,
but will it come in time?

61 See note 43 above.

62 This statement about death must be
kept in context: (a) David feels that
he cannot stand continuance of his
present trouble. Life itself is at risk. (b)
But should he die now, it will be death
under the wrath of God, and such
a death spells hopelessness: eternity
without divine fellowship.

63 In the Old Testament the name of
the 'place' where the dead live on. See
further Psalms 49:13–15; 73:23–24.

9. Please, let the evil of the wicked ones come to an end,
    and establish the righteous one.
    There is one who really does test minds and feelings[78] –
    a[79] righteous God!

C.3. The God of judgment

10. My shield is upon[80] God,
    the saviour of the upright in heart.
11. God[81] is a righteous judge:
    a transcendent God indignant every day.
12. If one does not turn back,[82]
    he will sharpen that sword of his;
    his bow[83] he is sure to[84] bend and make it ready.
13. And for his use he is sure to prepare instruments of death;
    his arrows he will make into incendiaries.

B.2. Sin and penalty[85]

14. Behold!
    He travails with mischief,
    and conceives trouble,
    and gives birth to a lie.
15. He sunk a pit and dug it out;
    and he has fallen into the chasm he made!
16. His trouble will come back on his head,
    and on his skull his violence will come down.

A.2. Praise

18. I will give thanks to Yahweh
    in accord with his righteousness,
    and I will indeed make music
    to the name of Yahweh, the Most High.[86]

64 *sachach*, simple active, Isaiah 25:11, to swim; here, *hiphil*, 'to cause to swim'; to flood, saturate.

65 *masah*, Joshua 14:8; Psalms 39:11; 147:18.

66 *ashash*, 31:9,10.

67 See Psalm 5, note 40 above.

68 'Voice' is often used (as here) meaning 'sound'.

69 Only here is the verb 'to take, accept' used in connection with prayer. It is, so to speak, the stage beyond 'hearing'. Yahweh has approved the request and 'taken it on board' for answering.

70 In this line both 'Yahweh' and 'prayer' are given places of strong emphasis. 'Yahweh himself has accepted this prayer – and it is my prayer that he has accepted.'

71 The 'shame' vocabulary in Hebrew goes beyond feeling shame/embarrassment to 'reaping shame', being disappointed of all one hoped for.

72 Much is obscure in this heading. *shiggayon* (compare Habakkuk 3:1) must be classed as 'unknown'. Most relate it to *shagah* 'to go astray', taking it in the sense 'to be distraught', hence a poem of emotional intensity. This seems far-fetched. Thirtle and Bullinger (op.cit. p.72) prefer *sha'ag*, 'to roar' (compare Amos 1:2), as in Psalm 38:9 of urgent crying to God. Possibly so, but no certainty. 'Sang' (*shir*, compare Psalm 45, heading). Cush is unknown. Benjamites could have been among David's critics in the court of the Benjamite king, Saul (compare 1 Samuel 22:7; 24:9; 26:19), but equally Benjamites were involved in Absalom's rebellion (2 Samuel 19:16–17). Either of these could provide the setting for Psalm 7. If the former, Psalm 7 could be included here on grounds of appropriateness.

73 'This' is both what Cush has accused David of, and the deviancies immediately listed; or either of them.

74 See Psalm 2:5.

75 *ebrah*, from *abhar* 'to cross over, go beyond the bounds', therefore 'outbursting/overflowing anger'.

76 David pictures Yahweh sitting on high in judgment over the world. This is the ultimate judgment that neither he nor his opponents can escape. But, even before that tribunal, he is confident he will be cleared of blame. It is the most striking way possible that he can claim guiltlessness in his present emergency.

77 Statements like this in Psalms must always be kept in context. This is not a claim to sinless perfection, but to innocence in the present situation.

78 Lit. 'hearts and kidneys': the former standing for mind, will, conscience, imagination; the latter for emotions. Together they comprise the whole of human nature considered internally.

79 Sometimes (as here) the indefinite article is more emphatic than the definite!

80 i.e. God is my shield-bearer (compare 1 Samuel 17:7; note 'on' (KJV) in 1 Chronicles 18:7 – 'which the servants … carried'). My defence is his responsibility.

81 Both words for 'God' come in this verse. The first is the plural, *elohim*, God in the fullness of the divine attributes; the second is the singular, *el*, God transcendent.

82 To 'turn back' is the Old Testament expression for repentance: turning away from … and turning back to …

83 Sword and bow together picture the inescapability of divine judgment: sword for those near; bow for those at a distance.

84 Perfect of future certainty.

85 **B** (verses 3–5 and 14–16) expresses two sides of the way the moral law works out in the world: verses 3–5 remind us that a just God is ruling in exact justice; verses 14–16 reminds us that sin itself is a boomerang.

86 The bracket round the whole psalm is (the first word) 'Yahweh' and (the last word) 'Yahweh the Most High'. Life is lived (including its severest trials) inside that bracket.

Pause for Thought

Whether Psalms 3–7 all belong in the time of Absalom's rebellion must be (apart from Psalm 3) to an extent a conjecture. What cannot be denied is that they all arise from a time (or times) of hostility. The comparatively buoyant spirit of Psalms 3 and 4 becomes a much sharper sense of enmity in Psalm 5, with a clearer awareness of the wickedness which David was facing. Next comes the 'terror' of 6:2, 3, 10, and, finally, the solemn sense of divine judgment – and eternal judgment – which pre-occupies Psalm 7. Psalms, indeed, for a time of trouble – and full of lessons for any and every troubled soul. A very fundamental lesson emerges from a simple observation. Of the fifty-five verses in these psalms, about fifteen are devoted to enemies and their threat, but about thirty to truths, thoughts of God and descriptions of prayer and praise. In whatever form trouble comes – the hostility of others, circumstantial problems and tragedies, personal sorrows – its tendency is to drive us inward, to make us 'retire hurt', urge us to find some corner in which to moan over our lot, marvel how unfair life is, 'chew the fat' of our own misery! David is too practical to say 'forget your problems'. Neither his nor our difficulties are negligible or inconsequential. No, don't try to forget them, but rather face and describe them – as these psalms do. The vague is so often more alarming than what is candidly and specifically faced. But always outweigh the problems, hurts, sorrows – whatever – by the great truths about the Lord, and by the practice of prayer and praise. See how our psalms begin: 'Yahweh' (3); 'God of my righteousness' (4); 'Hear ... Yahweh' (5); 'Yahweh' (6); 'Yahweh my God' (7). Look again at the truths shared in Psalm 4: the God who answers prayer (v. 1); who sets apart those he loves, protectingly (v. 3); gives a greater joy than earth affords (v. 7); and who keeps us in security and peace (v. 8). The mind stocked with truth is the mind fortified.

Day 3   Read Psalms 8–10

Psalm 8.
The Power of the Powerless

Belonging to the worship-leader;[1] set for the Gittith;[2] a song[3] of David's.

A.1. The sovereign Yahweh

1. Yahweh, our Sovereign,
    how magnificent[4] is your name[5]
    in all the earth!

B.1. Yahweh's rule

You who have placed your splendour
above the heavens –
2. out of the mouth of babies and unweaned infants[6]
    you have founded[7] strength,
    because of your adversaries,
    in order to quell[8] enemy and avenger!

C. Yahweh's condescension

3. When I look at your heavens,[9]
    the works of your fingers,[10]
    moon and stars which you have established,
4. what is mere man[11] that you remember him,
    and the son of man[12] that you visit[13] him! –
5. You caused[14] him to be a little less than God;[15];
    with glory and majesty you continue to crown him;

1   See heading to Psalm 4.

2   Uncertain significance. 'Gath' was a Philistine city. Was the Gittith a Philistine musical instrument? Or a Gittite melody? The singular *gath* means 'wine-press': was 'the Gittith' a melody associated with ingathering/harvest? Also Psalms 81, 84.

3   See heading to Psalm 3.

4   *addiyr* combines dignity/nobility of position with magnificence and power. Note the parallel with 'splendour'. Psalms 76:4(5); 93:4; Isaiah 33:21, 'majestic'.

5   The 'name' means that the reference is not to God in his divine reality, but to Yahweh as he has made himself known to his people. The unique revelation to Israel is for all the world.

6   Humans at their weakest, most vulnerable. Compare 1 Corinthians 1:27. David's deliverance from Absalom when he considered himself so exposed and helpless, as in Psalms 3–7; or, further back, his deliverance from Saul (1 Samuel 23:14f, 25–26).

7   i.e. 'laid the foundation of/for'.

8   *shabhat*, 'to rest, cease, silence', here in causative form, 'make to rest, cease, be still'.

9   The absence of reference to the sun makes this a night-time psalm, the awesome impressiveness of the night sky.

10 The 'hand' is the organ of personal involvement; 'fingers' carries the imagery further – attention to detail.

B.2. Yahweh's ruler

6.   you maintain him in rule over the works of your hand;
     everything you have placed under his feet:

7.   sheep and cattle – all of them –
     and also the beasts of the field,

8.   the birds in the heavens,
     and the fish in the sea,
     whatever passes along the paths of the seas.

A.2. The sovereign Yahweh

9.   Yahweh, our Sovereign,
     How magnificent is your name
     in all the earth!

Psalms 9–10.
A Triptych of Faith

Belonging to the worship-leader;[16] set to 'A son's death';[17] a song of David's.[18]

The evidence suggests that Psalms 9–10 were originally one psalm – a (very) broken alphabetic acrostic. In an alphabetic acrostic each successive verse begins with the next letter of the Hebrew alphabet – a sort of Hebrew 'A to Z' – and with the same intention of giving a full account of the chosen theme. See, for example, Psalms 34, 119, 145. A broken acrostic omits some letters of the alphabet and may reverse others – as is the case with Psalms 9–10. Usually commentators explain such 'irregularities' as errors that have crept into the text in the course of transmission – and even try to correct what is amiss and supply what is lacking (as does NIV, for example, in Psalm 145:13). It is more likely that the broken acrostic is a deliberate literary form, to be explained either because the theme is one which human thought cannot fully comprehend, or (as may be the case in 9–10) to reflect the

11   'mere man' represents *'enosh*, a word of uncertain derivation, but possibly the unused *anash*, 'to become weak'. At any rate, *enosh* is humankind in its vulnerability, feebleness.

12   Or 'son of Adam'. 'Mere mankind' expresses frailty; 'son of man' expresses mortality.

13   Widely used in the sense 'pay attention to, take care of'.

14   The verbs in verses 5–6 are perfect-imperfect-imperfect-perfect. The perfects expressed established fact, the imperfects recurring divine activity.

15   The Hebrew text 'God' was interpreted by the Greek translators as 'angels' (cf. Hebrews 2:7). Some see in 1 Samuel 28:13 a 'generic' use of 'god/gods' meaning 'spiritual being(s)'.

16   See Psalm 4, heading.

17   Of no assured meaning. Was it simply the name of a tune?

18   See Psalm 3, heading.

19   The personal commitment ('all my heart') is continued in four 'cohortative' verbs, whose emphasis is expressed by 'indeed' and by the introduction of an exclamatory 'how' governing the final three verbs.

20   The time-honoured 'wonderful' for the *pal'a* group of words can hardly be altered. Compare 'wonderful', Isaiah 9:6. The form found in Psalm 9:1 – and widely – means 'to be wondered at', 'rightly provoking wonder'. Basically, what requires a supernatural explanation.

21   Or 'because of'. The mere personal presence ('face') of Yahweh is sufficient to deal with the situation.

brokenness, unevenness and unexpectedness of life itself. This is somewhat supported by the fact that Psalms 9–10 fall into three sections, each covering six letters of the Hebrew Alphabet. Each of the three sections deals with an aspect of the life of faith: confidence (9:1–13), challenges (9:14–10:6), and prayer (10:7–18).

Psalm 9:1–12.
Confident Faith

A.1. Praise: personal commitment

1. I will give thanks, Yahweh, (*aleph*)
    with all my heart;[19]
    I will indeed recount
    all your wonderful acts.[20]
2. How I will rejoice and exult in you,
    make music to your name, Most High!

B.1. Divine justice: Yahweh enthroned

3. When my enemies turn back (*beth*)
    they stumble and perish from before[21] your face,
4. because you have worked for my judgment and my cause:[22]
    you sat on the throne, exercising judgment in righteousness.

C.1. The wicked destroyed

5. You have rebuked the nations, (*gimel*)
    destroyed the wicked:
    their name you have erased for ever and ever.

C.2. The enemy's destructiveness

6. O enemy (*he*)
    desolations have been completed in perpetuity!

22 'Judgment' is basically 'making the right decision' in a given situation; 'cause' is the situation as brought before a court. 'Exercising judgment' perfectly illustrates the main Old Testament meaning of 'to judge' – not a sentence of condemnation but making the 'right decision' which 'puts things to rights'.

23 There are noteworthy features in this section. Its first and last words (in Hebrew as in this rendering) are 'Yahweh'. In between, Yahweh is the subject of seven statements. Secondly, each verse begins with the letter *waw*. In an alphabetical acrostic this constitutes a huge emphasis – and shows that the alphabetical form is not a mere literary device, ornament or poetic skill but an adjunct to meaning.

24 *tebhel*, specifically the world of people and affairs, Psalms 18:15; 24:1.

25 See 2:1.

26 From *sagabh*, 'to be high, inaccessible', *misgabh* is a place of security, high out of the reach of the foe.

27 A word of uncertain meaning, but it must have some such meaning as 'distress, extremity'.

28 'Seek', not in the sense of looking for something that has been lost, but, as throughout the Old Testament, of coming again and again to the place where something is known to be available. Deuteronomy 12:5; Amos 5:6.

29 The verbs are perfects of certainty

30 Note the contrast with the confident 'I will recount' of Psalm 9:1. Now the recounting is conditional on some outpouring of grace, because the pressure of hatred, enmity, humiliation is so strong. Faith is under stress.

And the cities you uprooted –
their very memory itself has perished!

B.2. Divine justice: Yahweh enthroned[23]

7. And Yahweh (*waw*)
    for ever will sit enthroned:
    for judgment he has established his throne.
8. And he will himself judge the peopled-world[24] in righteousness, (*waw*)
    will settle cases for the states[25] with fairness.
9. And Yahweh will be a top-security[26] for the crushed, (*waw*)
    top-security for periods of distress.[27]
10. And those who know your name will put their trust in you, (*waw*)
    because you have not forsaken those who seek[28] you, Yahweh.

A.2. Praise: A worldwide message

11. Make music to Yahweh (*zayin*)
    sitting enthroned on Zion.
    Declare among the peoples his doings.
12. When he is seeking out blood-guiltiness
    he has determined to remember[29] them –
    he has determined not to forget the outcry of the downtrodden.

Psalms 9:13–10:6. Buffeted Faith

A.1. Present need: A cry for grace

13. Grant me your grace, Yahweh; (*cheth*)
    see my humiliation caused by those who hate me
    – you who raise me up from the gates of death –

31 Three certainties are asserted or assumed: (a) the boomerang nature of sin (verses 15–16). This is not a mere moral force in operation but a decision Yahweh has made and a work he performs. (b) Eternity awaits (verses 17–18). (c) Yahweh will act (verses 19–20).

32 Parallelism with verse 15b suggests that the hands of the wicked are meant: the topic is still the boomerang of sin.

33 As a word this means a 'meditation, musing'. It occurs in the text of Psalms 19:14; 92:3.

34 The Old Testament does not have a doctrine of eternal punishment, but there are hints (as here) that Sheol is in some sense the special destiny of those not right with God. Compare Psalm 49:14a; Proverbs 9:18.

35 *'ebhyon*, from *'abhah,* 'to be willing'; in a 'bad' sense, those who can be pushed around, the pliable, vulnerable to pressure from stronger 'interests'. (Its 'good' sense is those who gladly will the will of God.)

36 From *'anah*, 'to be low'. Those at the bottom of life's heap, the defenceless.

37 See Psalm 8:4.

38 The most likely rendering, meaning 'something that will strike fear'.

39 As note 36.

40 Yahweh's seeming absence (verse 1); the wicked's attitude to others (verse 2), his dismissal of commercial values (verse 3), confident atheism (verse 4), confidence for present and future (verses 5–6).

41 See Psalm 9:9.

42 See Psalm 9:12.

14. so that I may recount[30] all your praise
    in the gates of the daughter of Zion.
    How I will delight in your salvation!

B. Certainties[31]

15. The nations will surely sink into the chasm they have
    made. (*teth*)
    In the net they have hidden their foot is sure to be caught!
16. Yahweh is known by the judgment he has made:
    in the work of his hands[32] the wicked is sure to be snared!
    (*higgaion*,[33] *Selah*)
    The wicked will return to Sheol,[34] (*yodh*)
17. all the nations who forget God,
18. because not in perpetuity will the vulnerable[35] be
    forgotten; (*kaph*)
    nor will the expectation of the downtrodden[36] perish for
    ever.
19. Rise up, Yahweh!
    Do not let mere man[37] prevail.
    Let the nations be judged before you.
20. Appoint fear[38] for them, Yahweh;
    let the nations know they are merely human.[39] (*Selah*)

A.2. Present needs[40]

1. Yahweh, why are you standing at a distance? (*lamedh*)
   Why are you silent in periods of distress?[41]
2. In pride the wicked sets the downtrodden[42] alight:[43]
   they are captured in the plans which they have thought
   out.[44]
3. For the wicked boasts about his heart's desire,
   and blesses the one who makes profit by violence;
   he scorns Yahweh:
4. The wicked man –
   in accord with the pride of his anger –
   he is not seeking –

43 *dalaq*, to burn, set on fire. Compare Psalm 7:13, 'incendiaries'. Interpreted as meaning 'hotly pursue', Genesis 31:36. This is the intention here.

44 This understanding best suits the context: that the downtrodden are captured by the plans of the wicked. It is equally possible to translate, 'Let them be captured', i.e. the wicked, compare Psalm 9:15.

45 The Hebrew is just as abrupt as these five lines! Not because the text is in disarray but because poetry allows allusiveness, leaving it to the reader to fill in the gaps. 'The pride of his anger' could be 'the pride of his nose', meaning 'with his nose in the air'. On 'seek', see Psalm 9:10.

46 i.e. he knows how to look after himself!

47 As usual, the decisions God has reached.

48 More literally, 'higher than in front of him', 'too high from where he stands'.

49 i.e. suffer insecurity.

50 *r'a*, 'evil' in all its forms, anything from a bad taste to moral wrong. Here, the troubles of life, anything that threatens security.

51 This is not a mere recapitulation of verses 1–6. The focus is on the dangerous hostility of the wicked to the defenceless: i.e. the danger he constitutes in the actuality of daily life (verses 7–10) and its basis in practical atheism (verse 11). It is for this existent threat that prayer (verses 12–16) is the answer: hostile speech (7), hidden threat (8), deadly intent (9–10).

52 Lit. 'his eyes are hidden/under cover to the unfortunate'.

53 See Psalm 9:12.

there is no God –
all his plans!⁴⁵

5. His ways are stable in every situation.⁴⁶
   Too high are your judgments⁴⁷ for his sight.⁴⁸ (*mem*)
   All his adversaries – he puffs at them!

6. He has said in his heart,
   'I will not totter⁴⁹ –
   to generation after generation,
   one who is free of trouble.'⁵⁰

Psalm 10:7–18.
Praying Faith

A. The way of the wicked⁵¹

7. With cursing his mouth is full – (*pe*)
   and deceit, and tyranny;
   under his tongue is trouble and mischief.

8. He sits in ambush where there are settlements;
   in hiding he murders the guiltless;
   covertly he eyes the unfortunate:⁵² (*ayin*)

9. he lies in ambush in a hiding place like a lion in its lair;
   he lies in ambush to carry off the downtrodden;⁵³
   he carries off the downtrodden when he draws him into his net;

10. and he crouches down low⁵⁴ and the unfortunate fall by his strong ones.⁵⁵

11. He has said in his heart:
    'The transcendent God⁵⁶ has forgotten;
    he has hidden his face;
    he has never ever⁵⁷ seen'.

B. The way of prayer⁵⁸

12. Rise up, Yahweh! (*qoph*)
    O transcendent God,⁵⁹ lift your hand!

54 Heb. 'he crouches he is low'. When two verbs come together without conjunction, the second carries the main meaning, and the first is adverbial to it: 'He is crouchingly low'.

55 Even then the powerful surrounded themselves with 'minders'!

56 *'el*, God transcendent.

57 'Never ever' is the strong expression; 'in perpetuity'.

58 Divine intervention is sought (verses 12–13); truth is affirmed (verse 14) and prayer made (verse 15).

59 God transcendent. In verse 13a 'God' is *elohim*.

60 'Seek' in the sense 'enquire into'.

61 'Trouble' (*'amal*) is uniformly used of earthly trouble, endured, felt or imposed. The thought is that what troubles and vexes our lives is also a trouble and vexation to Yahweh.

62 'Requite' translates *nathan*, 'to give'. The full expression occurs in 1 Kings 8:32.

63 Lit. 'upon you', a 'pregnant' use: 'to come to rest upon you'.

64 A strong expression: 'leaves/deserts/abandons himself'.

65 The sense has to be 'until you find none'. Many alter the Hebrew text, but all the alterations require the same sort of expansion in translation, so why not leave the text as it is?

66 Psalm 9:12.

Do not forget the downtrodden!

13. On what ground has the wicked scorned God?
    On what ground has he said in his heart,
    'You will not seek[60] it?'

14. You have seen it! – (*resh*)
    because you personally do take note of trouble and
    vexation,[61]
    to requite by your hand.[62]
    To you[63] the unfortunate unreservedly consigns[64] himself;
    of the orphan you are ever the helper.

15. Break the arm of the wicked; (*shin*)
    and as for the evil man, do seek out his wickedness –
    may you find none![65]

16. Yahweh is king for ever and ever.
    The nations are bound to perish out of his earth.

17. The desire of the downtrodden[66] you have heard, Yahweh;
    (*tau*)
    you will establish their heart;
    you will make your ear attentive,

18. to judge the orphan and the crushed,
    that a mere man from earth may no more again be a
    tyrant.

Pause for Thought

Think of the contrast between a quiet night-time stroll in your garden and the bustle and demands of a busy, stressful day in your office, and you have exactly the contrast between Psalm 8 and Psalms 9–10! Psalm 8 is a worshipful meditation on the night sky; Psalm 9–10 (as originally one) is alive with the pressures, acrimonious words and hostile deeds of an unsympathetic world. There you are! Take them together, and we all say, Yes, life's like that! But what are Psalm 8 and Psalm 9–10 saying to us in our mixed up existence?

Like all prayer, worship involves talking to God. Psalm 8 is not sitting in the silent contemplation of wordless adoration; it is telling God about God. The emphasis (because it comes twice in verses 1 and 9) tells him that he is God our deliverer and redeemer, Yahweh, the God of Exodus 3:15 and 6:7. He is also the sovereign God – not a passive, ornamental Sovereign, but the active, executive, managing director, controller and detailed planner of his world, in all its aspects and activities. He is a God who is truly God. Thirdly, he is the one and only God of all the earth – not in whatever nature any given nation or society may design him, but according to his 'name', that is, the way he has revealed himself. There is no God except the God of the Bible!

> Jehovah, great I AM,
> by earth and heaven confessed;
> I bow and bless the sacred Name.

The fourth component of worship in Psalm 8 is a properly lowly estimate of ourselves, a deep, prevailing 'wonderment' that such a God concerns himself with such as me. By contrast, Psalm 9–10 teaches us about the sort of prayer that arms us to face the pressures of life with calm assurance. It is God-conscious prayer (9:1–2; 10:16–18; see how the psalm opens and closes), with a clear awareness of him to whom we are praying (9:9–10), and sounding a note of praise (9:11). It is 'count your blessings' praying, taking in God's 'wonderful works' (9:11–12) and past mercies. Prayer is need expressed in detail (10:3–11), and can be couched in vigorous words both to God (9:19; 10:12), and regarding man (10:14–15). The reverence of true worship guards our freedom of speech in prayer from unseemly familiarity; the activity of praise and intercession guards our worship from impractical pietism.

Day 4 Read Psalms 11–14

Psalm 11.
Not Flight but Faith

Belonging to the worship-leader; David's.

A. Safety (verse 1a) and misleading voices (verses 1b–3)

1.   In Yahweh I have taken refuge.
   How do you keep saying to my soul,
   'Flutter off, bird, to your mountain!'[1]
2.   For – behold! – the wicked bend the bow;
   they have set their arrow on the string,[2]
   to shoot, in darkness, at the upright in heart.
3.   When the foundations are being demolished,[3]
   what could even the righteous have done?[4]

B. Sovereignty (verse 4a–b) and a true view of life (verses 4c–6)

4.   Yahweh is in the temple of his holiness;
   it is in heaven that Yahweh has his throne![5]
   It is his eyes that gaze,
   his eyelids[6] that test[7] the sons of man.
5.   It is Yahweh who tests the righteous;[8]
   and the wicked, and him who loves violence his soul hates.
6.   He will rain down on the wicked traps[9] –
   fire and sulphur and raging heat,
   the measure in their cup.[10]

1   1 Samuel 18:8–16 describes the sort of background this psalm needs. Sadly, David did eventually 'flutter off to his mountain', but was there an earlier time when he was sure that, if the LORD could care for him as a fugitive, the LORD could equally care for him as a resident of Saul's court.

2   Very likely David had more jealous enemies at court than just the unpredictable king.

3   Saul's increasing paranoia at least illustrates what the siren voices were here saying to David: all the old certainties are gone, nothing is secure or stable; you can't tell how things will be from one day to another – and there's nothing you could have done about it!

4   Perfect tense. Possibly 'What could even the righteous have determined to do?'

5   The closeness of Yahweh to his people in his temple-home does not diminish the reality of his heavenly sovereignty over all things.

6   Used as a parallel to 'eyes' for the sake of variation, e.g. Psalm 132:4.

7   The trials of life (as in verses 1–3).

8   The emphasis in the Hebrew needs a translation that goes beyond the literal: 'It is Yahweh who tests and it is the righteous he tests.'

9   This fine mixed metaphor is what the Hebrew says; see RV. Many (sadly including NKJV) alter to 'coals'.

C. Confidence under divine scrutiny

7. Because Yahweh is righteous;
    it is genuine righteousness that he loves.
    It is at the upright one that his face gazes.[11]

Psalm 12.
The Tongue of Falsehood and the Word of Truth

Belonging to the worship-leader;[12] for the Eighth;[13] a song of David's.[14]

A.1. Appeal to Yahweh in a collapsing society

1. Oh do save, Yahweh,
    because the reliable person has come to an end,
    because trustworthy ones have disappeared from the sons of man.
2. They keep speaking falsehood each with his contemporary;
    with a lip of consummate flattery,[15] two-faced,[16] they keep speaking.

B.1. The words of man, false and forceful[17]

3. May Yahweh cut off all lips of consummate flattery,[18]
    the tongue speaking great things –
4. those who have said,
    'With our tongue we will prove our strength;
    our lips are at our disposal.[19]
    Who is our master?'

C. Yahweh's commitment

5. 'As a result of the devastation of the downtrodden,
    as a result of the groaning of the vulnerable,
    now I will rise up,'

---

10 'Cup' (compare Psalms 6:5; 75:8; 116:13) stands for life's experiences as decided upon and measured out by Yahweh.

11 The image is of the face of Yahweh turned favourably to those he loves. Compare Numbers 6:25; Psalm 80:3. It is not by flight (verse 1b) but by confidence in divine favour (verse 7) that life's challenges can be faced.

12 Psalm 4, heading.

13 Psalm 6, heading.

14 Psalm 3, heading.

15 Lit. 'a lip of smoothnesses', plural of amplitude; every sort of flattery.

16 Lit. 'with heart and heart', 1 Chronicles 12:33 (NKJV, 'stouthearted'), 'not of heart and heart', of uncertain commitment, hypocritical.

17 Vilification, critical and hostile words are easily seen as David's experience during the period of Saul's animosity and increasing, paranoiac jealousy. 1 Samuel 18. The Doeg incident (1 Samuel 22) shows the sort of people Saul was prepared to take seriously. 1 Samuel 26:19 indicates sly foes 'twisting the knife'. The people of Keilah (1 Samuel 23) – however praiseworthy their loyalty to Saul – must have dealt with David in a 'two-faced' way.

18 Note 15.

19 Lit. 'with us', meaning part of our equipment, on our side.

20 Somewhat interpretative translation. Lit. 'the generation this'.

21 i.e. move freely about.

22 So, literally. The sense is 'in the estimation of'.

Yahweh keeps saying.
'I will place him in the safety for which he pants.'

B.2. Yahweh's words, pure and purified

6. The words of Yahweh are clean –
silver refined in an earthly crucible,
purified seven times!

A.2. Confidence in Yahweh in a mixed society

7. You, Yahweh, will keep them;
you will preserve each from this generation for ever.[20]
8. All around the wicked go to and fro[21]
when triviality is exalted for[22] the sons of man.

Psalm 13.
Still Waiting, Still Trusting

Belonging to the worship-leader; a song of David's[23]

A. The fourfold 'How long': protracted anxiety[24]

1. How long, Yahweh, will you forget me; in perpetuity?
How long will you hide your face from me?
2. How long will I place plans[25] before my soul[26] –
grief in my heart each day?
How long will my enemy[27] be exalted over me?

B. The threefold 'in case': urgent threats[28]

3. Take notice,
answer[29] me, Yahweh my God;[30]
enlighten my eyes,[31]
in case I sleep in death;
4. in case my enemy say: 'I have proved able for[32] him';
in case my adversary delight that I have slipped.[33]

23 See Psalms 3 and 4, headings.

24 In turn, divine remoteness, personal indecision/uncertainty, human enmity. The causes of potential breakdown are supernatural, personal, circumstantial. What a recipe!

25 'Plans', plural of amplitude, here, 'set plan after plan before …'

26 'Before myself', lit. 'in/within'. Propose plan after plan to myself. 'Make proposals how to deal with the situation.' The reaction to the protracted anxiety.

27 No indication who was the enemy or what the cause. The situation leading up to 1 Samuel 27:1, with its counsel of despair.

28 The pressures under which he is living seem likely to terminate his earthly life (verse 3b, compare Mark 14:33–34), in which case the victory obviously lies with the opposition (verse 4a), but even if this does not happen, the unresolved situation leaves them triumphant (verse 4b).

29 'Take note answer' is another example of two verbs without conjunction. Compare on Psalm 10:10. Here 'answer lookingly' – a look is enough, reassuring David of favour, lifting the trouble, sending the enemy packing.

30 Notice 'my', personal faith remains under trial; compare Mark 15:34.

31 Compare 1 Samuel 14:27, NKJV 'countenance'; lit. 'eyes', of renewed vitality, resilience.

32 Regularly, 'to be able (for)' is used in the sense 'prevail over'.

33 David does not here ask for the destruction of the enemy but for his frustration – an indication that he may have had Saul in mind. Saul was always 'Yahweh's anointed' to him, compare 1 Samuel 26:11.

C. The twofold rejoicing: the fruit of trust

5.   And[34] in your committed love[35] I have trusted:
     O let my heart delight in your salvation;
6.   let me indeed sing to Yahweh
     because he is sure to deal fully[36] with me.

Psalm 14.
Three Voices:
Atheism Exposed and Countered

Belonging to the worship-leader[37]; David's.

A. The first voice (1a), the fool – with comment (1b)

1.   The spiritually unprincipled person[38] has said in his heart
     'There is no God.'
     They act with abominable corruptness.
     There is no one doing good.

B. The second voice (2–4), Yahweh – with comment (5–6)

2.   From heaven Yahweh looks down on the sons of man,[39]
     to see is there anyone acting prudently,
     seeking God.
3.   The whole lot has turned aside.
     Together they have become tainted.[40]
     There is no one doing good –
     there is not even one!
4.   Do they not know –
     all the trouble-makers[41] –
     those who eat my people eat bread![42] –
     upon Yahweh they have not called!
5.   There they were truly afraid,[43]
     because God is himself in the generation of the righteous.

34   We could translate the conjunction 'But', i.e. in contrast to the experience of trouble and distractedness. 'And' is more effective: throughout his troubles there was always this additional component.

35   See on Psalm 5:7.

36   Treating the verb as a perfect of certainty. Trust brings delight even when nothing has actually yet changed. Compare 1 Samuel 1:18.

37   Psalm 4, heading.

38   Heb. *nabal*, illustrated by Nabal of Carmel, 1 Samuel 25. He was not by any means a 'fool', but a successful and wealthy farmer, though he lacked any sense of obligation. Compare 2 Samuel 13:11–13; for the noun, *nebalah*, compare Genesis 34:7. Psalm 14 applies the word theologically: failure to grasp or to take into account the knowledge of God; as Isaiah 32:6, Romans 1:28.

39   The marks of the out-and-out atheist (verse 1) show themselves throughout sinful humanity. Romans 3:9–18.

40   Compare Psalm 53:3; Job 15:16. Commentators say, in cognate languages, of milk turning sour. Here of the inevitable way human nature 'goes to the bad'.

41   See Psalm 5:5.

42   So, literally. Usually understood as 'who eat my people like they eat bread', i.e. with the same thoughtless assumption of self-preservation, meaning 'they live by eating my people' – all natural and acceptable!

43   'There' sounds as if David is pointing to some past event in which the spiritually thoughtless were panic stricken, exposing the vulnerability of their position. As, for example, a reaction of fear unrecorded in 1 Samuel 26.

6.   The plans of the downtrodden will you disappoint,
     when Yahweh is himself his refuge?

C. The third voice (7a–b), Israel – with comment (7c)

7.   Oh that out of Zion were come the salvation of Israel[44] –
     when Yahweh restores the fortunes of his people!
     May Jacob delight![45]
     May Israel rejoice!

---

44 There is no verb in this sentence in the Hebrew text. 'Were come' is provided according to the sense.

45 The wish is that, even while still waiting for the coming restoration, the Lord's people may, in the interim, delight in him.

Pause for Thought

Periods of anxiety are something we all have to learn to deal with, and Psalm 13, for all its brevity, is a marvellous instruction. First, there are three areas of experience from which troubling worries may arise – the spiritual (v. 1), the personal (v. 2a), and the circumstantial (v. 2b). The first (meriting two cries of 'how long?') is given prominence. We know beyond question that Yahweh will never forget us, but the plaguing thought arises that maybe our sins and failures have so alienated him that he has withdrawn his favour (v. 1b). Even those who never entertained such a thought can well imagine its anguish. 'Grief in the heart' is something to be watched like a hawk. It is the tendency to retire into a corner and talk to ourselves about ourselves! It can only further focus attention on our miseries! The verses of Psalm 13:3–4, so to say, begin the real 'fight back' against the pressing anxieties. 'Answer' (3a) is asking Yahweh to break silence and come back into my life; 'enlighten' seeks personal relief from agony of soul, not by looking inwardly but by turning upwardly. The three 'in cases' raise disagreeable possibilities: that we should end this life under the cloud of apparent divine displeasure (3c), that the enemy should come out on the winning side (4a), and that, under all this anxiety, I might 'let the side down' by 'slipping' (4b). Now we come to what David proposes as the real winning reaction (vv. 5–6). Notice how four 'how longs' (vv. 1–2) were followed by three 'in cases' (vv. 3–4), and now by two exultations (vv. 5–6). By progressively narrowing its focus in this way, the Psalm lays a sharp emphasis on the last two verses – the delight and the song that follow from taking the nature of Yahweh's love into account and adopting a clear position of trust. In verse 5, his love is *chesedh,* not a potentially fleeting emotion, perhaps dependant on favourable conditions on our side of the relationship. No, it is love arising from a determination and unchangeable disposition of Yahweh's will – the love he expressed to us, his bride, when in return to the question, 'Will you love her?' he replied 'I will'. In the light of that love, thoughts of forgetfulness and the hidden face evaporate. The only response is to reply to very questioning thought or experience: I trust him! And to make that reply as each day starts, and, if necessary, moment by moment throughout the day.

Day 5   Read Psalms 15–17

Psalm 15.
Taking up Residence

A song of David's.[1]

A.1. The crucial question: acceptance with God

1. Yahweh,
    who will be a guest[2] in your tent?[3]
    who will take up residence in the mountain of your
    holiness?

B. Qualifications

(Lifestyle and conduct)
2. Whoever walks perfectly,[4]
    and works righteousness,[5]

(Speech)
    and whoever speaks truth in his heart,
3. has determined not to spread scandal with his tongue;

(Relationships)
    has determined not to do wrong to his fellow man,
    nor to raise a reproach[6] against his neighbour.

(Values)
4. A person rightly despised is properly scorned[7] in his eyes,
    and those who fear Yahweh he keeps treating as
    honourable.

(Integrity, trustworthiness)
    When he has sworn to his own hurt,[8] he does not change.

1   Psalm 4, heading.

2   *gur*, of the temporary resident, the
    resident alien, the person with specially
    granted, not inherited, rights, the
    lodger, 'the stranger within your gates'
    (Exodus 20:10).

3   The LORD's 'tent' was his home among
    his people. To whom will Yahweh
    extend the hospitality of his home?

4   Compare Genesis 17:1.

5   i.e. what is 'right with God'.

6   A somewhat unusual expression:
    possibly an ellipsis for 'to raise his voice
    in a reproach', or, maybe more simply,
    'to take up a reproach', to join in
    vilifying. Compare our expression 'to
    pick up gossip'.

7   'Rightly … properly' take into account
    that these verbs, in Hebrew, are
    niphal participles, equivalent to Latin
    gerundives.

8   The idea of 'his own' has to be
    understood as demanded by context.
    Compare, NIV, 'even when it hurts'.
    The prohibition here warns against
    sinful vacillation, not (compare
    Proverbs 6:1–5) against responsible
    second thoughts (such as Jephthah
    ought to have entertained, Judges
    11:30–31, 34, 39).

9   Heb. 'usury'.

10 The first line refuses exploiting
    someone's difficulties; the second,
    violating his rights.

11 i.e. from his place as a guest and
    resident in Yahweh's tent and on his
    hill.

(Probity)

5. His money he has determined not to place at exorbitant interest,[9]

   nor to take a bribe against the guiltless.[10]

A.2. Stability

Whoever does these things will never be shaken.[11]

Psalm 16.
Security in God

A *michtam*[12] of David's

A.1. Security in God as refuge: a prayer

1. Keep me, O God,
   because I have taken refuge in you.

B. Life in the divine refuge

(a.1) Yahweh

2. I have said[13] to Yahweh:
   'You are my Sovereign One;
   my good is not additional to you.[14]

(b.1) Yahweh's people, a pleasure

3. Regarding the holy ones on earth,
   they are indeed the mighty ones in whom is all my pleasure.

(c.1) Spiritual commitment (negative)

4. Many are their pains, who change to another.[15]
   I will not pour out their libations of blood,
   nor will I take up their names on my lips.

12 Uncertain meaning: also Psalms 56–60. *kethem* means 'gold' (e.g. Psalm 45:9), hence a 'golden truth', specially prized. *katham* (only Jeremiah 2:22) of something indelible, a permanent truth. But why would these psalms as compared to others be termed 'golden' or need emphasis on their permanency?

13 The formation of this verb is unusual, but best seen as a primitive first person singular.

14 Equivalent to 'Thou, O Christ, art all I want (need).' There is no need to seek anything beyond Yahweh.

15 That 'another god' is intended is made clear by the reference in the next line to false religious practice.

16 'Portion' is outward: the circumstances of life. 'Cup' is subjective: the experiences of life (as allocated by Yahweh, Psalm 75:8–9).

17 Lit. 'my kidneys', as the seat of emotions, instincts. Possibly, here, 'conscience'.

18 Yahweh in front is the one I follow, the standard to which I aspire; Yahweh alongside is the strength on which I draw for life's journey.

19 All that is honourable in me; everything in me that reflects the image of God.

20 Sheol in its broad usage is the 'place' where the dead live on. The Old Testament had a clear understanding that there is life after death, though clarity about the conditions of that life awaited the coming of Jesus (2 Timothy 1:10). Verses like Psalm 16:10 (compare Psalms 49:14–15; 73:23) indicate a fuller hope than merely living on in Sheol.

21 Or, by a Hebrew pun, 'corruption'.

(a.2) Yahweh

5. Yahweh is the measure of my portion and my cup;[16]
    you enlarge my allocation.

(b.2) Yahweh's provision: a delight

6. The measured-out portion has fallen to me in delightful
    ways:
    yes indeed, the inheritance is pleasing to me.

(c.2) Spiritual commitment (positive)

7. I will bless Yahweh who counsels me;
    yes indeed, night by night my feelings[17] instruct me.
8. I have put Yahweh in front of me continuously –
    indeed, at my right hand: I will not be shaken.[18]

A.2. Security in perpetuity: a certainty

9. Therefore my heart rejoices, and my glory[19] delights.
    Yes indeed, my flesh too will reside securely,
10. because you will not abandon my soul to Sheol;[20]
    you will not give over your beloved one to see the
    chasm.[21]
11. You will make me know the path to life:
    abundance of real joy comes with your face;[22]
    true delights are in your right hand in perpetuity.

Psalm 17.
Upward I Look:
A Threefold Appeal

A prayer of David's

A.1. The first appeal, based on righteousness

1. Yahweh, do hear righteousness![23]
    Oh pay attention to my cry!
    Open your ear to my prayer,

22 Lit. Satiation of every sort of joy (plural of amplitude) is with your face (the personal presence and favour of Yahweh's).

23 This striking use of 'righteousness' as a direct object, is a strong way of asserting that the appeal cannot be faulted as made in total righteousness. This is stressed throughout this section: 'undeceitful' (verse 1), 'upright' (verse 2), 'find nothing … not transgress' (verse 3), 'kept myself' (verse 4), 'within' (verse 5).

24 Lit. 'by not lips of deceit'.

25 'Judgment', the decision to be made in my case.

26 Illustrated by 1 Samuel 25:32–34.

27 e.g. 1 Samuel 24:4. 'Violent' (*'ariyts*), compare Isaiah 35:9; Jeremiah 7:11; Ezekiel 7:22; 15:10; Daniel 11:14.

28 The well-worn tracks made by wagons, hence plain, unmissible.

29 i.e. by your personal, direct action.

30 Or possibly, 'show how marvelous is your committed love'.

31 i.e. as enemies.

32 The 'pupil of the eye', something one moves instinctively to protect.

33 Lit. 'my enemies in soul/against soul'. If the reference is to the enemies' soul, then 'in soul' refers to their determination; if David's soul, then 'deadly'. Hence, I have included both!

34 Metaphor for all tenderness and sensitivity.

35 Of hooded glances.

36 *kephir*, usually translated 'young lion', but meaning (not a lion cub but) a lion in its youthful prime.

by undeceitful lips.[24]

2. It is from before you that my judgment[25] must come:
   your eyes – may they gaze at what is upright!

3. You have tested my heart;
   you have visited it by night;
   you have refined me till you find nothing.
   I have planned that my mouth will not transgress.

4. As regards the works of man,
   by the word of your lips,[26]
   I have kept myself from the paths of the violent.[27]

5. Support my steps within your tracks[28]
   lest my footsteps be insecure.

6. Myself, I have called to you,
   because you do answer me, O God.

A.2. The second appeal: against ruthless enemies

Turn your ear to me;
hear what I say.

7. By your right hand,[29] in your committed love,
   make the distinction,[30]
   Saviour, of those who take refuge from those who raise
   themselves up.[31]

8. Keep me as the apple of the eye;[32]
   in the shadow of your wings hide me

9. from the wicked who are set to destroy me,
   my deadly, determined[33] enemies who keep surrounding
   me.

10. Their fat[34] they have closed;
    with their mouth they speak in pride.

11. In our steps they now surround us;
    their eyes they fix, by turning them to the ground.[35]

12. His likeness is like a lion which longs to tear in pieces,
    and like a prime lion[36] crouching in a hiding place.

37 Verses 13–14 have all the allusiveness that often characterizes poetry, and commentators often allege corruption of the text, but in fact the text is very ordered: in Hebrew, there is alternation of two lines of two words with a third line of one word followed by three lines of two words followed by a third line of one word. The translation requires only the same use of imagination that allusive poetry needs in any language. The allegation of corruption is nothing but refusal to allow poetry to be poetry.

38 Both times in this verse *methim*, 'men', is used in a broad way but often with a slightly derogatory edge.

39 The sheer goodness of God to the unbelieving and undeserving. Matthew 5:45; Acts 14:17.

40 'Awakening' in the life to come, waking from the 'sleep' of death. Isaiah 26:19; Daniel 12:2; Psalm 49:15; 73:23–24.

A.3. The third appeal: for direct, divine action[37]

13. Rise up, Yahweh!
    Meet him face to face!
    Bring him down!
    Rescue my soul from the wicked one by your sword.
14. From men,[38] by your hand, Yahweh –
    from men from the world,
    whose portion is in life –
    with your treasure you fill their belly;[39]
    they are satisfied with sons,
    and what they leave they lay down for their infants.
15. As for me, in righteousness I will gaze at your face;
    I will be satisfied on awakening[40] with your likeness.

Pause for Thought

What do you make of Psalm 15? It sounds dreadfully like salvation by works, doesn't it? And commentators do not help when they describe it (as many do) as 'an entrance liturgy': someone comes seeking entrance, and in response to questions from the Gatekeeper lists his qualifications for being allowed in! But look again at verse 1. The point at issue is not entrance but residence, not being allowed in but being welcome to stay – as the invited guest and the accepted resident. Which is exactly what we who trust in Jesus are. We are in the kingdom of God not by nature but by grace; not by our initiative but by his invitation; accepted not by merit but 'in the Beloved' (Eph. 1:6; Col. 1:12–13). The topic the psalm addresses, then, is this: what should our lives look like now that we are on the inside? And the picture it paints is searching in the extreme. In general it spells out the abiding requirement (Lev. 19:2) that 'You shall be holy, for I, Yahweh your God, am holy': holiness of life and conduct (verses 2a–b; compare Matthew 5:48; 1 John 2:1a); controlled, pure speech, in both heart and tongue (verses 2c, 3a; compare 1 Peter 3:10–12; Ephesians 4:25, 29; 5:4; Colossians 3:9); wholesome relationships, whether regarding another's welfare (v. 3b), or their reputation (verse 3c; compare Leviticus 19:18; Luke 10:29–36). 'Love your neighbour as yourself' means 'exactly like you love yourself', with the love that exercises care and meets needs – even on days when we 'hate' ourselves! In social values, love means to side with everything that promotes sound morality and goodness, and always to identify with the LORD's people (verse 4a–b; compare 2 Chronicles 19:2; Proverbs 22:24; 2 Timothy 2:19–22). It means keeping one's promises (verse 4c, see note 8 above). And, not least, how we manage our money, never to allow it to become a minister to greed or a justification for injuring someone else (verse 5; compare Proverbs 15:27; 28:20; Luke 16:13; 1 Timothy 6:9-10). It's a tall order, to be sure, but, says verse 5c, the result is something to covet – stability and consistency.

Day 6 Read Psalm 18

Psalm 18.
What a Great God!

Belonging to the worship-leader; Yahweh's servant David's, when he spoke to Yahweh the words of this song on the day Yahweh delivered him from the grip[1] of all his enemies and from the hand of Saul. He said:

A.1. Devotion to the saving God

1. I love[2] you, Yahweh, my strength
2. Yahweh, my crag[3] and my fortress and my rescuer;
    my transcendent God,[4] my rock in whom I take refuge;
    my shield and the horn[5] of my salvation,
    my top security.[6]

B.1. Divine intervention (1): Yahweh in power

(Prayer)
3.[7] To the One rightly praised I call – Yahweh! –
    and from my enemies I am saved.
4. The cords of death wrapped around me,
    and the torrents of worthlessness[8] terrified me.
5. The cords of Sheol encircled me,
    the snares of death caught me unawares.
6. In the adversity I had I kept calling on Yahweh,
    and to my God I kept crying for help;
    from his temple he kept hearing my voice,
    and my cry before him for help kept coming into his ears.

1 'Grip' and 'hand' are two different words. The former is the palm of the hand turned upwards, ready to take hold of something: hence 'grip'. In many places it is not contextually possible to bring out a distinctive meaning.

2 'Love' here is the parent verb of the word often translated 'compassion, emotional love'. It is the only place where the verb is used in the simple active (*qal*) mode. It is also the only place where the verb is used of human love for God.

3 'Crag' or 'cliff', as affording secure hiding places in clefts in the rock-face.

4 *'el*, God in his transcendent deity.

5 'The horn or antler, symbol of strength'. Alongside 'shield' it makes a contrast between defence and attack.

6 See on Psalm 9:9.

7 Verses 3-6 are a poem in their own right, in an a-b-b-a formation where the a-lines deal with the effectiveness of prayer, and the four b-lines are respectively verb-subject, subject-verb, subject-verb, verb-subject.

8 'Torrents of *belial*', the latter word used widely of what is wicked/abhorrent. Literally, probably, 'not profitable'. 'Bringing no good' can easily modulate into 'up to no good'.

(Power)

7.[9] And the earth shook and shuddered,

     and the foundations of the mountains quaked and shook themselves,

     because he was incensed.

8. Smoke went up, in his exasperation,

     and from his mouth fire[10] was devouring;

     coals were kindled by it!

9. And he bent the heavens[11] and came down,

     and there was darkness[12] under his feet.

10. And he rode on a cherub[13] and flew,

     and he darted on the wings of the wind.

11. He makes darkness his covering;

     his shelter around him

     darkness of waters,[14] masses of clouds.[15]

12. Because of the brightness in front of him

     his clouds came over,[16]

     hailstones and coals of fire.[17]

13. And Yahweh thundered in the heavens,

     and the Most High uttered his voice,

     hailstones and coals of fire!

14. And he sent out his arrows and scattered them,

     and abundant lightning flashes,

     and he perturbed them.

15. And the channels of waters were seen.[18]

     And the foundations of the peopled-world[19] were exposed

     by your rebuke, Yahweh;

     by the breath of the wind of your exasperation.

(Rescue)

16.[20] He sends[21] from on high;

     he takes me;

     he draws me up[22] out of many waters;

17. he delivers me from my enemy – strong as he is![23] –

     and from those who hate me, for they are mightier than I.

18. They confront[24] me in the day of my calamity,

     and[25] Yahweh proves to be my support.

9 We read verses 7–15 and say, 'But nothing like this actually happened as recorded in 1 Samuel!' Quite so! What we have here is a behind the scenes depiction of Yahweh acting in power, using the great forces of nature in an imaginative way. In 1 Samuel we see divine providence quietly at work, bringing David out of deadly trouble and on to the throne according to the plan of God. The pictures of power and the workings of providence are two ways of seeing the same events. The imagery is regularly used of God intervening: Exodus 19:16–18; Judges 5:4–5; Psalm 68:7–8; etc.

10 'Fire … coal', as ever the fiery imagery of active, threatening, divine holiness.

11 Out of their usual position, to bring them near earth, facilitating the LORD's entrance on the earthly scene. Or, possibly, 'turned the heavens aside' – removed the usual barrier between heaven and earth.

12 Or 'cloud', the low cloud cover of a stormy day.

13 Compare Ezekiel 1: storm imagery and supernatural beings mark the advent of Yahweh in his glory. Ezekiel describes in detail the cherubim carrying the enthroned God. In Exodus 25:18–22 they cover the Ark and bear the invisible throne of Yahweh.

14 i.e. dark rain-clouds.

15 Lit. 'clouds of clouds'. Possibly the first word (*'abh*) is a concentrated cloud-formation, and the second (*shechaqiym*) dispersed misty clouds.

16 Clouds graciously shielding us from the unbearable brightness? All we see is the cloud, but the brightness – Yahweh in all his glory – is still there.

17 Exodus 9:23 – hail and fire signal the judgment of God.

19. He brought me out into a broad place –
    he extricates me because he is pleased with me.

B.2. Yahweh in righteousness

(Reward: Yahweh and me)

20. Yahweh rewards fully[26] with me,
    according to my righteousness;[27]
    according to the cleanness of my hands
    he makes return to me,
21. because I have kept Yahweh's ways,
    and I have not wickedly deserted[28] my God.
22. For all his judgments[29] are in front of[30] me,
    and his statutes[31] I did not set aside from me,
23. and I have been wholehearted[32] with him,
    and I have kept myself from my iniquity.
24. And Yahweh has made return to me
    according to my righteousness;
    according to the cleanness of my hands before his eyes.[33]

(Equity: you and me)

25. With the loyal you prove yourself loyal;
    with the perfect person you prove yourself perfect;[34]
26. with the pure you prove yourself pure,
    and with the crooked you prove yourself equivocal.
27. For it is the downtrodden that you yourself save,
    and the haughty eyes that you bring down.
28. For you yourself light my lamp;
    Yahweh my God brightens my darkness.
29. For by you I run against a troop,
    and by my God I jump a wall.

B.3. Yahweh in enabling

(Perfect: Yahweh and me)

30. The only transcendent God[35] – his way is perfect.[36]
    Yahweh's word is refined.[37]
    He is a shield to all who take refuge in him.

18 Probably an allusion to Exodus 14:21–22. The Exodus-God in action.

19 *tebhel*, specifically the inhabited world, the world of men, Psalms 9:8; 24:1.

20 The present tenses in verses 16–19 are the 'historic present' – the past described as though happening before our eyes. Nowadays it is called 'stream of consciousness' writing. The verbs are the Hebrew 'imperfect'. In 1 Samuel David was kept safe by what we would call 'natural causes': Saul calling off the chase because the Philistines invaded (23:27); Saul's conscience getting the better of him (24:16); the use of the Ephod (23:9). Where we see 'natural causes', David, in Psalm 18, sees the powerful hand of God.

21 Could be an ellipsis –'he reaches out his hand' (compare 1 Samuel 6:8).

22 Only otherwise used of Moses, Exodus 2:10. David sees himself as parallel to Moses in God's plan for his people: Moses and the law, David and the monarchy.

23 The adjective is not a qualification ('my strong enemy') but as an appositional adjective, 'my enemy, that strong one', compare Psalm 93:4.

24 'get ahead of me', 'anticipate me'.

25 Could be translated 'but'. 'And' is more effective: in every situation there is always the additional factor of Yahweh.

26 *gamal* has the broad sense 'to deal fully with', the nature of the 'dealing' to be determined by context. Here the connection with 'righteousness' requires 'reward'.

27 Not 'sinless perfection' but in the right/free of guilt in the present context, i.e. his dealings with Saul.

28 Lit. 'been wicked from my God'.

31. For who is God except Yahweh?
    And who is a rock apart from our God?
32. The God who equips me with power,[38]
    and has granted my way to be perfect:[39]
33. making my feet like a deer,
    and on my heights he makes me stand;
34. teaching my hands for war,
    and my arms bend a bow of bronze.

(Victorious: you and me)[40]

35. And you have given me the shield of your salvation,[41]
    and your right hand supports me,
    and it is your condescension that gives me increase.
36. You broaden my footing under me,[42]
    and my ankles did not twist.[43]
37. I pursue my enemies and overtake them,
    and I do not turn back until they are finished off.
38. I wound them,
    and they are not able to rise up:
    they fall under my feet.
39. And you have equipped me with power[44] for war:
    you bring down under me those who rise up against me.
40. And as for my enemies, you have given me their necks,[45]
    and as for those who hate me, I exterminate them.
41. They cry for help, and there is no one to save them;
    to Yahweh, and he did not answer[46] them.
42. And I pulverize them – like dust before the wind;
    like mire in the streets I empty them out.
43. You rescue me from the disputes of the people;[47]
    you make me head of the nations;
    a people I did not know serves me;
44. as soon as the ear hears they obey[48] me;
    foreigners[49] give every appearance of submitting[50] to me;
45. foreigners wilt away,
    and come quaking out of their fastnesses.

29 'Judgments', what he has authoritatively decided to be right.

30 As the constant target at which I aim.

31 From *chaqaq*, to engrave, what is carved in the rock for permanency.

32 *tamiym* is the perfect integration of all parts and aspects of a person, undivided commitment.

33 Note the 'inclusion' – how this paragraph begins and end with the same assertion.

34 'Perfect', *tamiym*, that which is as it should be in all its parts. Hence 'perfect', 'complete'. Possibly here, 'wholehearted' in loyalty to Yahweh and receiving 'wholehearted' divine devotion in return.

35 *'el* with the definite article, 'the transcendent God who is indeed *the* God'.

36 'Perfect'. See note 34. The LORD's way is the perfect and perfectly integrated lifestyle, the exactly right way for every aspect of life. Also verse 32.

37 David is thinking of how, through all the difficult days now past, the word the LORD spoke in 1 Samuel 16 about his coming kingship has proved reliable. He has been protected (verse 30c), and found his God reliable (verse 31b), who has kept him on course throughout a very tortuous path (verse 32b), given him surefootedness (verse 33a), finally brought him to the appointed heights (verse 33b), and given him ability and strength in battle where necessary (verse 34).

38 *chayil*, power, resources, wealth, ability, substance, armed force.

39 See note 34.

A.2. Devotion to the saving God[51]

46. Yahweh lives!
    And blessed[52] be my rock!
    And exalted be the God of my salvation!
47. The transcendent God[53] who grants me full requital,[54]
    and has subdued peoples under me:
48. rescuing me from my enemies –
    yes indeed, you lift me high from those who rise up
    against me;
    from the man of violence you deliver me.
49. Therefore I will give you thanks among the nations,
    Yahweh,
    and to your name I will make music –
50. he who magnifies the full salvation[55] of his king,
    and shows committed love for his anointed,
    for David, and for his seed for ever.

40 The translation of the Hebrew tenses in this section is by no means obvious. I have chosen to translate the imperfects as present tense, but bear in mind that this could be treated as 'historic present', or the verbs could be translated as continuous past. For the most part the incidents indicated can be related to items recorded in David's years under Saul.

41 Whom Yahweh saves he also shields.

42 As distinct from a narrow path where one has to pick one's steps, a broad path gives ease for movement without care.

43 Lit. 'slip, totter, prove infirm'.

44 See verse 32.

45 Made them turn their backs.

46 Or was determined not to answer, a perfect expressing fixed attitude.

47 e.g. all the in-fighting of Saul's court and the animosity against David throughout those outlaw years.

48 *sham'a*, 'to hear' easily merges into 'to give a hearing to', hence 'to obey'. The *niphal* mode here allows us to translate 'commit themselves to hearing'. The repeated verb is more effective in Hebrew than it sounds in English: at the hearing of the ear they commit themselves to hearing.

49 Lit. (here and in the next line) 'sons of the foreigner', 'son of', meaning 'in the condition of'.

50 *kachash*, to deceive; Deuteronomy 33:29 (*niphal*) of enemies coming to a show of obedience. On the assumption that the root sense of 'deception' remains, some such translation as 'give the appearance of' is suitable.

51 Verses 46–50 parallel to verses 1–2: note the words 'rock', 'salvation' and 'the transcendent God', but the ending goes beyond the beginning, taking the course of the psalm into account. Note therefore the presence of 'my enemies', 'those who rise up against me'; also the universality of the reference to 'nations', and David referred to now as 'his king'.

52 See Psalm 26:12.

53 *'el'*, the transcendent God, plus the definite article: *the* great God.

54 'Requitals', plural of amplitude.

55 Plural of amplitude.

Pause for Thought

So David finally came to the place of song – as the heading of Psalm 18 informs us. But, my word, it took time! We are not told how many years lay between his anointing (1 Sam. 16) and his initial acceptance as king of Judah (2 Sam. 2), and doubtless there were golden moments, as he basked in the loyalty of his men, rejoiced in the deliverances of Yahweh, or revelled in his new marriage to Abigail, but for the most part they were years of danger and toil, years in which David exchanged the luxuries of Saul's palace for the hardships of a cave dweller. Yet this was the man upon whom 'the Spirit of the LORD came … from that day forward' (1 Sam. 16:13). For the most part, the Holy Spirit in the Old Testament comes as an occasional 'filling' to a particular person for a particular task – corresponding to the filling with the Spirit in the New Testament, where Peter, for example, was filled with the Spirit on at last three occasions to cater for some special situation, but it was different for David. In his case, the Holy Spirit was a constant presence and reality. David's initial experience as a Spirit-endowed man – the former Shepherd is introduced into the royal court and becomes the King's favourite – prompts us readers to nod wisely. This is what we would logically expect – Saul's anointed successor is moving towards his destiny. But then everything goes wrong! Royal favour becomes jealousy; jealousy becomes murderous hate; David takes to his heels and to the hills! Not because the Holy Spirit was withdrawn, but because he was there, shaping everything according to the will of God. We forget all this to our cost. It is always the same, because it has to be so. The Spirit and the flesh are at war (Gal. 5:17); 'through much tribulation' we enter God's kingdom (Acts 14:22). No sooner was the Lord Jesus anointed with the Spirit at his baptism, and assured of his divine Sonship, than he was led by that same Spirit into the wilderness to be tempted by the devil (Matt. 4:1). The Holy Spirit and conflict belong together. David needed that his hand be taught for war (Ps. 18:34); he needed to bend a bow of bronze (v. 34); he needed that his feet be like a deer (v. 33) if he was ever to attain his destined high places. And for all this Yahweh was his teacher, his strength and his enabler.

Day 7 Read Psalms 19–21

Psalm 19.
Three Voices in Harmony

Belonging to the worship-leader; a song of David's.

A. The silent word of creation

(Space)

1. The heavens recount the glory of God.[1]
   And the expanse of the sky[2] declares the work of his hands.

(Time)

2. Day after day[3] pours out speech,
   and night after night reports knowledge.

(Universality)

3. There is no speech,
   and there are no words:
   their voice is not heard.

4. In all the earth their line[4] has gone out,
   and to the end of the peopled-world their utterances.

(The sun, the great marker of time and space)

   For the sun he has set a tent in them:

5. It, like a bridegroom, comes out from his chamber,
   and like a mighty man revels in running his pathway;

6. from the end of the heavens is his emergence,
   and his circuit is to their end,
   and there is nothing hidden from its heat.

1 *'el*, God transcendent.

2 The 'expanse' suggests the night sky. If we take 'the heavens' as the sky by day, then for David the vastness of the sky by day points to *'el*, God in his greatness; the night sky points to divine workmanship. Neither calls attention to itself but points away to him.

3 The regularity of days and nights is part of the unspoken truth, as is the fact that throughout the unbroken sequence the 'message' remains the same.

4 This is the most obvious translation: extending a line is a picture of ownership, domination/conquest, equivalent here to 'they extend their sway to all the earth'. Many change the Hebrew text from *qawwam*, their *qaw*/'line' to *qolam*, 'their voice'; others derive *qaw* from *qawah* meaning 'to call (upon)' which might be exemplified in Psalm 40:1 (usually translated, according to a familiar use of the verb, 'to wait patiently').

5 Note the change from 'God' (verse 1) to the six-fold Yahweh in verses 7–10 (seven-fold if we add verse 14). The silent word of Nature declares 'God'; behind the word of Scripture stands Yahweh, the covenant God of grace and redemption.

6 'Perfect', compare Psalm 18:30. 'Perfectly complete, completely perfect', neither needing addition nor permitting subtraction.

7 'Bringing back the soul', reviving one's personal vitality. Judges 15:19; 1 Samuel 30:12.

B. The perfect word of Yahweh[5]: nature and benefits

7. Yahweh's teaching is complete,[6]
    restoring[7] the soul;
    Yahweh's testimony[8] is trustworthy,
    Giving wisdom to the teachable;[9]
8. Yahweh's precepts[10] are straightforward,
    giving joy[11] to the heart;
    Yahweh's command is pure,[12]
    enlightening the eyes.
9. The fear[13] of Yahweh is clean,
    standing for ever;
    Yahweh's judgments[14] are true;
    righteous altogether!
10.[15] To be desired more than gold,
    than abundant fine gold!
    And sweeter than honey,
    even overflowing honey!

C. The acceptable word of the sinner[16]

11. Also, as regards your servant,
    he is warned by them;
    in keeping them there is an abundant outcome.
12 Mistakes[17] – who can discern them?
    From things kept hidden keep me innocent.
13. Also from presumptuousnesses restrain your servant;
    may they not rule over me!
    Then I will be perfect,
    and innocent of great rebellion.
14. May the words of my mouth accord with your favour,[18]
    and the musings of my heart accord with your presence.
    Yahweh, my rock and my redeemer.[19]

8   What Yahweh 'testifies to' about himself and about his truth. His *torah* (verse 7a) is his teaching; his 'testimony' is his personal authority, his vouching for his teaching.

9   *pethiy*: in a bad sense, 'gullible', the 'empty head' (Proverbs 1:22; 7:7), waiting to be filled with whatever comes its way; in a good sense, open-minded to Yahweh, ready to be taught by him, Psalm 116:6.

10 'Precepts … command' can be treated as synonymous, with the former possibly stressing the thought of application to the details of daily life. Together they insist that Yahweh's word is meant to be obeyed.

11 'Joy … enlightening', not a burden, not imposing a blight or regrettable restriction on life, but rather bringing happiness, relief, and illumination. 1 Samuel 14:27, 29.

12 Is there a distinction between 'pure' and (verse 9) 'clean'? 'Pure' is used of everything that is as it should be, free of what is questionable (whether in essence or by acquisition), Psalm 24:4; Proverbs 14:4; Song 6:9,10. 'Clean' (from the 'levitical' *tahar*), free of anything that would separate from Yahweh.

13 The Word of God fosters a response of reverence.

14 His decisions, what he 'judges' to be right, whether precept, command, prohibition. Compare Deuteronomy 5:1, one word in the vocabulary of revealed truth.

15 Verse 10a–b describes intrinsic value; verse 10c–d experienced pleasure.

16 The A-section above (verses 1–6) ended with the thought of the sun penetrating everywhere. Having reviewed the Word of God in verses 7-10, David now finds that his whole inner being is exposed to its searching.

Psalm 20.
Before Battle:
Prayer and Assurance[20]

Belonging to the worship-leader; a song of David's.

The first voice: a plea that the king's prayer be heard and his offerings acceptable

1. May Yahweh answer you in the day of adversity!
    May the name of the God of Jacob be your[21] top-security![22]
2. May he send you help from the holy place,[23]
    and from Zion may he support you!
3. May he remember all your offerings,
    and make rich your burnt sacrifices! (*Selah*)
4. May he grant you according to your heart,[24]
    and bring all your plans to fulfilment!

The second voice: the king speaks on behalf of his army

5. We will shout aloud in your salvation,
    and in the name of our God we will raise our banners.

The first voice again: a wish that the king's prayer be answered

5c. May Yahweh fulfil all your requests!

The second voice again: the king's confidence in Yahweh

6. Now,[25]
    I know that Yahweh has determined to save his anointed one.
    He will answer him from the heavens[26] of his holiness,
    with the all-sufficient might[27] of the salvation of his right hand.

17 A noun (*shegiy'ah*) from *shagah*. The usual translation 'to sin by inadvertence': an 'inadvertent sin' does not reflect the real intention of the word which is rather something that is out of keeping with the general tenor of life, a 'mistake' (as Genesis 43:12), a 'slip up'.

18 Lit. 'be for favour': 'favour' (*ratson*), compare Leviticus 1:4 ('accepted').

19 My *go'el* – the *go'el* is the next-of-kin whose right it is to take as his own the burden that his distressed kinsman is bearing. Compare Ruth 2:20; 3:9,12,13; 4:1–14; Psalm 72:14; 78:35; 103:4.

20 How are we to understand why verses 1–4 are prayers for 'you' (masc. sing.); in verse 5a–b 'we' speak of confidence in 'our God'; in verse 5c we seem to hear the first voice again, praying for 'you'; in verse 6 'I' speaks about Yahweh saving and answering 'his anointed'; verses 7–8 are 'we' verses, affirming reliance on Yahweh and assured of coming victory; and verse 9 addresses Yahweh as king and pleads for answered prayer? With some imagination, we can find here a number of participants in an act of worship preparatory to battle.

21 The person addressed as 'you' would appear to be the one on whom everything depends. Who could this be but the king, in this case David himself?

22 See Psalm 9:9.

23 Lit. 'from the holiness', but in conformity to the parallelism with 'from Zion', this is a reference to Yahweh in his earthly dwelling, the 'holy of holies'.

24 A literal rendering, meaning 'what your heart desires'.

25 The temporal 'now', at this time. As the first voice prayed (verse 5c) a fresh spirit of assurance came to the king.

The first and second voices together: united reliance on Yahweh

7. These in chariotry,
   and these in horses,
   and we – we will keep in mind the name of Yahweh, our God.
8. They are the ones destined to bow down and fall,
   and we to rise up and be restored.

The first voice again: a final prayer that Yahweh hears and answers

9. Yahweh, please save!
   True King,[28] answer us the day we call!

Psalm 21.
Royal Rejoicing:
Present Glories, Victories to Come[29]

Belonging to the worship-leader; a song of David's.

A.1. Yahweh's strength, the king's joy

1. Yahweh, in your strength the king rejoices,
   and in your salvation how greatly he exults!

B.1. Blessings granted and enjoyed

2. His heart's desire you have granted him,
   and the wish of his lips you have not held back. (*Selah*)
3. For you anticipate his needs with blessings of good;
   you set on his head a crown of pure gold.
4. Life he asked from you.
   You gave it to him –
   length of days for ever and ever![30]

26 The God who graciously lives in Zion (verse 2) does not cease thereby to be the heavenly God, supreme in sovereignty.

27 Lit. 'the mightinesses of the salvation …' a plural of amplitude.

28 Lit. 'The king', meaning 'the one and only real king'. Some (see ESV) alter the punctuation of the Hebrew text to read 'Yahweh, save the king. May he answer us …!' This is needless meddling. A final prayer on behalf of the earthly king to *The King* is a suitable and very effective ending.

29 Dating this psalm is not possible. Any high point in David's career when he counted his blessings and looked forward to the future glories associated, messianically, with his office.

30 It is with touches like this that we see David is moving easily between what he enjoys of divine blessings and the blessedsnesses of Messiah's reign. At some early point the dynastic promises of 2 Samuel 7 modulated into the expectation of an eternal king.

31 'Him' and 'blessings' are in apposition, implying that to say the one is to say the other. The thought, therefore is complex: (a) 'You appoint for him blessings' and (b) 'You make him to be (the means of) blessings.' The plural expresses amplitude: he enjoys and is the bestower of every possible blessing to the fullest extent.

32 Lit. 'with/in the company of your face'. 'Face' emphasizes personal presence.

33 Are the verbs in this section descriptive of coming events (the future victories envisaged by David) or are they in effect present tenses descriptive of Yahweh's customary acts for his Messiah and against his foes? I have opted for the latter, only because the balance of the Psalm as a whole seems to me to be in the messianic direction.

5. Great is his glory through your salvation:
    splendour and majesty you set on him.
6. For you make him blessings[31] for ever.
    You gladden him with joy in your presence.[32]
7. For the king is trusting in Yahweh,
    and through the committed love of the Most High he will
    not be shaken.

B.2. Blessings and victories anticipated[33]

8. Your hand finds out about[34] all your enemies;
    your right hand finds those who hate you.
9. You make them like an oven of fire[35] in the time of your
    face[36] –
    Yahweh in his exasperation swallows them up,
    and fire devours them.
10. From off the earth you destroy their fruit,
    and their seed from among the sons of man.
11. For they directed[37] evil against you;
    they devised a plan – beyond their ability! –
12. for you make them turn back;[38]
    with your bow-strings you make preparations against
    their face.

A.2. Yahweh's strength; his people's song

13. Be exalted, Yahweh, in your strength.
    We will indeed sing and make music to your mightiness.

34 The verb 'to find' followed by the
    preposition *le*. Only elsewhere
    Deuteronomy 22:14; 1 Samuel 13:22.
    The latter gives the sense, 'belonging
    to', but the former, 'to find out about'.

35 An oven was an earthenware pot which
    was heated for use by being filled
    with combustible material and set
    alight. Here 'an oven of fire' is such a
    pot set alight, a figure of intense, all-
    consuming fire. 'Fire' symbolises the
    active holiness of Yahweh.

36 i.e. one look is enough! When you look
    at them; or when you appear.

37 *natah*, to turn, bend, stretch, stretch
    out, extend. Nowhere else used of 'evil'.

38 Lit. 'you make them a shoulder'.

Pause for Thought

The trouble with the silent voice of creation (Ps. 19) is that it 'says' so many different things! On the one hand there is the sentiment that 'one is nearer God's heart in a garden than anywhere else on earth', and this can be extended to so many other experiences: the astonishing beauty of the sky at sunset, the grandeur of a mountain landscape. But I don't know of a poem that says 'one is nearer God's heart in an earthquake than anywhere else on earth'. It is exactly the same length of line; it scans properly; and it accords with the biblical assertion that 'the earth is the LORD's' (Ps. 24:1) – not just the 'nice' bits but the whole, the rough bits too. Indeed, we would be in a disastrously poor way if the Lord God Almighty were 'there' only in fair weather and not in foul! So then, as we listen to the unspeaking 'voice' of the natural world, we 'hear' a confused babble, a question rather than an answer: what is the Creator 'really' like? It's time, then, that Isaac Watts taught us to sing a different song:

> The heavens declare thy glory, Lord;
> In every star thy wisdom shines.
> But when our eyes behold thy Word,
> We read thy name in fairer lines.

How exact that is! 'Glory' shines in the created order: the glory of beauty; the glory of beneficence; yes, and the glory of awe-inspiring, terrifying forces! But the Word of God tells us *his name, who he is*. The One who is God, in all the multiplicity of ways his creation reveals, is, at heart, in his central, personal essence, Yahweh, the God of grace, the God who hears and acts, the God of our salvation. He is the God of the Word of God, and, like the Word he speaks, a God reviving the soul, making wise, bringing joy, illuminating; indeed, all righteous, but golden in grace, and honey to those who taste and see that Yahweh is gracious (Ps. 34:8).

Day 8   Read Psalms 22–23

Psalm 22.
The One and the Many:
One Suffering, Many Worshipping

Belonging to the worship-leader; set to 'The Hind[1] of the Dawn'; a song of David's.

A. Perplexity in suffering[2]

(An Unanswered Cry)

1. My God, my God,[3]
    why did you forsake me?[4] –
    Why distant from my salvation,
    from the words of my roaring?[5]
2. My God, I keep crying out by day,
    and you do not hear!
    And I the night,
    And I keep no silence.
3. And you are holy,[6]
    sitting enthroned in the praises of Israel.[7]
4. In you our fathers trusted.
    They trusted,
    and you rescued them!
5. To you they shouted out,
    and they escaped.
    In you they trusted,
    and they were not disappointed.

(Unrewarded trust)

6. And I am a worm and not a man;
    a taunt of mankind, and despised by people.
7. All who see me keep laughing at me;

1   The word (*'ayyeleth*) means 'hind', but it is very like a word (*'eyal*) meaning 'help' (Psalm 8:4). If so, 'Help in the Morning'. Either way, presumably the tune recommended for the Psalm.

2   The psalm goes beyond any experience of David's. While it could arise from some time of suffering it goes far beyond such to torture and death. We are listening to David the prophet (Acts 2:30) looking forward to the suffering Messiah.

3   Each time *'el*, God transcendent, God in power.

4   Matt. 27:46; Mark 15:34.

5   A strong word (*sha'agah*). The verb (*sha'ag*) is used in verse 13 of a roaring lion.

6   Whatever the severity of the trial, no reproach is allowed against God: he is still the Holy One; and since 'holy' expresses the central essence of the divine nature, however foes may seem to triumph he is still the God of power and might.

7   A compound thought: He is the enthroned God; his mighty acts are known to his people, therefore they praise him; as they praise him, so he is sovereignly with them.

8   Lit. 'Roll (it) to Yahweh', compare Psalm 37:5, 'Roll your way …'; Proverbs 16:3, 'roll your works …'.

9   Matthew 27:39–43; Luke 23:35–37.

10 Uncertain translation, suitable to context.

11 'From the womb'. In verse 9 the word translated 'womb' and in verse 11 'body', is, lit. 'the belly'.

they keep grimacing with their lips;
they keep wagging their heads:

8. 'Commit[8] it to Yahweh!' –
'He will rescue him';
'He will deliver him because he is pleased with him.'[9]

9. For you are the one who brought me out[10] of the womb,
who caused me to trust, at my mother's breasts.

10. Upon you I have been cast from birth;[11]
from my mother's body, you are my God.[12]

B. Prayer for divine nearness[13]

11. Do not be distant from me,
for adversity is near;
for there is no helper.

12. Many bulls have surrounded me;
mighty ones of Bashan have encircled me;

13. they have opened their mouth wide at me,
a lion ravaging and roaring!

14. Like water I have been poured out,[14]
and all my bones are dislocated.[15]
My heart has become like wax:
it has melted within my inner parts.

15. My strength has dried up like earthenware,
and my tongue is stuck to my jaws,[16]
and to the dust of death you have brought me down.

16. For dogs[17] have surrounded me,
an assembly of wicked men has closed me in,
piercing my hands and my feet.[18]

17. I can count all my bones.
They look, open-eyed,[19] at me.[20]

18. They share out my clothes for themselves,
and over my clothing they cast lots.[21]

19. And you, Yahweh, do not you be distant!
For my help, O my Strength,[22] come quickly!

20. From the sword deliver my soul,
from the hand[23] of the dog,[24] my unique one![25]

12 '*el*' as in verse 1.

13 Trouble is near (verse 11), enemies rampant (12–13), suffering intense (14–15), wickedness unrestrained (16–18). Renewed appeal and sudden sense of response (19–21).

14 Of strength evaporating under intensity of suffering?

15 A likely consequence of the unnatural position of the crucified person. The possibilities of the meaning of the verb (here in its Hithpael or reflexive mode of *paradh*): 'separate themselves, show themselves, come apart, stick out'.

16 John 19:28.

17 Used as a synonym for worthless, despicable, 2 Samuel 3:8. Like 'dogsbody'.

18 This remains the most likely translation of the Hebrew as we have it. Other suggestions involve highly dubious emendations.

19 The idiom of two verbs without a connecting particle: the second carried the sense; the first qualified. 'They take note they look', 'They look observantly', 'they goggle'.

20 Matthew 27:36; Luke 23:35.

21 Matthew 27:35; Mark15:24; Luke 23:34; John 19:23–24.

22 Noun '*ayyaluth*, compare heading.

23 'Hand' means 'power'.

24 Compare verse 16.

25 Compare Psalm 35:17, where again the parallel with 'soul' requires us to understand 'my one and only life'.

26 Quoted as messianic in Hebrews 2:12.

27 Singular, a reference to the sufferer of the earlier verses.

Save me from the lion's mouth,
from the horns of the wild oxen …
…YOU HAVE ANSWERED ME!! …

C. Praise on a universal scale

(Festival time for Israel)

22. I will recount your name to my brothers;[26]
    among the congregation I will praise you.
23. You who fear Yahweh, praise him!
    All you seed of Jacob, glorify him!
    And reverence him, all you seed of Israel
24. because he has not despised and he has not detested
    the humiliation of the downtrodden:[27]
    he has not hidden his face from him –
    when he cried to him for help, he heard!
25. From you comes my praise[28] in the great assembly;
    my vows I will pay in full in front of those who fear him.
26. The downtrodden ones will eat[29] and be satisfied;
    those who seek him[30] will praise Yahweh.
    May your heart live for ever!

(Festival time for the world)

27. They will remember and return to Yahweh,
    all the ends of the earth;
    and they will bow in worship before you,
    all the families of the nations.
28. For to Yahweh belongs the kingship,
    and he rules the nations.
29. They will surely eat and bow in worship,[31]
    all the prosperous[32] of the earth;
    before him will bow all who are about to go down to the dust,
    each who cannot keep himself alive.[33]
30. A veritable seed indeed[34] will serve him!
    It will be recounted about Yahweh[35] for the future.[36]
31. They will come out and declare his righteousness,

28 Yahweh is the source as well as the object of praise.

29 Paying vows (verse 25) involved a 'peace-offering', which included a family and communal feast (Leviticus 7:15-21; Deuteronomy 12:12). Here the 'guest list' includes those of the existing people of God (verses 25–26) and a worldwide people (verse 27).

30 See Psalm 9:10; 10:4.

31 Perfect tenses, here interpreted as perfects of certainty.

32 Lit. 'fat ones'.

33 A comprehensive gathering: those who might seem to be able to manage on their own, those about to perish, and the 'born losers'. They will all hear the glad cry; May your heart live (verse 26)!

34 Hebrew 'a seed' is treated here as the idiom 'indefiniteness for the sake of emphasis' (e.g. Isaiah 37:4, 'a living God!'). The 'seed' here is the worldwide Israel; all who are gathered to the messianic feast: Isaiah 25:6-9.

35 i.e. How Yahweh answered (verse 21) and created the universal people through the Great Sufferer.

36 Lit. 'for a generation'.

37 Matching the 'It is finished' at Calvary (John 19:30).

38 Lit. 'waters of rest', but the word has a wide range: rest, home, security, quiet.

39 See Psalm 19:7.

40 i.e. that match his righteous nature and lead to his righteous goals.

41 This is our security and confidence: his leadership does not arise from or correspond to anything in us or that we have done; it arises only from what is in his heart and nature.

to a people to be born,
that he has taken action.[37]

Psalm 23.
Shepherd, Companion and Host

A Song of David's.

(The Shepherd)

1.   Yahweh is my shepherd:
I will not lack.
2.   In pastures of fresh grass he makes me lie.
Beside secure waters[38] he guides me.
3.   He restores my soul.[39]
He leads me along tracks of righteousness,[40]
for the sake of his name.[41]

(The Companion)

4.   Even when I am walking in the valley of deadly shadows
I do not fear evil,[42]
Because you are ever with me:[43]
your rod and your staff[44] reassure me.

(The Host)

5.   You lay a table before me,
in front of my adversaries.[45]
You have refreshed my head with oil;
my cup is more than full![46]
6.   But indeed good and committed love
will pursue me[47]
all the days of my life,
and I will return[48] to Yahweh's house
for ever.[49]

42   This word (*r'a*) ranges from a nasty taste to full moral evil. Its meaning depends on the context. Here it would at least start with the general term 'harm'.

43   The more emphatic word for 'with' (*'imadiy*). If, as seems likely, this linked with the verb (*'amadh*) 'to stand', it merits the translation 'ever'.

44   'Rod' (*shebhet*) is used once (Leviticus 27:32) of shepherding; the second word 'staff' comes from the verb (*sha'an*) 'to lean on'. Together they constitute the idiom of reduplication to express completeness: comprehensive protection from every danger.

45   Very probably a recollection of 2 Samuel 17:24–29 – an incident bound to live on in memory.

46   Lit. 'my cup is saturation'.

47   If these verses recall the days of flight from Absalom then the choice of the verb 'to pursue' is very telling. Whatever danger pursues there is always a greater pursuit afoot – Yahweh's goodness and committed love.

48   So says the Hebrew, but the verb is similar to 'I will dwell' and possibly is meant to bring it to mind in a complex thought 'return and stay'; no more of the flittings inseparable from this life.

49   Lit. 'for prolongation of days'.

Pause for Thought

The two psalms read today provide a striking contrast between the holy and the homely. Psalm 22 is such holy ground that we take off our shoes and walk with careful, even hesitant steps. More than any other passage of Scripture it penetrates into the actual suffering of our crucified Lord: the pierced hands and feet, the body itself agonizingly pulled apart, the racking thirst, the mocking onlookers. Thank God for the reticence of the Gospel accounts: truly 'we may not know, we cannot tell/ what pains He had to bear'. Psalm 22 presses to the limit of what Scripture allows, and we do well to read it sparingly and with awe. We are face-to-face with the sheer reality of divine inspiration, for, 1000 years before the event, David not only foresaw suffering, but the suffering of the Crucified. We marvel as well as tremble. This is the unique miracle of Holy Scripture. We worship the Lord our God both for the extremity he suffered for us, and for the book he has written for our learning. But – and here is a lovely thing – the homely Psalm 23 is equally true! It can be seen (as we have noted) as a threefold picture. Now note that each picture – Shepherd, Companion, Host – asserts a truth: for the continuous present, as long as this life lasts, shepherding care guarantees that 'I will not lack'. This is the Shepherd's responsibility and since he will not fail neither will the supply! For the adversities and threats of life, 'I will not fear evil'. However black the next stretch of the journey through the valley may seem, verse 4 changes from the 'he' of shepherd-leadership (v. 3) to the 'you' of side-by-side companionship: 'My Shepherd is beside me.' But now, the Bible dares to go the further step: what of eternity? Verse 6 traces the pathway forward: 'all the days of my life' are catered for by goodness and committed love, and then there awaits the great return, 'I will return to Yahweh's house for ever', for the endlessly prolonged 'days' of eternal life.

Day 9   Read Psalms 24–25

Psalm 24.
Fling Wide the Gates

David's, a song.

Approaching[1]

1. To Yahweh belongs the earth and its fullness,
   the peopled-world[2] and those living in it,
2. because it is he who founded it on the seas,
   and establishes[3] it on the rivers.[4]

Welcoming[5]

3. Who may ascend Yahweh's hill?
   And who may rise up[6] in the place of his holiness?

(Personal integrity)
4. Clean of hands[7] and pure of heart;

(Spiritual Integrity)
   who has not lifted up his soul[8] to falseness;[9]

(Social Integrity)
   and has not sworn with deceitful intent.
5. He receives blessing from Yahweh –
   righteousness from the God of his salvation.
6. This is the characteristic[10] of those who seek him,
   those who seek[11] your face,
   Jacob.[12] (*Selah*)

1   An incident like 2 Samuel 6 suits this psalm. A procession bearing the Ark of the Covenant nears the gates, proclaiming Yahweh as creator and possessor.

2   *tebhel* is specifically the inhabited world. Psalms 9:8; 18:15; 19:4.

3   Note the continuous present tense: the Creator is the ever active maintainer.

4   Used here of 'ocean tides', the movement of the seas – seen as a constant 'threat' to the stability of the creation, therefore needing the constant vigilance and ongoing care of the Creator God.

5   The question raised in these verses (3–6) is not who can come in but who can stay. The procession contains not just the Ark, symbol of Yahweh's presence, but a whole retinue with him. May they too climb the hill and take their stand?

6   *qum,* to rise up. For its religious use as an attitude of worship, see Exodus 33:10; a forensic, legal use, to stand up in court, to make and maintain a case, see Psalm 1:5; 27:12. Who can take his place as a worshipper, make a case for his right to be there?

7   The hand as 'grip'; here, what the hand takes hold of and retains.

8   The major Hebrew Text reads 'my soul', but it seems best to follow many MSS in rather reading 'his soul'.

9   Heb. *shaw'*, not 'an untruth' but 'untruth'. Exodus 20:7: of any and every sort of religious aberration, identifying Yahweh with worthless gods.

Entering[13]

(Request)

7.   Lift up, O Gates, your heads,
      and be lifted up, everlasting doors,
      that the king of glory may come in.

(Interrogation)

8.   Whoever is the king of glory?

(Reply)

      Yahweh, strong and mighty!
      Yahweh, mighty in war!

(Request)

9.   Lift up, O Gates, your heads,
      and lift them up, everlasting doors,
      that the king of glory may come in.

(Interrogation)

10.   Who is this king of glory?

(Reply)

      Yahweh of Hosts![14]
      He is the king of glory!

Psalm 25.
An A – Z for Troubled Times[15]

David's.

A.1. Waiting on Yahweh

1.   To you, Yahweh, I lift up my soul.[16] (*aleph*)
2.   In you, my God, I have trusted. (?*beth*?)
      Do not let me be disappointed.[17]
      Do not let my enemies exult over me.

10 Lit. 'Generation', a 'circle' of folk held together by common factors. The interpretative translation 'characteristic' (or 'hallmark') suits this context: they have in common that they 'seek' Yahweh (see Psalms 9;10; 10:4), find him to be their saving God, and in consequence live the life of threefold integrity.

11 Two different verbs are used in this verse for 'seek'. No distinction in meaning seems to be involved.

12 In the Hebrew as here, 'Jacob' comes at the end. Unless we are to re-write the text and read 'God of Jacob' (see ESV), 'Jacob' must stand as a noun in apposition: the people just described 'are Jacob' (see NKJV); they bear the marks of the genuine people of God.

13 The procession stands at the gates, requesting admission, confidently answering the gate-keepers' questions.

14 For the most part 'Yahweh' and 'Hosts' have a genitive relationship ('of'), but in Psalm 59:5–6, where we have 'Yahweh God of Hosts', 'God' and 'Hosts' are nouns in apposition (see also Psalms 80:4–5, 7–8,14–15,19–20), requiring the meaning 'God who is Hosts'. This is the vital clue to the meaning intended: Yahweh is, in his own essence 'Hosts'; his unity (Deuteronomy 6:4) – as indeed the use of the word for 'one' here in Deuteronomy (*'echad*) can imply – is not a bare singularity but a unity comprising a multiplicity. Compare 'one' in Exodus 26:11. As 'Yahweh of Hosts' he comprises within himself every potentiality and power.

3. Also, as for all those who wait for you – (*gimel*)
do not let them be disappointed.
Let those be disappointed
who are acting treacherously without cause!
4. Your ways, Yahweh, make me to know;[18] (*daleth*)
teach me your paths.
5. Direct me by your truth and teach me,[19] (*he*)
because you are the God of my salvation:
it is for you I wait all day.

B.1. Dealing with sin (past): do not remember

6. Remember your compassions, Yahweh, (*zayin*)
and your committed loves,[20]
for they are from of old.
7. The sins of my youth, and my rebellions (*cheth*)
do not remember;
according to your committed love
remember me,[21]
for your goodness' sake, Yahweh.

C.1. Divine teacher: Who are his pupils?

8. Good and upright is Yahweh, (*teth*)
therefore he teaches sinners in the way.[22]
9. May he direct the downtrodden in judgment,[23] (*yodh*)
and teach the downtrodden his way.[24]
10. All Yahweh's ways are committed love and truth (*kaph*)
for those who preserve his covenant and his testimonies.[25]

B.2. Dealing with sin (present): forgive

11. For your name's sake, Yahweh, (*lamedh*)
forgive my iniquity, for it is abundant!

C.2. Divine teacher: Who are his pupils?

12. Who indeed is the man who fears Yahweh? – (*mem*)
he will teach him in the way he chooses.

15 Psalm 25 is 'alphabetic acrostic'. Each successive verse begins with the next letter of the Hebrew alphabet. Psalm 119 is the Golden Acrostic where the alphabet is complete and each letter is accorded eight verses. Psalm 25 is an incomplete or broken acrostic – for example, the letters *waw* and *qoph* are omitted; *beth* can only be found by readjusting the text. This brokenness is probably a literary device: the subject (life's troubles) is too complex to claim that it can be completely covered. See also Psalm 145 on the praises of God, where *nun* is missing (but is invented by NIV, ESV from other sources).

16 i.e. 'commitment, loyalty, dependence', Psalm 24:4. But the context in Psalm 25 points rather to seeing in Yahweh alone the solution to life's needs.

17 The verb 'to be ashamed' but, as usual, with the meaning 'to reap shame' rather than merely 'to feel embarrassment'. Hence 'to be disappointed of one's hope'.

18 The Hebrew word order here is shockingly awkward in English. 'Your ways' (*deracheyka*) provides the leading consonant (*daleth*) and is therefore in the emphatic position.

19 The sequence of verbs is important: verbs of knowing followed by verbs of doing: no true knowing without intent to practice the truth; no possibility of practicing the truth until it is known. The place of learning is the place of waiting (Proverbs 8:34); the place of waiting is the place of transformation (Isaiah 40:31).

20 'Compassion' is love in the heart of God: what he feels towards us; 'committed love' is love in the will of God: what he has decided and how he has obligated himself to us. Both words are plural: compassion always is plural; 'committed love' infrequently so. Plural of amplitude, love in its fullness, divine commitment without reserve.

13. His soul will lodge with good, (*nun*)
    and his seed will possess the earth.
14. The fellowship of Yahweh belongs to those who fear him,
    (*samech*)
    and he intends to teach them his covenant.

A.2. Waiting on Yahweh[26]

15. My eyes are constantly fixed on Yahweh,
    for it is he who will bring my feet out of the net.
16. Turn to me and grant me your grace, (*pe*)
    for I am on my own[27] and downtrodden.
17. The troubles of my heart have grown large; (*tsadhe*)
    bring me out of my pressures![28]
18. See my affliction and trouble, (*resh*)
    and bear all my sins away.[29]
19. See my enemies, for they are many, (*resh*)
    and with hatred expressed in violence they hate me.[30]
20. Oh keep my soul, and deliver me; (*shin*)
    do not let me be disappointed, for I have taken refuge in you.
21. Let integrity and uprightness preserve me, (*tau*)
    for I have determined to wait on you.

(David's wider concern)
22. O God, ransom[31] Israel from all his troubles!

---

21 A more complicated and emphatic set of words than can conveniently be expressed in English: 'remember for my advantage, you!'

22 A very remarkable 'therefore'. The goodness and uprightness of God – the very features which our sinfulness offends – are in fact the reason why he bothers to teach us.

23 'Judgment' is the authoritative decision of judge or king; the decision of authority as to what is right. Here 'according to what he has decided upon'.

24 'Direct' and 'way' are respectively verb and noun from the same root: 'Direct … his direction.'

25 i.e. the word of God as spoken by God himself. What he has 'testified to' about himself, and his ways and requirements.

26 The final section and the opening section have a wide range of thoughts and words in common: 'eyes' (15) match 'soul' (1); 'taking refuge' (20) matches 'trust' (2); both sections speak of 'enemies' (2,19), disappointment (2–3, 20) and 'waiting' (5, 21).

27 *yachidh*, used in Genesis 22:2 of the 'unique' Isaac, 'one on his own', 'solitary'. So, here, of David, sensing that he is totally isolated, bereft of association, no resource. In this way verse 16 confirms verse 15, the exclusive fixing of the eyes on Yahweh.

28 Verses 17–21 are closely integrated; 17 and 18 are thematically united by 'troubles'; 18 and 19 by the initial 'see' in each case; 19 and 20 by presence of enemies and the need for deliverance; 20 and 21 by the matching thoughts of taking refuge and waiting.

29 The picture of 'sin-bearing' looks back to Leviticus 16:21–22.

30 The strikingly forceful expression 'with hatred of violence' does not describe the violence of the hatred but the way the hatred shows itself.

31 There are two verbs used for 'redeem'. One is *ga'al* which provides the participle *go'el*, the next of kin whose right it is to take upon himself, and as his own, the burden (whatever it may be) of his kinsman. This verb, therefore, points to the *person* of the redeemer. The other verb (used here) is *padah* which focuses on the *price paid* to effect the ransom.

Pause for Thought

Alongside Psalm 24, Psalm 25 is profoundly comforting. Psalm 24:3–4 is the Old Testament counterpart of Hebrews 12:4. To take our stand in the presence of God, we must be holy as he is. It has always been so (Lev. 19:2), and always will be so (Rev. 21:27). But, if we are thinking of parallels between the Testaments, then the reference in Revelation 21:27 to the Lamb's book of life is a blessed and comforting recollection of the balancing truths of Psalm 25. The holy God, who insists on his holiness as the standard, is also the forgiving God. This means that he always has other things in mind than just our sinfulness and unworthiness. According to 25:6–7, he can look back over our sin-stained past and forget what he has seen! But, compared with what he banishes from mind and memory, three things are permanent: 'compassion' (his 'passionate love'), his solemnly 'committed love', and his 'goodness'. He never looks at us saving through these three 'windows'; indeed, says the remarkable verse 8, it is actually because ('therefore') he is good and upright that he bothers with sinners so as to lead and teach us. How good is that! Using the great, comprehensive word 'holy', we rightly tremble at the thought of standing before the holy God, and then, reading 25:8, we can say that it is because he is holy that he bothers! Verse 11 puts the same truth in another way: it is 'for his name's sake' – that is to say, because he is what he is; because his 'name' is an accurate shorthand for his revealed nature, he pardons my iniquity, great as it is. But look, too, at the matching truth in verse 16. In verse 11 we appeal to him on the ground of what he is; in verse 16 we can appeal to him on the ground of what we are, bereft and downtrodden. The recurring thought in Psalm 25 is its encouragement to 'wait on the Lord', bringing confidence (v. 3), concentrating on divine teaching (v. 5), summoning to holiness (v. 21).

Day 10 Read Psalms 26–28

Psalm 26.
Integrity, Past and Future

David's.

A.1. 'I have walked': the past reviewed

1. Judge[1] me, Yahweh,
   because, for my part,
   I have walked in my integrity
   and in Yahweh I have trusted:
   I have not slipped up![2]

B.1. Divine examination invited

2. Test[3] me, Yahweh,
   and try me;
   assay my feelings and my heart,[4]
3. for your committed love is before my eyes,[5]
   and I constantly walk about[6] in your truth.

C.1. Confession of innocence (negative): life before others

4. I have not sat with men of falsehood,
   and I do not go along with those with hidden motives.[7]
5. I have hated the assembly of evil doers,
   and with the wicked I do not sit.

C.2. Confession of innocence (positive): life before God

6. I wash my hands in innocence,[8]

1 As always with the basic meaning of 'make your decision about me'. David brings himself before the bar of Yahweh's scrutiny in relation to some situation in which he can claim integrity and needs to be differentiated from the wicked.

2 An imperfect (here continuous) tense, looking back over the past. It could be translated as a 'participial' imperfect, 'without slipping up'.

3 The three verbs for 'testing' here are broadly synonymous. If distinction is possible, then 'test' (*bachan*) is to test for purity, reality, reliability; 'try' (*nasah*), to test circumstantially for fidelity; and to 'assay' (*tsaraph*), to test for impurity (specifically of precious metal), to refine.

4 Physical organs used as 'seats' of psychological states: 'feelings' is 'kidneys', the seat of the emotions. The 'heart' is used generally of human nature 'on the inward side', but, alongside 'kidneys', more particularly the mind.

5 i.e. it is what I 'have an eye to', the target I aim at, the ideal I want to achieve.

6 The form of the verb here is imperfect tense, used of constant, characteristic action, and its mode is *hithpael*, as in Genesis 13:17, of Abram walking up and down, hither and yon in the land; in Genesis 17:1 of Abraham living out his life, in all its movements and activities, before God.

7 Lit. simply the plural adjective 'hidden', not used in this implied sense elsewhere. See Psalm 28:3 for the thought, and compare our suspicion of a 'hidden agenda'.

and I go around your altar, Yahweh,

7. to make people hear the voice of thanksgiving,
   and to recount all your wonders.

8. Yahweh, I have loved the dwellingplace[9] of your house,
   the place of the abode of your glory.

B.2. Divine response invited

9. Do not collect up my soul with sinners,
   nor with bloodguilty men[10] my life,

10. in whose hands is scheming,[11]
    and their right hand is full of bribes.

A.2. 'I will walk': the future pledged

11. And, for my part, I will walk in my integrity.
    Ransom me,[12] and grant me your grace.

12. My foot has taken its stand on a level place.
    In the great gathering[13] I will bless[14] you.

Psalm 27.
The Confident Life

David's.

A.1. Confidence

1. Yahweh is my light and my salvation:
   whom should I fear?
   Yahweh is the fortress of my life:
   whom should I dread?

2. When evildoers come near against me,
   to eat my flesh –
   my adversaries and my enemies –
   it is they who are doomed to stumble and fall.[15]

3. Should an army camp[16] against me,
   my heart will not fear;

8 For hand-washing, Deuteronomy 21:6.
   'In innocence' means 'in token of …'
   For priestly washing before entering on
   their duties, Exodus 30:17–21. David
   accepts this standard for himself.

9 i.e. where Yahweh dwells.

10 'Men of bloods', 'bloodthirsty',
    people who would stop at nothing; or
    'bloodguilty', actually with blood on
    their hands.

11 Lit. 'a scheme'. The word is almost
    entirely used in a 'bad' sense, hence
    'scheming'.

12 See Psalm 25:22.

13 Plural of amplitude – a feminine
    plural of the same word appears in
    Psalm 68:27, and as a place name in
    Numbers 33:25.

14 The simplest way to understand
    our 'blessing' Yahweh is to remind
    ourselves that when we ask him to
    'bless' someone it is shorthand for 'take
    note of his needs and meet them'. So
    when we 'bless' Yahweh it is shorthand
    for 'take note of his glories and
    excellencies and respond to them in
    wonder and adoration'.

15 Perfects of certainty: a future event
    so certain or inevtable that it can be
    described as having already happened!

16 Lit. 'should a camp camp'. This sort of
    repetition is effective in Hebrew but
    awkward in English

should war arise against me,
in spite of this I remain trusting.

B.1. Yahweh's house, my security in his shelter

4. One thing I have asked from Yahweh:
    that is what I keep seeking:
    that I may live in Yahweh's house
    all the days of my life –
    to gaze at the delightfulness of Yahweh,
    and to search things out[17] in his temple.

5. For he will hide me in his booth
    in the evil day;
    he will cover me with the covering of his tent;
    on a rock he will raise me high.

6. And now my head will be high,
    above my enemies around me.
    And I will sacrifice in his tent
    sacrifices with loud shouting:
    I will sing,
    and I will make music to Yahweh.

B.2. Yahweh's face, my security in his favour

7. Hear, Yahweh!
    With my voice I keep crying out.
    Grant me your grace, and answer me.

8. To you my heart has said –
    'Seek my face!'[18]
    'Your face, Yahweh, I will seek.'

9. Do not cover your face from me!
    Do not turn your servant away in exasperation!
    You have been my help.
    Do not leave me!
    And do not forsake me,
    God of my salvation.

10. When[19] even my father and my mother have forsaken me,

17 Other occasions of this verb (*baqar*) do not help us to understand what is meant here (Leviticus 13:36; 27:33; 2 Kings 16:15; Proverbs 20:25; Ezekiel 34:11–12). It may simply mean that the 'house' is the place to 'seek' Yahweh's presence in worship – the general meaning of both other verbs 'to seek', see Psalm 10:4. Or (as above) the house is the place where the solution to life's conundrums becomes clear (Psalm 73:17). Some favour the meaning 'to seek for divine answer'; others, relating the verb to *boqer*, 'morning', 'to come early'.

18 Since verse 8b is plainly something Yahweh has said to David, commentators tend to assume that the Hebrew Text has become dislocated, and they set about, by various expedients, to put it right. As the text stands, the first word of David's heart to Yahweh is to repeat Yahweh's invitation and then record his own response. In other words, the text as we have it is unexpected rather than impossible! The 'face' is the organ of favour (or disfavour), depending whether it is turned towards or away; whether it is shining or frowning. See Numbers 6:25; Psalm 13:1; Psalm 31:16.

19 'When' (KJV) can be used in the same sense as *'im* 'if', but with the hint that the condition at least has the likelihood of being fulfilled. Possibly, therefore 'If and when'. But there is no need to suppose that David was ever deserted in this way.

20 In verses 11–12, David, having realized that his security rests in Yahweh's favour, commits himself wholeheartedly to Yahweh's way for living (11) and safety (12).

it is Yahweh who gathers me in.

11.[20] Teach me, Yahweh, your way,
and guide me along a level path
because of those hostile to me.

12. Do not give me over to the desire of my adversaries,
for those who bear witness to a lie have risen against me,
each puffing out violence.

A.2. Confidence

13. Would that I had believed[21] to see Yahweh's goodness
in the land of living!

14. Wait for Yahweh!
Be strong,
and he will empower your heart!
Wait for Yahweh!

Psalm 28.
Deadly Danger: Prevailing Prayer

David's.

A.1. Prayer made: Yahweh my rock

1. To you, Yahweh, I keep calling out.
My Rock,[22]
do not turn in deafness from me,[23]
lest you turn in silence from me,[24]
and I be like those going down into the Pit.[25]

2. Hear the voice[26] of my plea for grace,
when I cry to you for help,
when I lift up my hands to the shrine[27] of your holiness.

B.1. David and the wicked: contrasting destinies

3. Do not drag me away with the wicked and with the
trouble-makers,[28]

21 I believe this to be the correct rendering of the text as we have it. It suggests some previous lapse on David's part. This is somewhat confirmed by the insistence of verse 14 on waiting on Yahweh. Others treat the words as an exclamation, 'Except I had believed…!' – i.e. just think what would have happened in that case!

22 'Rock', by its nature is a 'passive' metaphor, depicting strength, permanence, reliability, 'there-ness'. But in the Old Testament it is also linked with Exodus 17, the smitten rock, the source of life-giving water, an 'active' metaphor for Yahweh acting on behalf of his people, supplying, saving, reviving.

23 Lit. 'Be deaf from me'.

24 Lit. 'are silent from me'.

25 'Pit' is a general equivalent to Sheol, the 'place' where the dead live on (Proverbs 1:12; Ezekiel 26:20), but some verses (as here) suggest 'the Pit' is reserved for the wicked: death under divine anger (Psalms 30:3; 88:4); dying with God's face hidden (Psalm 143:7); cut off from God, a discreditable death (Isaiah 14:15,19). David's dread in Psalm 28 is not death as such but death with unmerited disgrace, dying while Yahweh remains 'deaf' and alienated, a death which seems to identify David with the wicked.

26 'Voice' is never redundant. It always expresses the verbalizing of prayer: a very important idea in the Old Testament.

27 *debhiyr,* the innermost shrine. Mainly used of Solomon's Temple, by which time *dehiyr* had become a standard term of reference. In essence it expresses here the idea of prayer 'penetrating' right into Yahweh's very presence.

who speak peace with their fellow-men
    while evil is in their heart.
4.   Give[29] to them according to their deeds,
    and according to the evil of their doings,
    according to the work of their hands give to them;
    bring back to them their full recompense.
5.   For they never discern Yahweh's deeds,
    nor the work of his hands.
    He will demolish them and not build them up.

A.2. Prayer heard: Yahweh my strength and shield

6.   Blessed[30] be Yahweh,
    for he has heard the voice of my plea for grace:
7.   Yahweh, my strength and my shield.
    In him my heart has trusted,
    and I am continually helped.
    My heart celebrates,
    and with my song I keep thanking him.

B.2. David and Israel: shared blessing

8.   Yahweh! – strength belongs to him,[31]
    and he is a fortress of full salvation for his anointed.
9.   Oh do save your people,
    and bless your inheritance.
    Shepherd them,
    and carry them for ever.

---

28 See Psalm 5:5.

29 It would be easy (and wholly wrong) to read these verses as the product of vindictiveness. Rather they express the ideals of a healthy society in which rewards are exactly apportioned according to deserving, and the rightness and inevitability of a day of judgment.

30 See Psalm 26:12.

31 The preposition used here (*lamo*) is ambiguous, being either third singular ('to him') or third plural ('to them'). Most interpret as 'to them', i.e. a reference to Yahweh giving strength to his people. But the parallelism with B.1 (verse 3), favours a reference to David throughout verse 8, as does the immediately preceding context which is wholly occupied with David.

Pause for Thought

Very central to the Old Testament is the thought of Yahweh's 'house'. It is one of the links between our three psalms: 26:8 has 'dwelling place', 'abode', 'house'; 27:4–5, 'house', 'temple', 'booth', 'tent'; 28:2, 'inner shrine'. Each word has its own significance to share, but together they express in common the one privileged thought that Yahweh actually 'localised' himself in an earthly address. Our churches are places to which we go to be with him; his 'house' was a place to which he came in order to be with us. Sometimes some of our English Bibles represent 'house' by 'temple'. This is very wrong, destroying the beautiful truth of the God who comes to live at the heart of his people's life. 'Tent' looks back to the wilderness days when Israel were a camping people, and the LORD in effect said: If you are camping, I want to camp too! Read Numbers 2 and arrange the lines of Israel's tents like a great cross, with the LORD's tent – the 'Tabernacle' – placed at the crossing. Doesn't that express visually the reality intended: Yahweh, the indwelling God, at the very heart of his people? Look at Psalm 34:7, the Angel of the LORD in a mobile home so that he is always free to move with his people. The use of 'booth' develops the idea of the sharing God. When Israel kept 'the feast of booths', they actually lived in makeshift shelters of branches of trees, to remind them of their travelling days: that they were travellers because they had been redeemed by Yahweh at the Exodus; that Egypt and bondage were behind them for ever; and that, however flimsy their dwelling places, they were safe and provided for in his keeping. And now, living in his own 'booth', he actually shares their hardships, their vulnerability. When his dwelling is called a 'temple' we are reminded that the reality of his presence among us is a call to worship. In the same spirit, his 'house' is where his glory dwells (26:8) – the unapproachable glory of Exodus 40:35 – and his 'inner shrine' is 'the shrine of his holiness' (28:2). The homeliness of Yahweh taking an earthly address, and the intimacy of his actually coming to live among his people, must never degenerate into casualness. He is with us in all his glory; in the fullness of his holiness. The place on which we stand is holy ground, and without the precious blood of atonement we dare not enter his presence.

Day II Read Psalms 29–31

Psalm 29.
The Storm and the Glory

A Song of David's.

A.1. Heavenly supremacy and worship

1.   Give to Yahweh, sons of God,[1]
     give to Yahweh glory and strength.
2.   Give to Yahweh the glory due to his name.
     Bow in worship to Yahweh in[2] the majesty of holiness.

B. Voices in the storm

(b.1) Storm at sea
3.   Yahweh's voice over the waters!
     The transcendent God of glory has thundered!
     Yahweh over many waters!
4.   Yahweh's voice in power!
     Yahweh's voice in majesty!

(b.2) Storm in the north[3]
5.   Yahweh's voice is breaking the cedars –
     Yahweh has broken the cedars of Lebanon:
6.   he has made them skip like a calf –
     Lebanon and Sirion[4] like a young wild ox!
7.   Yahweh's voice is cleaving the flames of fire!

(b.3) Storm in the south
8.   Yahweh's voice makes the wilderness writhe:
     Yahweh makes the wilderness of Kadesh[5] writhe.
9.   Yahweh's voice makes the deer give birth,
     and has stripped the forests bare,
     and in his temple everything is saying 'Glory!'[6]

1   In Psalm 89:6–7 the identical words refer (as the parallelism with 'who in the heavens' indicates) to heavenly beings. We can treat 'sons of' as the idiomatic use indicating state or condition – as when the 75 year old Abram (Genesis 12:4, lit.) is described as 'son of 75 years'. 'God' is the plural of *'el*, probably used here in its vocabularic sense of 'strength/might'. Hence 'mighty ones'. Compare, ESV, text and margin.

2   i.e. 'in regard to', as his holiness merits.

3   The storm sweeps inland: first (verses 5–6) the wind lashes the trees; then, along with thunder (verse 7), come flashes of forked lightning. Or, perhaps, translate: 'Yahweh's voice cuts (the trees) asunder with flames of fire.'

4   Sirion is Mount Hermon, in the anti-Lebanon range, the highest mountain in Palestine.

5   In the extreme south of Judah. Is the storm here accompanied by an earthquake? Or is the magnificent poetry just continued, 'convulses the wilderness'?

6   The description begins (verse 5) and ends (verse 9) with 'glory'. To many the storm is simply awesome (verses 3–4), or destructive (verses 5–7), or a meaningless display of power (verses 8–9). Those who know Yahweh in his temple see it as his glory: he, in all his glory, is there in the storm.

7   *mabbul*, only used in Genesis 6–9: the reference here is to the great Flood, Yahweh reigning supreme in holy judgment.

A2. Earthly sovereignty and blessing

10. It was Yahweh who sat enthroned at the Flood:[7]
    Yahweh has taken his seat as king for ever!
11. It is Yahweh who keeps giving strength to his people;[8]
    it is Yahweh who keeps blessing his people with peace.

Psalm 30.
Only by Grace

A song. A hymn[9] at the dedication of the house.[10] David's.

A.1. Out of the pit: prayer leading to praise

1. I will exalt you, Yahweh,
    for you have drawn[11] me up,
    and you have not let my enemies[12] rejoice over me.
2. Yahweh, my God, I cried out to you for help,
    and you healed me.
3. Yahweh, you brought my soul up from Sheol;
    you have quickened me so that I should not go down to
    the pit.[13]

B.1. Truth for all

4. Make music to Yahweh,
    you who are his beloved,[14]
    and give thanks to the reminder of his holiness,[15]
5. for there is but a moment in his exasperation,
    and lifetime in his favour;[16]
    in the evening weeping may stay overnight,
    but, in the morning, joyful shouting!

B.2. Truth for David

6. As for me,
    I said in my prosperity:
    'I will not be disturbed for ever.

8   Just as Yahweh has 'sons' in heaven (verses 1–3) who worship responsively to his glory, power and holiness, so, on earth, he has his people who, in a world deservedly under judgment, live within his blessing and peace.

9   *Shiyr*, another word for 'song'. 'Hymn' is suggested simply for variety.

10   What 'house'? NIV and ESV pre-empt discussion by representing 'house' by the word 'temple'. The heart of the psalm is David's confession of a complacent spirit, assuming that divine favour and grace could be taken for granted, and asserting that he learned better through a visitation of severe illness which put in jeopardy his monarchy, called in question his standing before God, and gave his enemies a handle to use against him. It is certainly easy to fit this scenario into 2 Samuel 5; 1 Chronicles 21–22 – even though illness is not recorded there – and therefore to see 'house' as David's own newly-built residence.

11   A vivid image: *dalah*, of drawing a bucket up from a well, Exodus 2:16.

12   Right up to the time of Absalom's rebellion (2 Samuel 16:5) there were Saul loyalists cursing David. There must have been even more such at the earlier date of the dedication of David's house, ready (as we might say) 'to rain on his parade'.

13   See Psalm 28:1.

14   Plural of *chasiydh*, the recipients of Yahweh's *chesedh*, his 'committed love'.

15   See Exodus 3:15. Yahweh's name is what keeps him in mind, as the summary statement of what he has revealed of himself, and therefore the encapsulation of his holiness.

7. Yahweh, by your favour,
    You have established strength as my mountain.'[17]
    You hid your face;
    I became terrified!
8. To you, Yahweh, I kept crying out,
    and to the Sovereign I kept making my plea for grace.
9. What profit is there in my blood,
    in my going down to the pit?[18]
    Does dust give you thanks?
    Does it declare your truth?
10. Hear, Yahweh,
    and grant me your grace.
    Yahweh, be the help I need!

A.2. Out of mourning into exaltation: transformation leading to thanksgiving

11. You have turned my mourning right round for me into
    dancing;
    you have unfastened my sack-cloth,
    and girded me with joy!
12. In order that glory may make music to you[19] and not be
    silent.
    Yahweh, my God,
    for ever I will thank you!

Psalm 31.
At the End of One's Tether, a Place called Prayer

Belonging to the worship-leader; a Song of David's

A. The trap set; prayer and commitment

(Be my rock)

1. In you, Yahweh, I have taken refuge.
    Do not let me ever be disappointed.[20]
    In your righteousness, rescue me.

16 David does not make his personal testimony a truth for all: he would have all Yahweh's people rejoice in what is true of their God: that his holiness includes a capacity to move at speed from anger to favour.

17 The thought is not that his mountain was strong but that his strength was mountainous. Here an expression of David's complacency.

18 David is not here speaking about every death, but death at a time when Yahweh has hidden his face and withdrawn his favour.

19 Or 'in order that one may make music to you gloriously'. This, at any rate, gives good sense.

20 'Put to shame'/'reap shame'. See Psalm 25:2, note 17.

21 See Psalm 18:2, note 3.

22 See Luke 23:46. The Lord Jesus did not quote verse 5b.

23 *padah*, see Psalm 25:22, note 31.

24 i.e. *'el*.

25 Plural, expressing intensity.

26 i.e. where there is plenty of footing, room to stand firmly.

27 The 'eye' looks ahead, fixes goals, focuses longings. The failing eye is a picture of loss of hope and expectation.

28 'Soul and body' stand for the whole person in its inner and outer aspects. There seems nothing left to live for ('eye'), nor any resilience left to 'take any more vexation'. 'Body' (*beten*), cf. Habakkuk 3:16, may refer to failure of 'nerve'.

2. Turn your ear to me.
   Deliver me quickly.
   Be a fortress-rock for me,
   a fortified house to save me.

(You are my crag)

3. For you are my crag[21] and my fortress:
   for your name's sake lead me and guide me.
4. Bring me out of the net they have hidden for me,
   for you are my place of safety.
5. Into your hand I commit my spirit:[22]
   you have ransomed[23] me,
   Yahweh, transcendent God[24] of truth.

(Trust, joy, security)

6. I hate those who keep to empty things of falsehood.
   As far as I am concerned,
   it is in Yahweh that I have put my trust.
7. Oh, I exult and rejoice in your committed love,
   in that you have seen my humiliation;
   you have known of the deep distress[25] of my soul,
8. and you have not consigned me into the hand of my
   enemy;
   you have made my feet stand in a broad place.[26]

B. Isolation, prayer and trust

(No further capacity to endure)

9. Grant me your grace, Yahweh, for I am distressed.
   My eye,[27] my soul and my body[28] have become weak
   through vexation.

(Iniquity)

10. For my life has come to an end with sorrow,
    and my years with groaning;
    my strength[29] has stumbled through my iniquity,
    and even my bones[30] have grown weak.

29 *koach* is often used in balance with
   chayil, where the latter points to wealth
   and other externally available resources
   (in the case of a king, his army), and
   the former to inner resource, personal
   resilience, ability – as here, but eroded
   by moral causes, as when David's
   ability to face up to the challenges of
   life presented by his own family was
   weakened by his sin over Bathsheba
   and her husband (2 Samuel 11). Was
   this the setting of Psalm 31?

30 The physical constitution, here with its
   robustness virtually gone.

31 'Away from the heart', equivalent to
   'out of sight, out of mind'.

32 'Like a thing perishing/exterminated'.

33 'Time' here is *'eth*, not a date but a
   period marked by some characteristic.
   For example 'May' is a date, but
   'Spring' is a characteristic, a particular
   sort of time. 'Times' here is pretty well
   equivalent to 'experiences', the whole
   course and content of life, the way
   things work out.

34 It is always important to note the
   context of references like this to the
   dead: here it is specifically the destiny
   of the wicked that is in mind. Hence
   'silent'.

35 From *'athaq*, 'to move forward',
   hence the noun 'forwardness' in an
   objectionable sense, going beyond the
   bounds.

36 'Face' stresses the personal, distinctive
   presence of Yahweh (just as we
   recognize people by face), i.e. in all his
   reality and individual distinctiveness.

37 A likely but slightly insecure
   translation.

(Enmity, isolation, defamation, conspiracy)

11. Through all my adversaries I have become a thing of
    reproach –
    and to my neighbours especially –
    and a source of dread to my acquaintances –
    and those who see me out of doors fly from me!

12. I have been forgotten –
    like someone dead – out of mind![31]
    I have become like something obliterated![32]

13. For I have heard the whispering of many –
    fear all around –
    while they close ranks together against me,
    plot to take my life!

(Trust, looking for deliverance, favour, mercy)

14. And as for me,
    on you I place my trust, Yahweh:
    I have said: 'You are my God!'

15. In your hand are my times;[33]
    deliver me from the hand of my enemies,
    and from those that pursue me.

16. Oh, make your face shine on your servant!
    Save me, in you committed love!

17. Yahweh, do not let me be disappointed,
    for I have called to you.

C. Contrasting destinies

(Sheol and silence)

   Let the wicked be disappointed.
   Let them be dumb in Sheol![34]

18. Let lips of falsehood be silenced
    which speak against the righteous
    in an unrestrained way,[35]
    with pride and contempt.

38 On 'booth' see on Psalm 27:5. Such
   an unusual thought can only be
   explained by a reference to the 'feast
   of booths', with its deliberate recall
   of Israel's safety during the vulnerable
   days of desert travel. Hence, the truth
   of our safety in the invisible 'refuge' of
   Yahweh's face.

39 See Psalm 26:12.

40 'Love' is the Old Testament's
   broadest word, covering a wide area
   of affections. It pitches our love for
   Yahweh at the level of the manageable
   rather than using the great word for
   'committed love', that is his undying
   love for us. 'Beloved' is passive noun
   linked to *chesedh*, 'committed love',
   'those who are loved with Yahweh's
   committed love.'

(Goodness and protection)

19. How abundant is your goodness,
    which you have secreted away
    for those who fear you,
    and prepared for those who take refuge in you,
    in front of the sons of man!

20. You will cover them with the covering of your face[36]
    from men's plots;[37]
    you will secrete them away in a booth[38]
    from the strife of tongues.

D. Responses: personal and communal

(Divine love and answered prayer)

21. Blessed[39] be Yahweh,
    for he has shown how marvellous is his committed love for me
    in a city under siege.

22. And for my part,
    I said when I was alarmed,
    'I have been cut off
    from in front of your eyes.'
    But in fact
    you heard the voice of my plea for grace,
    when I cried out to you for help.

(Love returned; confidence maintained)

23. Love Yahweh,
    all you his beloved.[40]
    Yahweh really does preserve the faithful,
    and requites to the last degree whoever acts in pride.

24. Be strong,
    and let your heart prove mighty,
    all you who are waiting for Yahweh.

Pause for Thought

The revelation of God in the Bible is full of contrasts, and one of our greatest mistakes (and temptations) is to try to reduce the number of such contrasts so as to bring the great God of Scripture within the confines of what our logic can manage. We saw something of this in our thoughts about Psalm 19 – how it is easy to think of God's heart in a garden but not so easy in an earthquake! The Bible will not let us off that hook – and how glad we should be that it does not. We would indeed be in queer street if the LORD God was not in charge when the sun goes in and the clouds threaten. That is exactly where today's readings come in. In Psalm 29 David's marvellous poetic gift watches the storm sweeping in from the sea, marching spectacularly down the country, causing havoc: trees crashing down, open country devastated. In Yahweh's temple there is only one word, maybe shouted in exultation; maybe whispered in awe: 'Glory!' Yahweh in all his glory is in the storm. But now review the four sections of Psalm 31. It is Yahweh's eye that is expected to note who, in all the flux of earthly life, is right with him and acting in righteousness, and who is wicked, arrogant, beyond the beyonds. It is Yahweh who is expected to apportion due reward, up to the utmost degree of requital to those who act in arrogance. In other words, here is detailed sovereign rule over the world of moral choices, moral consequences; here is a God who searches and knows hearts, motives, intentions, outcomes. He is there in all his glory in the broad sweep of the storm; he is there in all his glory as the searcher of hearts. He is there when the storm brings disruption; he is there as the enforcer of moral order. He is there in macromanagement; he is there in micromanagement. He is God!

Day 12 Read Psalms 32–33

Psalm 32.
'That moment … a pardon receives'[1]

David's. A Maskil.[2]

A.1. Statement one: the blessedness and fulness of forgiveness

(Sin forgiven)

1.   Blessed is he with iniquity[3] borne away,[4]
     with sin covered.

(No charge; no stain)

2.   Blessed is the human to who Yahweh does not reckon iniquity,
     nor is there in his spirit deceit.

B.1. Testimony: confession and forgiveness

(Delay)

3.   When I kept silent,[5]
     my bones[6] wore out
     through my roaring[7] all the day.

4.   For, day and night,
     your hand was heavy upon me.
     My moisture[8] was changed right round[9]
     as by the all-consuming heat[10] of summer.

(Confession and response)

5.   My sin – why, I let you know[11] it,
     and my iniquity I did not cover[12] over!

1   From the wonderful verse 2 of Fanny van Alstyne's hymn, 'To God be the Glory'.

2   The first of thirteen psalms to which this description is given. From *sakal*, to be prudent, well thought-out action leading to the desired result, *maskil* (part of the *hiphil* mode, to ponder, think through; act with prudence) is probably rightly understood as 'didactic' (compare verse 8). A teaching poem.

3   Two of the leading words in the sin-vocabulary. 'Iniquity' is the 'warped' human nature; 'sin' the specific misdemeanour. (The third word is 'wilful rebellion'.)

4   'To bear away' sin is a regular Old Testament idiom for forgiveness. Its root is in the 'scapegoat' ceremony of the Day of Atonement when the High Priest 'put' Israel's iniquities, rebellions and sins (note, all three words) on the head of the goat, and it then 'bore' them away, never to be seen again. This 'sin-bearing' concept is basic to Old Testament atonement theology.

5   This psalm may well be a further insight into the David-Bathsheba incident (2 Samuel 11). There could well have been a period during which David thought he had 'got away' with his sins and crimes, and during which, none the less, he suffered agonies of conscience.

6   Reference to decreasing physical resilience.

7   A very dramatic word to choose: it basically refers to the roar of a lion as it pounces on its prey, Judges 14:5.

I said, 'I will make confession of my rebellions to Yahweh,
and for your part,
you bore away the iniquity of my sin,[13]. (*Selah*)

A.2. Statement two. Conclusion drawn: prayer and safety

6.   On this account,
     every beloved will pray to you
     in a season of finding:[14]
     surely, in the inundation of abundant waters
     To him they will not reach.

B.2. Testimony: preservation and guidance

(Human testimony: security in Yahweh)

7.   You are a covert for me.
     From trouble you will preserve me.
     With ringing cries of rescue you surround me. (*Selah*)

(Yahweh's testimony: what he promises and what he expects)

8.   I will give you insight and I will teach you
     in the way you are to go;
     I will counsel you,
     my eye fixed on you!

9.   Do not be as a horse, as a mule –
     without discernment:
     with bridle and halter its ornament for restraining.
     No approach to you![15]

A.3. Statement three: trust brings love and joy

10. Many are the pains of the wicked,
     but whoever is trusting in Yahweh –
     committed love surrounds him.

11. Rejoice in Yahweh,
     and exult,
     you righteous ones,

8   *Leshadh,* only elsewhere in Numbers 11:8 ('a juicy thing of oil'). The present use is unexemplified, but refers to 'vitality', vital juices.

9   *haphak,* to overturn, virtually a technical term for what God did to Sodom (Genesis 19).

10   Lit. 'heats', a plural of amplitude, hence some such word as 'all-consuming' or 'enervating'.

11   Lit. 'I caused you to know'.

12   Of these two verbs, the first is imperfect tense and the second the expected perfect tense of past action. The imperfect must be used here to give vividness to the change of mind involved.

13   This immediacy of forgiveness following penitence reflects 2 Samuel 12:13.

14   The fuller, comparable phrase occurs in Isaiah 55:6 ('in his being found'); so here: '*eth* (compare Psalm 31:15, note 33) 'a time giving the opportunity of finding (you).'

15   The Hebrew is as abrupt as this rendering, but we are dealing with allusive poetry and the sense is clear. Yahweh desires conscious, thoughtful obedience to his word of direction, not the enforced conformity of the harnessed beast, dressed for show in accoutrements which are actually not 'ornaments' to it at all but evidences of subjugation. The last line could be a statement 'No coming near you' – a reference to the essential wildness of an animal not yet 'broken'. Or 'Else it will not come near you' – an obedience of compulsion.

and shout aloud,
all you who are upright in heart.

Psalm 33.
The Creator, the Word,
the Nations, the People[16]

A.1 The voice of praise

1. Shout,[17] you righteous,[18] with joy in Yahweh.
    For the upright, praise is fitting.
2. Give thanks to Yahweh with the lyre,
    with a ten-stringed harp make music to him.
3. Sing to him a new song.[19]
    Play well on the strings with triumphant shouting.[20]

B.1. Yahweh's world, Yahweh's word

(His word, his love and his creation)
4. For Yahweh's word is upright,
    and all his work is in truth.
5. He loves righteousness and judgment.[21]
    The earth is full of Yahweh's committed love.
6. By Yahweh's word the heavens were made,
    and by the Spirit[22] of his mouth all their host.
7. He gathers, like a heap, the waters of the sea.[23]
    He puts the deeps in storehouses.[24]

(His word and the peopled world)
8. Let all the earth be afraid[25] of Yahweh.
    Let all the inhabitants of the peopled-world go in dread
    of him.
9. For it is he who spoke and it came to be.
    It was he who commanded and it stood.
10. It is Yahweh who makes[26] the counsel of the nations
    ineffectual,

16 This very stylish poem is unattributed. It consists of opening and closing sections (verses 1–3, 20–22) each of six lines (of Hebrew), and between them four stanzas of eight lines each: the first two dealing with Creation (verses 4–7, 8–11), the second two with Yahweh's special people (verses 12–15, 16–19).

17 *ranan*, to give a ringing cry, to shout aloud. The added idea of joyful, exuberant praise, etc., depends on the context.

18 'Righteous' always has a primary meaning of 'right with God'. Just as forensically it means 'acquitted at law', so it means at one with Yahweh, acquitted before him.

19 The idea expressed by 'a new song' is of a song freshly responding, as when a new truth is grasped or an old truth freshly appreciated.

20 *teru'ah* is the war cry of Joshua 6:20; the religious shouting of 2 Samuel 6:15. Psalm 27:6 speaks of 'sacrifices of shouting'.

21 When they occur together like this, 'righteousness' refers to righteous principles and 'judgment' to righteous application and practice.

22 Or 'spirit' or 'wind' or (presumably) 'breath' (Hebrew would have used a different word missing if it meant 'breath'). A reference to the Spirit of God suits the recollection of Genesis 1:2 (compare NKJV) on which the Psalm is based here.

23 The sea is the only aspect of earthly creation picked out for mention – possibly because its ceaseless turbulence is often symbolic of opposition to the Creator, and the poet wishes to remind us that this restless element is nevertheless subordinate to its Creator and his word.

frustrates the plans of the peoples.

11. It is Yahweh's counsel that for ever will stand,
the plans of his heart to generation after generation.

B.2. Yahweh's world, Yahweh's people

(The blessed people)

12. Blessed[27] is the nation whose God is Yahweh!
The people he chose to be an inheritance for himself!
13.[28] From heaven Yahweh looks.[29]
He sees all the sons of man!
14. From the established place of his dwelling he gazes
at all the inhabitants of the earth,
15. he who altogether shapes their heart,
he who discerns all their works.

(The people of reverence and hope)[30]

16. There is no king saved by the abundance of his resources,
nor an individual[31] delivered by the abundance of
strength.
17. The horse is a falsehood for salvation,
nor by the abundance of its might can it rescue!
18. Behold! Yahweh's eye is on those who fear him,
on those who hope for his committed love,
19. to deliver their soul even from death,
and to preserve them alive in famine.

A.2. The heart of joy

20. Our soul waits[32] for Yahweh:
our help and our shield is he.
21. For our heart will rejoice in him,
because in his holy name we have trusted.
22. May your committed love, Yahweh, be on us,
according as we have hoped in you.

24 A poetic way of saying that all the forces of nature, including the hidden movements in the depths of the seas, the deepest ocean currents, are at Yahweh's disposal, and come out into operation by his direction.

25 Or ' … will be afraid … will go in dread …' It is a matter of judgment which suits the context.

26 'Makes … frustrates' are both perfect tense, the perfect expressing what is invariable.

27 See 1:1.

28 The intention of verses 13–15 is to enhance the reality of verse 12. A real choice was involved. The Creator has the whole world at his disposal, every individual known in heart and life. Out of all this conglomerate he really did choose the people he desired to have.

29 'Looks … sees … gazes' are perfects as in note 24, but in verse 15, 'shapes … discerns' are participles – the unvarying relationship of Creator to created, stressing a moment by moment 'shaping' and 'discerning', character and conduct alike.

30 Neither position (16a), ability (16b) nor resource (17) can save, only a relationship with Yahweh of reverence and trustful hope (18).

31 Or 'warrior, mighty man'.

32 Perfect tense; see note 24.

Pause for Thought

Psalm 32 achieves no mean feat by alerting us – dramatically – to the seriousness of sin. Even though it is, in fact, the least aspect of the problem of sin, the psalm underlines the personal pity of it all. Sin burdens, diminishes and blights the life of the sinner (vv. 3–4). It may not be felt but in fact it is like carrying around a sack of sand. Proverbs 7:23 says sexual promiscuity is the equivalent of being shot in the liver by an arrow! Paul (1 Cor. 6:18) teaches that the adulterer sins against his own body! Not, we might say, the common view, but exactly what Psalm 32 implies about David's 'roaring'. Then at a deeper level is the alienation and hostility of God, whose hand goes out heavily against the sinner. We need to take this on board. David is writing as a believer and of a believer's sins. The hurt done to our holy God alienates him, grieves his Holy Spirit (Eph. 4:30), and leaves us diminished – vitality turned to aridity. 'Flee childish lusts' counsels Paul (2 Tim. 2:22); 'follow righteousness'. What a relief, then, to note the miracle (no less) of repentance (Ps. 32:5). The sheer simplicity of it! 'I let you know … you forgave.' Yes, even though he alone knows 'the iniquity of my sin' – 'my sin in iniquity!' See the same thought in Psalm 51:1–3 (note 'because') – and the very incident recorded in 2 Samuel 12:13. This simplicity of dealing with sin by repentance is made possible through substitution. The principle of one standing in the place of another goes back at least as far as Abraham: recall how, without instruction, he knew he could kill the ram 'in the place of his son' (Gen. 22:13). The same principle pervades the levitical sacrifices – everywhere we read of the sinner laying his hand on the sacrifice (e.g. Lev. 1:4). He is enacting on a personal level what the High Priest did nationally in Leviticus 16:21–22: transferring sin in all its penalties to another, appointing a substitute. Isaiah foresaw that ultimately only a Person could be a true substitute for persons (53:4–6), foreshadowing Jesus, when

> In my place, condemned he stood;
> Sealed my pardon in his blood.

In this way (Ps. 32:1), sin is 'covered' – not by being hidden out of sight but as a debt is 'covered' by the price which pays for it. Wonder of all wonders, my sin is no longer put to my account, but is 'imputed' (Ps. 32:2) to Another.

Day 13   Read Psalm 34

Psalm 34[1]

David's. When he changed his sense[2] in the presence of Abimelech,[3] and he drove him away, and he went.

A.1. Framework: shared testimony[4]

1. Oh, I will bless[5] Yahweh on every occasion.[6] *(aleph)*
    Continually his praise will be in my mouth.
2. In Yahweh my soul will make its boast[7] *(beth)*
    The downtrodden will hear and rejoice.

B.1. Full deliverance

3. Magnify Yahweh with me. *(gimel)*
    Let us raise up his name together.
4. I sought Yahweh and he answered me, *(daleth)*
    and from all my terrors he delivered me.

C.1. Look and be saved

5. They looked to him and they were beaming, *(he)*
    and their faces were certainly not abashed.[8]
6. This downtrodden one called, and Yahweh himself heard,
    (zayin)
    and out of all his troubles saved him.

D.1. The camping angel

7. The Angel of Yahweh[9] is ever actually camping[10] *(cheth)*
    around those who fear him, and has extricated them.
8. Taste[11] and see that Yahweh is good. *(teth)*
    Blessed[12] is the individual who takes refuge in him.

1   A 'broken acrostic' psalm: see introduction to Psalms 9–10.

2   The incident is recorded in 1 Samuel 21:10–15. See further the following 'Pause for Thought'. The verb *ta'am* (apart from Psalm 34:8; Proverbs 31:18) is only used of tasting food. The noun is also used of what one 'senses' to be right, right behaviour (e.g. 1 Samuel 25:33; Job 12:20; Psalm 119:66; Proverbs 11:22 and 26:16; Jeremiah 48:11; Jonah 3:7). 'Changed his taste' is usually understood as 'put common sense to one side', 'feigned madness'. It speaks of changing from what would have been ordinarily 'proper' in such a situation.

3   In 1 Samuel, Abimelech is called Achish. Probably Achish was the king's personal name and Abimelech his throne name – just as Edward VII was 'Bertie', or George VI 'Albert'.

4   Verses 1–2 introduce the psalm: Yahweh is to be praised in every circumstance. Verses 11–12 mark a change from testimony to teaching, drawing lessons from what is known of Yahweh. Verses 21–22 offer a conclusion: Yahweh who ransoms, and the security of those who take refuge. The intervening verses (3–10, 13–20) balance testimony and matching truths.

5   See Psalm 26:12.

6   *'eth*, see Psalm 31:15.

7   This idea of 'boasting' must be purged of any sense of arrogance. The verb does mean 'to boast' but the sense is 'to express joyful confidence'.

E.1. Fearing Yahweh, finding provision

9.   Fear Yahweh, you his holy ones, *(yodh)*
   for there is nothing lacking to those who fear him.
10. Even lions[13] go in want and are hungry, *(kaph)*
   but those who seek Yahweh lack nothing good.

A.2. Framework: shared teaching

11. Come, sons, listen to me: *(lamedh)*
   The fear of Yahweh is what I will teach you –
12. who is the man who desires life, *(mem)*
   who loves days so as to see good?

E.2. The mark of the God-fearing life[14]

13. Preserve your tongue from evil, *(nun)*
   and your lips from speaking deceit.
14. Turn from evil and do good; *(samech)*
   seek peace and pursue it.

D.2. The nearness of Yahweh[15]

15. Yahweh's eyes are to the righteous, *(ayin)*
   and his ears[16] to their cry for help.
16. Yahweh's face is against those who do evil *(pe)*
   to cut away remembrance of them from the earth.

C.2. Cry out and be saved[17]

17. They cry[18] and Yahweh is listening, *(tsadhe)*
   and from all their troubles he delivers them.
18. Yahweh is near[19] to the heart-broken, *(qoph)*
   and those crushed in spirit he saves.

B.2. Full deliverance[20]

19. Many are the evils of a righteous one, *(resh)*
   and from them all Yahweh delivers him.

8   Hebrew uses the imperative to express a future event so certain that (so to say) it can be commanded to happen. Thus, Genesis 12:2 'you will be a blessing' is, lit. 'be a blessing'. The negative imperative here ('do not be abashed') expresses a certainty as to what cannot be.

9   The Angel of Yahweh is both identical with Yahweh and distinct from him. See Genesis 16 where we meet 'the Angel' for the first time: he both speaks as Yahweh and as distinct from Yahweh. Exodus 33:2–3 reveals him as accommodating Yahweh's holy presence to the company of sinful Israel. The Angel is an Old Testament preview of the Lord Jesus.

10 The verb is both a participle, expressing an ongoing situation, and also here stands in the emphatic position.

11 See 'taste' in the heading to this psalm (note 2).

12 *'ashrey*, see Psalm 1:1.

13 *kephiyr*, often translated 'young lion', i.e. the lion in its prime.

14 This title is justified by the fact that verses 15–16 begin to fulfil the purpose stated in verse 12, to teach the fear of Yahweh. The link with **E** is thematic. **E.1** tells of the blessing brought by fearing Yahweh; **E.2** teaches the foremost mark of the God-fearing life. This huge emphasis on sins of speech is typical of the whole Bible.

15 The **D**-sections are linked by how close Yahweh is to his own people – camping with them, watching them.

16 Yahweh is interested not only in what he sees about us but also in what we have to say about ourselves and our needs.

17 The **C**-sections open with the matching ideas of 'looking' and 'crying out'. They both also affirm total salvation.

20. He keeps all his bones: *(shin)*
    not one of them is broken.

A.2. Framework (3): shared security

21. Evil will put the wicked to death,[21] *(tau)*
    and those who hate the righteous will be held guilty.[22]
22. Yahweh indeed ransoms[23] the soul of his servants, *(pe)*
    and none who take refuge in him will be held guilty.

_____

18 The verbs in verses 17–18 present the usual problems of interpretation. 'Cry' and 'delivers' are perfect tense: are they perfects of fixed attitude – therefore to be represented by English present (as stating what is always so), or do they look back to some notable past action? 'Saves' is an imperfect used as a 'frequentative': what is customarily the case.

19 'Near' *(qarobh)* is used of the Next-of-kin (Ruth 2:20; 3:12), the one whose right it is to take on himself as his own all the needs of his troubled relative.

20 The **B**-sections share the vocabulary of deliverance and totality.

21 Here again is the 'boomerang' nature of sin: it always infects us with the seeds of its own destruction.

22 'Held guilty' is the verb of the 'guilt offering' – in connection with which the sinner was obliged to take into account the manward consequences as well as the Godward. Correspondingly, to be 'held guilty' implies that in judgment nothing will be overlooked, absolutely everything will be brought into the light. Likewise 'not to be held guilty' is to be given a total clearance of every charge.

23 See Psalm 25:22. 'Indeed' is introduced in the translation because 'ransom' is in the emphatic position in the sentence.

Pause for Thought

The heading throws an interesting light on Psalm 34. It agrees with 1 Samuel in attributing David's escape from the Philistines to his clever stratagem of pretending to be deranged. In this it contrasts sharply with content of the psalm, but in a way which is both easy and fascinating to explain. One does not need much imagination to think what a good story David would have made of his pretended loopiness, and how he fooled his way out of danger in Gath. So think of him recounting his cleverness yet once more, when suddenly it came over him that in fact there was a 'real' story hidden inside the 'good' story – a real story of prayer made and prayer answered. Yes, he had played the madman, yes he had written up insulting graffiti about Achish on the doors, yes he had made his personal behaviour unacceptable, but he had also prayed, he had also looked ceaselessly to Yahweh. He had looked, he had cried out, he had found his God to be near at hand in the hour of terror – and wasn't that the real story? Wasn't that what he ought to be telling his friends? Not boosting his own cleverness but boasting and rejoicing confidently in his saving, delivering God? Did he suddenly stop telling the tale, and say 'Please excuse me' and slip off to some solitary place where he could write what we call Psalm 34? There is no situation where we cannot 'bless Yahweh' (v. 1), for 'blessing him' means dwelling on his unchanging glories and excellencies, and they remain the same no matter how dark the earthly scene. There is no situation from which the 'downtrodden' – those at the bottom of life's heap – cannot cry out and be heard, because Yahweh's eye never flickers from watching over his servants, his ear is ever open to their cry (15–16). There is no situation where he is anything but 'near' (18), with his mobile home pitched alongside so as always to be with us (7). There is no situation where his face is not set against our adversaries to cut them down (16). The life-changing way is to look to him (5), to taste the sweet savour of his goodness (8), to

> Fear him, ye saints, and you will then
> Have nothing else to fear …

The story within the story is the one to listen to, and it is written for our learning in Psalm 34.

Day 14 Read Psalms 35–36

Psalm 35.
Deeply Hurt, Deeply Endangered[1]

A. Uncalled-for danger[2]

1. Please, Yahweh, plead my case[3] with those who propose a case against me;
   make war against those who make war against me.
2. Grip hand-shield and body-shield,[4]
   and, please, rise up as my help.
3. Draw a spear,
   and block the approach[5] of my pursuers.
   Say to my soul,
   'I am your salvation.'
4. Let them be disappointed and dishonoured
   who are seeking my soul.
   Let them be repulsed and abashed
   who are planning evil for me.
5. Let them be like chaff before the wind –
   the Angel of Yahweh[6] urging them on!
6. Let their way be darkness,
   and totally slippery,[7]
   with the Angel of Yahweh pursuing them.
7. Because, without cause, they have hidden their netted pit for me,
   without cause they have dug it out for my soul.
8. May destruction come to him when he does not know it,[8]
   his net which he has hidden catch him!
   To destruction may he fall into it![9]
9. And how my soul will exult in Yahweh,
   be glad in his salvation!
10. All my bones will say:

1 Linked thematically with Psalm 34 – divine intervention in a critically dangerous day. Both psalms feature the Angel of Yahweh (34:7; 35:5–6) in contrasting roles. Psalm 34 looks back to deliverance; Psalm 35 is still looking forward, and teaches us how to handle the waiting period. It is divided into sections by promises to praise (9–10, 18, 27–28). Internally, each section offers a reason why David is asking for retribution (7, 11–16, 19–21), but otherwise it is hard to see any internal pattern in the sections. The psalm is more an outpouring of a troubled spirit than a carefully crafted poem.

2 See verse 7.

3 'Plead' and 'make war' are the two sides of David's need: the latter seeks the end of the physical threat; the former a vindication before the law respecting charges laid against him.

4 All that can be said for certain is that two sorts of shield are mentioned. The former (*magen*) arises from *ganan*, to surround; the latter (*tsinnah*) from *tsanan*, to preserve.

5 As near a translation as is possible of the Hebrew text as we have received it. Maybe, more literally, 'close it off to meet those who are pursuing me'.

6 See Psalm 34:7.

7 'Slippery places' or 'slipperinesses', a plural of amplitude.

8 i.e. does not know it is coming.

9 The boomerang capacity of sin.

10 See verses 11–16.

'Yahweh, who is like you?
One who delivers the downtrodden
from one stronger than he,
yes, the downtrodden and vulnerable
from one who is plundering him.'

B. Undeserved danger[10]

11. Witnesses intent on violence[11] keep rising up –
    what I know nothing of they keep asking of me.[12]
12. They pay me back, to the full, evil for good –
    bereavement to my soul![13]
13. But as for me,
    when they were sick,
    sackcloth was my clothing;
    I humiliated my soul with fasting –
    and as to my prayer, it used to return to my bosom.[14]
14. As for a friend, as for a brother I had, I went about my life.[15]
    As in lamentation for a mother I was bowed down in
    black mourning!
15. But when I limped they rejoiced and gathered together:
    they gathered together against me.
    Attackers[16] – and I did not know them –
    mauled[17] me, and were never still!
16. As people alienated from God –
    every sort of mockery[18] all around –
    grinding away at me with their teeth![19]
17. O Sovereign One,
    how long will you see?[20]
    Oh, bring back my soul from their destructions,
    from prime lions my unique life.[21]
18. I will give you thanks in the abundant assembly,
    among mighty people I will praise you.

11 Lit. 'witnesses of violence'.

12 i.e. 'require of me', require recompense regarding, make me responsible for.

13 'Bereavement' (*shekol)* is specifically loss of children. This is what David's foes wished for him. 'To my soul': we might say 'heartfelt bereavement'.

14 There is no need to introduce (as many do) the thought that unanswered prayer returns with blessing on the intercessor – true though that may well be. David simply says that praying for his foes brought blessing to himself.

15 'I walked up and down/went about.'

16 A form of the word (*nekeh*) not found elsewhere. Some render 'smitten', presumably referring to social outcasts; others 'smiters', or attackers.

17 'Tore' as of a wild beast with its claws.

18 Plural of amplitude, 'mockeries'.

19 While a certain amount of doubt attaches to the translation of this verse, it is justifiable at each point, without altering the text as many do.

20 Be a mere onlooker.

21 See Psalm 22:20 where again 'unique one' is parallel to 'soul'.

22 See verses 19–21.

23 Look askance at me; look at me with hooded eyes.

24 Plural, 'with words of deceits'.

25 i.e. 'sneer openly'.

26 The answer to the jibe 'we saw' is 'you saw'. The seeing God: Genesis 16:13; Exodus 3:7; 2 Kings 19:16; Acts 4: 29.

27 To make the right and authoritative decision about me – in contrast to all the lies.

C. Malicious danger[22]

19. Do not let those who are, through falsehood, my
    enemies rejoice!
    Those who hate me without cause screw up their
    eyes.[23]
20. For it is not peace that they speak;
    and against those who are quiet in the land,
    with words of utter deceit[24] they plan:
21. they broaden their mouth against me;[25]
    they have said: 'Ho, ho! Our eyes saw it!'
22. You saw it,[26] Yahweh!
    Do not keep silence!
    Sovereign One, do not be distant from me!
23. Rouse yourself and wake up for my judgment;[27]
    my God and Sovereign One, for my case!
24. Judge me in accordance with your righteousness,
    Yahweh, my God,
    and do not let them rejoice over me!
25. Do not let them say in their heart:
    'Aha! Just what we wanted!'[28]
    Do not let them say: 'We have swallowed him whole!'
26. Let them be disappointed and abashed altogether,
    who rejoice over my evil![29]
    Let them be clothed with disappointment and
    dishonour,
    who magnify themselves against me!
27. Let them shout aloud and rejoice,
    who delight in my righteousness,[30]
    and let them say continually,
    'Let Yahweh be magnified,
    Who delights in the peace[31] of his servant!'
28. And my tongue will muse of your righteousness;
    all the day, of your praise!

28 Lit. 'Our soul'. Soul (*nephesh*) is
   regularly used in the sense of 'desire,
   longing'.

29 'When I am in trouble'. 'Evil' ranges
   in meaning from bad tasting to moral
   evil. Many references are simply to
   'trouble, ill-fortune, going through a
   bad patch'.

30 When things turn out right for me,
   when I am vindicated.

31 'Peace' has a threefold reference: peace
   with God, peace with those around
   and peace in the heart: i.e. total wellbeing.

32 At the centre of this psalm is a section
   dealing with the nature of Yahweh
   and the benefits he bestows (5–8); it is
   flanked on each side by, respectively,
   the wicked (2–4) and Yahweh's people
   (9–11). The structure of the psalm
   therefore suggests the question, which
   side are you on? But since the psalm
   opens (1) with the wicked as rebellious
   and ends (12) with their fate, the
   whole poem seeks to tip the scales in
   one direction, and to dissuade us from
   siding with the wicked.

33 The voice the wicked listens to is
   rebellion's voice.

34 Poetry is by nature allusive, suggesting
   rather than 'spelling out' in detail.
   Thus, David's injects here: 'and this is
   my heart's central conviction'; I mean
   this with all my heart.

35 'It' refers to the voice of rebellion in
   verse 1. 'In his own eyes (estimation)'
   subtly indicates that all the time the
   wicked is simply listening to himself,
   hearing what he wants to hear.

36 A compressed thought (suitable to the
   allusive wording of this psalm): first,
   he is safe in his concealment; secondly,
   should he be found out, no one would
   find his behaviour unacceptable.

Psalm 36.
Wickedness: A Dissuasive[32]

Belonging to the worship-leader; Yahweh's servant, David's

A.1. The hallmark of wickedness

1. Rebellion's word to the wicked[33] –
   at the centre of my heart[34] –
   'There is no terror of God before his eyes.'

B.1. The wicked and his delusions

2. For it flatters him (in his own eyes)[35]
   regarding the finding out of his iniquity so as to hate it.[36]
3. The words of his mouth are trouble[37] and deceit;
   he has ceased to act prudently so as to do good.
4. He plans trouble in his bed;
   he positions himself on a road[38] that is not good.
   Evil is a thing he does not scorn.

C. Consider Yahweh

5. Yahweh –
   your committed love is in the heavens,
   your trustworthiness is up to the clouds.[39]
6. Your righteousness is like the mountains of the transcendent God.[40]
   Your judgments are like a great deep.[41]
   Mankind and beasts you save, Yahweh!
7. How precious is your committed love, O God –
   and the sons of man take refuge in the shadow of your wings![42]
8. They are saturated with the fatness of your house,
   and the stream of your delights you make them drink.

37 'awen: the word found in the expression 'trouble-makers' in Psalms 5:5; 6:8; etc. People who know how to twist the knife in the wound stir up trouble and strife.

38 i.e. the direction he deliberately adopts for his life.

39 The heavens and the clouds do not depict remoteness but sovereignty. These are the ruling factors: permanence, they belong in the very fabric of things; pre-eminence, they are Yahweh's first consideration.

40 'God' here is 'el, God transcendent. Very probably the description is intended to express, 'very great indeed/ supremely great' – so great that even God transcendent would think them great!

41 Note the telling contrast: mountains towering up, depth extending down. A wonderfully poetic expression of what Isaiah 55:8–9 spells out. The folly of turning from such a God to listen to oneself (verse 2)! 'Judgments': the decisions he makes by which he rules the world.

42 The implication of this exclamation is clear: with this privilege as ours, the folly of not running to Yahweh for refuge! Not least when the alternative is self-reliance!

43 Verse 9 follows seamlessly from verse 8, but the transition from 'they' to 'we' indicated a new subject: the testimony of the righteous.

44 This could refer to the gift of righteousness which Yahweh gives to those whom he saves (compare Isaiah 54:17b: what the New Testament calls the imputed righteousness of Christ, Philippians 3:9). It would in any case include Yahweh's righteous government of the world and our lives, which is the guarantee of our security.

B.2. Life and light for Yahweh's devotees

9. For with you is the spring of life:
    in your light we see light.[43]
10. Prolong your committed love to those who know you,
    and your righteousness[44] to the upright in heart.
11. Do not let the foot of pride come against me,
    nor the hand of the wicked make me homeless!

A.2. The destiny of the wicked

12. There[45] they fell,
    the trouble-makers:
    thrust down,
    and unable to rise.

45 'There' points to a place, and 'fell' is a past tense. David is here singling out some defeat of the ungodly which he can pinpoint with accuracy. We are not told what it was or where, but the definiteness assures us that it was so, and, within the psalm, it has the force of a sure principle. There will always be a 'there'!

Pause for Thought

Right through Psalm 35 runs a very practical truth – what actually to *do* during a difficult patch of life. It makes no difference whether the difficulty arises from people, circumstances or within our own natures, Psalm 35 has a programme for us. Take first what lies at the heart of the psalm and is also probably the hardest piece of its guidance: wait patiently and trustfully for the LORD's timing. It may seem prolonged to us, and it is permitted to cry out 'How long?' (v. 17), provided the cry is made in faith and not in criticism. Timetabling is one of the major ways our thoughts are not his thoughts (Isa. 55:8), but he always knows exactly what he is doing; the when, where and how have been in his mind since all eternity; all is well. We used to sing the hymn,

'Hold the fort, for I am coming,'
Jesus signals still.
Wave the answer back to heaven,
'By thy grace, we will!'

This rule is always the same. Then, secondly, Psalm 35:5–6 teaches us that it is actually in the very nature of our God to deal with our foes. It is not just something he does from time to time: it belongs in his nature; it is part of what he is. We met the Angel in Psalm 34:7 where he was living in a mobile home so that he is always alongside, at the ready, to move when we move. Now we learn that he is active to chase and pursue. Remember that the Angel is Jesus in the fullness of his deity as Son of God, in the fullness of his distinctiveness as Son of man, always with us (Matt. 28:20), never leaving or forsaking (Heb. 13:5), constantly holding (John 10:28–29). Finally, we have the resource of prayer, telling Yahweh, knowing that he is himself the counterweight to everything the enemy can do. They gloat hurtfully even though falsely, 'We saw it'; but we can take the matter at once, calmly, to Yahweh: 'You saw it' (Ps. 35:23). Our counter-attack is to bring him in on our side, and to ask for his active engagement in the battle (v. 23). This is the recipe, then, for the troubled day: waiting with believing patience; watching out for the Angel at work; praying and leaving the outcome to him.

Day 15 Read Psalm 37

Psalm 37.
An A-Z for Life's Tensions[1]

David's.

A. Prospering wickedness: responses

1. Do not upset yourself[2] over the evil-doers; (*aleph*)
    do not become jealous of workers of deviancy,[3]

2. because like grass, quickly, they will fade away,[4]
    and like green growth they will wither.

3. Trust in Yahweh, (*beth*)
    and do good.
    Live in the land,
    and tend[5] trustworthiness

4. and find your pleasure in Yahweh,
    and he will give you your heart's requests.

5. Commit[6] your way to Yahweh (*gimel*)
    and trust in him,
    and he will take action.

6. And he will bring out your righteousness[7] like the light,
    and your judgment like the noonday.

7. Be still[8] before Yahweh, (*daleth*)
    and wait with keen anticipation[9] for him.
    Do not upset yourself over one who is making his way
    prosperous,
    over the man who is making plans.[10]

8. Let exasperation drop, (*he*)
    and leave rage.
    Do not upset yourself –
    only to doing evil![11]

9. Because evil-doers will be cut down,

1   Psalm 37 is very much a psalm to
    read at one sitting, so as to grasp the
    message of the whole. The theme is
    announced in verse 1: the presence
    of 'evil-doers' causes perturbation.
    The true way of life is the way of
    faith, which, ultimately, is the way of
    triumph (1–11). Each section, from
    verse 12, opens with 'the wicked'
    (12, 21, 32): the developing hostility
    between righteous and wicked
    (12–20); the greater wealth of the
    righteous whereby they can afford to be
    unworried (21–31); the final difference
    of destiny (32–34) – the life of faith is
    the true life now and for ever. Psalm
    37 is a virtually complete alphabetic
    acrostic (see heading to Psalm 9–10).
    The letters *ayin* and *tau* both are
    preceded by the conjunction *waw*.

2   'Heat yourself' (in anger/vexation).

3   '*awelah*, from the unused '*ul*, 'to
    deviate'.

4   Or 'be cut down' – identical imperfects
    from different verbal roots. 'Fade …
    wither' teach that sin contains the
    'seeds' of its own impermanence; it has
    no lasting potential.

5   Lit. 'Shepherd trustworthiness'.

6   'Roll your way to Yahweh', compare
    Psalm 22:9; Proverbs 16:3.

7   'Righteousness' here is 'vindication' in
    the tensions and disparities of life; you
    are, after all, in the right. 'Judgment' is
    the consequent decision in your favour.

8   As in English, 'be still' refers to both
    speech and activity. In any of life's
    tensions, neither rush into speech, nor
    into frantic action.

while those who wait for Yahweh will inherit the land.[12]

10. And yet a little while, (*waw*)
    and there will not be a wicked one,
    and you will look searchingly at his place,
    and he will not be there,
11. and it is the downtrodden who will inherit the land,
    and will find their pleasure in an abundance of peace.

B. Hostile wickedness: insights

12. The wicked plots against the righteous, (*zayin*)
    and grinds his teeth at him.
13. The Sovereign One laughs at him,[13]
    because he has seen that his day will come.
14. The wicked have drawn their sword, (*cheth*)
    and bent their bow
    to make the downtrodden and vulnerable[14] fall,
    to slaughter those whose way is upright.[15]
15. Their sword will enter their own heart,
    and their bows will be broken.[16]
16. Better is a little belonging to the righteous (*teth*)
    than the abundance of many wicked,
17. because the arms of the wicked will be broken
    and Yahweh is indeed upholding[17] the righteous.
18. Yahweh indeed knows the days of the person of integrity
    (*yodh*)
    and their inheritance will be for ever.
19. They will not be disappointed[18] in a period of evil,
    and in days of famine they will be satisfied.
20. Because the wicked will perish, (*kaph*)
    and Yahweh's enemies are like the splendour of pastures:[19]
    they come to an end;
    like smoke, they come to an end!

C. Insecure wickedness: who inherits?

21. The wicked borrows and does not pay back; (*lamedh*)

9 'Wait with anticipation' tries to offer the best of all possible worlds! Is the verb *chiyl*, or *chul*? 'To writhe (in excited anticipation)', or 'to wait'?

10 'Plans' is a neutral word, depending on context to suggest whether it is wholesome planning or deviousness. The context here possibly suggests 'successful plans', plans leading to prospering, someone doing better than I am.

11 An allusive exclamation expressing the tendency of exasperation and rage. Note that moral obligations must take priority over feelings: compare 'do good' verse 3.

12 Or 'the earth', but 'land' is better, referring to the land promised to Abraham, now the kingdom not of this world, the heavenly Jerusalem: i.e. they will prove to be the true people of Yahweh, the inheritors of his promises.

13 Having set the scene (hostility) in verse 12, the 'insights' follow: verse 13, a peep behind the scenes; verses 14–15, the boomerang nature of sinful animosity; verses 16–19, the evanescent nature of the prosperity of the wicked, but the enduring wealth of the righteous; verse 20, destiny.

14 'Downtrodden' describes a fact: they are without resource, status or influence. 'Vulnerable' describes an attitude: they accept the adversity of life. They are (lit.) 'willing' – in the good sense, ready for Yahweh's will; in the 'bad' sense, capable of being pushed around.

15 No matter what their position or fortune in life, their obligation remains the same: to live uprightly.

but the righteous acts with grace, and gives.

22. Because[20] those whom he blesses will inherit the land,
    and those whom he curses will be cut down.

23. It is from Yahweh that a person's steps are established,[21]
    (*mem*)
    and he delights in his way,

24. because, when he falls, he is not hurled to the ground,
    for Yahweh continues upholding him with his hand.

25.[22] A young man I was; (*nun*)
    also I have become old.
    And I have not seen the righteous forsaken,
    nor his seed seeking bread.

26. All the day he acts with grace and lends,
    and his seed are destined for blessing.

27. Turn from evil and do good and dwell for ever, (*samech*)

28. because Yahweh loves judgment,
    and he does not forsake his beloved ones.
    For ever they are kept (*ayin*)
    but the seed of the wicked are to be cut down.

29. It is the righteous who will inherit the land,
    and will dwell in it for ever.

30. The mouth of the righteous muses of wisdom, (*pe*)
    and his tongue speaks of judgment.

31. The teaching of his God is in his heart;
    his steps will not be shaky.

D. Impermanent wickedness

32. The wicked keeps watch on the righteous, (*tsadhe*)
    and seeks to put him to death.

33. Yahweh
    does not leave him in his hand,
    and does not pronounce him guilty when he is judged.

34. Wait for Yahweh, (*qoph*)
    and keep his way,
    and he will raise you high to possess the land.
    When the wicked are cut down, you will see it.

16 Not only will their weapons turn against themselves but, ultimately, the weapons (their means of hurting others) will be destroyed. Note the broken arms in verse 17, their ability to use their weapons!

17 'Upholding' (verse 17) is what Yahweh does; 'knows' (18) is what he thinks. The act is the product of an unchanging mind, a thought-out position. Both verbs are in the emphatic position, noted by including the word 'indeed'.

18 The inner and outer aspects of experience: an assured mind as well as a satisfied body.

19 'Pastures' are here today, gone tomorrow. The word can be understood as 'young lambs', in their prime, chosen for sacrifice – all given to the service of Yahweh.

20 That is, it is because his future is secure that the righteous is liberated to be generous.

21 See verse 31. Steadiness on life's pathway is the 'inclusion' (the bracketing truth) of the whole section.

22 As a statement of one person's experience verse 25 can be taken as it stands; alongside verse 24 we would understand it as intended to leave room for transient adversities. Something broadly true and always ultimately true.

35. I have seen the wicked in might, (*resh*)
    spreading himself like tree luxuriant in its native soil.
36. And he passed away and he was not,
    and I looked for him,
    and he was not to be found!
37. Keep (note of) the person of integrity (*shin*)
    and look out for the upright,
    for the man of peace has a future.
38. But those rebelling are sure to be destroyed together.
    The future of the wicked shall surely be cut off.
39. And the salvation of the righteous is from Yahweh, (*tau*)
    their stronghold in a period of adversity.
40. Yahweh is resolved to help them and rescue them:
    he will rescue them from the wicked, and save them,
    because they have taken refuge in him.

Pause for Thought

The idea of submissiveness – doing nothing, leaving it to God – is both the strength and weakness of Psalm 37, because there is a time for 'letting go and letting God', and there is a time for the intense and often costly activity of fighting back, and these can be confused to our peril. For example, as young Christians we heard notable preachers teaching that sanctification was a matter of 'letting go and letting God', and we were grievously led astray, because it's not! The Bible urges us to resist even unto blood in striving against sin (Heb. 12:4); it describes our armour for the war, as we wrestle with 'principalities' and 'powers' (Eph. 6:10–17, KJV). When it calls us to 'present' our 'bodies' (Rom. 12:1–2, KJV) it does not have in mind a future of dressing gown and slippers, but the arduous road of Christlike virtues (Rom. 12:4ff.) and the demanding task of putting on the Lord Jesus Christ (Rom. 13:14). We have a race to run with demanding discipline (1 Cor. 9:24–27); we are in the tough trades of soldiers, athletes and farmers (2 Tim. 2:3–6). But there is also a time for non-retaliation, for leaving it to God (Rom. 12:19), for waiting silently for God, holding our tongues and turning the other cheek (Lam. 3:25–30; Matt. 5:39). In such a time, says Psalm 37, our active response is to trust and delight in Yahweh (3–4), to be still and wait (7), to live in the visible world of trial seeing clearly the invisible world of divine sovereignty and justice (13, 18), to look to the end, secure in Yahweh's care, even sharing in his laughter (v. 13; Ps. 2:4). Alongside Psalm 37, Isaiah 53: 79 and 1 Peter 2:20–25 make good reading: we are called to be like the Son of God in all things; he is our inspiration and model as well as our Redeemer.

Day 16 Read Psalms 38–39

Psalm 38.
Turning to a Justly Offended God[1]

A psalm of David's; To bring to remembrance.[2]

A.1. Plea for forbearance in a time of wrath

1.   Yahweh,
   do not, in your exasperation, discipline me,
   nor, in your rage, chasten me.
2.   For your arrows are dropped down onto me,
   and your hand comes down on me.

B.1. Extremity of need: sin and sickness[3]

3.   There is no soundness in my flesh,
   on account of your indignation;
   there is no peace in my bones on account of my sin.
4.[4] Because my iniquities have reached over my head,
   like a heavy burden, they are too heavy for me.
5.   My wounds stink with decay[5] on account of my silliness.[6]
6.   I am bent right down[7] exceedingly.
   I have walked around, mourning, all the day,
7.   for my muscles[8] are full of inflammation
   and there is no wholeness in my flesh.
8.   I am numbed and crushed exceedingly;
   I have roared because of the groaning of my heart.

A.2. Openness to God: nothing hidden

9.   Sovereign One,
   in front of you is all my desire,
   and from you my moaning has not been hidden.

1. The psalm consists of four **A**-passages in which David addresses Yahweh (1–2, 9, 15, and 21–22). The essential truth the psalm declares is in these: Yahweh is rightly offended and hostile (1–2), yet he can be asked not to forsake but to help and save (21–22). The God of wrath is the God of salvation. All is known to him (9), yet he is our ground of hope (15). The intermediate **B**-passages (3–8, 10–14 and 16–20) are first person singular, in which David respectively describes his case, outlines reactions and, in the teeth of mounting opposition, makes his commitment to 'pursue what is good' (1 Thessalonians 5:15, NKJV).

2. The content of the psalm suggests that its purpose was to bring to Yahweh's remembrance David's deep need. Compare Psalm 70.

3. It could be that David is describing sin and its felt consequence in terms of bodily sickness, but it is more likely that an onset of severe illness brought to light sin as its underlying cause. Verse 3 would appear to make sickness and sin parallel but distinct causes of the trouble.

4. A double metaphor: 'reached over my head' depicts rising flood waters; and a burden too heavy to be borne.

5. The construction of two verbs without conjunction: '… they smell, they decay …' – 'they decay malodourously'.

6. *'iwweleth*, noun related to *'ewiyl*, the downright fool, the fat head, the ceaselessly flippant person who can take nothing seriously, including moral principles and values. The implication is that David's sin was a conscious flouting of moral rectitude, which he now regrets as silly beyond words.

B.2. Reactions: inwardly (10), socially (11–2), personally (13–14)

10. My heart palpitates;
    my strength has left me;
    and the light of my eyes –
    they too are not with me.
11. Those who love me, and my friends stand away from my plague,
    and my nearest relatives stand at a distance.
12. And those who are seeking my life set snares,
    and those who are seeking my evil[9] speak of destruction,
    and they muse about deceitful things all the day.
13. And as for me,
    like a deaf man I do not hear,
    and like a dumb person who does not open his mouth.
14. And I have become like a man who is not hearing,
    and in whose mouth there are no rebukes.

A.3. Profession: confident hope

15. Because[10] in you, Yahweh, I have set my hope.
    You yourself will answer,
    O Sovereign One, my God.

B.3. Confesson of sin in the crisis

16. Because[11] I said –
    Lest they rejoice over me,
    act grandly[12] against me when my foot slips!
17. For I am ready to trip up,
    and my pain is before me continually.
18. For[13] I will declare my iniquity;
    I am anxious about my sin.
19. And[14] my enemies are alive!
    They are mighty![15]
    And those who hate me on false grounds are many.

7 Two verbs without conjunction: 'I am twisted/convulsed, I am brought low'.

8 A likely meaning is *kesalay*, my fatnesses.

9 Here in the simple sense of 'my hurt'.

10 In verse 15 ('because') David explains his readiness and motive for adopting a policy of deafness and silence in the face of vociferous enemies: his determination to leave the outcome to Yahweh, and his certainty of answered prayer.

11 Just as the 'because' of verse 15 explains the policy of verses 13–14, so the 'because' of verse 16 explains the confidence of verse 15. It is confidence in prayer made. The situation has been made clear to the sovereign God and confidently left there.

12 From *gadhel*, to be great/big. Here (*hiphil*) to act the big one, to put on airs and graces.

13 The initial 'for' in both 17 and 18 offer parallel reasons why David looks for a speedy answer to his prayer: first his fragile state, and secondly his readiness to own up to sin and his concern about his position as a sinner.

14 We would catch the force of verse 19 as we emphasize *And*. David is adding a further reason to the double 'for' of the preceding verses.

15 'Alive' could be treated as an appositional adjective: 'My enemies – alive as they are – are mighty!'

16 A further reason why Yahweh should act on David's behalf: his enemies are provoked by his perseverance in what is good.

20. And those who are paying me back evil for good are my
    opponents,
    in return for my pursuit of good.[16]

A.4. A plea for God not to forsake but to help

21. Do not leave me, Yahweh![17]
    My God, do not be distant from me!
22. Oh, hurry to my help!
    O Sovereign One, my salvation!

Psalm 39.
The Pity of Life's Transience[18]

Belonging to the worship-leader, Jeduthun;[19] a psalm of
David's.

A.1. Silence before the world

1. I said:
   'I will keep my ways, so as not to sin with my tongue.
   I will keep my lips in a muzzle
   As long as the wicked are in front of me.'[20]
2. I kept myself dumb – silence! –
   I kept quiet – no use! –
   My pain was unassuaged.[21]

B.1. Talking to God: living with life's brevity

3. My heart grew hot within me;
   in my musing, the fire burned.[22]
   I spoke with my tongue:
4. 'Make me know, Yahweh, my end,
   and what is the measure of my days.
   Let me know how transient I am.[23]
5. Behold!
   Mere handbreadths you have appointed my days,

17 The wording here ('Do not leave me,
   Yahweh') is the reverse of the wording
   with which the psalm opened (verse
   1, 'Yahweh … do not discipline me')
   making a neat inclusion, but also
   affirming a wonderful truth: the God
   who acts against our sin is the God to
   whom we can appeal for help.

18 As in Psalm 38, David is hurting
   through divine action against sin
   (verse 11), but the focus is different.
   In Psalm 38 sickness has exposed sin,
   and the theme is sin-wrath-confession-
   forgiveness; in Psalm 39 sickness
   exposes the brevity of life, the need to
   face this in such a way as to give a good
   testimony to the watching world, and
   the desire for relief in the brief time
   remaining. David speaks to all our
   hearts; the full knowledge of eternal
   life which we have in Christ does not
   diminish our sense of this life's brevity,
   its preciousness, and our desire to
   'make a good death'.

19 One of the three worship-leaders,
   who, with their sons, were appointed
   by David to give thanks and play
   instruments: Asaph, Heman, Jeduthun
   (1 Chronicles 16:41; 25:1-3).

20 Under stress of an imminent death,
   David is understandably concerned
   not to say a wrong, misleading or
   unworthy thing.

21 Uncertain translation; possibly 'was
   stirred'. Compare NKJV, ESV.

22 See Jeremiah 20:9.

23 David knows that he is not going to
   be told the date of his death, and these
   verses show that he already knows how
   transient he is. We should therefore
   understand 'know' on both occasions
   as 'make me aware'/'teach me to
   acknowledge'.

and my duration is as nothing in front of you.
Yes indeed, all humankind stands as firm as a mere breath!
(*Selah*)

6. Yes indeed, it is as a shadow that a man walks around!
    Yes indeed, as no more than a breath they bustle around!
    He heaps things up,
    and does not know who will gather them![24]

C. The essential issues[25]

7. Now then, what am I waiting for, O Sovereign One?
    My hope is in you.
8. From all my rebellions deliver me.
    Do not make me the reproach of the unprincipled.[26]

A.2. Silence before God[27]

9. I kept myself dumb;
    I did not open my mouth,
    because it was you who did it.
10. Remove your stroke from upon me.
    I – as a result of the vigour of your hand – I am finished!
11. By corrections of iniquity you discipline a man,
    you make what he desires melt away like a moth!
    Yes indeed, all mankind is but a breath!

B.2. Talking to God: desiring relief before the inevitable end

12. Oh, hear my prayer, Yahweh,
    and to my cry for help turn your ear.
    Towards my tears do not be dumb,
    because I am a refugee[28] with you,
    a sojourner like all my fathers.
13. Avert your gaze from me,
    so that I may brighten up,
    before I go and am not.

24 Note how, from the end of verse 5, through verse 6, the general and plural alternates with the singular. What is true of all is true of each.

25 As the analysis shows, this is the 'heart' of the psalm. In the transience, fragility and insecurity of life three things are important: sure hope fixed on Yahweh; deliverance from the consequences of rebellious sin; a life above criticism.

26 *nabhal*, often translated 'fool' (see ESV). Illustrated by Nabal in 1 Samuel 25 (compare verse 25), the *nabal* is the person insensitive to moral rules and obligations, suffering from an ethical blind-spot. Compare 2 Samuel 13:11–13.

27 Note the repetition of 'I kept myself dumb' (verse 2) in the parallel **A.1**. There it was silence before the watching world, here before God: first (verse 9b) out of recognition that David's pains were divinely imposed ('your hand'); secondly, seeking an end of the time of duress, recognising human transiency.

28 Refugee … sojourner are *ger … toshabh*. The words occur together in Genesis 23:4. The *ger* seeks political asylum from some difficulty; the *toshabh* seeks permission to stay. Both words are used of Israel living in Yahweh's land (Leviticus 25:23). The words therefore do not express uncertainty but confidence – confidence in a God-given position and inheritance. They are words that belong to Yahweh's redeemed people.

Pause for Thought

It would have been helpful (Ps. 39:2) if David had felt able to tell us the sort of thing he was fearful he might say in the presence of someone with no profession of faith. We can, of course, try to guess. We have all heard Christians speak in such a carelessly confident way about dying that their testimony sounded glib and brash, failing to take into account the solemnity of death, or that in the majority of cases it comes as an unwelcome intruder into a life we are loathe to leave. Again, have we not heard Christians speak of death – or pray for someone seriously ill – as if death was the very worst thing that could possibly happen (whereas the truth is that for a Christian, considered solely as an individual, setting aside relationships and responsibilities, to die is the very best thing that can happen)! David discovered that the ending of earthly life and the advent of death was, putting it mildly, a hurdle to be faced, and a task to be prepared for. First, be careful what we say – and maybe best say nothing. Dying without being afraid is one of the pearls of great price of being a Christian, so be careful, in the words of Jesus, not to cast this pearl before swine. A calm and unanxious demeanour could well speak louder than words. And, secondly, David certainly does tell us how we can go about cultivating this – in the threefold directive implied in 39:7–8. As ever that great old song 'Turn your eyes upon Jesus' strikes the essential note – or as David put it: 'my hope is in you'. Are you in the prime of life? Are you in the later years when death waits round the corner? Are you, by divine sovereign appointment, in a terminal illness? Whatever: turn your eyes on Jesus and keep them fixed there. Beyond this, we must take up Paul's motto – to have a conscience void of offence towards God and man always (Acts 24:16), for is that not what David is saying in Psalm 39:8? Yes, of course, all our sins were anticipated at Calvary and covered there, but what was done once and for all on the Cross becomes real all over again in our experience as we obey the divine command that all men everywhere should repent (Acts 17:30). The third strand in a 'good death' is the repute among others that we leave behind – a 'savour of Christ among those who are being saved and among those who are perishing' (2 Cor. 2:15, NIV).

Psalm 40.
Needs Met, Needs Continuing[1]

Belonging to the worship-leader; David's; a psalm.

A.1. The effectiveness of waiting

1. I just waited for Yahweh,
    and he turned to me,
    and he heard my cry for help.
2. And he brought me up from the pit of ruin,
    from the muddiest mire,[2]
    and he raised my feet onto a crag:
    he made my steps firm.
3. And he put a new song in my mouth,
    praise[3] to our God.
    Many will see and fear and trust in Yahweh.

B.1. Blessing

4. Blessed is the individual who has made Yahweh his object
    of trust,
    and has not turned to the bombastic,
    and to those who fall away to what is deceptive.[4]
5. Many things you yourself have done,
    Yahweh, my God,
    your wonderful works,
    and your plans for us –
    there is no way of setting them out in order for you.
    I would declare and speak –
    they are too many to recount!

1   Psalm 40 is linked by theme with Psalms 37–39 and, for all we know, arises from the same experience of adversity and opposition, and belongs to the same period of composition. The great topic of 'waiting' was focused in Psalm 37, followed through in Psalms 38–39, and now its triumphant outcome is recorded. Rescue from the pit (verse 2) aptly depicts the deliverances sought in the two preceding psalms. Deliverance (1–3) is now traced forward into a threefold testimony: personal dedication (6–8), public declaration (9–10) and confession of continuing need and exhaustion in the face of external pressures (11– 12). The psalm reveals the same two classes of people in tension: those under blessing, and those meriting shame (13–16). The opening and closing sections highlight the important theme that past deliverances (1–2) are always followed by fresh challenges and needs (17).

2   Two synonyms, 'the mire of mire'.

3   'Praise' is a noun (in apposition to 'song').

4   The unacceptable alternatives to a position of trust in Yahweh is to turn to people with huge and unwarranted self-confidence ('bombast': compare Isaiah 30:7, Egypt, the 'big mouth' promising everything, delivering nothing), or to the deceptivity of false gods – and this against the abundance of evidence Yahweh has provided in what he has done (verse 5).

C.1. The receptive, responsive heart[5]

6. Sacrifice and offering you have not wished.[6]
   My ears you have dug out[7] for me.[8]
   Burnt offering and sin offering you did not ask.[9]
7. Then,[10] I said:
   Behold!
   I have come –
   in the roll of the book it is written[11] about me –
8. to do your good pleasure, my God, I delight,
   and your teaching is in my inner being.[12]

C.2. The testifying heart

9. I have told the good news of righteousness[13]
   in the large assembly.
   Behold!
   My lips I will not restrain,
   Yahweh, you yourself know.
10. Your righteousness I have not covered inside my heart.
    Your faithfulness and your salvation I have spoken.
    I have not hidden your committed love and your truth[14]
    from the large assembly.

C.3. The fainting heart[15]

11. You, Yahweh
    you will not hold back your compassion from me,
    your committed love and your truth.
    Continually they will preserve me.[16]
12. Because evils past counting have surrounded me
    my iniquities have caught up with me,
    and I am not able to see.[17]
    They are more numerous than the hairs of my head
    and my heart has deserted me![18]

5 David is, in the first instance, pondering his own response to Yahweh's deliverance, but being the messianic, responsive dedication the true Messianic King would make (Hebrews 10:5–10).

6 David means that *in this case* divine deliverance is so wonderful that (mere) offering could not match what Yahweh would wish: nothing but total self-dedication could suffice. He is not commenting on the sacrificial system as such, but assessing what is suitable in response to verses 1–2 (compare Hebrews 10:5–10). The sacrificial system in Leviticus is God's provision for his people (Leviticus 17:11) but fell short of full reality in that only another human can be the full substitute human sinners need.

7 The verb *karah* is used of digging wells (Genesis 26:25), a grave (Genesis 50:5), pit (Psalm 57:6). There is surely a sidelong glance at Exodus 21:6 and the ceremony of lifelong devotion (a different verb is used), but the thought here is the opening of the ear (compare Isaiah 50:4–5) to receive a revelation of what Yahweh desired. A very vivid portrayal of special revelation.

8 'For me' is what is called a 'dative of advantage', for my good/benefit.

9 Compare note 5. So, here, 'you did not ask (in this instance)'.

10 A temporal 'then', 'at that point'. Along with the realization that something beyond sacrifices was required came the truth of personal dedication.

11 Compare Deuteronomy 17:18–20.

12 The three **C**-sections are linked by reference to the 'inner man', see verses 11, 13, 'my heart'. In verse 8 'within my intestines', meaning 'my very being', the dedication of a person gripped at centre by divine truth imparted by special revelation.

B.2. Blessing and blighting

13. Let it be your favour, Yahweh, to deliver me;
    Yahweh, to be my help make haste!
14. Let them reap shame and be abashed all together,
    who are seeking my soul, to sweep it away.
    Let them slip away backwards and be dishonoured,
    who take pleasure in my evil.
15. Let them be appalled on account of their shame,[19]
    who are saying to me, 'Aha! Aha!'.
16. Let them be happy and rejoice in you,
    all who are seeking you;
    let them say continually:
    'Yahweh is great' –
    those who love your salvation.

A.2. Still waiting

17. But as for me –
    I am downtrodden and vulnerable.
    The Sovereign One makes plans for me.
    You are my help and my rescuer.
    O my God,
    do not delay!

Psalm 41.
A Passport to Divine Care

Belonging to the worship-leader; a psalm of David's.

A.1. Divine deliverance: proposition 1[20]

1. Blessed[21] is he who is thoughtful towards the poor.[22]
   In an evil day Yahweh will make him escape.
2. Yahweh will keep him,
   and preserve his life.
   He will be blessed[23] in the land.[24]

13 David feels that Yahweh has acted righteously in delivering him. But in calling his deliverance 'righteousness' he intends us to see it not as something that simply happened on a specific occasion but as a revelation of the divine nature.

14 'Righteousness' means Yahweh is unchanging in his own nature; 'faithfulness' means he keeps his pledged word; 'salvation', that he stands by and acts on behalf of his people; 'committed love' is his motive; and 'truth' means all that he has revealed about himself and which can be relied on.

15 Though signally delivered (verses 1–3), such deliverance in this life is not final: sin remains (12), as do enemies (13–15); weakness remains (17), and so does Yahweh (13, 16, 17).

16 'Compassion' (*rachamim*) is the love of 'being in love', love as a passion, love in the *heart*; 'committed love' (*chesedh*) is the love professed in the Marriage Service, the love which says 'I will', love as a conscious commitment of the *will*.

17 The blindness and incapacity sin brings. 'See', in every sense in which we use the word: grasp of truth ('I see that'), ability ('I can't see my way to…'), seeing and deciding which direction to take in life.

18 As we say 'I had no heart for …', enthusiasm, 'gusto', general vitality. e.g. Joshua 2:11.

19 i.e. when they 'reap shame'. In the Old Testament 'shame' always goes beyond embarrassment to 'reaping shame' because disappointed of some hope or another.

And you will never give[25] him over to the desire[26] of his
enemies.
Yahweh will support him on a couch of illness;
all his bed you rearrange[27] in his sickness.[28]

B.1. Plea for grace in respect of sin

4. For my part,
   I said:
   'Yahweh, grant me your grace.
   Oh, heal my soul, because I have sinned against you.'

C.1. Enmity

5. My enemies,
   they speak evil against me:
   'When will he die, and his name perish?'
6. And if he has come to see, he speaks vacuously:[29]
   his heart gathers mischief to itself;
   he goes outside;
   he speaks.

C.2. Hatred

7. Together against me,
   all who hate me whisper to one another;
   against me they plot evil for me.
8. 'Something horrible[30] has been poured out on him,
   and since he has taken to his bed he will not get up
   again.'
9. Also, a man at peace with me,
   in whom I trusted,
   one eating my bread,
   has made his heel great[31] against me.

B.2. Plea for grace in respect of justice

10. But as for you,

20 Psalm 41 belongs to the same
    situation of sickness-sin-enmity as
    Psalms 38–40. And consequently the
    ending (verses 11–12, Proposition
    2) is understandable. It is not clear
    how Proposition 1 fits in. 2 Samuel 9
    illustrates David taking time to be
    thoughtful for the needy. We can only
    assume that some such circumstance
    prompted this psalm, which then
    enabled David to focus on his
    crucial current need with increased
    confidence. For the rest of the psalm
    care for the needy disappears as David
    squares up to sin-sickness and enmity.

21 'ashrey, see Psalm 1:1. Is the word
    used here as an 'inclusion', bracketing
    the first book of Psalms? Ps. 1, the
    blessedness of devotion to Yahweh; Ps.
    41, the blessedness of devotion to the
    needy.

22 dal is used of the financially distressed
    (e.g. Ruth 3:10; Job 34:19, contrasted
    with 'rich'); it is also used more widely
    of those at the 'lower' end of the social
    scale (e.g. Psalm 72:13 where it is
    linked with 'the vulnerable'). Psalm
    41 therefore addresses the idea of a
    sensitive social conscience.

23 'ashar, the verb which provides 'ashrey
    (note 21).

24 Or 'on earth'. See Psalm 37:9, note 12.

25 An example of the idiom of a future
    event considered so impossible that
    it can be commanded not to happen
    ('Do not hand him over'), hence a very
    emphatic negative ('never').

26 Lit. 'to the soul', nephesh, here in the
    sense of 'heart's desire, dearest wish'.

27 haphak, often 'to overturn' (specially
    of Sodom and Gomorrah!). Here of
    'turning over' bedding, etc.

Yahweh.
Grant me your grace, and raise me up,
in order that I may pay them back in full.[32]

A.2. Divine deliverance: Proposition 2[33]

11. By this I know that you are delighted with me –
    that my enemy will not raise a shout[34] over me.
12. And as for me,
    in return for my integrity you will be sure to grasp hold of
    me,
    and to give me a position before you for ever.

(Editorial conclusion to Psalms, Book One)[35]
13. Blessed be Yahweh,
    the God of Israel,
    from everlasting to everlasting.
    Amen and Amen.

28 The alternation (verse 2bcde) between the statement about Yahweh and address to him is an effective way of stressing (as though to say, no matter from what point of view you come) how Yahweh cares for the poor.

29 Lit. 'he speaks emptiness'.

30 'A thing of *belial*'. On 'belial' (*beliya'al*) see Psalm 18:4. Always to be understood contextually. It is used seriously of moral deviance, social disruptiveness, religious apostasy, sometimes as a parallel to 'death/ Sheol' – this indicates its seriousness. In the present case 'offensive, revolting, disgusting'.

31 I can only offer this literal translation of a phrase of uncertain precise meaning. Quoted, John 13:18, with the sense of base betrayal. As in Psalm 40:6–8, David's experience as messianic king was a taste of the experience of the real Messianic King casting its shadow before it. Did 'heel' become a metaphor for sneaky, underhand behaviour from someone who should have known better? Arising from Jacob and Esau (Genesis 25:26; 27:36; Hosea 12:3)?

32 This intention to 'pay back in full' is to be understood in relation to David as king (not David as private individual). It is the king's duty to apply exact justice and to purge the society over which he rules (Psalm 101).

33 David now pleads his personal integrity (compare verse 1), and looks confidently for Yahweh's favour to uphold his cause and to keep him in his own presence. As ever, this is not a concession to 'salvation by works', but a biblical expectation that Yahweh will be faithful to his own.

34 Equivalent to 'crow over me'.

35 Compare Psalms 72:18; 106:48. In the present case the initial *baruk* ('blessed be') is not unsuitable as an inclusion with the first word of verse 1 (*'ashrey*, 'Blessed is'). On 'blessing' God, see Psalm 26:12.

Pause for Thought

Did David know, in Psalm 40:6–8, that he was writing of his greater son, yet to be born? Or, being a prophet, did it 'just happen'? Either way, as Hebrews 10:5–10 shows, David was not only accurately forecasting the 'mind' of the Lord Jesus Christ as he approached his death, but was, in fact, providing the key-stone of the arch of atonement teaching. The principle of substitution – one standing in the place of another – was well established by the time of Genesis 22:13. Abraham had said that 'God will provide for himself the lamb' (Gen. 22:8, ESV), and when his hand was stayed from sacrificing his son, and he saw 'a ram, caught in a thicket', he knew what to do: the ram 'instead of his son' (22:13, ESV). In this way, all through the period of the levitical sacrifices animals were a perfect expression of substitution. Leviticus 16:21–22 both explains the ever-present ritual of the laying on of the hand (Lev. 1:4; 3:2; 4:4) – the appointment of a substitute – and also illustrates how the substitute is thus constituted as a sin-bearer. This went on year after year, driving home the fundamental truth that this is God's way of dealing with his people's sins. By his will, it is possible that the sins of the guilty should pass to the account of the innocent, and be dealt with, in subtitutionary fashion, by the death of the beast instead of the human, the 'innocent' instead of the guilty. By the time Isaiah wrote 52:13–53:12, his towering genius was seeing things at a further stage. He found no fault with the principle of substitution, but he saw that, ultimately, only a Person could substitute for persons. When we think about it, the reason is obvious: we are sinners because our wills revolt against the will of God. But an animal has no 'will' in the matter! Without knowledge or consent, it receives the task of being the sinner's substitute – which, in fact, leaves us without substitution at the very heart of our sinfulness. Hence the importance of, 'to do your good pleasure' is my 'delight' (Ps. 40:7–8), and the huge significance of those words applied to Jesus: at last a sinless Person accepts, consciously, voluntarily, the sins of those he came to save. The age-long principle of substitution receives its perfect fulfilment.

Day 18   Read Psalms 42–43

Psalms 42–43.[1]
Downcast Soul: Up-beat God

Belonging to the worship-leader; a teaching poem;[2] belonging to the Sons of Korah.[3]

A.1. Looking back: God in the past

1. Like a deer craves for channels full of water[4]
   just so my soul craves for you, O God.
2. My soul is thirsty for God,
   for the living, transcendent God.[5]
   When will I come
   and be seen before God?[6]
3. My tears have been bread for me
   by day and night,
   while they say to me all the day,
   'Where is your God?'
4. These are the things I keep remembering
   and pouring out my soul, to my sorrow[7] –
   that I used to pass along in the throng;
   I used to lead them to the house of God,
   with the voice of shouting and thanksgiving,
   a crowd celebrating a feast.
5. Why are you downcast, my soul,
   and disturbed, to my sorrow?[8]
   Hope in God,
   because yet again I will thank him
   for the salvation of his face.[9]

1 Psalms 42–43 belong together. They are united by the refrain (42:5, 11; 43:5). The intervening stanzas consist of two of equal length (42:1–4; 43:1–4), and the slightly longer 42:6–10, with coinciding wording linking them together. The theme is continuous, as the analysis shows.

2 *masakiyl,* see Psalm 32.

3 A guild/choir of singers. 1 Chronicles 6:33 where Heman, son of Korah, is entitled 'the singer'.

4 The noun 'water' is always used in the plural. In this verse I have, nevertheless, chosen to treat it as a plural of amplitude, 'full of'.

5 *'el.*

6 A slight adjustment of vowels would yield 'and see the face of God', possibly a technical expression for appearing before God at the sanctuary (Exodus 23:17; Psalm 84:7). It seems the writer is far from Jerusalem, surrounded by hostile company – possibly some such 'captivity' as 2 Kings 14:13–14. This induces a depression, and a questioning how to face the present and the future, in their stark contrast with past joys. The 'refrain' implies the writer's sense that his faith should be able to rise to the occasion; the psalm is a case-study of dealing with a downcast spirit.

7 The preposition *'al,* in an extension of its meaning 'against', it is used to express 'to my disadvantage/detriment/sorrow'.

8 See note 7.

A.2. Looking around: God in the present

6. To my sorrow,
    my soul is downcast :
    therefore I keep remembering you,[10]
    from the land of Jordan,
    and the peaks of Hermon,
    from the hill Mitsar.[11]

7. Deep[12] to deep is calling,
    at the voice of your cataracts:
    they are all your breakers and waves that have passed over
    me!

8. Daily Yahweh will command his unfailing love,
    and in the night his song will be with me,[13]
    a prayer to the transcendent God[14] of my life.

9. I will say to the transcendent God, my crag,
    'Why have you forgotten me?
    Why do I go, mourning, through the enemy's
    oppression?'

10. With a shattering in my bones my adversaries have
    reproached me,
    while they say to me all the day:
    'Where is your God?'

11. Why are you downcast, my soul?
    And why are you disturbed, to my sorrow?
    Hope in God,
    because yet again I will thank him,
    the salvation of my face,[15] and my God.

A.3. Looking ahead: God in the future

1. Judge me,[16] O God, and take up my case
    against a nation devoid of grace.[17]
    From a man of deceit and deviancy do rescue me,

2. because you are my fortress God.[18]
    Why have you spurned me?
    Why do I go around this way and that, mourning,
    through the enemy's oppression?

9   The salvation that the mere fact of his personal presence brings. Many alter the Hebrew text here to make it match verse 11 and 43:5. Nothing suggests this change except the passion of Old Testament commentators to provide their own re-writing.

10 Contrast the 'remembering' in verse 4. Nostalgia only increases pain for a past that is gone'; this 'remembering' is a present turning to the God who is always there – even in the far distant north country.

11 Not a name elsewhere known. We could translate 'from the small hill' – possibly a belittling reference to Mount Hermon itself, the highest peak in the north country, but (so to say) nothing compared with Mount Zion! As part of his remembrance of Yahweh (6), he recalls: the superiority of Zion (6); the sovereign rule of Yahweh whereby his troubles, rightly understood, are Yahweh's waves (7); Yahweh's unfailing love and the divine presence (8).

12 *tehom,* 'the deep' was (in pagan thought) considered as an independent force antagonistic to the ordered work of the Creator. There may be a suggestion here that, behind his human adversaries, there lie hidden dark forces of evil – regarding which he reminds himself that any and every power at work is but a tool in Yahweh's hand: Satan's breakers are Yahweh's waves.

13 A contrast and antidote to the 'day and night' of verse 3.

14 *'el.*

15 An unexpected expression but perfectly understandable: depression shows itself in a downcast face (Genesis 40:7; Nehemiah 2:2); salvation is directed to the point of need.

16 'Put everything to rights for me', a regular, indeed fundamental, sense of 'judge'.

3. Send out your light and your truth:
    it is they that will lead me;[19]
    they will bring me to the hill[20] of your holiness,
    and to your great dwellingplace,[21]

4. and I will come to the altar of God,
    to the transcendent God of the joy of my exultation,
    and I will give you thanks with the lyre,
    God, my God.

5. Why are you downcast, my soul,
    and why are you disturbed, to my sorrow?
    Hope in God,
    because yet again I will thank him,
    the salvation of my face, and my God.

17 *Chesedh* is Yahweh's committed love; *chasiydh* is a passive adjective from the noun, 'beloved', a recipient of Yahweh's committed love. Here it describes people outside the sphere of covenant grace within which Yahweh's committed love (as distinct from his general benevolence) operates.

18 'The God of my strong place/ stronghold'.

19 We can understand this literally – that Yahweh, acting in light and truth will bring the exile back home – or 'spiritually', that if the exile faithfully follows Yahweh's light and truth he will come to experiences equivalent to the 'holy hill', etc. Either way, God's blessings are not dependent on places and buildings.

20 A mounting experience of privilege: first the hill (the place Yahweh chose), dwelling (the house he inhabits), altar (the approach he has provided), then God (the personal fellowship he extends).

21 Plural of amplitude.

Pause for Thought

Nine times the question 'why?' rings out in Psalms 42–43. A good time, therefore, to remind ourselves that question are not doubts. So often a person can be heard to say, 'I have so many doubts' when, in fact, all they have is what we all have –'so many questions'. And so it will be till we get to heaven (where, very likely, we will be so caught up in glory that the answers will no longer seem to matter). Look at the two halves of the refrain (42:5,11; 43:5): sure about God (the second half), battered by circumstances (the first half). This is a perfect cameo of life on earth. Don't be afraid to raise questions, just make sure they are believing questions. But sometimes our questions develop a life of their own and take over, and we find ourselves 'downcast'. This too can happen to any of us, a common hazard arising because we are not yet in glory. What then? A double remedy lies on the surface of today's psalm. Neither of its components may prove easy, but together they are effective. First look at the sequence of 42:5–6. Verse 5 surely implies that, with God as our hope, we have no need to be downcast; then verse 6 chips in, 'My soul is downcast.' What a frank prayer; I know it's foolish to be down, but I am! This sort of openness with God runs through the psalm – what 42:8 calls 'a prayer to the transcendent God of my life'. Just as his love never falters, so his ear is always open (8). Think of the middle hours of the night, when sleep flees and anxieties grow a hundred times as big. What then? Have you tried, 'in the night his song will be with me'? The remedial effect of one of the great hymns of yesterday or today. Then, secondly, there is our mind. Romans 12:1–2 speaks of being transformed 'by the renewing of your mind, NIV'. The mind is 'renewed' by feeding on new thoughts. If we are only being anxious about our anxieties, worrying over our worries, stewing our problems, we are only nourishing the old mind, the downcast spirit. No, says Psalm 42:4, 6, I will turn from old memories, 'I keep remembering you.' The mind feeding itself on divine truth, dwelling on the promises of God, recalling his endless mercies and unchanging love, turning its eyes upon Jesus – that mind is walking the pathway of renewal.

Day 19 Read Psalms 44–45

Psalm 44.
Faith and Faithfulness Unrewarded

Belonging to the worship-leader; belonging to the Sons of Korah; a teaching poem.[1]

A.1. The glorious past

1. O God,
    with our ears we have heard,
    our fathers have recounted to us
    the work you worked in their days,
    in days gone by.[2]
2. You – your hand[3] – dispossessed nations,
    and you planted them;[4]
    you injured states,[5]
    and gave them freedom.[6]
3. Because it was not by their sword that they possessed the land,
    nor was it their arm that brought them salvation,
    because it was your right hand and your arm[7]
    and the light of your face,[8]
    because you favoured them.

B.1. An undimmed faith[9]

4. You are my king, O God;[10]
    command full salvation[11] for Jacob!
5. By you we will push down[12] our adversaries;
    by your name we will trample those who rise against us:
6. because it is not in my bow that I will trust,
    nor is it my sword that will save me;

1 On Korah and *maskiyl*, see heading to Psalm 42.

2 Lit. 'the days of beforetime'.

3 'You, your hand', i.e. 'You, by your personal intervention'. 'Hand' is the organ of intervention – as we talk of 'taking a hand' in something.

4 'Them' – both times, refers to the 'fathers'.

5 'States' is a somewhat arbitrary translation of *le'ummim*. The unused *la'am* is said to mean 'to bind together/ bring together'. *'le'um* is therefore a 'people', some distinct group.

6 Or 'and you sent them in'. But *shalach*, 'to send out', is used in Jeremiah 34:14 in parallel to the full phrase 'to send out free'; and in Isaiah 32:20, of animals roaming unrestricted; compare Isaiah 45:13.

7 As 'hand' symbolizes personal intervention, so 'arm' symbolizes personal strength in action: compare, Deuteronomy 7:19; Isaiah 51:9; 52:10; 53:1.

8 Compare Numbers 6:26; Psalm 42:5.

9 The psalmist turns from recounting the past to affirming his creed: this is the heart of the problem this psalm tackles. There is continuity of faith with the past, but it is not bringing corresponding benefits: belief is maintained (4–8) and, indeed, (17–21) conduct is conformed to what is believed, but it is only reaping a harvest of trouble (9–16).

7. because you are committed to save[13] us from our
adversaries,
and to make those who hate us reap shame.
8. In God we have boasted all the day,
and to your name for ever we will give thanks. (*Selah*)

A.2. The dismal present[14]

9. But – yes, incredibly![15] –
you have spurned and dishonoured us,
and you do not go out with our hosts.
10. You make us turn back from an adversary,
and those who hate us plunder at will.[16]
11. You have given us over like sheep for food,
and scattered us among the nations.
12. You have sold your people in return for no wealth,
and you have not increased by their sale-value.
13. You make us an object of reproach to our neighbours,
a thing of mockery and disdain to those around us.
14. You make us a by-word among the nations,
a wagging of the head[17] among the states.
15. All the day my dishonour is before me,
and the shame of my face has covered me:[18]
16. through the voice of the one who reproaches and vilifies;
because of the enemy and the one who takes his revenge.

B.2. An undeviating faithfulness[19]

17. All this has come upon us –
though[20] we have not forgotten you,
nor have we played false with your covenant![21]
18. Our heart has not backslidden,
nor have our steps turned aside[22] from your path,
19. though you have crushed us in the place of jackals,[23]
and covered us over with deadly darkness.[24]
20. If we have forgotten the name of our God,
and spread our hands out to a strange deity[25]

10 Note how verses 4 and 6 record 'my'
testimony; verses 5 and 7 speak of
'us'. It is possible we have here an
'antiphonal' liturgy in which the king
is the speaker in verses 4 and 6, and
the people respond in verses 5 and 7,
with verse 8 spoken by both as a united
affirmation of faith.

11 'Salvations', plural of amplitude.

12 The verb, *nagach*, used of the 'he-goat'
in Daniel 8:7.

13 Verse 7 has two verbs in the perfect
tense. These look back to the past: 'you
saved … made …', i.e. in distinction
from what you are doing to us now.
Alternatively, in conformity to verse 6,
I have chosen to treat them as perfects
of determination. Or we could render
'because you save … make …', timeless
presents, the perfect representing fixed,
invariable action.

14 The antiphonal structure can be seen
in this section – even if not quite so
obviously. The sense of the verses is
suited to a king-people responsive
liturgy. The king feels for the defeat
of his army (9); the people respond
as having suffered defeat (10); the
king laments slaughter and loss (11);
the people take note of the seeming
pointlessness of it all (12); the king's
shame and embarrassment (13);
the people likewise (14); the king's
disappointment (15); the people (or
all) sense the gloating enemy (16).

15 I apologise for such an awkward
rendering of the apparently simple
particle *'aph*. The conjunction *gam*
('also') adds one fact to another, but
'aph heaps one fact on another, very
often with an element of incredulity
– an air of 'would you believe it!'
Compare Isaiah 42:13 (NKJV) 'yes'. In
many cases the obsolete English word
'forsooth!' catches the meaning.

21. would God not search this out,
      because he knows the hidden things of the heart?
22. Because, on account of you,[26] we have been killed all the day;
      we have been thought of as sheep for slaughter!

A.3. The desired future

23. Rouse yourself!
      Why are you asleep,
      O Sovereign One!?
      Wake up!
      Do not spurn us for ever!
24. Why are you hiding your face,
      forgetting our humiliation and oppression?
25. Because our soul has been prostrated to the dust,
      our body cleaves to the earth.
26. Rise up,
      be a help for us,
      and ransom us[27]
      for the sake of your committed love.

Psalm 45.
The Royal Wedding

Belonging to the worship-leader; Set to Lilies[28]; belonging to the Sons of Korah; a teaching poem;[29] a song of true love.[30]

A.1. The king[31]

1. My heart is astir with a good word:
     I am going to speak of my works about the king.
     My tongue is like the pen of a fluent scribe.
2. You are doubly more beautiful[32] than the sons of man.[33]
     Grace had been infused into your lips[34] –

16 Lit. 'for themselves', i.e. as and when they feel like it.

17 Amusement, derision, amazement.

18 The shame which shows itself in my face is actually everywhere: 'I am covered with embarrassment'.

19 Matching the confession of faith (4–8), this is a confession of innocence. Verses 17–22 are equivalent to an extended question: Why? In a world ruled by a moral God we have an expectation that virtue will be rewarded, and an element of surprise when it is not. Psalm 44 must be a difficult Scripture to anyone inclined towards a 'prosperity gospel'!

20 The conjunction, 'and', is versatile, adaptable to every context.

21 A comprehensive claim of innocence covering the inner reality of heart and mind ('not forgotten') and the outward reality of obedience within the covenant.

22 A plural subject with a singular verb. Possibly this is intended to have 'distributive' force – 'nor has any single one of our steps turned aside'. This is certainly exemplified where persons are involved (Genesis 27:29, 'those who curse … cursed be he/may every one be cursed …').

23 Jackals, says Isaiah (34:13), inhabit ruins, but the brevity of our expression above would need a lot of imagination in order to become 'you have crushed us and made us a ruinous den of jackals'! Could 'the place of jackals' be metaphorical for a field of battle (where jackals would scent blood an prowl as scavengers? Again a great deal of imagination is involved. Such a use is not exemplified elsewhere.

24 *tsalmaweth*, or 'shadow of death'.

25 *'el.*

therefore[35] God has blessed you for ever.

3. Gird your sword on your side, mighty One! –
   your majesty and your splendour!

4. And in your majesty
   ride successfully in the cause of truth –
   humility – righteousness[36] –
   and may your right hand teach you awesome things!

5. Your arrows – what sharpened ones! –
   (peoples are falling beneath you!) –
   right into the heart of the king's enemies![37]

6. Your throne, O God,[38] is for ever and ever.
   A sceptre of uprightness is the sceptre of your kingdom.

7. You have loved righteousness and hated wickedness,
   therefore God, your God, has anointed you
   with the oil of gladness more than your associates.

8. All your clothes are myrrh –
   aloes – cassia[39] –
   from palaces of ivory whence[40] they made you rejoice.

9. Kings' daughters are your precious ones;
   the queen has taken up her position at your right hand,
   in gold from Ophir.[41]

A.2. The queen[42]

10. Hear, daughter,
    and see, and turn your ear,
    and forget[43] your people and your father's house,

11. and let the king desire your beauty:
    for he is your sovereign,
    and bow down to him.

12. And the daughter of Tyre, with a gift –
    the richest of people will seek your favour.

13. The daughter of a king, indoors,
    in her clothes woven with gold,
    is glorified in every way.

14. In multicoloured robes she will be conducted to the king.
    Young women, following her, her companions, are

26 i.e. on account of our commitment to you. The 'innocence' claimed through these verses is impressive: covering heart and life (17–18), in spite of adversity (19); spiritual devotion (20); innocence under the searching gaze of God (21). Far from having acted disloyally, they have been ready to pay a heavy price for fidelity (22).

27 Pay on our behalf whatever price is needed to bring us out of our predicament.

28 The name of a melody?

29 *maskiyl*, see heading to Psalm 42.

30 Plural ('of loves') expressing intensity.

31 Following the announcement (1) that the king is his subject, the poet recounts seven features of the king: God's blessing of grace (2), the king's standing for truth and righteousness (3–4), his victory (5), his deity (6a), anointing for righteous rule (6b, 7), the king's clothing (8) and his entourage (9).

32 The verb, *yaphah*, 'to be beautiful' is found here in an unusual reduplicative form which gives the emenders a field day. Some say similar forms are found in cognate languages. It may be (as I have chosen to believe) a specially devised form to express the exceptional beauty of the king.

33 Or 'of Adam'.

34 How greatly the Bible values purity and beauty of speech! Luke 4:22; John 7:46; James 3:2.

35 Here in the sense 'Giving proof that'.

brought to you.[44]

15. They are conducted with rejoicing and exultation;
   they are brought into the palace of the king.

A.3. For the future

16. Taking the place of your fathers, there will be your sons.[45]
   You will appoint them to be princes in all the earth.
17. I[46] will keep your name in memory by all generations,
   therefore peoples will give you thanks for ever and ever.

36 This is exactly how the Hebrew stands – hyphen and all! 'Humility' and 'righteousness' are nouns in apposition – a humble righteousness and a righteous humility – and together they define the way in which 'truth' is to be promoted: a truth matching what is 'right with God' – God's truth – and expressed in the context of humility of life-style. On the king's meekness: Zechariah 9:9; Matthew 11:29.

37 I have translated verse 5 just as the Hebrew is presented to us. No need to re-write the text: we are dealing with poetry, not an academic thesis, and we must allow its vivid allusiveness and flexibility. The adjective 'sharp' is in apposition to the noun 'arrows' and therefore merits emphatic translation ('your arrows – those sharp ones!').

38 An unequivocal assertion of the deity of the Messiah, but this, coupled with 'your God' (7), poses an Old Testament enigma. How can Messiah be both God and also be a devotee of God? The answer has to await the New Testament.

39 The structure of wording here parallels that in verse 4, note 36. Another example of nouns in apposition: so impregnated with scents are the king's clothes that they seem identical with their perfume.

40 'Whence' is highly dubious. Possibly – through questionable reasoning – 'stringed instruments made you glad'.

41 Location uncertain, a specially prized gold (1 Chronicles 29:4; Job 22:24; 28:16; Isaiah 13:12).

42 Seven truths about the Queen: detachment from the past (10), devotion (11), pre-eminence (12), glory (13a), clothing (13b–14), companions (14), homecoming (15).

43 The 'heaping up' of four verbs of command places enormous emphasis on the bride's need to put the past behind, and find her all in her new relationship.

44 i.e. to the king. He is the centre and focal point of everything.

45 The words are addressed to the king: the personal pronouns are masculine. It is not just the bride who is called to put the past behind her (10). The bridegroom (compare Genesis 2:24) too must fix his eyes on the future, represented by his sons.

46 The poem ends with the poet speaking again as he did in verse 1. There he promised a poem about the king; he rounds it off with a note of satisfaction: his poem will keep the king for ever in remembrance.

Pause for Thought

'From palaces of ivory' (8) … 'into the palace' (15) sums up the 'movement' of Psalm 45, does it not? But it was not from any earthly palace that the Messiah King emerged when he came out to claim his bride. It was the perfume of heaven itself, of the Father's house and presence, that clung to him when he came to earth, but his mission was essentially the same: that of our heavenly bridegroom seeking and saving his beloved to be his bride. Just think of our privileges. The earthly bride of the earthly king was summoned to put the past behind her (10) and to live only in and for the king's devoted love (11). In the deepest, truest sense we can forget 'the things that are behind' (Phil. 3:13, KJV), for they are all 'under the blood', and what has been cleansed and forgiven on earth will not even be remembered in heaven (compare Jeremiah 31:34). As Revelation 7:14 records, we stand before the throne as those whose robes are both 'washed' and 'made white' – that is to say, not a single spot or stain (however faint) remains. Pure white has replaced the scarlet of our sinfulness – and all through the blood of Jesus, our Bridegroom-King. Secondly, the model for our subsequent lives is that of a perfect honeymoon in perpetuity: 'let the king desire your beauty … bow down to him' (11). His attention is constantly focused on us – the Shepherd-Lamb (and who could know what shepherding should be, better than a lamb?), ever attentive to our needs; and, correspondingly, our longing for him – to 'know him, and the power of his resurrection, and the fellowship of his sufferings' (Phil. 3:10, KJV). Thirdly, we are robed for the occasion (13–14; see Philippians 3:9; Romans 13:14) –

> Clothed in His righteousness alone,
> Faultless to stand before the throne!

Finally, our home is in the palace (14–15). Whether we think, with Philippians 3:20, of our heavenly citizenship, or, with Revelation 7:15 ('will spread his tent over them') of living in the divine tent-home, we are fully, totally, irrevocably, eternally 'accepted in the Beloved' (Eph. 1:6, KJV).

Day 20 Read Psalms 46–48[1]

Psalm 46.
Not a Storm, a River[2]

Belonging to the worship-leader; belonging to the Sons of Korah; set to Alamoth; a Song.

A. God in control

1. God is on our side:
   refuge and strength,[3]
   help for us in adversity;
   exceedingly to be found![4]
2. Therefore we will not fear
   when the earth changes –
   when mountains[5] shift[6] into the heart of the seas.[7]
3. Its waters boil up boisterously;
   mountains shake by its swelling – (*Selah*)
4. a river![8]
   Its streams gladden the city of God,
   the holiest of the dwelling-places of the Most High.
5. God is at its centre;
   it will not be shifted.
   God will help it at the approach of morning.
6. Nations were boisterous;[9]
   kingdoms shifted;
   he uttered his voice;[10]
   the earth melts![11]
7. Yahweh of Hosts[12] is with us;
   top-security[13] for us is the God of Jacob.

1. These psalms are sometimes explained on the assumption that there was an annual 'enthronement festival' in Israel, celebrating Yahweh's kingship (as we now celebrate Ascension Day) – compare Psalm 47:5. It is more illuminating to think of them as poetically meditating on 2 Kings 19:35–37, the eleventh hour deliverance of Jerusalem from Sennacherib; Psalm 46, the international uproar and clash of arms that threatened the city, hushed by the voice of God; Psalm 47, Yahweh's triumphant return to heaven after demonstrating his sovereign ownership of all earth's powers; Psalm 48, a triumphant tour of inspection to note a city that emerged unscarred from such a threat.

2. Psalm 46 is as neat a poem as could ever be planned. Putting aside the uniting force of the 'refrain' (7,11), the psalm opens with the voice of man (1) and closes with the voice of God (10). Each of the two main sections ends with God speaking (6,10).

3. 'Refuge' shields us in danger; 'strength' empowers us in weakness.

4. i.e. 'exceedingly available'.

5. 'Mountains' depict creation in its passive solidity; 'waters' (3) are creation in its destructive powers. Both alike are subject to the Creator.

B. God in action

8. Come, gaze[14] at the deeds of Yahweh –
   how he has placed desolations in the earth:
9. making wars cease to the end of the earth;
   the bow, he shatters;
   and he cuts the spar in pieces;
   the wagons[15] he burns with fire.
10. Relax, and know[16]
    that I am God;
    I will be exalted among the nations;
    I will be exalted in the earth.
11. Yahweh of Hosts is with us;
    top-security for us is the God of Jacob.

Psalm 47.
The Exalted God of all the Earth[17]

Belonging to the worship-leader; belonging to the Sons of Korah; a song.[18]

A. Victorious God: victorious people

1. All you peoples,[19]
   clap hands!
   Shout aloud to God,
   with the voice of great ringing cries.
2. Because Yahweh, the Most High, is to be feared,
   a great king over all the earth –
3. driving[20] back peoples under us,
   states under our feet;
4. choosing for us our inheritance,
   the pride[21] of Jacob whom he has loved. (*Selah*)
5. God has gone up[22] with a triumph shout,
   Yahweh with the sound of a ram's horn.

6. This verb, *mot*, occurs three times (2,5,6). It means 'to move/move about/slip, slide'. I am not wholly content with the translation 'shift' but I could not think of a better which could be used in all three places, and that is the essential: the instability (of the physical mountains), the political (nations) but the stability of the spiritual (the city of God).

7. Genesis 1:9. The psalm depicts the undoing of the work of creation: the land going back under the waters.

8. We could make this a statement, 'There is a river', exposing a contrast between the turbulent waters of the world and the calm waters of the city. I believe the truth is rather different, taking 'a river'(4) as in apposition to the boiling waters of verse 3. To the untaught eye all is unrest, threatening, turbulent (3); but the instructed eye (4) sees more clearly. All is ordered in the hand of God, blithely doing his will, running his course. Isaiah depicted Assyria as a river in flood (Isaiah 8:6–8) – but the threat turned out to Jerusalem's advantage (2 Kings 19:35–36).

9. A change of theme, from the physical world and its 'forces' to the world of men, nations, history, politics.

10. Three perfect tenses hold three facts in balance: on the one hand international turmoil and instability; on the other, the mere sound of Yahweh's voice!

11. The fourth verb is imperfect tense, intended to impart vividness to what is described, as if we were watching it happen: Why, look, it's melting!!

12. See Psalm 24:10.

13. See Psalm 9:9.

B. Victorious God: universal people

6. Make music to God, make music;
   make music to our king, make music,

7. because God is king[23] of all the earth:
   make music with a teaching poem.[24]

8. God is king over the nations;
   God sits on the throne of his holiness.

9. The nobles of the peoples will assuredly gather[25]
   to be[26] the people of the God of Abraham,[27]
   because the Shields[28] of the earth belong to God;
   he is exceedingly to be upraised.

Psalm 48.
The King and the kings

A Hymn;[29] A Song belonging to the Sons of Korah.

A.1. 'Our God' and his city

1. Yahweh is great,[30]
   and exceedingly to be praised
   in the city of our God,
   the mountain of his holiness.

B.1. The beautiful city

(a.1. Kept by the king)
2.[31] Beautiful in elevation,
   the joy of all the earth
   the mountain of Zion,
   the very apex of Zaphon,
   the city of the great king.

3. God is in its palaces;
   known to be top-security.

14 It is easy to link this double command with the Sennacherib incident. We can imagine the crowds flocking to gaze in amazement and joy at the detritus of the Assyrian army. It is not easy to associate the commands with some national festival of Yahweh's exaltation. Note the parallel with Psalm 48: Psalm 46 invites inspection of the enemy's defeat; 48 invites inspection of the city's untouched preservation.

15 'Wagons' are the support vehicles bringing and holding supplies. Think of them drawn up in a defensive circle, but now defending nothing, simply encircling the leavings of a departed threat!

16 i.e. 'realize' in the light of your recent deliverance.

17 The two halves of this psalm (1–5, 6–9) traverse the same ground, but with fascinating differences. They start with exuberant praise (1, 6), move to kingliness (2, 7–8), continue with the contrasting notes of subdued peoples (3–4) and incorporated peoples (9ab), and end with divine exaltation (5, 9c). The first section, dealing with 'subdued peoples', starts by calling 'all peoples' to rejoice; the second section, dealing with one universal people, starts by exalting 'our king' – the God of Israel. Verses 1 and 9c form an inclusion binding the whole psalm into one.

18 *mizmor*, see heading to Psalm 3.

19 The first half of the psalm implicitly asks a question which the second half answers. The question is why the nations should clap their hands at being subdued by Israel. The answer is that this 'subjugation' turns out to be incorporation into the universal Israel (compare Isaiah19:25; 45:14–25; Ephesians 3:6).

(b.1. Secure against the kings)[32]

4. For, behold!
   The kings gathered,[33]
   they came by, all together;

5. They saw for themselves;
   just so! – they were astonished;
   they were terrified;[34]
   they betook themselves to flight.

6. Trembling gripped them there,[35]
   writhing like a girl in travail.

7. By an east wind you shatter ships of Tarshish.[36]

B.2. The established city

(a.2. Yahweh's right hand)

8. Just like we have heard,
   so we have seen,
   in the city of Yahweh of Hosts,
   in the city of our God.
   God will establish it for ever! (*Selah*)

9. In the midst of your temple, O God,
   we have contemplated[37] your committed love.

10. Just as your name is, O God,
    just so is your praise,
    to the ends of the earth.

(b.2. The unmarked city)

11. Let mount Zion rejoice;
    let the daughters of Judah exult,
    on account of your judgments.[38]

12. Go around Zion;
    encompass it;
    count its towers;

13. set your heart[39] on its battlements;
    review its palaces,[40]
    in order that you may give an account to subsequent
    generations,

20 I am treating 'driving' and 'choosing' as the participial use of the imperfect, here offered as proof of Yahweh's kingship. The defeat of the conglomerate armies of Sennacherib would be a perfect background to the psalm, not to mention historical memories of the Exodus and conquest of Canaan. The reference to 'the pride of Jacob', i.e. the land, mean that the conquest is included in the picture.

21 'Pride' in the sense of 'confident exultation' in Yahweh who made the gift of the land.

22 Isaiah (31:4) predicted that the Asssyrian threat would be ended when Yahweh 'came down' to fight for Mount Zion. Having 'come down', he now goes up home in triumph. Another part of the background is 2 Samuel 6:15; compare Psalms 18:9; 68:18.

23 Our king (6) is The King (7). this is typical Old Testament monotheistic thinking. In Israel's king the world finds its king, just as in Israel's salvation the world is saved.

24 *maskiyl*. If it is correct to see the word as a noun, then the call is to turn the mind to the task of discerning the truth embodied in Yahweh's intervention to save his people from Assyria, or to discern the truth expressed in Yahweh's kingship (compare 1 Corinthians 14:15). Alternatively, we could treat *maskiyl* as a participle: 'make music to him who acts with practical prudence'.

25 A 'prophetic' perfect: something so sure to happen that it can be stated as an accomplished fact.

26 'The people of the God of Abraham' is in apposition to 'the nobles of the peoples'. They are not grudgingly admitted to a secondary citizenship, nor are they simply 'like' the people of Abraham. They are actually such, as in Ephesians 3:6.

A.2. 'Our God' and his people

14. because this is God,
    our God for ever and ever.
    It is he who will guide us unto dying.[41]

27 The designation is deliberately chosen: it was Abraham to whom world conquest was promised, and through whom the world would be blessed (Genesis 22:17–18).

28 Description of kings in their official duties, Psalms 84:10; 89:18.

29 See Psalm 30, heading.

30 The topic of the psalm is chiefly the security and preservation of Jerusalem under threat, but the emphasis throughout the psalm, and the inclusion which binds it together (1, 14), is the greatness of Yahweh. Nothing is great except he lend it his greatness.

31 'The mountain of Zion' is flanked on one side by two aspects of its earthly reality and on the other two aspects of its spiritual reality. Ideally considered, we have its beauty, and its central place in the consideration of the nation. We might so speak of the heavenly Zion that now is (Hebrews 12:22), and the eschatological Zion we are yet to experience (Revelation 21:2). In mythology Zaphon was the mount-home of the 'god' Baal. Its location was not precisely fixed, but the psalmist affirms that the real divine mountain-home is Zion.

32 A test case: is Zion really protected by 'top-security'?

33 Compare Sennacherib's boast, Isaiah 10:8.

34 A highly poetical account of the Assyrian approach and flight, of course, but the heart of the matter is true: they did no more than look at the city. Isaiah's prediction (37:33–35) was fulfilled.

35 Specifying a place ('there') roots the psalm in some verifiable incident – and none suits it better than the Assyrian invasion and the rout of Sennacherib's forces.

36 'Ships of Tarshish' were the largest ships, capable of the longest sea voyages. The location of Tarshish is disputed. Some hold that Tarshish is not a place-name but a word descriptive of the open sea. We can only presume that this is a proverbial saying illustrative of Yahweh's easy power over even the chief accomplishments of man.

37 *damah* , in the simple active mode (*qal*), means 'to be like, resemble'. Many urge that in the intensive active (*piel*) –which we have here – the meaning is 'to make a resemblance of, to portray' (as in a visual representation). This, of course, suits the idea that Psalm 48 presupposes a dramatic presentation (in the temple) of Yahweh's kinship over the kings of the earth. The fact is, however, that every use of the *piel* in the Bible refers to mental activity, pondering, contemplating, thinking, purposing, plotting (Numbers 33:56; Judges 20:5; 2 Samuel 21:5; Psalm 50:21; Isaiah 10:7; 14:24; Esther 4:13.

38 The decisions you have made – to rescue Zion and overthrow Assyria.

39 'Fix your attention on'.

40 The city as such is intact ('go around, encompass'), its defences remain unchallenged and undamaged (towers, battlements); it is still the city of the king (palaces). 'Review' represents an otherwise unknown and indeterminate verb.

41 Possibly 'against (even) death' is the intention of the text; 'Till our dying day' would offer an interpretation in parallel with 'for ever and ever'. esv leaves the words out altogether!

Pause for Thought

Our three psalms cover in turn Christmas, Ascension and the Second Coming. In Psalm 46 our God is Immanuel, he who is 'with us' in all his deity of power as 'Yahweh who is Hosts', who, in himself, is every power, resource and sufficiency; but he is with us, too, in all his condescending tenderness, patience and care, for he is 'the God of Jacob', the patriarch who is portrayed as the least worthy, the most crafty. Abraham likely towers above us in faith; Isaac outshines us in patient, quiet godliness and continuance; Jacob, with all his frailties, compromises, and shortcomings speaks to our condition: yes, this God, the God of Jacob, is our God for ever, and 'with us' for ever. The Ascension proclaims that the work undertaken has been accomplished; did you sing this as a child?

> All his work is ended, joyfully we sing:
> Jesus hath ascended: glory to our king!

So in Psalm 47:5 'God has gone up' because what he 'came down' to do, he has done. Our great High Priest has done what no previous priest could afford to do: he has 'sat down' because what he came down to do – 'one sacrifice for sins for ever' (Heb. 10:12, KJV) – he has done. In Psalm 46 we are at rest *in his care*; in Psalm 47 we are at rest *on his finished work*; in Psalm 48 we are at rest *in hope*, for he will guide us to our dying day – yes, and beyond that into eternal glory. To walk, in our mind's eye, around our Zion-home, and view its perfections, its towers and battlements intact, its palaces awaiting – it is a picture that runs wider than itself, for this glorious, intact, perfect beauty is also the portion of each and every redeemed sinner as we step through Zion's gates: we shall be like him for we shall see him as he is (1 John. 3:2).

Day 21 Read Psalms 49–50

Psalm 49.
Beyond Life and Beyond Death[1]

Belonging to the worship-leader; belonging to the Sons of Korah; a Song.

A.1. To share discernment

1. Hear this, all you peoples;[2]
   open your ears, all you who inhabit this world of time,[3]
2. both all mankind alike, and also every individual man.[4]
3. My mouth keeps speaking a true wisdom,[5]
   and the thoughts of my heart a true discernment.[6]
4. I keep turning my ear to a proverb;[7]
   on the lyre I will open up my riddle.[8]

B.1. Wealth: its limits[9]

5. Why should I be afraid of days of evil,
   iniquity at my heels surrounds me?[10]
6. Those who are trusting in their resources,
   and keep making their boast in the abundance of their wealth –
7. not one will in any way whatsoever ransom even a brother,[11]
   nor give to God an atonement-price for him:
8. the ransom of their soul is a costly matter,
   and one must give it up for ever,
9. that he might live on in perpetuity,
   not see the pit.[12]

1   This is the heart of Psalm 49. The great truth the poet wants to share is that though all people die (12), there is a life beyond Sheol (the 'place' where all the dead live on) for those who die with 'discernment' (20), the 'upright' (14), those who are right with God and have ordered their lives accordingly. To this life God will himself 'take' them, having paid the price to do so (15).

2   The psalm claims a universal truth, applicable to all people at all times.

3   *cheledh*. The unused verb means 'to continue'. *cheledh* expresses 'duration of life' (e.g. Psalm 39:4–5). In the sense of 'the world' as here, it is the world of time and space, the world as transitory, lasting only as time lasts.

4   Lit. 'sons of Adam/mankind ... sons of *'ish*/the individual man'.

5   'True ... true'. Wisdom and discernment are plurals of amplitude. Wisdom etc. in the fullest possible meaning.

6   i.e. not a casual statement as of one thinking on his feet, but a well pondered truth.

C.1. Beyond this life[13]

10. Because he sees wise people die;
    together the superficial[14] and the unspiritual[15] perish,
    and leave their resources to those after them.
11. Within themselves,[16]
    their houses are for ever,
    their dwellingplaces for generation after generation.
    They have called lands by their[17] names!
12. Man,[18] in spite of preciousness, does not remain.[19]
    He is similar to the beasts which are destroyed.

C.2. Beyond Sheol[20]

13. This is the way with them!
    Folly[21] belongs to them!
    And their following approve what they say![22]
14. Like sheep they have consigned[23] them to Sheol;
    death itself will shepherd them,
    and the upright are destined to dominate them in the
    morning.[24]
    And their form is destined for fading away in Sheol:[25]
    no honoured place for any.
15. Surely, however, God[26] will himself ransom my soul from
    the hand of Sheol
    because he will take[27] me. (*Selah*)

B.2. Wealth: its limits

16. Do not become afraid when someone grows rich,
    when the glory of his house multiplies,
17. because when he dies he will take nothing whatsoever;
    the glory of his house will not follow him down.
18. Because while he lives he blesses his soul –
    and they congratulate you when you do well for yourself –
19. it[28] will go to the generation of his fathers;
    for perpetuity they will not see light.

7   Following the claim to universal truth
    (1–2), and to a fullness of discernment
    (3), verse 4 adds that this is a truth
    received by revelation: the open ear
    preceded the opened mouth. Compare
    Isaiah 50:4–5. 'Proverb' (*mashal*)
    is very versatile in use – a succinct
    saying (1 Samuel 10:12), an object
    of ridicule (Deuteronomy 28:37), an
    allegory needing interpretation (Ezekiel
    27:2), etc., but also truth received by
    revelation (Numbers 23:7, 18; 24:3;
    etc.). This last is plainly the sense
    in Psalm 49, a capstone to the huge
    claims the writer makes for what he is
    about to write.

8   i.e. present the truth as a song to be
    sung to accompaniment. 'Riddle'
    because this aspect of life is a 'riddle' to
    people, but he is about to unravel it.

9   We meet here the problem which
    lay behind the writing of the psalm:
    not the problem of inequality – that
    the world's wealth is so inequitably
    distributed – but the fact that wealth
    brings power, a power that is so often
    used oppressively.

10 '(when) iniquity dogs my footsteps
    from behind – indeed surrounds me
    on every side.' Thus he describes what
    might make him afraid – the iniquity
    of more powerful vested interests.
    The implication of the unannounced
    verse 6 is that these vested interests are
    people trusting in their wealth. But
    how foolish to trust what is so limited
    in its reach!

A.2. The key factor: discernment

20. Man,[29] in spite of preciousness,
     when he does not discern,
     is similar to the beasts which are destroyed.

Psalm 50.
The High Court

A Song; belonging to Asaph.[30]

A.1. The court assembled

1. The transcendent God,
    God,[31]
    Yahweh has spoken,
    and he has called the earth –
    from the sun's rising to its setting.
2. Out of Zion,
    the perfection of beauty,
    God himself has flashed forth.
3. Our God comes,
    and oh! let him not be silent.[32]
    Before him fire devours,
    and around him storm rages.[33]
4. He calls out to the heavens above,
    and to the earth,[34]
    that he may try his people's case.[35]
5. 'Assemble for me my beloved ones,[36]
    those in covenant[37] with me based on sacrifice.'
6. And the heavens will declare his righteousness.[38]
    Because God is judge.

B.1. The first defendants: ritualistic formalists[39]

7. Hear, my people, and I will speak! –

11 Whatever leverage wealth gives them on earth, it has no currency in heaven. The ideas of 'ransom' and 'atonement' raise the question of sin and of being 'right with God'. No earthly wealth touches this problem. 'Ransom' (*padhah*) emphasizes payment; 'atonement-price' (*kopher*) is the payment that 'covers' (*kaphar*) the debt (not by hiding it out of sight, but by cancelling it). The emphasis on 'brother' ('even a brother') underlines a situation in which, for love's sake, no expense would be spared, no effort withheld. But all to no effect; the need is beyond our resource. Compare Exodus 21:30 where both *kopher* and *pidhyon* (atonement-price and 'ransom') occur and where the price-paying concept is so clear.

12 Psalm 16:10; 55:23–24; 103:4; Isaiah 51:14. In Psalm 49:9, figurative of death and burial.

13 This is the first of two **C**-sections that form the heart of the psalm. **C.1.** faces the inevitability of death itself. In this regard 'man' is part of the animal creation. It comes to all alike (10); cannot be cheated by a phoney effort at immorality (11), and, left to himself 'man' faces death just as an animal does (12).

14 *kesiyl*, usually translated 'fool'. Typically this type of 'fool' is the thickhead, wise in his own eyes, but lacking all spiritual insight or concern.

15 'Brutish' (not brutal), lacking spiritual perception (Psalm 92:6). You cannot 'get through' to him. Apparently untouched by grace, unspiritual.

16 So literally, *qirbam*, 'their inner part'. Many, compare NIV, would read *qibram*, 'their grave'. It is often easy, like this, to smooth out the linguistic shortcuts that are natural to a poet.

Israel, and I will witness against you.

8. It is not for your sacrifices[40] that I will admonish you –
   your burnt offerings are before me continually.

9. I will not take a bull from your house,
   from your enclosures goats,

10. because every living thing of the forest is mine,
    the beasts on the mountains of a thousand.[41]

11. I know all the birds of the mountains,
    and the throngs of animals in the open country are
    available to me.

12. If I were hungry, I would not say it to you,
    because the inhabited world and all its contents are mine.

13. Do I eat the flesh of mighty beasts?
    And drink goats' blood?

14. Sacrifice to God a thank-offering,[42]
    and fulfill your vows to the Most High,

15. and call me in the day of adversity.
    I will set you free,
    and you will glorify me.

B.2. The second defendants: creedal formalists[43]

16. And to the wicked God has said:
    What business of ours is it to recount my statutes,
    and that you should take my covenant in your mouth[44]

17. – you who have hated correction,
    and have thrown away my words behind you?[45]

18. If you saw a thief, you were pleased with him,
    and your portion was with adulterers.

19. Your mouth you let go free with evil
    and you keep linking your tongue with deceit.

20. You sit:[46] against your brother you keep speaking;
    against your mother's son give voice[47] to a fault.

21. These are the things you have done,
    and I kept silent.
    You considered I am to be like you.[48]
    I will reprove you,

17 i.e. 'their own'. A vain reaching after
   a personal perpetuation which the
   brevity of life and the certainty of
   death deprives them of. The irony is
   that this is in fact the perpetuation
   they achieve – a name on a tomb!

18 'adham, 'mankind'. Something true
   universally.

19 liyn, to lodge overnight, be a temporary
   guest. Here 'lodge for long'.

20 **C.2.** takes the next step: what happens
   after this death which is common to
   all? The answer is that there is a life
   beyond Sheol to which Yahweh 'takes'
   his upright ones.

21 'Fat-headedness'. With the same
   baseless self-confidence that they
   evidenced all their earthly lives they go
   swanning into eternity.

22 Lit. 'approve their mouth'. A subtle
   implication that there is nothing
   behind their assured utterances. It is all
   mouth.

23 Third plural indefinite: as when we
   report that 'they say', meaning 'It is
   being said'.

   So here 'they are consigned' means
   'have been consigned'.

24 Resurrection morning, or the morning
   that greets them at the other side of the
   grave (Daniel 12:2; Psalm 17:15).

25 Or possibly 'Sheol is destined to erode
   the form'. It is uncertain what 'form'
   might mean in this context. It makes
   sense to think that none can flourish
   in Sheol, but all must find it a place of
   diminishing.

26 The subject, 'God', is given the
   emphatic place, preceding its verb. The
   thought is the equivalent to Abraham's
   'God himself will provide' (Genesis
   22:8).

and set it out[49] in order for you to see.

A.2. The court's decision[50]

22. Discern this, please,
    you who forget God,
    lest I savage you,[51]
    and there is none to deliver.
23. Whoever sacrifices a thank-offering glorifies me,
    and whoever appoints a way[52] for me to show him the salvation of God.

---

27 On this use of the verb 'to take', cf. Gen. 5:24; 2 King 2:3, 9, 10; Ps.73:24 ('afterwards take me to glory…')

28 'It' refers to 'his soul' in verse 18. The verb in verse 19 is feminine; 'soul' is a feminine noun. To go to the fathers is a general expression for dying, e.g. Genesis 15:15.

29 'adham, see verse 12. The psalm has centred on the wealthy but the truth the psalmist reveals in their case applies to all. It is not wealth that disqualifies but lack of spiritual discernment.

30 Named among the levitical singers and instrumentalists (1 Chronicles 15:16–17; 16:5, 7). Head of a levitical choir (1 Chronicles 25:1, 2, 6; 2 Chronicles 5:12); a composer of songs (2 Chronicles 29:30; compare 35:15). See Psalms 73–83.

31 'God' the first time is 'el, God in his transcendent majesty and power; the second 'God' is 'elohim, God in the completeness of the divine attributes, a plural of amplitude. Compare Joshua 22:22, where the context suggests that this impressive formula was the standard way of making a loyalty oath.

32 For this sort of enthusiastic interjection, compare Zechariah 3:5 (when the watching high priest intervenes to make sure everything is done). The appeal for divine speech is, in effect, a request for Yahweh to explain what he is doing, action accompanied by words, an unmistakeable work of God.

33 These elements accompanying a theophany are drawn from Exodus 19, a suitable background to the emphasis in this psalm on Covenant (5) and Decalogue (16).

34 The heavens and the earth are always present all the time, seeing everything therefore they figure as witnesses in imaginary courts scenes like this; compare Isaiah 1:2.

35 The whole world is brought to court (1), but those on trial are Yahweh's people, and the misdemeanours charged are such as they alone could be guilty of.

36 The adjective chasiydh is a passive formation related to chesedh, Yahweh's committed, steadfast love: those who are the recipients of that love.

37 'Those in covenant' is a participle. This means that the psalm is not looking back to a past covenanting, but examining present loyalty to covenant obligations.

38 In this imagined court scene, verses 1–2 and 5–6 deal with the gathering of the court – the judge, the defendants and the witnesses. In between we hear three voices describing what they see: verse 3a, the advent of God the judge; verse 3, he is attended by the symbols (fire, storm) of his holiness and awesomeness; verse 4, he summons the witnesses he desires.

39 The heart of this section is verse 13. Their devotion to offering sacrifice was aimed at doing God a favour. The direction of their religion was from man to God, a religion of 'brownie points', of getting into God's good books, of human meritorious works.

40 The two central sections of the psalm (**B.1** and **B.2**) focus in turn on the two aspects of the revelation at Sinai: the sacrifices (7–15) and the moral law (16–21).

41 A literal rendering of a unique and unexpected wording. The time-honoured 'cattle on a thousand hills' is difficult to refuse but it is not what the Hebrew obviously means. Possibly the sense meant is 'beasts on the mountains where thousands of beasts are to be found'. But why express it so obscurely?

42 True religion is a recognition of how God meets our needs: therefore thanksgiving; it is serious commitment and devotion: therefore fulfilling vows – and it is trustful expectancy expressed in prayer.

43 Creedal formalists say the right things in the right places in the right way at the right time – but the truth is that they hate divine truth (16–17)! Behind their attitude is the unspoken assumption that God does not worry about truth either (21).

44 Deuteronomy 31:10–11; Moses commanded a covenant renewal ceremony every seven years. This psalm sounds as if it was designed for such an occasion.

45 The charge (18–20) specifies Commandments 7–9, i.e. applies the test of observable conduct, not of the hidden things of the heart. Exactly the sort of things a court would deal with.

46 The picture is of the 'armchair' critic. Calmly assured of his own rightness and his right to pass judgment.

47 An ellipisis. Lit. 'you give a fault'. The verb stands for 'to give tongue, to utter'.

48 A very literal rendering. In the Hebrew the verb 'I am' stands where one would expect a noun as subject of the clause following 'considered (that) …' Very likely there is an intentional recalling of 'I AM', the Exodus name (Exodus 3:13–15).

49 A reference to the case being brought, the charge-list.

50 The Court's decision is to caution rather than to condemn out of hand. The LORD is reluctant to execute judgment; he delights in mercy. Sacrifices as such are of no interest to him, but sacrifices properly used are acceptable, hence the command here to sacrifice a thank-offering. Properly used they were divine ordinances for man's welfare and God's pleasure.

51 Tear you in pieces, like a beast of prey.

52 The customary 'orders his way aright' may be correct but does require a good number of 'understood' words. For the translation above, see *Revised Version* margin. It refers to the one who disposes himself to receive God's way of salvation. At last he sees that the initiative must rest with God, and what he proposes to do for us.

Pause for Thought

Only the New Testament brings the full revelation of the life to come; only Jesus can bring 'life and immortality to light through the gospel' (2 Tim. 1:10, KJV). Nevertheless the Old Testament provided enough to be going on with! First, the Old Testament affirms that the dead are alive. 'Abraham' it says, in a perfectly lovely expression, 'was gathered to his people' (Gen. 25:8, KJV) – an expectation just as certain to delight the Christian heart. Jacob knew that, in time, he would 'go down to Sheol to my son', speaking of the presumed dead Joseph (Gen. 37:35, NRSV). David was sure, regarding his dead infant, 'I shall go to him' (2 Sam. 12:23, KJV). Sheol, as such, was not a wholly attractive prospect, and how could it be? Death broke up the body-soul unity that is human life. The body went to the grave; the soul lived on (Eccles. 12:7). Sheol was a sort of half-existence, so that Isaiah can call its residents 'the shadowy ones' (14:9, *repha'im*, NKJV 'the dead'). The prospect of Sheol was frightening for those who knew (or felt) themselves to be astray from Yahweh. We saw this in Psalm 30, the dread of dying if God's favour has been withdrawn (compare Psalm 6:5; etc.). But, in contrast, there is the bright expectation of life and light for those who belong to him. The saying is true: 'Death is not the extinguishing of the light, it is putting out the lamp because dawn has come.' To those right with God, death brings a reversal of the inequalities of our present life (Ps. 49:14b); it leads to a blessed 'taking', undefined in Psalm 49:15 (NKJV 'receive'), but which Psalm 73:24 says leads to 'glory'. The night is over (compare Romans 13:12); morning has come (Ps. 49:14). Shadows have passed away, death is 'swallowed up', let the feasting begin (Isa. 25:6–10a)!

Day 22   Read Psalms 51–52

Psalm 51.
Repentance: Abundant Pardon:
Individual and National renewal[1]

Belonging to the worship-leader; a song of David's. When Nathan the prophet came to him when he had gone to Bath-Sheba.[2]

A. The wonder of repentance: individual experience

A.1. Sin, grace, and cleansing

1. Grant me your grace,[3] O God,
    according to your committed love;
    according to the abundance of your compassion
    wipe[4] away my rebellions;[5]
2. abundantly launder me from my iniquity,
    and purify me from my sin,

A.2. Sin and conscience

3. because[6] personally I know[7] my rebellions,
    and my sin is in front of[8] me all the time.

A.3. Sin and God

4. Against you – only you – I sinned,
    and what is evil in your eyes I have done,
    in order that[9] you may be in the right when you speak,
    in the clear when you judge.

1   This psalm begins on the individual level (1–6) and ends (16–19) by moving to the national level – the renewed city. The clue to understanding this is to accept the heading: the author is David, and the occasion that of his great multiplex sin as recorded in 2 Samuel 11. The king's sin imperilled the welfare of his kingdom – and his restoration restored its vitality. One of the sillier ideas floated by commentaries is that verses 1–15 deny the God-given nature and validity of sacrifices, proposing a wholly 'spiritual' religion, and that verses 16–19 (approving of sacrifices) were added to make the psalm suitable for general use. In other words, one makes the psalm acceptable by adding a stanza contradicting its teaching! Psalm 51 is the Old Testament's central text on repentance.

2   2 Samuel 11:1–12:25. The psalm records David's subsequent meditation on the significance of 2 Samuel 12:13.

3   The first of three words describing God as David the sinner sees him: 'grace', the unmerited, undeserved goodness of God, specifically shielding us from his wrath (as the first reference to grace – Genesis 6:8 – shows). 'Committed love' (*chesedh*), love as a decision of the unchangeable will of God; 'compassion', emotional, passionate love.

A.4. Sin and human nature

5. Behold!
    In iniquity I was brought to birth,[10]
    and in sin when my mother conceived me.[11]
6. Behold![12]
    It is truth gives you pleasure in what is concealed,[13]
    and in what is covered over you will make me know[14]
    wisdom.

B. Evidence of true repentance

B.1. Longing to be right with God[15]

7. Deal with my sin[16] by hyssop[17]
    so that I may be purified;
    launder me,
    and I will be whiter even than snow!
8. Make me hear gladness and joy.
    Let the bones[18] you have crushed exult.
9. Hide your face from my sins,
    and wipe away all my iniquities.

B.2. Commitment to newness of life[19]

10. A purified heart create for me, O God,
    and within me make a new and steadfast spirit.
11. Do not cast me away from your face,
    and the Spirit of your holiness do not take from me.
12. Oh, bring back to me the gladness of your salvation,
    and with a willing Spirit sustain me.

B.3. Sharing the truth

13. Oh, I would teach[20] rebels your ways,
    and sinners will turn back[21] to you.
14.[22] Deliver me from blood-guiltiness,
    O God,
    God of my salvation:

4   The first of three words describing what God can do with our sin: (i) 'wipe away' (*machah*), sin leaves a mark God can see and which he can erase; (ii) 'launder' (*kabas*), the infection and stain of sin gets right down into the fibres of our nature – God alone knows a detergent which can reach and cleanse away; (iii) 'purify' (*tahar*), mostly used in Leviticus of purifying from some offence that excluded them from the congregation of God's people, i.e. here, removal of that which separates from God.

5   The first of three words dealing with the offence: (i) 'sin', the specific offence committed, 'missing the mark' (cf. Judges 20:16, 'not miss'); (ii) 'iniquity', the 'twist' or 'warp' in human nature from whence sin springs; (iii) 'rebellion', willful, responsible refusal of God's way.

6   The appeal for the saving mercies in verses 1–2 is based on the 'because' of verse 3, the key factor of acknowledgement. Compare Psalm 32:3–4 which (if the psalm belongs – as it could well do – to this incident) suggests that for a time David lived by self-deception, and paid the price.

7   'To know', often used as here, in the sense 'to realise, acknowledge'. 'Knowledge' in the typically biblical sense is not just an item in the mind, but a truth so grasped by the mind that it changes the life.

8   Compare Psalm 38:17. 'In front of', not a statement of its place 'out there ahead', but describing what is a constant in felt experience. Hence v.3 is saying 'I acknowledge – and I feel what I acknowledge.'

My tongue will shout out aloud of your righteousness.

15. Sovereign One,

do open even my lips,[23]

and my mouth[24] will declare your praise.

C. Acceptable sacrifices: the community of penitents[25]

16. Because[26] you are not pleased with sacrifice[27] –

I really would give it!

Burnt offering you do not accept with favour.

17. God's sacrifices are a broken spirit;

a broken and crushed heart,

O God,

you will not treat with contempt.

18. In your favourable acceptance,

do good to Zion;

do build the walls of Jerusalem.

19. Then[28]

you will accept with favour

sacrifices of righteousness,[29]

burnt offering and whole burnt offering;[30]

Then

they will offer bulls on your altar.

Psalm 52.
Contrasts

Belonging to the worship-leader; a Song of David's. When Doeg the Edomite came and declared to Saul and said to him: David came to the house of Abimelech.[31]

A.1. The evil boast

1. How you make your boast[32] in evil, big-fellow![33]

The committed love[34] of the transcendent God[35] is all the day![36]

9 The conjunction (*lema'an*) expresses purpose, and should not be weakened in any way. Divine purposeful working is so all embracing that, while God cannot at all be held responsible for man's sin, yet man's sin has its intended place in revealing the righteousness and justice of God. The sinner might cry out, 'You can do all things. Why did you not stop me?' The Lord would reply, 'Because I purposed that you should come to the place where you would recognise your sin, face the reality of my righteous justice, stand judged before my holiness – this is my choicest blessing for the sinner!'

10 Lit. 'I was writhed with', referring to the pains of childbirth. 'Conceived', 'was hot', used in Genesis 31:10, 41 of animals being 'on heat'. David is not casting any doubt on the morality of the sexual aspect of procreation, but just tracking sinfulness back to the earliest existence of a moral being.

11 David traces back the presence of sin first to the moment of birth, and then, beyond that, to the moment of conception. These verses are important evidences in any discussion of abortion: the infant at birth, and the foetus at conception, is a moral and personal being,

12 The double 'behold!' throws these two verses into contrast: verse 5, the human reality – sin as a constituent of human nature; verse 6, sin as contrary to divine desire.

13 A slightly uncertain – but substantially confident – translation.

14 Imperfect tense, therefore possibly (as above) a future tense may be intended: God has a better plan for David than that he should be eternally consigned to what human birth has made him. Alternatively, 'you make me know wisdom'; it is by divine action that he is aware of his birth-inheritance.

B.1. The cutting tongue

2. Total destruction[37] is what your tongue plans –
   sharpened like a razor,
   you worker of deceit![38]
3. You have loved evil rather than good,
   falsehood rather than speaking righteousness. (*Selah*)
4. You have loved all words of annihilation,[39]
   you tongue of deceit!

C. God the Uprooter[40]

5. There is also the transcendent God[41] –
   he will demolish you perpetually;
   he will scoop you up;
   and he will drag you away, without a tent;[42]
   and he will uproot you out of the land of the living. (*Selah*)

B.2. The last laugh

6. And the righteous will see, and fear,
   and they will laugh over[43] him –
7. 'Behold!
   The fellow who does not make God his fortress,
   and trusts in the abundance of his wealth,
   is strong in his destructiveness!'[44]

A.2. The good name[45]

8. And as for me,
   I am an olive tree[46] flourishing in the house[47] of God.
   I have put my trust in the committed love of God
   for ever and ever.[48]
9. I will thank[49] you for ever,
   because you have acted;
   and, in the presence of your beloved ones,
   I will await your name
   because it is good.

15 On the verbs in these verses, see verses 1–2.

16 Suitably to the situation indicated by the heading: no sacrifice was provided for David's sins of murder and adultery, therefore recourse to a priest was out of the question. Therefore David appeals directly to God to apply some hyssop-cleansing which he has reserved to himself.

17 On hyssop, see: Exodus 12:22 (Passover: the blood achieved propitiation – the satisfying of God's wrath, the blessing of peace with God); Leviticus 14:6ff. (the 'cleansing' of the leper: dealing with personal defilement); Numbers 19:16–19 (chance uncleanness, by touching a dead body). Hyssop was the means of application throughout.

18 Compare Psalm 32:3. Sin debilitates the sinner.

19 Each verse in this section refers to 'spirit'. Since the topic in verse 10 is God's creative work, the 'spirit' in question is the new spirit God will create in David (corresponding to 2 Corinthians 5:17; compare Ezekiel 36:26). Verse 11 follows verse 10 in the same way that Ezekiel 36:27 follows 36:26. The new-created human spirit is the work of the divine Spirit. The plea is for intimate personal union; David with God (verse 11a) and God by his Spirit with David (verse 11b). In v.12 'Spirit' or 'spirit' could be equally argued.

20 The saving instrument is the communication of the truth.

21 The verb 'to turn back' links this section with the previous verses: 'bring back to me … [they] will turn back'. It is the returned sinner who can lead sinners back. Notice the balance between the desire expressed in verse 13a and the certainty of return in verse 13b.

22 Verse 14 sounds as if it should belong with verses 10–12, the desire for newness of life, but it is firmly in place between two verses dealing with the opened mouth of testimony. It expresses the hugely important truth that it is precisely as sinners declared righteous (the verse begins with 'blood-guiltiness' and ends with 'righteousness') that we testify to our salvation. We are living illustrations of the fact that God bothers with sinners; only as such can we speak to others. He deals with our sins in his absolute righteousness.

23 'My lips' is emphatic. Lips that shame would keep silent, the Sovereign LORD will 'open' and use! Only he can save; only he can liberate into speech.

24 The Sovereign One opening the lips creates personal responsibility to use the lips he has opened.

25 See how accurately these verses belong with the foregoing psalm. Verses 16–17 obviously do; verse 19 ('you will accept with favour') picks up the same verb in verse 16; the reference in verse 19 to sacrifice and burnt offering looks back to verse 16; verses 16 and 18 coincide in the thought of acceptance with favour. The whole section insists that only when verses 16–17 are true can verses 18–20 be true.

26 'Because' is, in effect, 'namely that'. It looks back to verse 13, 'teach … your ways', explaining that the ritual act of offering a sacrifice as such means nothing to God. What rebellious sinners need to know is God's insistence on a consenting and participating spirit.

27 When 'sacrifice' and burnt offering are mentioned together, 'sacrifice' means the 'peace' or 'fellowship offering' – they are the rituals specifically that pointed to living for and with God. The burnt offering symbolises the sinner coming in full consecration to God; the peace offering, God coming in peace to the sinner. They were the sacrifices of 'getting back together'. The life of consecration (burnt offering) and fellowship (peace offering) is not a matter of correct ritual but of getting right with God, knowing and teaching his way with sinners, singing of his righteousness.

28 The two occurrences of 'then' are temporal – 'at that time'. When things are such as the preceding verses describe, not the restoring of walls, but the penitential return of sinners.

29 Sacrifices representative of a spirit and heart right with God.

30 'Whole burnt offering' is the single word *kaliyl*, emphasising totality. Compare a secular use in Judges 20:40. In the psalm it is an explanatory and emphatic addition, the entirety of the offering (Leviticus 6:15–16, 22–23; Deuteronomy 33:10; 1 Samuel 7:9).

31 1 Samuel 22:6-23. Commentators find difficulty relating the psalm to the incident – largely because they are expecting something Hebrew poetry does not provide. There is no such thing in the Bible as 'narrative poetry' in the English sense. The Hebrew poets did not record events but meditated on the truths and principles inherent in the events. Doeg was a sneaky eavesdropper to things not meant for his ears, and he reported them in a manner 'economical with the truth'. This more than covers what the psalm requires.

32 In the bad sense of self-confident, self-satisfied glorying. Compare 49:6–7; Jeremiah 9:22–24.

33 *gibbor. gabhar,* to be strong, prevail, hence *gibbor,* 'mighty'. *Gebher* is used as a general term for an adult male (Exodus 10:11); human being (Job 22:2); ironically, of a 'big shot' in Isaiah 22:17 ('great as you think you are'); 'person, chap, fellow, individual' (Numbers 24:13; Josh. 7:14). In the psalm very ironic – what a 'big shot' to put a settlement of unarmed priests to the sword!

34 *Chesedh,* God's committed, unchanging love set against man's self-satisfied boasting.

35 *'el,* the transcendent God in power. What is Doeg's brutality compared with real strength?

36 The implication is that while Doeg's moment of ascendancy is transient, God's love and power is for ever.

37 Plural of amplitude.

38 The accusation is of intent to mislead and cause mischief. Doeg only told the truth up to the point where it would do harm. 'You worker of deceit'; we would say 'you con-man'.

39 Lit. 'words of swallowing up' – i.e. whereby the thing spoken of disappears from sight. Some prefer the meaning 'confusion'.

40 Lines 2, 3, 4 of verse 5 picture a building demolished, its bits and pieces raked together, and the whole carted away. Line 5 pictures the uprooted tree. The doubling of the imagery expresses certainty (Genesis 41:32). The end of any security of tenure; the cutting off of life.

41 Making these words (lit. 'also the transcendent God') into a separate sentence slightly (but only slightly) overstresses the emphasis the Hebrew gives them.

42 Or (compare, ESV) 'far from (your) tent'; or 'from the Tent' meaning God's Tabernacle. This links with verse 8: to Doeg, God's dwelling would have been a mere tent, to David a house of God, secure home.

43 Not the laugh of vindictiveness or malice (compare, Job 31:29; Proverbs 24:17), but of satisfaction at seeing the just judgment of God and the vindication of the right.

44 The singular of the word which opened verse 2, bracketing the whole centre of the psalm.

45 Note the links with verse 1, forming an inclusion round the psalm: 'committed love' occurs in both **A.1.** and **A.2.** The same word reappears in a different form in 'beloved ones' – those who have had his committed love bestowed on them. 'Good' contrasts with 'evil'; 'ever and ever' matches 'all the day'.

46 There may be a symbolic force in 'olive tree'. In Genesis 8:11, the olive leaf seems to be a symbol of peace come back; in Jeremiah 11:15–16 and Hosea 14:6, a picture of beauty and fresh life; in Zechariah 4:3,11–12, nourished by divine life.

47 Compare verse 5, the 'big-shot' loses his tent; the house of God remains!

48 The parallel with **A.1.** (verse 1) shows that it is not David's trust that is for ever but God's committed love.

49 Another contrast with verse 1. The 'big shot' glories arrogantly in his evil prowess; David bows in thankfulness to God.

Pause for Thought

There can hardly be a psalm in the whole collection that speaks so plainly to the world of the twenty-first century as Psalm 52. We don't have to name names or specify localities or identify causes to remind ourselves that the spirit of Doeg the Edomite lives on. There are those everywhere all too ready to forward their interests, as he did, at the point of a sword. It is the world we live in: a world in which some advance by force of arms, and the rest seek security behind force of arms. Doeg on a universal scale! So what does Psalm 52 reply? First, that the power of committed, unchanging divine love is the sufficient alternative to the 'big fellow' and his arrogant tongue (1). David was in the thick of a life-threatening situation, with Saul's death squads as ruthlessly after him as ever Doeg was after the priests. He (almost blandly) looks danger in the eye, and replies that God's steadfast love remains every day. Secondly, it invites us to keep in mind the great settlement that is on its way, the final showdown, the total overthrow of the Doeg-spirit and its practitioners (verse 5 – the heart of Psalm 52). Do remind yourself of the heaping up of verbs of destruction – four altogether! The terminator truly terminated! So we are allowed to appraise every threat: it won't last; its end may be soon; it may continue longer than we would wish; but the end is written. Thirdly, the way forward is the way of faith. Psalm 52 deals with contrasts – the bracketing contrast between evil self-confidence (1) and the good name (9) – there's something worth pondering! But look also at the contrast between the two trees – one uprooted (5), the other flourishing (8). And then there is the contrast between trusting one's own resources (7), and trusting in steadfast love (8) – a trust sustained by delightful fellowship (9c) and restfully, confidently awaiting the fulfillment of all the 'good name' pledges (9d).

Day 23 Read Psalms 53–55

Psalm 53.
Unafraid[1]

Belonging to the worship-leader; set to Machalath;[2] a song of David's.

A.1. Rejection of God

1. The spiritually unprincipled person[3] has said in his heart
   'There is no God.'
   They bring ruin,
   and they practice abominable deviancy.
   There is no one doing good.

B.1. Divine assessment[4]

2. From heaven
   God looks down[5]
   on the sons of man,
   to see if there is anyone acting prudently,
   seeking God.
3. Each and every one[6] has backslidden,
   together they have become tainted.[7]
   There is no one doing good;
   There is not even one.

B.2. Divine action

4. Do they not know –
   all the trouble-makers[8] –
   those who eat my people eat bread![9] –
   upon God they have not called!
5. There[10] they were truly afraid,

1. Psalm 53 is largely identical with Psalm 14, but it has been editorially adapted to meet a new situation. The crux lies in the interpretation of verse 5, which here refers to fear felt by 'my people', and the psalm celebrates a miraculous deliverance when a sudden panic fell on the threatening enemy. In a psalm which opens 'there is no God', the word 'God' appears seven times! The opening denial (1) is balanced by the concluding longing (6).

2. Compare Psalm 88. Uncertain meaning. Is it a musical term whose significance has been lost? Is it related to chalal, to be sick/weak? Or to chiyl, to writhe, whirl, dance?

3. See Psalm 14:1.

4. In the **B**-sections, the opening and closing lines affirm the reality of God: appraising ... scorning. There are five references to 'God' in these verses.

5. Compare Genesis 18:16 (no judgment without preliminary examination); Exodus14:24 (looking so as to keep the threat to his people in mind and deal with it).

6. This focus on the individual differentiates Psalm 53 from Psalm 14. A singular enemy and threat is in mind.

7. See Psalm14:3.

8. See Psalm 5:5.

9. See Psalm 14:4.

10. As in Psalm 14 'there' points to a specific situation.

(there was no cause for fear!)[11]
because God has himself scattered[12] the bones of him who
camps against you.
You have disappointed them.[13]
Indeed[14] God has scorned them!

A.2. Longing for God

6.   Oh that out of Zion were come the salvation of Israel
      when God restores the fortunes of his people!
      May Jacob exult!
      May Israel rejoice!

Psalm 54.
'His name – by faith in his name'[15]

Belonging to the worship-leader; set for strings;[16] a song
of David's. When the Ziphites came and said to Saul: 'Is
not David hiding himself with us?'[17]

A.1. The saving name: prayer

1.   O God,
      by your name,[18] save[19] me,
      and by your mightiness plead my cause.
2.   O God,
      hear my prayer.
      Open your ear to the words of my mouth.

B.1. God ignored

3.   Because strangers[20] have risen up against me –
      terrifying people have sought my soul;[21]
      they have not placed God in front of them. (*Selah*)

11   'Cause for' is an interpretative addition
     to (lit.) 'there was no fear'.

12   Or 'determined to scatter'.

13   These last two lines of verse 5 first
     address God and then describe God.
     This sort of change of stance is typical
     of Hebrew writing – as it were, seeing
     something from two different points of
     view confirms it as certain.

14   Or 'because'.

15   Acts 3:16, ESV.

16   See Psalm 4, heading.

17   David had rescued the people of Keilah
     and then escaped from Saul into the
     wilderness of Ziph where (1 Samuel
     22–23) 'God did not give him over to
     Saul' (23:14). But the Ziphites took
     action to inform Saul about David,
     promising to arrest him themselves
     (23:20). David moved south of Ziph
     and was threatened with encirclement
     by Saul (23:26), who was called
     away by news of a Philistine invasion
     (23:27–28), whereupon David went
     east to En-gedi on the Dead Sea. Over
     and above the hostility of Doeg (Psalm
     53), Psalm 54 reflects disillusionment
     following rejection by men of his own
     tribe of Judah. Keilah and Ziph were
     both Judahite towns (Joshua 15:24,
     44). We need to keep in mind the
     tensions of the situation. Both Keilah
     and Ziph were showing commendable
     loyalty to their king, Saul.

18   i.e. by everything that is true of you
     as revealed in your name. The name
     characterizes the person – illustrated by
     1 Samuel 25:25!

19   'Save' alludes to the threat to David;
     'plead' to the accusations made against
     him. As always, there can be no
     salvation unless justice is satisfied.

B.2. God upholding

4. Behold!
   God is my helper.[22]
   The Sovereign One is the chief upholder[23] of my soul.
5. He will return the evil[24] to my foes.[25]
   In your truth[26] exterminate them!

A.2. The delivering name: praise

6. With a freewill offering I will sacrifice to you.[27]
   I will give thanks to your name,
   Yahweh,[28]
   because it is good,
   and my eye is sure to see the last of my enemies.[29]

Psalm 55.
The Balanced Life

Belonging to the worship-leader; set for strings;[30] a song of David's.

A. Turmoil

(Prayer)
1. Turn your ear, O God, to my prayer,
   and do not hide yourself from my plea for grace.
2. Attend to me, and answer me.
   I am restive[31] in my musing,
   and I am distraught,

(Enmity)
3. because of the voice of the enemy;
   because of the pressure of the wicked.
   For they keep bringing down trouble on me,
   and in exasperation they bear a grudge.

20 'Strangers' describes how they were behaving: Judahites though they were, they were acting as only aliens could; 'terrifying' indicates what they were capable of; 'not placed' is the final straw! Without God, they are devoid of moral or spiritual restraint or value.

21 Compare the wording with 1 Samuel 23:15.

22 Lit. 'a helper for me/of mine', on my side. An immediate contrast to the end of verse 3.

23 Or 'among those who uphold …' David was not bereft of help, but among their company he saw also the Sovereign – treating the preposition 'be' in its sense of 'among', but it could also (as above) be what is called the *beth essentiae* (in the character of), and the plural 'helpers' could be a plural of amplitude. This suits the appeal to God as Sovereign.

24 Compare Deuteromy 19:19. The LORD's law was to return to the false accuser whatever he would have wished done to the one he maligned.

25 See Psalm 5:8.

26 'Your trustworthiness', your fidelity to your own nature and word. Recall the appeal to his 'name' and 'mightiness' (1).

27 The LORD's acts of goodness and deliverance are stepping stones to greater and fuller devotion.

28 This lovely appeal directly to 'Yahweh' rounds out David's theology: 'God', *elohim*', possessor of the full total of divine attributes; 'sovereign' (adonay), absolute in sovereignty and rule; Yahweh', the Exodus God who saves his people and overthrows his foes.

(Distress)

4. My heart writhes inside me,
   and deadly terrors[32] have fallen on me.
5. Fear and trembling come on me,
   and shuddering has covered[33] me.

(Longing to escape)

6. And I said:
   'Oh that I had wings like a dove;
   I would fly,
   and take up my dwelling.[34]
7. Behold!
   I would distance myself as a wanderer,
   and stay a while in the wilderness.[35] (Selah)
8. I would hasten to my place of escape
   from the rushing[36] wind,
   from the tempest.'

B.1. The 'all round the clock' distress

(Plea)

9. Swallow them up,[37]
   O Sovereign One.
   Divide their tongues.[38]
   Because I have seen violence and contention in the city.

(24 hour hostility)

10. Daily and nightly,
    they go around on its walls;
    and there is mischief and trouble inside it.
11. There is total destruction[39] inside it,
    and from its streets oppression and deceit do not move
    away.[40]

(Distress)

12. Because it is not an enemy who reproaches me:
    I would bear it!

29 Lit. 'upon my enemies my eye will look' – not gloating but observing. David registers the coming fact of their extermination and his own presence to see it.

30 Psalm 54, heading.

31 Four leading 'I' sayings reveal the 'movement' of the psalm: 'I am restive' (1), 'I said' (6), 'I will call out' (16), 'I keep trusting' (23).

32 'Terrors of death', but the idea of finding death a terror would be out of context with the rest of the psalm, whereas treating 'terrors of death' as expressing an adjective suits.

33 Compare Exodus 14:28, the waters 'covering/overwhelming' Pharaoh's forces.

34 This is the 'absolute' use of *shakan*, i.e. 'to dwell' without saying where, hence 'to take up a dwelling place/settle down'; compare Psalm 102:28 (NKJV 'continue'; ESV 'dwell secure').

35 'Wilderness' is a very versatile word (*midhbar*). It does not necessarily mean a 'howling wilderness' (e.g. Deuteronomy 8:15); often it refers to the 'green belt' or 'open country' (1 Kings 9:18). Here the thought is remoteness.

36 Uncertain rendering.

37 David is beginning to develop the prayer outlined in verses 1–2. Prayer is the solution, not flight.

38 i.e. divide their counsels, give them clashing plans. Compare 2 Samuel 15:31.

39 Plural of amplitude, 'destructions'.

Not someone who hates me who has advantaged
himself[41] against me:
I could hide from him![42]

13. But you,
a man of my own class,[43]
my confidant,[44]
and my known friend!

14. Together we enjoyed sweet fellowship.
In the house of God we walked in the hub-bub.[45]

(Retribution)

15. Desolations[46] upon them!
May they go down living to Sheol![47]
Because rank evil[48] is their true[49] home –
Right among them!

B.2. The 'all round the clock' solution

(Resolve)

16. As for me,
I will call out to God,
and Yahweh himself will save me.

(24-hour prayer)

17. Evening and morning and noonday,[50]
I will muse and murmur,
and he is sure to hear[51] my voice.

18. In peace he has ransomed[52] my soul from the battle I had,
because in their abundance[53] they were with me.

19. The transcendent God will hear and bring them down –
he who sits enthroned from of old –
because real change[54] does not come to them[55]
and they do not fear God.

(Conflict and confidence)

20. He stretched out his hands against those at peace with
him;
he defiled his covenant.

40 The abundance of David's danger is felt if we note the movement from the encircling walls, to the inside of the city (twice), and then to the individual streets. A very poetic way of saying 'absolutely everywhere' – just as 'daily and nightly' express all the time. It must have felt like this in 1 Samuel 23:7,12. Note also the heaping up of hostile words: mischief, trouble, destruction, oppression, deceit – a rounded list: the first is matched by the last (the character or 'mind' of the opposition), the second by the fourth (their aim), and at the centre 'total destruction'.

41 Lit. 'made himself great'. What we call the 'rat race'.

42 Escape his clutches.

43 *'erek*, from *'arak*, to set out in rows, order, classify. The idiomatic use here is not exemplified elsewhere. 'Such a one as I myself'.

44 *'alluphiy*, from *'alaph*, to be familiar with. Proverbs 23:25 (NKJV 'learn' = 'become familiar with').

45 The joyous festal procession; compare Psalm 42:4.

46 Or, possibly, 'may death surprise them!'

47 David associates himself with Moses' words in Numbers 16:30 when he called for proof that in resisting him the rebels were resisting God's appointed agents. In the same way, David knows himself to be the sacrosanct person, here, expressing a pure anger – leaving the outcome to God. Romans 12:19.

48 Plural of intensity, 'evil itself'.

49 Or 'in their lodging place', but I think the preposition is the *beth essentiae*, as above.

50 The biblical way of describing the 24 hours of a day.

21. Smoother than butter were his mouthings,
    and war was his heart!
    Softer than oil were his words,
    and they were drawn swords!
22. Throw whatever comes your way[56] on Yahweh,
    and he will himself sustain you.
    Not ever will he permit insecurity to the righteous.

(Destinies)
23. And for your part, O God,[57]
    you will bring them down
    into the well of the pit.
    Blood-guilty and deceitful men,
    they will not halve their days![58]
    And, for my part,
    I keep trusting in you.

---

51 Perfect tense expressing certainty of future action (i.e. so certain that it can be stated as having happened).

52 What is called a 'pregnant' construction: 'he has ransomed my soul, bringing it into peace.'

53 Lit. 'in terms of the many', 'as the many'.

54 Plural of intensity.

55 Or 'to him', the enthroned God who does not change.

56 An attempt to represent *yehabheka*, a word of uncertain meaning. Some say it comes from an unexemplified *yahabh*, meaning 'to give', hence what is allocated to one in the changes and chances of life. Whatever else, this gives a suitable meaning in context.

57 The 'For your part … For my part' balance of these concluding verses is striking: every situation and every opponent can be left to him; our part is continuing trust.

58 Understood to mean 'not live out half their days', a way of stressing the essential transiency of life's hostilities.

Pause for Thought

Regularity, setting specific times apart for prayer – and keeping to them in a disciplined way – is something the Bible encourages. We all find the story of Daniel's practice in prayer moving to read (Dan. 6:10). How, in spite of the king's foolish, self-glorifying edict, he went to his upper room, with its windows towards Jerusalem, and knelt down three times a day. We sense not only the old man's yearning heart for the city of God, but his confidence in prayer and his commitment. I wonder if Daniel had caught the vision of the threefold discipline from Psalm 55:17, 'evening and morning and noonday'? How to end one day and begin another; how to stop in the middle of a busy life and turn to God. Isaiah made a forecast that the Servant of the LORD – the Lord Jesus – would practice the discipline of what we used to call 'the morning watch' (see Isaiah 50:4), and Mark 1:35 records an occasion when he did just that. In Acts 3:1 we find Peter and John keeping the statutory hour of prayer, the ninth hour, and the devout Cornelius testifies to the same prayer discipline (Acts 10:30). Should we be 'evening, morning and noon' people? The answer is 'Why not?' Two truths are important before we make excuses about the busyness of life today. First, prayer is a simple thing, not necessarily prolonged (Matthew 6:7–8), and secondly, none of the passages we have referred to says anything about the time when we pray or for what length of time. As soon as we think of starting the day with God, our minds begin thinking about four or five a.m. or some other unearthly hour – because we read somewhere that some great prayer-warrior was always up and about by then! 'Setting aside time' means just that – doing what is possible for us within our God-given day and our God-given abilities. Time to read a verse of the Bible; time to call upon God. And here's a final thought: Psalm 55 begins with prayer (1) and ends with trust (23). If we say we are those who trust, those who are saved by faith, then a primary way this shows itself is to balance life's demands with life's prayers.

Day 24   Read Psalms 56–58

Psalm 56.
The Sure Foot on the Right Road[1]

Belonging to the worship-leader; set to 'The Dove of Silence in the Distance'; David's, a Miktham,[2] when the Philistines held him in Gath.[3]

A.1. God's grace, man's hostility

1.   Grant me your grace, O God,
     because mere man[4] pants[5] after me.
     All day, making war, he oppresses me.
2.   My foes pant all the day,
     because many are at war with me,
     Most High.[6]

B.1. Not fear but trust

3.   The day I am afraid[7]
     I personally turn in trust to you.
4.   In God[8]
     – I keep praising his word! –
     in God I have put my trust;
     what can flesh[9] do to me?

C.1. David's words twisted; his steps dogged

5.   All the day they manipulate[10] my words.
     Against me for evil, are all their plans.
6.   All gathered together,[11] they hide.
     Themselves, they dog[12] my heels,
     according as[13] they wait for my soul.

1   Regarding the outline offered, **A.1.** has one line about God, three about human hostility; **A.2.**, one line about hostility, three about God. **B.1.** majors on the idea of 'trust', also **B.2.**, which, in the place of the first reference to trust, has 'call', introducing a fresh thought. In **C.1.** David feels the weight of human misrepresentation; in **C.2.** he accepts the burden of his own vows. The threat to his soul becomes divine deliverance of his soul.

2   See Psalm 16, heading.

3   See 1 Samuel 21:10–15. The heading of the psalm makes explicit what we would only have surmised from 1 Samuel – namely, that David was, if not under arrest at least under strict observation and restriction in Gath, a prized hostage in the Philistine hostility to Saul. See also Psalm 34, heading. 1 Samuel offers the bare bones of the situation, and chooses to tell a good story; Psalm 34 probes behind the scenes (the real cause of David's escape was not cleverness, but prayer); Psalm 56 meditates on how to walk carefully and surefootedly in a menacing situation.

4   *enosh*, Psalms 8:4; 9:19; 10:18. Humanity in its frailty, compare verse 4, 'flesh'. The opposition is strong, but at base what is it but 'mere' humanity?

5   A vivid metaphor for a covetous, grasping hostility. Compare Amos 2:7.

6   Or as an adverb referring to David's foes, 'loftily, arrogantly'.

A.2. Man's iniquity, God's grace

7. Notwithstanding mischief,[14]
   is there escape for them?
   In exasperation bring down[15] the peoples,[16] O God.
8. Of my wandering[17] you have yourself taken account.
   Do put my tears in your bottle!
   Are they not in your book?[18]

B.2. Not fear but trust[19]

9. Then my enemies will turn back
   in the day I keep calling.
   This I know,
   because God is mine.
10. In God –
    I keep praising his word! –
    In Yahweh –
    I keep praising that word!
11. In God I have put my trust:
    I will not fear.
    What can man[20] do to me?

C.2. David's vows kept: his feet secure

12. Binding on me,[21] O God, are your vows.
    I will render thanks[22] in full to you,
13. because you have delivered my soul from death.
    Have you not delivered my feet from stumbling,
    so that I may walk about before God in the light of life?

7 David's experience in Gath (1 Samuel 21:12) is the only time he is recorded as being afraid. Note the sequence here; 'the day I am afraid' (3) … I will not be afraid (4).

8 The Hebrew *batach,* to trust, usually 'governs' the thing or person trusted by the preposition 'in' (*be*). In this case the second 'in' (*be*) God' recapitulates the first, therefore there is considerable emphasis on God as the one trusted. At the end of verse 3 trusted, 'you', is governed by the preposition 'to', hence the different translation 'turn in trust to'.

9 On this antithesis of 'God' and 'flesh', compare Isaiah 31:3.

10 *'atsabh,* taken here in its meaning 'to shape, fashion', e.g. Job 10:8. Alternatively, a verb of the same spelling = to pain, hurt – 'they twist/torture my words'.

11 *gur*, here taken as the verb 'to gather'. A verb of the same spelling means 'to attack', 'Moving in to the attack, they hide'.

12 Lit. 'they keep my heels', in the sense 'keep watch at', i.e. sneakily, from behind.

13 i.e. they manipulate, plan, hide, gather, dog – all in the interests of their master objective to 'wait for' David's life.

14 The gratuitous trouble David's enemies have caused – not the Philistines but Saul and his duplicitous courtiers.

15 Compare Psalm 55:23.

16 Possibly signifying 'these peoples', the hostile Philistines and the pursuing emissaries of Saul. Or, as in Psalm 7:7–8, David may be seeing his trials in an eschatological setting and longing for the LORD's final settlement, putting all things to rights.

Psalm 57.
My Darkness, His Wings[23]

Belonging to the worship-leader; 'Do not destroy';[24] David's, a miktam,[25] when he fled from Saul into the cave.[26]

A.1. Plea for divine grace

1. Grant me your grace, O God.
    Grant me your grace,
    because in you my soul has taken refuge,
    and in the shadow of your wings I continue to take refuge
    until this great destruction passes.

B.1. Confident prayer

2. I keep calling to God Most High,[27]
    to the transcendent God
    who settles everything[28] for me.
3. He will send from heaven and save me,
    whenever he who pants for me has taunted. (*Selah*)
    God will send his committed love and his truth.

C.1. Deadly foe

4. My soul – in the middle of – lionesses –
    lie down I must – inflamed ones[29] – sons of men –
    their teeth – spear – and arrows –
    and their tongue – a sword – sharp![30]

D.1. Refrain: the exalted glory of God

5. Oh be exalted above the heavens, O God,
    over all the earth your glory![31]

17 Or 'my grief', if *nudh,* to wander, is taken in the sense 'to shake one's head', be agitated, grieved. This is less likely than a reference to David's current situation as a homeless wanderer.

18 That God has a double memorial of our miseries filed away – tears stored, events recorded – makes his intervention certain.

19 In the parallel verse 3–4 the specific thought was that faith, resting on the word of God, is the antidote to fear. In verses 9–11 the thought is that faith, resting on the word of God, turns to prayer. Verse 3 thinks of 'the day I am afraid'; verse 9, of 'the day I keep calling'.

20 *'adham,* i.e. man as human. Compare verse 1, *'enosh* ('man' in his frailty), verse 4, *basar* ('flesh', man as contrasted with God).

21 Heb. simply 'upon me'. The preposition *'al* is regularly used to express being under obligation, e.g. 2 Samuel 18:11 ('I would have given' = 'It would have been incumbent on me to give').

22 Or, maybe better, 'a thank offering'. Sacrifices in fulfillment of vows made in times of stress, and sacrifices of thank offerings to mark deliverance. The 'vow' marked a move forward in consecration; the 'thank offering' a grateful acknowledgment of blessings received.

23 This is a notably precisely planned psalm. If we isolate the refrain (5,11), then we have three stanzas of four lines, five lines and four lines, each set of three followed by the refrain. The psalm marks a night passed in the cave: going to bed (4); waking up (8). The title places David 'in the cave' but David places himself 'in you … in the shadow of your wings' (1), a very different shaded place!

C.2. Doomed foe

6.   A net they prepared for my footsteps;
     my soul bowed down;
     they dug a pit in front of me;
     they are destined to fall right into it![32] (*Selah*)

B.2. Confident praise

7.   My heart is fixed,[33] O God;
     my heart is fixed!
     I will indeed sing and make music!
8.   Awake, my glory![34]
     Awake, lute and harp!
     I will indeed awake the dawn!

A.2. Praise for divine love

9.   I will give thanks among the peoples,
     O Sovereign One.
     I will make music to you among the states,[35]
10.   because your committed love is great, up to the
     heavens,
     and up to the clouds, your truth.

D.2. Refrain. The exalted glory of God

11.   Oh be exalted above the heavens, O God,
     and over all the earth, your glory.

24   Compare Psalms 58, 59, 75. Maybe the opening line of a song – see Isaiah 65:8, possibly a vintage-song. Note also David's words in 1 Samuel 26:19.

25   See Psalm 16, heading.

26   1 Samuel 22:1 or 24:3.

27   'God Most High' only occurs here, compare Psalm 7:17 ('Yahweh Most High'), 78:35 ('Transcendent God Most High'). But see, specially, Genesis 14:18–22 where Abram identified 'God Most High' with Yahweh.

28   'Settles everything', *gamar*, 'to come or bring to an end', hence 'to complete, deal completely with'.

29   We might say 'all fired up'.

30   The Hebrew of verse 4 is just as 'jumpy' as this rendering! Three significant words in each line. It sounds like the beating of David's heart! Or maybe, in his imagination, the steadily approaching footsteps of his pursuers. 'Lionesses', savage strength; 'spears and arrows', human power to injure whether at a distance or at close quarters; 'sword', the deadly power of the tongue.

31   This 'refrain' sets the psalm on a different footing: not David, his danger and his deliverance, but the manifestation of the greatness and glory of God. In verse 3 he is all-powerful over David's foes; what is now sought is that he display how all important he is.

Psalm 58.
Righteousness Violated and Vindicated

Belonging to the worship-leader; 'Do not destroy';[36] David's; a miktam.[37]

A.1. Deterioration

1. Is it the case that by silence you can speak righteousness,
    pass judgment with fairness,
        you sons of man?
2. Truly, at heart, it is deviancy you practice;
        on earth it is the violence of your hands you measure out.

B.1. Why?

3. The wicked are estranged from the womb;
        they err from birth, speaking falsehood.
4. They have poison,
        in the likeness of the poison of a snake;[38]
        like a deaf reptile which shuts its ear,
5. which does not listen to the voice of charmers,
        each one a fully knowledgeable weaver of spells!

C. Intervention

6. O God,
        break their teeth in their mouth!
    The fangs of the prime lions[39] shatter,
    Yahweh![40]

B.2. Whither?

7. May they flow away like waters,
        which go their own way, here and there;
        as he aims his arrows, let them, as it were, wither![41]

32 It is impossible to know whether to translate 'they have fallen' or 'they are sure to fall'. Is David recording something that happened there and then: as his soul reached rock bottom, so did his foes as they fell into their own pit? Without historical verification, we ought rather to follow the sequence of thought in the psalm. The thought of the glory and greatness of God (5) forms a bridge between David's panicky realisation of how deadly the foe is (4), and his confidence that his exalted God (5) will see to it that their animosity boomerangs back on themselves (6).

33 i.e. despondency and the panicking heart are things of the past; David now has a settled attitude of praise and confidence.

34 There is no consensus as to what 'my glory' means. Probably a general sense; all within me capable of praising God.

35 'Peoples ... states'. David is already aware of God's worldwide plans for his kingship and dynasty. He is determined so to live in the present as to create a testimony for the future. On 'states' see Psalm 2:1.

36 See Psalm 57, heading.

37 See Psalm 16, heading.

38 There is a double illustration here: first, the deadly menace of the wicked, their inherent danger to others; secondly, that they are impervious to influences that might make them different, like a deaf reptile cannot be directed by a snake-charmer. (Not that the psalm fancies such a thing as a reptile that can shut its ears; it is an excellent and hypothetical illustration of inherent and irreformable menace.)

39 The conventional translation 'young lions' is misleading in that it suggests lion cubs. The thought is rather youthful strength at its peak.

8. Like a slug,[42] which goes to melt-down;
   like a woman's aborted foetus –
   such as do not gaze on the sun![43]

9. Before your pots discern the brambles![44]
   As the living One, as Rage itself,[45] he will blow each away.

A.2. Rectification

10. The righteous will rejoice when he has contemplated vengeance,
    when he washes his steps in the blood of the wicked,
    when man says:
    'Yes indeed, there is fruit for the righteous.
    Yes indeed, there is a real God exercising judgment[46] on earth.'

---

40 The second illustration (lions) explains the first (teeth). What is sought is destruction of power to injure.

41 'He', here, is the unrighteous ruler. His inherent malevolence is pictured as an arrow directed at the object of his malice. There are two verbs spelled the same way: *malal,* to fade, wither; or 'to circumcise'. From the former is derived the picture of the launched arrow becoming like a dead leaf falling to the ground; from the latter, an arrow with its head cut off or blunted.

42 *shabhlul* is not exemplified elsewhere. If it derives from *balal,* to mix up, blend, moisten (Genesis 11:7, 9; Exodus 29:2; compare Psalm 92:10), 'something moist'. If it means a 'snail', the reference is to the empty shell which is all a snail leaves when it 'goes'. If a 'slug' then literally it melts to nothing.

43 Live long enough to look around.

44 This is a strange half-statement. I treat it as a proverbial saying, like, 'Before you can say Jack Robinson!' A cooking-fire only of thorns would flare up and die in an instant.

45 Heb., simply 'like a living thing like rage'. I have opted to treat both words as referring to God acting against the unjust ones in his life and anger, but I do not know of an example of 'rage' being personified like this.

46 Ordinarily the plural noun *elohim* is treated as a singular because it represents the One God in the fullness of the divine attributes. In the present verse the participle 'exercising judgment' is plural, which has the effect of emphasizing the idea of God who is God indeed. I have tried to reflect this by the word 'real'.

Pause for Thought

What a challenge Psalm 58 is to our feebleness in prayer, our lack of rigour and our limited awareness of the scope and power of 'praying about it'! The situation the psalm envisages is one familiar enough to us: Unrighteous rulers; rulers that look on in silence when unrighteousness is being perpetrated. Even looking no further than verse 1 we could write a book about planet earth in the twenty-first century! In the face of wicked powers and crafty powers, how often we contemplate those earthly rulers whom we are well aware know better, and we shake our heads sadly and say, 'But they don't know what to do?' Then we look into ourselves and admit, 'Neither do we.' Psalm 58 would confront our defeatism with its straight questions, 'Don't you? Have you thought of praying about it?' David does not tell us whom he had in mind – the Bible often leaves gaps like that, so that we can fill them in with our own problems – but he knew what to do: Take it to the LORD! In the psalm, verses 1–5 raise problems: unrighteous rule (1–2), and the problem of original sin infecting wicked rulers (3–5 – whatever can alter that!). After verse 6, the unrighteous ones are leaking away, melting away, their weapons falling to the ground uselessly, gone before you can say Jack Robinson! The living, raging God has acted – because his people asked him to do so (6). Mind you, the prayer made in verse 6 is vivid, practical, resolute, realistic: Dare we pray like that? We admit it: when we pray on a world-scale we like to concentrate our thought on the more bland request that suffering be relieved, the hungry fed, persecuted Christians be delivered, prisoners released. But, to say the least, there are situations when these desireable ends can only be realistically met if unjust governments (and their representatives) are overthrown, cast down and deprived of their power to injure. Is it time we too began to pray about teeth being broken and fangs drawn?

Day 25　Read Psalms 59–60

Psalm 59.
A Trial of Strength[1]

Belonging to the worship-leader; 'Do not destroy';[2] David's; a miktam[3]; when Saul sent and they set a watch on the house to put him to death.[4]

A.1. Prayer: deliverance and security

(Deliverance)

1. Deliver me from my enemies,[5] O God;
    from those raising themselves against me, grant me top-security.[6]
2. Deliver me from trouble-makers,
    and from blood-thirsty men save me.
3. Because, behold!
    They have set an ambush for my soul;
    strong ones are gathering against[7] me –
    not for rebellion[8] of mine,
    not for sin of mine,
    Yahweh.
4. Not for iniquity (of mine)[9]
    they are running and making ready.
    Rouse yourself to meet me, and see!
5. But as for you,
    Yahweh,
    the God who is Hosts,[10]
    the God of Israel,[11]
    awake to visit all the nations;[12]
    grant no grace to any troublous deceivers.[13]

1　This title for Psalm 59 derives from the fourfold reference to 'strong' and 'strength' around which the psalm is written: the first reference is to how strong the enemies are (3). The exclamation in verse 9, 'his strength', the strength of David's God, 'your strength' (16), and finally God as 'my strength' (17).

2　Psalm 57, heading.

3　Psalm 16, heading.

4　1 Samuel 19:1–18. It is clear that over an unspecified period of time, leading up to the crisis recorded in 19:10, David lived in danger. Psalm 59 implies a longer period of house arrest that 1 Samuel suggests, but the historical record leaves plenty of room for this.

5　David's description of his opponents mounts in intensity: the fact ('enemies'), their active intent (raising themselves), capacity to hurt (trouble-makers), ruthlessness (blood-thirsty). In its extreme sense 'trouble-makers' are those who 'play havoc'.

6　From *sagabh*, 'to be high', the idea of putting something, someone out of reach. Beyond the reach of the enemy, secure on high, inaccessible. See verses 9,16,17.

7　Or 'stirring up strife'.

8　A strong assertion of innocence in the situation: he has not rebelled (against Saul), committed any fault (sin), nor has there been an ill motive in his heart ('iniquity', the inner aspect of sinfulness, cf. 51:2). As is usual in similar passages, David is not claiming sinless perfection but innocence as charged.

(The return of the dogs)

6. They keep returning[14] in the evening;
   they growl like dogs, and encircle the city.

7. Behold!
   They pour out with their mouths –
   swords in their lips! –
   Because, who is listening?[15]

(Top security)

8. But you,
   Yahweh,
   you will laugh at them!
   You mock at all nations![16]

9. Oh, his strength![17]
   For you I will stay on watch,
   because God is my top-security.

10. My God of committed love will anticipate my needs;

A.2. Prayer: requital and security

God himself will let me look on my foes.[18]

11. Do not kill them,[19]
    lest my people forget.
    Make them totter by your strength,
    and bring them down,
    our Shield,
    Sovereign One.

12. The sin of their mouth,
    the word of their lips[20] –
    let them be taken captive for their pride,
    and because of the cursing,
    and because of the falsehood
    which they spell out.

13. Finish them off in rage;
    finish them off –
    and they are no more!
    And let them know that it is God who rules in Jacob,
    to the ends of the earth! (*Selah*)

9 There is no real need to put 'of mine' in brackets. According to the norms of Hebrew poetry it is legitimate to understand it from the preceding lines.

10 This is one of the occasions when 'God' and 'Hosts' are nouns in apposition, therefore not 'God of Hosts', but 'God who is Hosts', see Psalms 24:10; 46:7,11; 48:8.

11 His character is 'Yahweh' (the God who saves and overthrows); his power is absolute ('hosts'), his people is Israel. Also (verse 1) 'my God', and judge of all the world (verse 5 – think of how, in moments of personal trial, we let our minds dwell on the Second Coming of Jesus). It is indicative of David's awareness of innocence that he is prepared even to face the final judgment.

12 Often David views the solution of his own problem in the eschatological setting of world rectification. Maybe, through the spectrum of private sorrows, he suddenly became aware of a world of like suffering and longed for its settlement.

13 Lit. 'treacherous ones of trouble'.

14 The narrative in 1 Samuel (19:10–12) only relates what is necessary to the history, and we get the impression of no more than a brief stay at David's home. But Saul need not have acted at once when he learned of David's departure. We need to remember how publicly popular David was; Saul would have had to use his private army circumspectly, and some more prolonged observation of David's house and movements could well have followed, as the psalm indicates.

15 This, of course, is the unspoken thought of David's pursuers – they will get away with it!

(The return of the dogs)

14. And let them[21] go on returning in the evening!
    Let them growl like dogs, and encircle the city!
15. Let even them totter around for food,
    and if they are not satisfied, remain overnight.[22]

(Top security)

16. But as for me,
    I will sing of your strength;
    I will shout aloud in the morning of your committed love,[23]
    because you have been top-security for me,
    my place to flee to in the day I experienced adversity.
17. My strength,
    to you I will indeed make music,
    because God is my top-security,
    my God of committed love.

Psalm 60.
The Banner of Prayer

Belonging to the worship-leader; set to 'The Lily of Testimony';[24] a miktam;[25] David's; to teach.[26] When he struggled with Aram of the Two Rivers and Aram of Zobah, and Joab went back and struck down Edom in the Valley of Salt, twelve thousand.[27]

A.1. Promises and prayer: part 1

(Promises under threat)

1. O God,[28]
    you have rejected us;
    you have broken out violently on us;
    you have been angry.
    Do restore us![29]
2. You have shaken the earth;

16 The thought here is, 'even if all the nations were to gather against David'. Not divine mockery of nations as such, but divine dismissal of their collective strength. Hence the following exclamation regarding Yahweh's strength.

17 LXX (predictably) offers 'my strength', and many (equally predictably) alter the Hebrew text accordingly (cf. NIV, ESV). But, as the foregoing note indicates, a sudden realization of 'his strength' is extremely appropriate.

18 Not with malicious glee at their downfall; rather 'let me be there to see the last of them', a statement of coming fact. 'Foes' (see on Psalm 5:8) may be related to a verb 'to watch', in which case the idea of the watchers watched is a neat turn around!

19 Verses 11–13 show that David is not concerned about personal vengeance but with the moral issues involved – a lesson for Israel (11), a due punishment (12), a universal revelation of Yahweh (13).

20 No reference to the hurt given to David; only their sins of speech – a typical Old Testament (and biblical) emphasis.

21 The translation 'let them return … growl … encircle … totter …' has been chosen to take into account the greater confidence expressed in these verses as compared with verses 6ff. Compare verse 9 ('for you I will stay on watch'); verse 17 ('to you I will indeed make music'); or again in verse 6 the 'dogs' refrain is followed (verse 8) by, 'But [as for] you', and in verse 16 by 'But as for me'.

you have split it open.[30]
Heal its broken places, for it has tottered.

3.   You have made your people see harsh things;
     you have made us drink wine which induces trembling.[31]

(The banner of prayer)

4.   To those who fear you, you have given a banner,[32]
     to be unfurled because of the truth.[33] (*Selah*)

5.   In order that your beloved ones may be set free,
     save, by your right hand,
     and answer me.

A.2. Promises and prayer: part 2.

(Promises reaffirmed)

6.   God has himself spoken in his holiness:[34]
     'Exultingly, I will divide out Shechem,[35]
     and measure out the valley of Succoth.

7.   Mine is Gilead,[36] and mine is Manasseh;
     and Ephraim is the protection for my head;
     Judah is my law-giver's staff.

8.   Moab[37] is my wash-basin;
     on Edom I throw my shoe;
     over me,[38] Philistia, shout in acclamation.[39]

(Prayer exercised)

9.   Who will conduct me into the fortified city?
     Who is ready to lead me into Edom?

10. Is it not you, O God,
     you who have rejected us,
     and who are not, O God, going out with our armies?

11. Give us help from the adversary,
     for human salvation is falsehood!

12. By God we will act valiantly.
     He it is who will trample on our adversaries.

22 *lun* 'to lodge, stay overnight, be a temporary guest'. There is also *lun,* 'to murmur against', which some suppose can mean here 'to howl'. The more obvious understanding is that while at the new day they are still hungry, David and Michal have something to sing and shout about!

23 How striking this must have been to the ambushers as they crept close to the house to see if they could learn anything, and returned to report, 'they are singing and shouting for joy'!

24 Presumably the name of a melody.

25 See Psalm 16, heading.

26 The only psalm-title where this occurs. Is it a direction that this psalm be publicly taught? Compare 2 Samuel 1:18.

27 Compare 2 Samuel 8:1–14; 1 Chronicles 18:1–13. Hadadezer, king of the Aramean kingdom of Zobah, to the north of Damascus, was concerned with his northern frontier and David, opportunistically, catching him with his back turned, invaded from the south, winning victories, taking prisoners and masses of war equipment. Meantime, however, Edom caught David with *his* back turned and invaded the south of Judah, threatening the very continuance of David's fledgling kingdom. Maybe the Aramaeans negotiated with Edom to open a second front. David detached Joab (cf. 'went back') who marched south and dealt with the Edomite threat. David saw the whole situation – the Edomite invasion, possibly too his own ill-advised, gratuitous invasion of the north, as a threat to the promises of God regarding him and his throne. The psalm does not, of course, retell the historical events – Hebrew does not practice narrative poetry – but meditates on the principles and problems involved.

28 The problem is not the Edomites but God! He has been alienated. David could possibly have made out a case for attacking the Philistines – they had been immediate aggressors against his kingship (2 Sam. 5:17-25) – but Moab and Ammon (see Deut. 2:9,19) were out of bounds, and the invasion of Zobah was naked aggression – doing what the kings of the world did - 'Am king will make war'!

29 From *shubh*, 'to turn back' (intransitive), the form here is *polel*, both transitive (e.g. Isaiah 47:10) and intransitive (e.g. Jeremiah 8:5). But here, uniquely, the form is followed by preposition *le*, 'Make a turning back to/for us.' But what is the object of the turning back? Is it 'restore us' or 'turn back to us'?

30 Compare Numbers 16:28–34. The psalm does not refer to an actual earthquake but is using earthquake terminology as figurative of divine hostility and anger.

31 The metaphor of the cup whose contents are the LORD's will for his people at that point; compare Psalm 75:8; Isaiah 51:17ff. In Psalm 60 'wine' and 'trembling' are nouns in apposition: 'wine (which is) trembling', i.e. the strongest intoxicant.

32 The word for 'banner' is *nes*. Some relate this to the *nus*, 'to flee'. The army's banner is the rallying point to run to. Alternatively *nes*, 'banner' gave rise to a verb, in the Hithpael mode, 'to unfurl/wave as a banner'. This is the more obvious derivation. Exodus 17:8–16 is the background to the psalm. Moses saw his uplifted hands as a banner, and also as hands reaching out to and touching God's throne – both banner and prayer. The banner of prayer will avail against Edom too.

33 Some prefer to alter the vowels of this word to make it 'the bow' –'to flee to because of the bow'. This involves introducing an Aramaic word. Why should not David see his kingdom as holding the 'truth' and 'truth' as threatened when pagans sought to overthrow his kingdom?

34 Not, so to speak, a casual statement but words spoken with the full authority of the holy nature of God.

35 On Succoth and Shechem see Genesis 33:17–18. They were the first places at which Jacob made any sort of gesture towards settling: he built at Succoth and bought land at Shechem. Succoth was in the Transjordan; Shechem in Canaan.

36 Gilead and Manasseh, in the north of the Promised Land, straddled the Jordan from east to west; Ephraim and Judah were the twin divisions of the classical Palestinian homeland. The place-names in verses 6–7 review in principle God's promises regarding what his people would possess, right from the unobtrusive beginning with Jacob to the essential kingdom of David.

37 The dimensions of the land promised to Abraham (Genesis 12:7; 13:14–15; 15:18–21) included Transjordan. At a time when Edom was making a credible bid to destroy David's kingdom, he reminded himself of the word of God's promise. 'Wash-basin' and shoe-rack depicts menial services to the overlord.

38 Or 'as you stand in attendance on me' (preposition *'al*: compare Genesis 18:8; Isaiah 6:2 ('in attendance on him stood')). Philistia will come to the day when its triumph will be (not to conquer Israel but) to acknowledge Yahweh.

39 Psalm 108:9 reads 'over Philistia I will shout in triumph' and, inevitably, there are those who would alter Psalm 60 to match. This is needless.

Pause for Thought

Psalms 59 and 60 make an interesting pair. Like the rest of the psalter of which they are part they are psalms of 'taking it to the LORD'. Isn't that, indeed, one of the main lessons of the Psalms – that there is nothing we cannot pray about, and no situation in which the LORD will fail to hear and answer prayer? In Psalm 59 David is in trouble through no fault of his own (3–4), and, as we read the parallel passages in 1 Samuel, we find that this is indeed the case He had even been an exemplary servant to Saul; he had ministered to the nervously unstable king, and fought his battles; he was truly free of blame. He did, of course, choose to become a fugitive, and that may not have been a right decision, but we must assume David felt there was no other course open to him. At any rate, as far as the problem the psalm faces is concerned – human, savage, enmity – he was blameless, and in dire straits! On the contrary, David's trouble in Psalm 60 is entirely of his own making. I am afraid that we have to say becoming king rather went to his head. How else are we to explain the fact that, in relation to Saul, David was totally content to do nothing but wait for God to keep his promise of the kingdom – and he did so even against the most persuasive advice (1 Sam. 24:4–7; 26:7–11). But when he became king he at once started military operations against the sad 'rump' of Saul's kingdom (2 Sam. 2:3; 3:6). What happened to the policy of waiting for God to keep his promises? And then there was this imperialistic nonsense of marching north to wage war gratuitously against Hadadezer – just because he was vulnerable and a land-grab was possible! What has become of the David of 'waiting faith'? Even the golden king could be a silly billy! But … but … but (and this is the wonderful thing), whether we are wholly innocent, or whether we are seriously and very much at fault, the way of prayer is still open – and effective!

Day 26 Read Psalms 61–63

Psalm 61.
Shelter Fit for a King

Belonging to the worship-leader; set for strings;[1] David's.

A.1. Prayer: a plea to be heard

1. Hear, O God, my loud cry;
    pay attention to my prayer.

B.1. Security: a fivefold picture[2]

(The rock)

2. From the extremity of the earth,[3]
    to you I keep crying out
    when my heart is fainting:
    to the rock that is higher then I[4]
    do lead me!

(The refuge and tower)[5]

3. Because you have been a refuge for me,
    and a tower of strength from the enemy.

(The tent)[6]

4. Oh, I will seek asylum[7] in your tent truly for ever;

(The wings)

    I will take refuge under the covering of your wings.

B.2. Security: a clearly defined relationship

(Possession)

5. For you, O God, you have listened to my vows;[8]

---

1   Psalm 4, heading.

2   The first three speak of security *from*; the last two of security *in*.

3   Earth as remote from heaven.

4   i.e. too high for me to reach unaided, therefore unreachable.

5   Complementary images of flight into security (refuge), and security after flight (tower).

6   With 'tent' and 'wings' the list seems to descend into the realms of increasing insecurity, frailty. Biblically speaking it is the reverse: the 'tent' is the LORD's 'tabernacle' – same word. Where could one be safer? Refuge in the tent (compare Exodus 40:34–35) was a daring but wonderful flight of thought. The wings speak of welcome into his personal care (like small chicks under the wings of a mother bird) – who dare touch us there! The pictures, again, express a contrast between a situation where we have no natural right but seek grace and favour (tent), and a situation where chicks have a birth-right to their mother-bird's wings.

7   The verb, *gur,* expresses just this, seeking asylum, finding safety where one has no natural claim to register; where everything depends on the exercise of hospitality.

8   Whatever vows a king makes: e.g. 2 Samuel 5:3; 2 Kings 11:17.

9   'Fearing' God is the common mark of his people (Psalm 31:19), the mark of those who are at peace with God (Psalm 2:11). It is evidenced by right living (34:11), worship (5:7), etc.

you have given the possession of those who fear[9] your
name.

(Royal promises)[10]

6. Days in addition to the days of the king you will add;
    his years, as it were generation after generation.

(Acceptance)

7. He will sit enthroned for ever before God.
    Committed love and truth –
    appoint them, that they may preserve him.

A.2. Praise: a daily duty.

8. In this way I will make music to your name for ever,
    so as to fulfil my vows day after day.

Psalm 62.
The Awe-inspiring God[11]

Belonging to the worship-leader; set to Jeduthun;[12]
a song of David's.

A.1. Silence, Salvation and Stability

1. Yes indeed,
    in relation to God,
    my soul is silence.[13]
    From him is my salvation.
2. Yes indeed,
    he is my rock and my salvation,
    my top-security:
    I will not be much shaken.[14]

B.1. By contrast, instability; moral decline

3. How long will you intimidate a person,

10 The terminology here is not to be
    taken literally but seen as conventional
    language wishing the king prosperity,
    e.g. 1 Kings 1:39; Daniel 2:4. All
    unknowingly thinking ahead accurately
    to the Messiah.

11 This psalm could equally be called
    'the psalm of certainties', seeing that
    the affirmative particle 'yes indeed'
    comes six times; or, again, 'the psalm
    of contrasts'. The great affirmation of
    unshakeableness (1–2) contrasts with
    the shaken wall (3–4), and the call to
    trust (verse 8, based on the assurances
    of verses 6–7) contrasts with what not
    to trust (9–10). Verses 11–12 contrast
    'committed love' with exact requital
    of works. The psalm ends with the
    greatest contrast: human voices are
    silenced (1, 5), the voice of God speaks
    (11). But the overwhelming impression
    of the psalm is reverential silence
    before an awesome God.

12 1 Chronicles 16:41–42, a leader of
    temple choirs and musicians.

13 Nouns in apposition: 'my soul is
    silence itself'.

14 Lit. 'greatly/abundantly shaken',
    obviously an ironic statement with the
    sense 'easily shaken' from such a secure
    position.

15 This translation requires a small vowel
    change in the Hebrew. As the text
    stands it could possibly be translated
    'you will, all of you, be murdered',
    but this form of the verb is not found
    elsewhere, and the idea does not fit
    well with the initial question 'How
    long?' It seems best to accept the small
    adjustment.

all of you keep on breaking down? [15]
Like a bulging wall![16]
A fence – a shaken one at that![17]

4. Yes indeed,
    from his dignity they make plans to banish him.
    They favour falsehood.
    With his mouth they each bless,
    and inwardly they curse! (*Selah*)

A.2. Silence, hope, security, refuge

5. Yes indeed,
    for God be still,[18] my soul,
    because from him is my hope.
6. Yes indeed,
    he is my rock and my salvation,
    my top-security:
    I will not be shaken.[19]
7. Upon God
    is (depends) my salvation and my glory.[20]
    The rock of my strength,
    my refuge,
    is in God.

B.2. Trust, the reliable and the insubstantial

8. Trust in him in every circumstance,[21] O people.
    Pour out your heart before him:[22]
    God is the refuge we have. (*Selah*)
9. Yes indeed,
    the sons of man[23] are insubstantial;
    the sons of every man are falsehood.
    In scales they are bound to rise up –
    all together they are lighter than the insubstantial!
10. Do not trust in oppression;
    and do not become insubstantial through robbery.
    When riches make a profit, do not set your heart (on them).

16 Does the endangered wall and fence refer to the beleaguered person under attack or does it describe the real condition of the attackers, in spite of their apparent invincibility? More likely the latter. Appearance says the strong are attacking the weak; reality speaks otherwise. They are the ones at the point of collapse; their victims are the ultimately unshakeable ones of verse 2.

17 The adjective 'shaken' is written here with the definite article (which many recommend should be removed). But the Bible contains examples of a noun without the article followed by an adjective with the article, an idiom designed to throw emphasis on what the adjective describes: e.g. Psalm 104:18; Jeremiah 6:20; 17:2.

18 The verb includes both silence (from speech), and stillness (from motion), expressive of confident waiting 'for God' to act.

19 Now even the ironic qualification of verse 2 is omitted. Any sense of partial confidence has been replaced with full assurance.

20 In verse 4 the thought of the opponent was to pull him down from his dignity, but his 'glory' is secure in God.

21 *'eth* means 'time' as distinguished by certain characteristics: e.g. 'May' is a date in a calendar; 'spring' is a characteristic set of circumstances.

22 A vivid way of saying that he is a God for all seasons and experiences.

23 The balanced descriptions 'sons of mankind' (*'adham*) and 'sons of individual man' (*'ish*) are understood in various ways: 'ordinary folk … individually known people' (compare NKJV, ESV), or the generality and the individual. The latter suits the psalm, but, either way, the double description is intended to say 'humans without exception'.

C. A voice in the silence: power, love and justice

11. Once God has spoken;
      twice, what I have heard:
      that God has strength.[24]
      And you, O Sovereign One, have committed love,
      because[25] you will yourself fully requite each man
      according to his work.

Psalm 63.
Beginning and Ending the
Day with God

A song of David's when he was in the wilderness of Judah.[26]

A. At dawn

(The present)

1. O God,
        you are my transcendent God.
        As day dawns I seek you.[27]
        My soul is thirsty for you.
        My flesh faints for you,
        in a land of drought,
        and fainting, without water!

(The past)

2. Just as I have gazed[28] on you in the sanctuary,
        to see your strength and your glory,

3. just so[29] your committed love is better than life:
        my lips will acclaim[30] you.

(The future)

4. Just so, I will bless[31] you during my life:
        in your name I will lift up my hands.

24 Strength compared with the insubstantiality (9) and insubstantial resources (10) of man; committed, changeless love as compared with human animosity (3) and shakiness.

25 Reinforcing the call to trust, because in a morally questionable and hostile world the Sovereign One can be relied on to act.

26 Since David was king (Psalm 63:11), this heading can be dated to the time of his flight from Jerusalem when Absalom rebelled (2 Samuel 15:13–17:29). David's escape route led through the northern part of the wilderness of Judah (2 Samuel 15:28; 16:2,14).

27 This combines two possible associations of *shachar*. On the one hand it seems impossible to resist a link with the noun *shachar*, 'dawn'; on the other hand, it is found in parallel with the verbs 'to seek', expressing a like thought (Psalm 78:34; Hosea 5:15). Jeremiah (e.g. 7:25) uses the idea of 'rising early' (see NKJV) as a metaphor for zeal.

28 David has past spiritual experiences and memories ready at hand to fortify him for present emergencies. The force of what David says is this: 'When formerly I experienced this longing, you responded to me in the sanctuary, revealing yourself in power and glory. Let it be so now in the desert.'

29 Circumstances and places change, changeless love and responsive praise do not.

30 *shabhach*, 'to praise', is synonymous with the other praise-verb. The translation 'acclaim' is simply for variety.

31 On 'blessing' God, see Psalm 26:12.

5. As with choice and succulent food[32] my soul will be
    satisfied,
    and with loud-shouting lips my mouth will offer praise.

B. At night

(The past)

6. Whenever I remember you on my couch,
    I keep musing on you in the night-watches;[33]
7. because you have been such a help[34] to me,
    and in the shadow of your wings I keep shouting aloud.

(The present)

8. My soul has determined to stick close behind you;
    your right hand ever holds me firmly.

(The future)

9. And as for those, bent on destruction, who keep seeking
    my soul,
    they will go to the lower places of the earth.
10. They[35] will consign him[36] to the mastery[37] of the sword.
    A portion[38] for jackals they will be.
11. And as for the king, he will rejoice in God.
    All who swear by him[39] will give expression to their praise,
    because the mouth of those who speak falsehood will be
    closed.

32 'As with fatness and fatness', two
    synonymous words. The eating of
    the fat was forbidden to worshippers
    (Leviticus 3:17). There is therefore a
    complex thought here: in worship,
    divine revelation and responsive praise,
    David will be nourished with 'food'
    only God himself can share with him.

33 See Judges 7:19; 1 Samuel 11:11;
    Lamentations 2:19.

34 David uses here the extended form of
    the noun 'help', hence 'such a help'.

35 A third person plural indefinite,
    equivalent to a passive – as in our usage
    'they say', meaning 'it is said'.

36 Either referring to the chief adversary,
    or (more likely) individualizing the
    plural 'they' of the previous line. In this
    case 'him' = 'each'.

37 Lit. 'into the hand of the sword'.

38 The dead left for scavengers

39 Make their oaths of loyalty to Yahweh.

Pause for Thought

A sleepless night is just as much a gift of God as is a night's sound sleep! Not that we usually look on it that way – but David did! Those 'watches of the night', so often occasions of restlessness, always time when the day's 'mole hills' become mountains of anxiety, he turned into opportunities to 'muse' about God (Ps. 63:6), and to come, not to a fresh place of worry, but to a fresh place of joy and all-round assurance (63:7–11). Silence – even before God – is not necessarily helpful. It depends what we are doing with it, where our minds are. Left to themselves they flit hither and yon, and add to our restlessness. But learn from David. He lets us into his five leading thoughts: 'my salvation (Ps. 62:1), the rock, top-security (62:2), hope (62:5), and refuge (62:7). From Psalm 63:7 we can add 'such a help' and the 'shadow of your wings'. There's a fruitful galaxy of thoughts for you. 'Salvation' leads our thoughts into the past, to the Cross where Jesus died, the wonderful 'one sacrifice for sins for ever' (Heb. 10:12, KJV), the eternal security that is our 'hope'. In earthly terms, hope is certainty of time, uncertainty of event ('I hope it will be fine tomorrow'); in the Bible 'hope' is uncertainty of time, certainty of event (We shall be with him '… see him as he is', 1 John 3:2.). The 'rock' (which David mentions three times in Psalm 63) pictures permanence, stability – and the 'smitten rock', life-giving, of Exodus 17. It is also the 'rock that is higher' (Ps. 61:2), the perch for our 'top-security'. Loveliest of all, in our tinyness and insignificance, try being a day old chick and run to the sheltering wings (Ps. 61:4; 63:7). We are 'transformed by the renewing of [our] minds' (Rom. 12:2). Minds are 'renewed' by fixing themselves on new topics (Col. 3:1–2).

Day 27 Read Psalms 64–65

Psalm 64.
The Shooters Outshot

Belonging to the worship-leader; a song of David's.

A.1. Prayer for preservation: the hiding place

1. O God,
    hear my voice[1] in my thoughts.
    From dread[2] of the enemy preserve my life.
2. Provide a hiding place for me from the partnership[3] of
    evil doers,
    from the rowdiness of trouble-makers.

B.1. Sudden attack

3. They are the ones who sharpen their tongue like a sword,
    fit their arrow to their bow – the bitter word –
4. to shoot, in hiding places,[4] the perfect.[5]
    Suddenly they shoot him and do not fear!
5. In their own interest, they strongly affirm[6] the bad word.
    They reckon to hide snares.
    They have said[7] who takes a look at them![8]
6. They search out all sorts of wrong:
    'We are perfectly ready![9]
    The search is fully researched!'

B.2. Sudden counter-attack[10]

    The inner being of a man and the heart are deep.[11]
7. God will shoot an arrow at them:
    suddenly their fatal wounding[12] is sure to happen.
8. They[13] will make him stumble –

1 References like this to the 'voice' are always important. They call attention to verbalizing our prayers, our personal talking to God.

2 *pachadh* calls attention to fear as felt by the fearful person.

3 The word *sodh* always needs to be contextualized. Basically, it means 'council' or 'counsel' – the consultative body or the decision reached. Typically used in Jeremiah 23:18, 22. In the present instance I was tempted to translate 'gang', a group held together by questionable intent. This would suit the tone of the psalm. Compare Genesis 49:6; Psalm 25:14; 55:14; 89:7; Amos 3:7.

4 Or, as a plural of amplitude, 'under complete cover'. Nowadays we hear of 'a source close to', an 'unattributable' statement, 'a leaked document'.

5 Lit. simply 'the perfect' – i.e. as regards the 'bitter' (3) and 'bad' (5) charges, innocent, blameless.

6 Lit. 'they strengthen the bad word'.

7 The verb 'to say' often used in the sense 'they have made up their minds/ decided'.

8 'Them' maybe either the conspirators (of being 'caught out' and held to account) or their hidden snares. (of the trap being discovered before it is sprung).

9 Lit. 'we are perfect'. This maybe a counter claim to 'the perfect' in verse 4 – we are the ones who have right completely on our side.

they against whom was their tongue.
They will shake their heads[14] –
every one[15] who looks at them.

9. All humankind will fear,
    and they will determine to declare the act of God,
    and acknowledge the prudence of his work.

A.2. Taking refuge

10. The righteous will rejoice in Yahweh,
     and take refuge in him,
     and all those who are upright in heart will utter their
     praise.

Psalm 65.
The All-Sufficient God

Belonging to the worship-leader; a song of David's; a
hymn.

A. The God of atonement

(Prayer heard)
1. Praise is constantly[16] yours,
    O God,
    in Zion,
    and to you the vow[17] will be paid in full.
2. O hearer of prayer,
    right up to you all flesh[18] will come.

(Sin covered)
3. There are matters of serious iniquity;[19] –
    our rebellions are too powerful for me.[20]
    You will yourself provide atonement.[21]

10 Note the coincidence of words with **B.1.**: Shoot, arrow, suddenly, tongue. Divine reaction is exactly retributive; their own weapons are turned on them.

11 Verse 6b and 7a have no stated link in the Hebrew but it would be allowable to translate them as 'though …. yet …'

12 Plural 'woundings' expressing fullness or intensity, hence 'fatal'.

13 'They' may refer to the instruments God uses for the downfall of the enemies; or it may be third person indefinite (= 'he will be made to stumble'); or, as above, the victory of the oppressed; or 'they will cause it – their tongue – to stumble against themselves' (the boomerang effect of sin).

14 In concern, derision, astonishment?

15 Note the development from eyewitnesses, to humanity (compare Isaiah 26:9), to those who are right with God and live conformably.

16 'Praise to you is stillness/silence.' Possibly, arising from stillness = motionlessness, there all the time.

17 In the context of verses 1–4, the vow which responds to Yahweh's work of atonement.

18 What Yahweh has done in atonement is open to all alike, and is the only place where all alike can find atonement.

19 'Iniquities', plural of amplitude, intensification.

20 'our … my'. Corporate identity and individual responsibility in sin. Compare Isaiah 6:5.

21 See Psalm 49:7. 'Atonement' (*kaphar*), in the simple active mode, 'to cover' (Genesis 6:14); in the *piel,* intensive active, mode, to pay the covering price – the price which 'covers' the debt by paying it.

(Blessedness enjoyed)

4. Blessed[22] is whoever you choose and bring near.[23]
   He will have his dwelling in your courts,[24]
   be well satisfied with the goodness of your house,
   the holy reality[25] of your temple.

B. The God of salvation

(The awesome answer)

5. By awesome things in righteousness you answer us,[26]
   O God of our salvation:
   the object of trust[27] for all the ends of the earth and of
   the sea
   – far off though they are.[28]

(The power of God)

6. He who makes the mountains stable[29] by his strength,
   he who is girded with mightiness,
7. who soothes the roaring of the seas,
   the roaring of their waves,
   and the hub-bub of states.

(The world overawed)

8. Those who live in the furthest parts are afraid of your
   signs.[30]
   The outgoings[31] of morning and evening you make to
   shout aloud.

C. The God of bounty

(God's care of the earth)

9. You visit the earth and irrigate it,
   abundantly you go on enriching it.[32]
   God's channel is full of water.
   You make their corn sure,
   for in this way you make it sure:
10. its furrows drenching;
    its clods leveling out;

22 See Psalm 1:1.

23 e.g. Leviticus 1:1. The sacrifices were,
    lit. 'a bringing near' and their purpose
    was 'to bring near'

24 Note progressive nearness: the (outer)
    courts, the house itself, the most holy
    place. Divine atonement really does
    what it sets out to do, to bring near.

25 'Holy' here is an adjective, 'the holy
    thing of your temple', signifying 'your
    temple in all its holiness'.

26 'Salvation' in these verses is God's
    ability to care for his people's safety
    amid all the huge powers that the
    world contains and which life in
    this world sees brought into play. In
    answer to prayer, Pharaoh's power
    was thrashed, the Red Sea subdued
    (Exodus 14), the wilderness conquered
    (Deuteronomy 8), Jordan crossed
    (Joshua 4), Jericho overthrown (Joshua
    6), etc. As Joshua 2:9–10 shows,
    these things were a testimony to the
    Gentiles, and the Psalm sees such
    events as a worldwide call to trust this
    unique God.

27 Not that they do, but that they should,
    and that he is worthy of their trust.

28 This is the gist of the Hebrew but as a
    translation it is no more than a shot.

29 Mountains look stable in their own
    right; seas are naturally boisterous;
    states (compare Psalm 2:1) and nations
    are unpredictable. All alike are under
    Yahweh's control and only remain by
    his 'say-so'.

30 A reference to pagan superstition
    and bewilderment when faced with
    'natural' phenomena.

31 Psalm 19:6, of sun-rise. The advent of
    morning ... of evening; the regularities
    of time, day and night. As in Psalm 19,
    the 'voice' of the ordered creation sings
    loudly to its Creator.

with showers[33] you soften it;
its growth you bless.

(God's enrichment of the Earth)

11. You crown the year of your goodness,[34]
    and your tracks[35] trickle with fatness.
12. They trickle on the pastures of the countryside,[36]
    and with exultation the hills gird themselves.
13. The pastures dress themselves with flocks;
    and the valleys envelop themselves with grain.
    They shout aloud.
    Oh yes, they sing!

32 The first two verbs are perfects of unvarying habit; the third, an imperfect of recurring action.

33 Or 'abundant dew'. The word (*rebhiybhiym*) from *rabhabh*, 'to be much, many' should simply mean 'copiousness': 'Copious showers'… 'heavy dew'.

34 The whole year is an experience of goodness and harvest time comes like a crown.

35 Strictly a track made by a cart-wheel. The picture seems to be of Yahweh bringing the harvest home, and wherever his cart goes there is prospering.

36 The word is *midhbar,* usually rendered 'wilderness', but its meaning includes 'green belt', 'open country' as well as barren desert.

Pause for Thought

Even though the Bible opens with God the Creator, by the end it would, I think, like Psalm 65, only approach creation through redemption. The hymn is right when it says,

> Heaven above is softer blue,
> Earth around is sweeter green;
> Something lives in every hue,
> Christless eyes have never seen …

This is true. The river estuary we once overlooked was filled with fresh beauty by the realization that (whatever about the ice-age and water erosion and all that) this lovely watered valley was scooped out by our Saviour-Creator's hand for our enjoyment. That is why it is so beautiful, and that is its heart of beauty. The world is his world, and as Psalm 65, part 2, reminds us, all its mighty 'forces' are his forces, there only to do his bidding, at his command, subject to his control. The God of salvation is the God who makes it safe for us to live in a world of potentially destructive forces and people. Everything is beautiful in his time. But was Psalm 65 intended for singing at Harvest Thanksgivings? The last five verses would suggest so, and they provide another deep lesson about the world around. Why does grain grow? What makes the soil fertile? Why are there flocks and herds to 'clothe' pasturelands? Nothing happens without our Creator-Saviour-Sovereign God. There is no life apart from his life. The farmer or gardener plants but he does not 'co-operate' with God. No, he obeys the rules and principles discovered or revealed (Isa. 28:23–29) in creation, and unobtrusively taught by the Creator. Fertilizers have no power of life unless he makes them fertilize; potatoes have no power of growth unless he makes them grow. He is the LORD and giver of life, who, in the same mercy that prompted the work of salvation, and with the same power that controls creation and history, 'crowns the year with his goodness'.

Day 28 Read Psalms 66–67

Psalm 66.
The Power of Testimony[1]

Belonging to the worship-leader; a hymn; a song.

A. 'All'

(His name and his praise)

1. Shout aloud to God, all the earth.
2. Make music to the glory of his name.
   Ascribe glory: the praise due to him![2]
3. Say to God:
   How rightly[3] to be held in awe, your works!
   Through the abundance of your strength
   your enemies will cringe[4] before you.
4. All the earth will bow in worship to you,
   and make music to you:
   they will make music to your name. *(Selah)*

B. 'All/they/we'

(Power over creation and people)

5. Come and see the actions of God:
   rightly awesome are his doings towards the sons of man.
6. He turned the sea into dry land![5]
   Through the river they crossed over on foot:
   there we will indeed rejoice in him.
7. Ruling by his mightiness for ever;
   on the nations[6]
   his eyes
   keep watch.[7]
   As for the stubborn, do not let them exalt themselves.

1 The course of this psalm is marked by changes in the pronouns used. Throughout it has a worldwide scope (1, 4, 5, 8, 16). 'All the earth' (1, 4) … 'you peoples' (8), by the end of the psalm are addressed as God-fearers (16) and we are left to assume that they have been won over by the testimony of God's people to his works. Verses 1–5 focus on 'all'; verses 5–12 focus on 'they' (6) who become 'we' (6b–12); verses 13–20 express the 'I' of personal testimony. Comprehensively, the psalm is saying this: God's past actions are the permanent possession of his people, for their blessing; what he did for 'them' he did for 'us', and what he did for 'us' he did for 'me'.

2 A legitimate development in translation from, lit. 'Ascribe glory, his praise!' Or 'glory' could be understood adverbially, 'Ascribe his praise gloriously.'

3 The *niphal* mode of the verb (here a participle) often supports this sort of 'gerundival' emphasis, what must or ought to be.

4 In the sense of 'make themselves small' – cut themselves down to size.

5 We can trace the allusions to the whole experience of the Exodus/wilderness generations here: the Red Sea and the overthrow of Egypt (6–7; Exodus 14), and the song that followed (Exodus 15). 'We will … rejoice' (6) could equally be 'we were rejoicing'. 'We will rejoice' points to the present enjoyment of God's past acts of salvation.

6 This separating out of the three components of the sentence tries to reflect the emphasis which the Hebrew places on each word in turn.

(Providence: preserving, testing, purposeful)

8. Bless, O you peoples, our God;
   and let them hear the voice of his praise,
9. who places our soul in life,[8]
   and has not consigned our feet to tottering.[9]
10. Because you have tested us, O God;
   you have refined us like the refining of silver;
11. you brought us into the net;[10]
   you imposed pressure on our loins;[11]
12. you make mere men[12] ride over our head;
   we went through fire and through water –
   and you brought us out to superfluity![13]

C. 'I/all'[14]

(Personal devotion expressed through the house and its sacrifices)[15]

(Worship)

13. I will go into your house with burnt offerings;
   I will pay my vows to you in full;
14. what my lips expressed so generously,[16]
   and my mouth spoke when I was in adversity;
15. burnt offerings of fatlings I will offer to you,
   with the incense[17] of rams;
   I will prepare cattle with he-goats. (*Selah*)

(Answered prayer)

16. Come! Hear!
   And I will recount,
   all you who fear God,
   what he has done for my soul:
17. To him
   with my mouth
   I called out,
   and high praise was on the tip of my tongue.[18]
18. Had I countenanced anything offensive[19] in my heart,

7   This is the only place in Scripture where *tsaphah* is followed by the preposition *be*, meriting the slight emphasis 'to keep watch on'.

8   Both 'kept us alive' and 'assigned us to enjoy life'.

9   Deuteronomy 8:4; Psalm 121:3.

10   Exodus 14:2, 9 would be a case in point.

11   This seems to be what the Hebrew says. The 'loins' signify preparedness for action ('girding up the loins'). Possibly, therefore the sense is 'imposed limitations on our ability to act'. Or, compare ESV: 'a crushing burden on our backs' – though that is not exactly what the Hebrew says.

12   Psalm 8:4. Some translate here 'at our head', the successful leadership of 'mere men' like Moses and Joshua.

13   Lit. 'saturation', i.e. a land flowing with milk and honey!

14   Testimony must become personal. No one is saved by association with group testimony

15   Burnt offerings and thank-offerings (vows) pledged in time of trouble are not making ritual a bargaining with God. They are using life's challenges to promise to come to a fresh and increased pace of consecration. The lavishness of the sacrificial expression symbolizes how total is the gratitude felt, and how full is the dedication intended.

16   Lit. 'that with which my lips gaped wide'. Compare Judges 11:35, 36; Job 35:16.

17   i.e. the sweet aroma. Compare Genesis 8:20–21.

18   Lit. 'under my tongue', i.e. right there ready to be spoken.

the Sovereign One would not hear!

19. But indeed God has heard;
    he has paid attention to the voice of my prayer.
20. Blessed be God
    who has not turned my prayer aside
    nor his committed love from being with me!

Psalm 67.
Put to Rights at Last[20]

Belonging to the worship-leader; set for strings; a song; a hymn.

A.1. The blessed people

1. May God grant us his grace, and bless us.
   May he illuminate his face among[21] us, (*Selah*)

B.1. The instructed world: the purpose of the blessing

2. in order that your way may be known on earth,[22]
   among all nations your salvation.

C.1. The praising world

3. The peoples will give thanks[23] to you, O God;
   the peoples, all of them, will give thanks to you.

D. The world set to rights[24]

4. States[25] will rejoice and shout out aloud,
   because you will set the peoples to rights[26] with fairness,
   and guide[27] the states on earth.

19 *'awen,* a versatile word always needing contextualization. It means anything and everything from trouble to idolatry to iniquity. Here, what would be troubling to God.

20 This perfectly balanced psalm centres on verse 4 (nations and states all 'set to rights') flanked by the identical verses 3 and 5, universal praise and thanks. Leading up to this focal point: blessing is sought for 'us' (1) in order that knowledge of salvation may come to the world (2). As a result of the central truth, the earth is at last fruitful (6), and both we ('us') and all the ends of the earth unite in blessing and reverence.

21 Lit. 'with us', which is shorthand for 'through being present with us'.

22 The sequence of thought here reflects the Abrahamic blessing: the blessed people become a channel of blessing to the world. Gen. 12:1-3; 22:17-18.

23 Or 'Let the people give thanks …'

24 Note how this central verse has three lines as distinct from the two-line verses of the rest of the psalm. This is a literary device calling attention to its centrality and importance.

25 See Psalm 2:1.

26 'Set to rights' translates 'judge', and is the basic Old Testament sense of 'passing judgment' – make the right decision which settles all issues.

27 Kingly rule ('judge'/'set to rights') is balanced by shepherding care; compare the use of 'to guide' in Psalm 77:20.

C.2. The praising world

5.   The peoples will give thanks to you, O God,
      the peoples, all of them. will give thanks to you.

B.2. The fruitful world:[28] The consequence of the blessing

6.   The earth itself has given its produce;
      God, our God, is blessing us.

A.2. The blessed people

7.   God will bless us,
      and all the ends of the earth will fear him.

28 This is one way of understanding verse 6: there has been such an abundant harvest that it has prompted thought of the final harvest of earth yet to be gathered in (Joel 3:13; compare Revelation 14:14–16). Alternatively, the verbs could be understood as perfects of certainty (future events so sure that they can be described as having already happened). When all things have been 'set to rights', the blight of sin (Genesis 3:17–19) will be lifted off creation and proper fertility will be restored.

Pause for Thought

Two convictions unite today's psalms. First, that there is only one way of salvation for the whole world. Look no further than Psalm 66:3, 5–6. 'All the earth' is invited to consider Yahweh's awesome works, but these works are none other than the Exodus-redemption, and the crossing of the Red Sea; the Passover Lamb, and the consummation of that victory by the final rout of Egypt in the sea; the Cross of Jesus and his resurrection. Secondly, confidence that the world will yet come to know this salvation; that 'all peoples' will yet give Yahweh praise and worldwide reverence (Ps. 67:2, 7). It is good to be reminded of these (biblically) commonplace truths, not least at times when the forces against the gospel of Christ seem to be on the increase. So far so good, but this is all 'vision'. What about a 'policy', that is, a practical programme for making the vision happen? For this we need to take the psalms in reverse order. The teaching of Psalm 67 is that God blesses us so that the world may come to know his salvation 67:2. It is, of course, true that he blesses us for our own enrichment, because he loves us, and delights to share himself with us. But there is another side to 'blessing': it comes to us for the sake of somebody else. 'Blessing' puts us under responsibility – whether it is that we so respond to God's blessing that others see the difference in our lives, or that there is someone waiting to be told of this generous God. Whatever. Blessing is granted *in order that* the world may know his salvation. When it comes to the spoken word, Psalm 66 is very direct: 'I will recount … what he has done for my soul' (66:16). It is not a matter of having all the answers (John 9:25), or of total Bible knowledge, or of theological expertise; it is a matter of 'May I tell you how it has been for me.' In a word: a closer walk with God whereby we come under his blessing, and have an up-to-date testimony to his grace.

Day 29 Read Psalm 68

Psalm 68.
On the March[1] : the Great Panorama

Belonging to the worship-leader; David's; a song; a hymn.

(Walking with God)

1. God rises up![2]
   His enemies are scattered!
   And those who hate him flee[3] from before him!

2. Like the scattering of smoke[4] you scatter them;
   like the melting of wax in front of a fire,
   the wicked will perish in front of God,

3. and as for the righteous,
   they will exult rejoicingly[5]
   in the presence of God,
   and they will be glad with rejoicing.

(Lessons from the wilderness)

4. Sing to God!
   Make music to his name!
   Build a highway[6] for him who rides through the steppe-lands.[7]
   It is by his name Yah[8] that you must exult before him!

5. Father of orphans,[9]
   arbitrator[10] for the widow,
   God in the dwelling-place of his holiness.[11]

6. God who makes those absolutely on their own[12] live in a house;[13]
   who brings out bond-slaves[14] into true prosperity,
   but, yes, the stubborn are destined to dwell in a bare land.[15]

1 Psalm 68 is not the easiest psalm to follow. It is clearly a 'processional', possibly belonging with 2 Samuel 6:12–17. At any rate the psalm recapitulates the movement from Egypt to Canaan: verses 1–3, the start of the great march (with verse 1, compare Numbers 10:35); verses 4–6, God's care of his freed prisoners and needy people through the wilderness; verses 7–10, entering Canaan, the land of rainfall (compare Deuteronomy 11:10–11, 14); verses 11–14, conquest, kings fleeing; verses 15–18, Canaan possessed, the Lord's dwelling-place for ever; verses 19–23, life in the land, bounty and mastery; verses 24–27, Yahweh in his sanctuary; verses 28–31, the submission of the kings; verses 32–35, worldwide praise. This is the sweep of this great panorama; individual verses remain difficult, but it is essential to start by seeing where the psalm is going, from the Exodus-redemption to the eschatological vision.

2 In Numbers 10:35 Moses said, 'Please God, Arise!' but David, on the basis of historical experience, can speak affirmatively: 'God will arise!'

3 Exodus 14:25, 27.

4 Two similes: 'smoke', what is insubstantial; 'wax', what is vulnerable.

5 Exodus 15:1, 20–21.

6 Developing the 'onward march' theme, based on Exodus experience. Make a high road for the Lord to lead his people into a great future.

(From Sinai into Canaan; Yahweh's provision for his people)

7. O God,

    when you went out ahead of your people;[16]

    when you stepped out in Desolation,[17] (*Selah*)

8. the earth quaked;

    indeed, the very heavens rained because of the presence of God,

    Sinai indeed,[18]

    because of the presence of God, the God of Israel.

9. Generous rainfall you sent in waves,[19] O God.

    Your inheritance, when it was weary,

    you yourself established it.[20]

10. Your company of people lived in it.

    You establish[21] it, in your goodness, for the downtrodden, O God.

(Conquest)

11. It was the Sovereign One who gave the word;[22]

    The women bringing the good news were an abundant host.[23]

12. Kings of hosts – they flee, they flee,[24]

    and she who stayed at home was the one who was dividing out the spoil!

13. Though you men were lying[25] within the enclaves[26] –

    the wings of a dove overlaid with silver,

    and its feathers with yellow gold![27]

14. When Shaddai[28] scattered kings in it,[29]

    let it snow in Tsalmon.[30]

(Settlement, Yahweh's mountain dwelling)[31]

15. Mountain of God, mountain of Bashan;[32]

    mountain of ruggedness, mountain of Bashan.

16. Why are you glowering, you mountains of ruggedness,

    at the mountain God desired for his resting place?

    Oh yes, Yahweh himself will dwell there in perpetuity.

17. The chariotry of God[33] is twice ten thousand,

7 *'arabbah* is often translated 'desert' or 'wilderness'. The arid land west of the Dead Sea, which Joshua 3:16 calls 'the Sea of the Arabhah'.

8 A diminutive of endearment from Yahweh. First used in Exodus 15:2; compare Isaiah 12:2; etc.

9 Compare Deuteronomy 10:18.

10 *dayan*, from *diyn*, used mostly of judicial decisions at law; e.g. 1 Samuel 24:15.

11 The point of this additional description is that care for the orphan and widow is no occasional or marginal divine concern, but is part of the essential holiness of the divine nature.

12 The word used here (*yachidh*) is that for a solitary, unique 'one' (e.g. Genesis 22:2, 12).

13 It would be legitimate, in context, to say 'in a household', for that is the implication.

14 Compare Deuteronomy 15:15.

15 *tsechiychah*, adj. *tsachiach*, shining, bare; in Ezekiel 26:4, 14 of 'the top of a rock' (NKJV). *tsachach*, 'to be white', Lamentations 4:7. In context here, the stubborn would remain in the desert, not enter the joys of Canaan.

16 Numbers 10:33.

17 'in *jeshiymon*', from *yasham*, 'to be desolate'. In Deuteronomy 32:10 (NKJV), 'howling wilderness' (of Israel during the wilderness days).

18 Exodus 19:16–18. 'Sinai indeed' is lit. 'This Sinai'. Some say it means 'the One of Sinai', defining the preceding 'God', just as 'God of Israel' defines 'God' in the next line.

outstanding[34] thousands!
The Sovereign One is among them.
Sinai is in the sanctuary![35]

18. You have gone up to the height.[36]
   You have captured captives,
   to take gifts instead of men[37] –
   and, yes, the stubborn ones[38] –
   so that Yah, God, might make his dwelling.

(Life in Canaan)

19. Blessed is the Sovereign One;
   day after day
   he bears the burden for us.
   The transcendent God is our salvation. (*Selah*)

20. The transcendent God is ours,
   a transcendent God intent on saving acts:
   to Yahweh, the Sovereign One, belong
   the exits[39] that belong to death!

21. But yes indeed, God will himself shatter the head of his
   enemies,
   the scalp of hair of anyone going about in his persistent[40]
   guilt.

22. The Sovereign One has said:
   'Even from Bashan I will bring them[41] back –
   I will bring them back from the depths of the sea'[42] –

23. in order that you may crush them –
   your feet in blood –
   your dogs' tongue with its portion of your enemies!'[43]

(God enters his sanctuary)

24. They have seen your progress, O God –
   the progress of my transcendent God, my king,
   into the sanctuary.

25. Ahead went the singers,
   behind, the musicians,
   in between[44] virgins playing tambourines.

26. In the assemblies, bless God –

19 This is the best I can make of David's use here of *nuph*, 'to wave to and fro'. It is not a verb used elsewhere of rainfall. But compare Proverbs 7:17 'perfumed/sprinkled'. Also *nopheth*, honey oozing from the comb (Psalm 19:11). If it can mean 'waves' of rain, it is suitable to the idea of nourishing rather than flooding showers.

20 We have now moved from Sinai into Canaan, about which Moses (Deuteronomy 11:10–14) emphasizes rainfall as one of its distinctions from Egypt.

21 The use of the imperfect for this verb gives the sense 'you still establish …' (just as you did then).

22 This is the key-note of the section: the whole exercise of conquering Canaan was a sovereign work of God. He commanded the victory, and so it was.

23 As an illustration, 1 Samuel 18:6.

24 The idiom of two verbs without intervening conjunction, the first verb being adverbial to the second: 'they flee fleeingly', 'they took themselves wholly to flight'.

25 The verb here is second plural masculine, hence 'you men', in contrast to the women of the preceding line.

26 No certainty of the translation of this word. Some say 'saddlebags', 'sheepfolds', 'by the hearths'. The idea is non-participants in the battle who nevertheless share the spoils (compare 1 Samuel 30:24, 25).

27 Presumably illustrative of the richness of the spoil shared.

Yahweh,
you who are from the spring of[45] Israel.

27. Benjamin[46] is there, the insignificant one, dominant among them,
the princes of Judah, their jubilant crowd,[47]
the princes of Zebulun,
the princes of Naphtali.

(Out to all the Earth)[48]

28. Your God has commanded your strength.[49]
Be strong, O God,
you who have acted on our behalf.

29. Because of your temple[50] set over Jerusalem
kings will bring along homage-gifts to you.

30. Rebuke the animal of the reeds,
the herd of bulls, with the calves of the peoples[51] –
each[52] humbling himself with items of silver.
He has scattered[53] the people who take pleasure in wars.

31. Ambassadors[54] will come out of Egypt;
Kush will stretch urgent hands[55] to God.

(Universal praise)[56]

32. Kingdoms of the earth,
sing to God;
make music to the Sovereign One. (Selah)

33. To him who rides in the heavens[57] of the heavens of old.
Behold!
He utters his voice, a voice of strength.

34. Ascribe strength to God –
his majesty over Israel,
and his strength in the clouds.

35. O[58] awe-inspiring God out of your supreme sanctuary![59]
He is the transcendent God of Israel,
who gives strength and true durability to the people.
Blessed be God!

28 El Shaddai was the great patriarchal title by which Yahweh was known; compare Genesis 17:1; 28:3; 35:11; 43:14; Exodus 6:3. The meaning of 'Shaddai' is the subject of speculation, but it is mostly thought to signify 'almighty'. The places where the title is used in Genesis suggest that El Shaddai was thought of as the God who was at his most powerful when man was at his most vulnerable.

29 i.e. in Canaan.

30 Presumably Mount Tsalmon near Shechem (Judges 9:48). 'Let it snow in Tsalmon' could be/probably is an apt proverbial expression, but even if so its significance is now lost. In the text as it stands the verb is jussive: 'Let it'. Many alter it to 'It will', but the change brings no clarification.

31 Yahweh's choice of Mount Zion (cf. 132:13-14) is made the centerpiece of settling in the land.

32 With poetic brevity, the thought is that Yahweh had a wide area of choice. But out of all possible candidates – like Bashan or other rugged peaks – divine choice fell on Zion – so, let that be an end to jealousy and jockeying for position!

33 The conquest was a work of irresistible divine power.

34 Or 'multiple thousands', depending whether the word, shin'an, is to be derived from shanah, 'to repeat', or shan'a, 'to shine'.

35 Yahweh has neither changed nor deserted his people. Rather he is now with them in the land just as he revealed himself at Sinai. This is the supreme dignity Zion possesses above all possible claimants.

36 i.e. of Zion, viewed here as the chosen and greatest mountain. In David's procession, this was represented by the entry of the Ark into Zion.

37 Those conquered became tributary, being allowed to buy themselves out of captivity. Treating the preposition *be* (which could mean 'among mankind') as expressing 'price or value'. Or it could be *beth essentiae* – 'gifts, namely, people – even the stubborn – …'

38 Possibly a reference to a policy of mercy, allowing even the stubborn to pay a ransom instead of being executed there and then.

39 The termini of life, and the many ways life may be terminated by death. All this belongs to Yahweh in his sovereign government.

40 Lit. 'in his guilts', plural taken here to express many acts of guilt, persistency. Yahweh is still the holy God of Sinai (compare verse 17). The favour he has shown his people in the gift of the land must not be mistaken for leniency.

41 'Them' is not expressed in the Hebrew but according to the rule governing omitted pronominal objects, there is a reference to the last stated noun i.e. Yahweh's guilty enemies.

42 The contrast between land (Bashan) and sea expresses totality. Nowhere to escape. 'Bashan' probably chosen as the furthest extent of the land from Zion.

43 The poetic allusiveness of lines like these should not be 'smoothed out' into rounded grammatical sentences. It is of the nature of poetry to allow ideas to crash together like this.

44 i.e. the procession was flanked on each side by girls with tambourines. Compare Exodus 15:20; Judges 11:34; 1 Samuel 18:6–7.

45 i.e. trace your descent from.

46 Four tribes are selected in illustration of 'from the spring of Israel' – two southern tribes (Benjamin, Judah) and two northern tribes (Zebulun and Naphtali). The southern names are the obvious ones, but why were Zebulun and Naphtali singled out? 1 Chronicles 15:6–28 gives some details of the way David organized processions for the Ark. Some contemporary reason prompted the names here. 'Dominant' is *radhah*, found in Psalm 49:14 as 'getting the better of'; in Leviticus 25:43 of a caring employer or 'boss' not acting ruthlessly; in Genesis 1:28 of man's position as responsible 'lord' of creation. So, here, of Benjamin 'taking the lead' in the procession.

47 The word *rigmah*, only found here, is given the meaning, 'a shouting crowd'.

48 These verses return to a main theme of the psalm. Yahweh's march from Sinai to Canaan was an historical demonstration of his kingship over the nations; the procession of the ark to Zion is a symbolic enactment of the same idea. So, reaching Zion, entering the Sanctuary, he is taking his rightful place as king of the world.

49 The victorious Yahweh shares his victory with his people. The quick change of focus here (and elsewhere in this psalm), now speaking as from Yahweh, now addressing him, may indicate an original 'liturgy' incorporated in the processional, with a leader speaking one line and the people responding with another.

50 Because of all the temple means – the enthroned Yahweh in his house, his universal lordship, his victorious march to ascend his throne – the day will come when the world submits. It is at points like this that the essential 'messianic' thought of Psalm 68 comes out.

51 The 'animal of the reeds' is Egypt, the ancestral genocidal enemy. Its submission would indicate the total collapse of worldly opposition. 'Bulls' are national leaders, 'calves', the 'common herd' (Psalm 22:12).

52 The participle 'humbling' is masc. sing., individualizing the bringing of tribute to Yahweh.

53 The Hebrew text is a perfect tense: Yahweh's march from Sinai as a victory march over the nations. Most (following LXX) alter to imperative, but with no significant advantage.

54 Word only found here, of uncertain meaning. 'Ambassadors' is offered as contextually suitable.

55 Lit. 'will make its hand run to God'.

56 This final stanza matches the first (1–4), where 'the righteous' (those right with God) are left undefined. Now that we have followed the victory march and Yahweh's conquest of the nations, it is a universal people who acclaim him. Following the preceding stanza (28–31) the final stanza is one of reassurance: submission and the paying of homage does not initiate the nations into a state of bondage but unites them into a worldwide Israel of praise.

57 Recall verse 4, the rider through the steppe-land, i.e. the God who is mighty on earth, conquering the nations, is now seen in his true sphere as the God of heaven.

58 Or 'Awesome is God out of your supreme sanctuary', addressing Israel as the temple-guardian.

59 Plural of majesty; your 'sanctuaries'.

Pause for Thought

'Aslan is a lion', said Mr. Beaver, '*the* Lion, the great Lion.' ... 'Then he isn't safe?' said Lucy. 'Safe?' said Mr Beaver ... 'Course he isn't safe! But he's good. He's the King.' And the *Chronicles of Narnia* got it exactly right: 'not safe but good.' It's straight out of Psalm 68. Here is a psalm for the threatening day when Jesus' enemies seem to be on top, their power let loose, their arguments unanswerable. But not so! The wicked will perish (20), kings will flee (12), heads will be wounded (21), and lives forfeited (23). It's as sure as the truth that the Rider in the skies (33) is also the Rider on earth (4). Meantime, the same Sovereign One is the defender of the defenceless (3), the deliverer of captives (6), the provider for the poor (10), our daily beneficiary and Saviour (19), and he holds 'the keys of death and of Hades' (v. 20; Rev. 1:18). We may be as insignificant as Benjamin (27) but we too have our place in the victory march, and it is our God who has ascended on high and has captured captives (18). The victory has already been won, the King is already on his throne, and – look around you – from all the earth people are every day making their way to pay homage-gifts to the King of kings and Lord of lords. At first sight Psalm 68 seems a curious collection of bits and pieces, but, as we have seen, it is not so, but an ordered representation of a victory parade. The enemy has been overwhelmed and his armies scattered; the throne has been won. No psalm can give us a sharper or more helpful, reassuring perspective from which to view the world we live in, or a more perfect vantage point from which to secure and maintain a balanced perspective for our demanding days.

Day 30   Read Psalm 69

Psalm 69.
How to handle Opponents and Opposition; Bringing God into our Needs[1]

Belonging to the worship-leader; set to 'Lilies'; David's.

A.1. Great need[2]

1.   Save me, O God,
     because the waters have risen up to my soul;[3]
2.   I have sunk down into the mud of a marsh;
     with nowhere to stand;
     I have come into the depths of waters –
     flood-waters have overwhelmed me.
3.   I am weary through my calling out;
     my throat is parched;
     my eyes have failed, while waiting for my God.
4.   More numerous than the hairs of my head
     are they who hate me without reason;
     those who are destroying me are mighty,
     my enemies falsely;
     what I did not steal,[4]
     I then kept restoring.

B.1. Telling God what he already knows: intervention sought

5.   O God, you know yourself my silliness,[5]
     and from you my guilt-offerings have not been hidden.[6]
6.   Do not let those who wait for you reap shame[7] because of me,

1   The most quoted of the psalms in the New Testament: John 2:17; 15:25; 19:28; Acts 1:20; Romans 11:9; 15:3. If we are to know on what occasion it was written, we must try to deduce it from the contents. It fits easily into the time when David was preparing resources for the future building of the Temple. He was never without critics and enemies, and all the troubles mentioned in Psalm 69 could easily have arisen then – false accusation, misappropriation of funds, possibly 'national security' being imperiled by a royal obsession. The psalm is a passionate outpouring of prayer, grief, near despair, expostulation, and (finally) confidence.

2   Three 'triads': illustrations of danger – waters, mud, floods; evidence of weariness – unanswered prayer, dehydration, failing faculties; causes – hatred, strong opposition, injustice.

3   *nephesh*, 'soul' is versatile in its significance; often, as would suit here, yielding the meaning 'neck'.

4   The implication is of a series of charges of malpractice, to which David found the best solution was to make repayments, while claiming innocence.

5   One of the Hebrew words for 'folly/foolishness' (*'iwweleth*). The corresponding noun, 'a fool', is typically the 'fathead', the irremediably flippant person.

O Sovereign One, Yahweh of Hosts;
Do not let those who seek you be dishonoured because of
me,
God of Israel.

7. Because, on your account, I have borne reproach;
    dishonour has covered my face.
8. I have become a stranger to my brothers,[8]
    and a foreigner to my mother's sons,
9. because[9] zeal for your house has eaten me up,
    and the reproaches of those reproaching you[10] fell on me.
10.[11] When I wept –
    my soul keeping the fast[12] –
    it became a reproach to me.
11. When I made sackcloth my clothing,
    I became a proverb[13] to them!
12. Those who sit in the gate were chatting[14] about me,
    and the beer drinkers made[15] songs.

C.1. The testimony of a troubled soul. Sorrows turned to prayer

13. But as for me,
    my prayer goes to you,
    Yahweh,
    at an acceptable season;[16]
    O God,
    in the abundance of your committed love,[17]
    answer me,
    in the truth[18] of your salvation.
14. Deliver me from the mire,[19]
    and do not let me sink.
    Let me be delivered from those who hate me,
    and from the depths of the waters.
15. Do not let the floodwaters overwhelm me,
    and do not let the marshes swallow me,
    and do not let the pit close[20] its mouth on me.
16. Answer me, Yahweh,

6   How are we to understand David's references to 'silliness' and (more lit.) 'guiltinesses'. 'Guilt' here is the word used in connection with the 'guilt' offering (Leviticus 6:1–7), in which not only was an offering made but restitution was required to the injured party. We should understand verse 5 in relation to the end of verse 4. David now sees that he was 'silly' to think making 'restitution' for wrongs he did not commit would solve anything.

7   David fears that because he had acted as if guilty, a potential for insult had been created against the whole company of those who were devoted to Yahweh, but (7) he did it for Yahweh's sake.

8   'Brothers' includes all male relatives, but 'mother's sons' means full brothers in the family – where certainly the early David was subject to criticism and accusation (1 Samuel 17:28–29).

9   David gives two reasons for the opposition he experiences: (7) 'on your account' and (9) 'zeal' for Yahweh's house. Both of these fit easily into the narrative of 1 Chronicles 28–29. David could readily be charged with obsessiveness, and opponents could well have sought occasion to accuse him of 'having his fingers in the till'. But, as in Psalm 22, 'the king' was foreshadowing 'the King'.

10 Another element in David's sorrows was that there were those who vented on him their spleen against Yahweh. Why this was we can only guess, but the expenditure of so much money on the temple cannot have passed without comment. Compare Mark 14:4–5.

11 Verses 10–12 are a wonderful description of a person who has reached the point where, in the opinion of others, he cannot do right!

because your committed love is good,

in accordance with the abundance of your compassion

turn to me.

17. And do not hide your face from your servant,

because I am in adversity.

Answer me quickly.[21]

18. Come near to my soul;

redeem it,

because of my enemies, ransom[22] me.

B.2. Telling God what he already knows: retribution sought[23]

19. You know yourself[24]

my reproach,

my shame, my dishonour;

in front of you are all my adversaries.

20. Reproach has broken my heart;

I am sickened –

I waited for condolence, but nothing!

And for comforters, but found none!

21. And as my food they gave me venom,

and for my thirst they made me drink vinegar.[25]

22.[26] Before them let their table become a trap,[27]

and their welfare a snare.

23. Let their eyes be darkened so that they cannot see,

and make their loins tremble continually.

24. Pour out your indignation on them,

and make the rage of your exasperation overtake them.

25. Let their enclave become desolated;

in their tents let there be no one living.

26. Because, as far as you are concerned,

what you have struck they have pursued,

and about the pain of our wounded ones they tell stories.

27. Add iniquity to their iniquity,[28]

and do not let them come into your righteousness.[29]

28. Wipe them out of the book of life,[30]

12 A tentative but exact translation of the Hebrew as we have it. Emendations have been suggested.

13 This versatile word (*mashal*) could be rendered 'a joke' here.

14 *siach*, to muse, murmur, talk, complain.

15 There is no verb in this line, which allows us to 'understand' a verb from the previous line.

16 *'eth*, which is not time as a date on the calendar, but a time with certain characteristics. Here, of acceptability to Yahweh; e.g. Psalm 1:3; 4:7; 9:9; 21:9; 32:6; 34:1; etc.

17 David appeals in turn to 'committed, unchanging love', and 'salvation' (from threats, as spelled out in verses 14–15). In verse 16 'committed love' is balanced by 'compassion': the latter is passionate love, love in the emotions, 'being in love'; the former is love as an expression of the will or determination, love as a vow or commitment.

18 i.e. 'reliability' (of Yahweh's power to save).

19 A return to the imagery of verse 2.

20 *'atar*, not used elsewhere. Said to mean 'to bend', here given the contextual meaning 'to shut'.

21 A good example of the idiom of two verbs without intervening conjunction, 'make haste, answer', therefore 'answer with haste'.

22 'Redeem … ransom', respectively *ga'al* and *padhah*. The former predominantly the verb of relationship, the act of the 'next-of-kin', the latter predominantly the verb of payment. See Psalms 19:14; 25:22.

and with the righteous let them not be written.

C.2. The testimony of a troubled soul: sorrows turned to joy

29. But as for me,
    I am downtrodden[31] and in pain.
    O God,
    let it be your salvation that gives me top-security.[32]
30. I will indeed praise the name of God with a song,
    and I will magnify him with thanksgiving.
31. And this will be good for Yahweh –
    more than an ox,
    a bull, with horn, with hoof.[33]
32. When the downtrodden have seen it,
    they will rejoice;
    You who are seeking God,
    let your heart live!
33. Because Yahweh is ever listening to the vulnerable,[34]
    and his prisoners[35] he has determined not to despise.

A.2. Great assurance[36]

34. Let heaven and earth praise him,
    the seas, and everything which moves around in them,
35. because God will himself save Zion,
    and he will build the cities of Judah,
    so that they will live there and possess it.
36. And the seed of his servants –
    they will inherit it,
    and those who love his name will dwell in it.

---

23 This section is notable for the frightful retribution asked. It is to be noted that verses 19–21, which set the scene, clearly portray the Lord Jesus in his rejection and suffering; verses 22–28 are the penalties due to us for putting him on the cross, and which would be ours had he not borne our sin in his body on the tree. Remember too that in expressing these elements of retribution David was (1) praying; (2) leaving it all to Yahweh what actually to do; (3) neither himself feeling rancour, nor planning to take revenge. The whole passage should be read in the light of Leviticus 19:18 and Romans 12:19. Bear in mind that Jesus spoke of those who he would 'deny before the Father' (Matthew 10:33); he represented himself as saying 'depart, you cursed …' (Matthew 25:41). David, in his imprecations, is foreshadowing 'the wrath of the Lamb' (Revelation 6:16), while giving expression to the righteous judgment of God.

24 Note identical opening word in **B.1.** (verse 5).

25 Spoken metaphorically here; compare Jeremiah 8:14; 9:15. But actually true of Messiah. Matthew 27:34.

26 The list of imprecations covers earthly well-being (22–23), divine favour (24), earthly home (25), peace with God (27) and eternal home (28).

27 Note the close connection of this first imprecation with the immediately preceding charge, compare Deuteronomy 19:19. Throughout, the imprecations seek for them what they had unjustly brought on David: bodily exhaustion (3) and a broken heart (20). So may they suffer (23); the Lord had hidden his face (17). May it be their portion (24, 27); an alienated family (8, 25) and accusations of guilt (4–5, 27).

28 The meaning is 'let their iniquities accumulate without overlooking any or cancelling any through forgiveness' –'add one iniquity after another to their account'.

29 Into the experience of being 'right with God'.

30 Exodus 32:32; Isaiah 4:3; Daniel 12:1: compare Psalms 56:8; 139:16.

31 From *anah*, 'to be low', those 'at the bottom of life's heap'.

32 The first word following the emphatic personal pronoun 'I' is 'down low' and the last word in the line is 'high out of harm's way'. A very neat contrast, a transformation only Yahweh could achieve; compare Psalm 113:7–8.

33 The horns indicate the age of an animal (age was often important, Exodus 12:5), its hooves tell if it is a 'clean' animal (Deuteronomy 14:6) acceptable to Yahweh. In other words, if it is an absolutely 'right' sacrifice. But personal joy in God and explicit praise means more to him than even the most punctiliously correct ritual.

34 From *abhah*, 'to be willing', hence in its good sense, those who will the will of God, are willingly obedient; in its bad sense, those who are pliant, able to be pushed around, even 'molded', by more powerful forces and interests.

35 Here the godly who find themselves caught up in forces too strong for them. Ephesians 4:1; 6:20.

36 As at the end of Psalm 51, David turns from his personal concerns to the stability and welfare of his kingdom. If his adversaries had their way and brought him down, David, aware that all the promises of God centred on his monarchy, knew that the city too would fall. Therefore, in assurance that Yahweh will prevail in the present emergency, he looks forward also to the security of Zion and its satellite townships.

Pause for Thought

'What would Jesus do?' is a good question to ask – and it often yields worthwhile answers both in general and in particular for our conduct. When we read Psalm 69 the question has to be different: 'What would Jesus say?' Can we hear verses 22-28 on his lips? First go off, we say, 'No … certainly not!' Jesus would have said, 'Father, forgive them, for they do not know what they are doing' (Luke 23:34, NRSV), and that has a sound of rightness about it, for as a general principle he instructed us to love our enemies and do good to those that hate us (Matt. 5:44). But it doesn't do to rush to a decision. Jesus is the bridegroom who shuts the door so that his welcomed guests are secure in his presence; but the same shut door excludes those who are dismissed as not known (Matt. 25:10–11). He sees worldwide guests at his heavenly banquet, but others cast into outer darkness (Matt. 8:11–12). As the Son of Man all judgment has been committed to him by the Father (John 5:26–27), and those bearing the mark of the beast will be 'tormented … in the presence of the Lamb' (Rev. 14:9–10, NRSV). In his judicial capacity our Lord Jesus is the executor of the holy will of God and the enforcer of his word – and Deuteronomy 19:19 teaches that the false accuser must receive what he planned unjustly to inflict. David could only pray for divine action; Jesus in judgment would take David's prayers and turn them into pronouncements of condemnation, merited sentences to be carried out. We need to read these verses with serious self-awareness, and very solemnized minds and hearts. Our only escape from the Son of Man, our Judge, is to flee to the Son of Man our Saviour. He who said, 'Depart from me, you cursed' also said, 'Come, you who are blessed of my Father' (Matt. 25:34, 41, ESV). The awesome 'throne of his glory' (Matt. 25:31, NKJV) is also the throne of grace (Heb. 4:16).

Day 31   Read Psalms 70–71

Psalm 70.
God in a Hurry![1]

Belonging to the worship-leader; David's; to bring to remembrance.[2]

A.1. Hurry!

1. God,
    to deliver me,
    Yahweh,
    to my help,
    hurry!

B.1. Those seeking to hurt

2. Let them reap shame,
    and be abashed,
    who are seeking my soul.
    Let them be repulsed
    and dishonoured,
    who delight in my evil.[3]
3. Let them turn back
    on account of their shame,[4]
    who are saying, 'Aha! Aha!'

B.2. Those seeking God[5]

4. Let them be glad,
    and rejoice in you,
    all who are seeking you.
    And let them say continually, 'May God be magnified!' –
    those who love your salvation.

1   Attention is often called to the similarities between this psalm and Psalm 40:13–17. Psalm 70 may be an adaptation of the other psalm for an occasion of sharp need and danger. The language in Psalm 70 is much more urgent and taut.

2   Psalm 38, heading.

3   i.e. 'evil' in the sense of a 'bad' experience, a calamity.

4   The shameful way they have behaved.

5   It is notable that this is not a prayer for changed circumstances, but for a glad and praising spirit. To have 'salvation' provides for a heart of praise irrespective of conditions.

6   Psalm 71 reads as an extended version of Psalm 70. Whether arising from the same time, we do not know, but the absence of a heading to Psalm 71 suggests a link between them. Certainly we find the same situation of enemies determined to do him evil (70:2; 71:13, 24). Compare also 71:2, 5–12; 70:2; 71:13, 24. The emphasis on a God faithful from birth, through life, to old age (verses 5–6, 18) provides a central truth for Psalm 71.

7   i.e. meaning 'be disappointed in my hopes; take refuge in you and find you have failed me.'

8   Your inflexibly righteous character and pursuit of righteous aims.

9   A dwelling as firm, secure and durable as a rock; but always Exodus 17 lies in the background, the smitten rock with its life-giving water.

A.2. Hurry!

5. But as for me,
   I am downtrodden and vulnerable.
   God, hurry to me!
   You are my help and my rescuer.
   Yahweh,
   do not delay!

Psalm 71.
The Life-long God[6]

A.1. The God of past and present

1. In you, Yahweh, I have taken refuge.
   Do not let me ever reap shame.[7]
2. In your righteousness[8],
   deliver me and rescue me.
   Turn your ear to me and save me.
3. Become for me a rock of a dwelling place[9]
   to go to continually:[10]
   you have commanded to save me,
   because you are my crag[11] and my stronghold.
4. My God,
   rescue me from the hand of the wicked[12] one,
   from the grip of the deviant and ruthless person,
5. because you are my hope,
   O Sovereign One, Yahweh,
   where my trust is placed[13] from my youth.
6. On you I have supported myself from birth;[14]
   from the body of my mother it was you who severed me;
   in you is my praise continually.
7. Something of a wonder[15] I have been to many;
   and you have been my refuge – what a strength![16]
8. My mouth will be filled with your praise,
   all the day with your beauty.

10   With continually sheltering here compare continually praising (6) and continually expecting (14).

11   or 'cliff' where fissures provided safe hiding places.

12   'wicked … deviant … ruthless', respectively character, conduct and relationships. Bad, deviant, oppressive.

13   Lit. 'my trust from my youth', but 'trust' is more specifically 'place of trust' (*mibhtach*), i.e. that on which my trust rests.

14   'From the belly', regularly used as synonym for 'womb, birth'.

15   In the expression 'signs and wonders', a 'sign' is something that points (to some truth), a 'wonder' something that attracts attention. What made the onlookers 'marvel' at the writer here? The opposition he excited; the misfortunes his enemies brought on him; the troubles that beset his course of life – this is what the context suggests, illustrative of the truth that troubles are an opportunity for testimony. Did they 'marvel' at his consistency of faith under trial?

16   This line is parallel to the preceding; as they were 'marvelling' he was turning to God. What is important is not what they think of me but what I find in him! 'A strong refuge' is too weak for the Hebrew: 'strength' is an added noun in apposition, giving it special emphasis.

17   *'eth*, see Psalm 69:13.

18   The thought is spelled out more fully in the parallel, verses 17–18.

19   The verb 'to keep' used in the sense 'to keep hostile watch on', as in the heading to Psalm 59.

B.1. The unforsaking God

9. Do not cast me away in the season[17] of old age;[18]
    when my strength is done do not forsake me;

10. because my enemies speak of me,
    and those who keep[19] my soul have taken counsel together,

11. saying,
    God has himself forsaken him;
    pursue and seize him,
    because there is no one to deliver.

C. Commitment: the God of hope, strength and reliabiity

12. O God,
    do not stay far from me;
    my God,
    to my aid hurry!

13. Let them come to a shameful end[20]
    who are the opponents of my soul.
    Let them envelop themselves in reproach and dishonour,
    who are seeking my evil.

14. But as for me,
    continually I will hope,
    and I will add to all your praise.

15. My mouth will recount your righteousness,
    all the day, your salvation,
    because I do not know the full number.[21]

16. I will go in the all-sufficient might[22] of the sovereign Yahweh,
    I will prompt memory of your righteousness, of you alone.[23]

B.2. The unforsaking God

17. O God,
    you have taught me from my youth,

20 The idiom of two verbs without connecting particle: 'let them reap shame, be finished off'. The second verb expresses the main thought and the first verb is an adverbial qualification. 'Let them come to an end in shame/disappointment.'

21 Plural, 'the numbers', 'the complete tale'.

22 Plural of amplitude, 'mights', here 'all-sufficient' seems an allowable emphasis.

23 Maybe we are intended to understand 'your righteousness, yours alone', but this is not the ordinary use of the added 'you alone'.

24 The 'arm' is the symbol (not simply of strength but) of personal strength in action. Compare Isaiah 52:10 (Yahweh with his sleeves rolled up for intervention and action); Isaiah 51:9–11; 63:12; Psalm 44:1; Luke 1:51.

25 Plural of amplitude, 'great things'.

26 For the terminology here and in verse 20, see Exodus 15:5, 11. Present troubles are seen in the light of the greatest of past deliverances. Compare Romans 8:11; 2 Corinthians 1:9.

27 Compare Psalm 40:2.

28 The hand on the strings, lips of praise, the soul caught up in the wonder of ransom, the tongue occupied with the truth of God's righteousness.

and up to now I keep declaring your wonders,

18. and to old age as well, and grey hairs, O God,
     do not forsake me,
     until I declare your arm[24] to a new generation,
     to all to come your mightiness;

A.2. The God of past and future

19. and your righteousness, O God, is to the height;
     what you have done is truly great.[25]
     God, who is like you?[26]
20. You who have made me see many adversities and evils
     you will give me life again,
     and from the depths of the earth you will bring me up
     again.[27]
21. You will multiply my greatness,
     and comfort me all around.
22. Also for my part
     I will give you thanks with the instrumentality of the
     lute,[28]
     your truth, my God.
     I will make music to you with the harp,
     O Holy One of Israel.
23. My lips will shout aloud when I make music to you,
     and my soul which you have ransomed.
24. Also my tongue, all the day, will muse of your
     righteousness,
     because they have been put to shame,
     because they have been dishonoured,
     those who were seeking my evil.

Pause for Thought

How far back in your life can you trace the hand of God? If you have never done this, I venture to think you will be surprised! In my earliest infancy I was left for a weekend with my maternal grandmother – and the weekend stretched out for my first seven years! The direct result of this is that I cannot remember a time when I did not love the Bible as the Word of God. Was this not the hand of God? I could tell you of more 'coincidences' (as they are called), and 'accidents' (as they seem), and the right person being in the right place at the right time – but I have no doubt your 'story' is similar. Consciously or unconscious to us, Yahweh has been our support since birth (Ps. 71:6); it was he who caused us to be born at the time and place of his choice. Not accident but design, not coincidence but plan, not chance but divine direction – that is the story of every believer, the secret history of every conversion. It is the direct implication of the wondrous title of 'Sovereign One' (vv. 5, 16), a God who truly is God, who holds in his hand not only the broad sweep of world history, but the tiniest details of personal stories; a God whom no circumstance or adversary – or collection of adversaries – can defeat; present in every place, master of every situation, deciding and controlling at every time. And so it will continue to be as long as earthly life shall last.

> E'en down to old age, all my people shall prove
> My sovereign, eternal, unchangeable love;
> And then, when grey hairs shall their temples adorn,
> Like lambs they still shall still in my bosom be borne.

See Isaiah 46:3–4. Our old age is as much his loving concern as our youth and prime (Ps. 71:9, 18).

Day 32 Read Psalm 72

Psalm 72.
A King Larger than Life[1]

Solomon's.[2]

A.1. Imitating God: the world and its people set to rights

1. O God
   give your judgments[3] to the king,
   your righteousness to the king's son.
2. He will try[4] your people's case with righteousness,
   and your downtrodden[5] ones with judgment.
3. The mountains[6] will bring peace to the people,
   as will the hills, in righteousness.[7]
4. He will judge the downtrodden ones of the people;
   he will save the sons of the vulnerable,[8]
   and crush the oppressor.

B.1. Endless abundance under the king

5. They will fear you[9] as long as[10] the sun,
   and in the presence of the moon,
   generation after generation.
6. He will come down like rain on mown grass,[11]
   like heavy dew,[12] a distillation[13] on earth.
7. The righteous will blossom[14] in his days,
   and abundance of peace till there is no moon.[15]

C.1. The nations: world dominion

8. And he will have dominion from sea to sea,[16]
   and from the River[17] to the extremities of the earth.

1 This is a psalm of the Messianic King. In other words it outlines some aspect of the royal promises which God linked with the house of David. Like (for example) Psalm 2, Psalm 72 holds up before the actual king (in this case, Solomon) some of the dimensions of the ideal which he is meant to embody, a reminder of his high calling. But the 'dimensions' always exceed what is possible for any merely human king in David's line (see this day's *Pause for Thought*) – in this case, for example, the length (verses 7, 17) and extent (verses 8, 11) of his rule. The Messianic Psalms consciously await him whose right it is to reign.

2 The expression 'To Solomon' most naturally means 'ascribed to Solomon as author/By Solomon', 'belonging' to him because written by him. There is no persuasive reason to question this. The psalm can be seen as an extended and poetic development of the kingly ideals Solomon voiced in 1 Kings 3:6–9. Solomon, more assuredly than any subsequent king, could describe himself as 'the king's son' (1).

3 This plural implies 'your judgment in all its aspects'/covering every situation. 'Judgment' here (as in *The Book of Common Prayer* Collect for Whitsunday, 'a right judgment in all things') refers to the ability to make the right decision at the right time. 'Righteousness' is right principles for the government of life and kingdom.

4 Throughout verses 2–4 the verbs could be treated as concessive, 'May he try …' etc.; compare ESV.

5 Those thrust to the lowest place in life, at the bottom of life's heap.

9. Before him the desert folk[18] will bow down,
   and as for his enemies, they will lick the dust.
10. Kings of Tarshish[19] and distant coasts[20] will bring back a gift;
    kings of Sheba and Seba will bring a tribute near –
11. all the kings will bow in reverence to him;
    all the nations will serve him.

C.2. The nations: the magnetic, caring rule

12. Because[21]
    he will deliver the vulnerable who cries for help,
    and the downtrodden,
    and the one who has no helper.[22]
13. He will pity the poor and vulnerable,
    and the souls of the vulnerable ones he will save.
14. From injury and from violence
    he will redeem[23] their soul,
    and their blood will be precious in his eyes.

C.3. The nations: responding in devotion

15. Long may he live![24]
    And let them give him of the gold of Sheba,[25]
    and pray for him continually:
    and all day long bless him.

B.2. Shared abundance under the king

16. May there be an abundance of grain[26] on earth –
    on top of the mountains[27] let it wave about,[28]
    like Lebanon[29] its fruit!
    And out of the city may they[30] flower like grass on earth!
17. May his name go on[31] for ever!
    In the presence of the sun,[32]
    may his name propagate itself.
    May they find their blessedness[33] in him!
    May all nations pronounce him happy![34]

6   A poetic way of saying that the whole creation will be delivered from the curse (Genesis 3:17–18) brought by human sin. Earth's product will no longer be 'thorns and thistles' but 'peace', all round prosperity and wellbeing.

7   I have chosen to follow here one of the conventions of Hebrew parallelism where the formation of the first line of the parallel extends its meaning to the second. Here the verb 'will bring' is carried over. Alternatively 'in righteousness' could be an example of what is called the *beth essentiae* underlining the reality of the righteousness conveyed, i.e. 'and the hills in veritable righteousness'.

8   *'ebhyon*, 'willing one', in a good sense, one who 'wills the will of God'; in a bad sense, one who is pliant to the will of stronger forces and 'interests' in society, one who can be 'pushed around'.

9   In verses 1–4 the psalm records how creation responded to the reign of the king in ceasing its opposition to man in sin and becoming his partner in prosperity; in verses 5–7 is recorded the people's response – their reverential fear of Yahweh. 'You' picks up 'your' in verses 1–2. In Psalm 72 the king is always 'he'/him (compare verse 8), not 'you'.

10 Lit. 'with', parallel to 'in the presence of'. 'Keeping company with the sun' has the sense 'as long as the sun lasts'. Likewise 'in the presence of the moon'/ standing before the moon', as long as the moon is there.

11 Probably in the sense 'when the grass has been cut', i.e. making the ground ready for a second growth (compare Amos 7:1). Or could the psalm be thinking of the lovely scent of rain falling on freshly cut grass – the sweet aroma of creation in its reality?

A.2. Reflecting God: the Earth filled with his glory[35]

18. Blessed be Yahweh, God,
    the God of Israel,
    who works things to be marveled at –
    he alone!
19. And blessed be the name of his glory for ever,
    and may it be filled with his glory –
    the whole earth!
    Amen and Amen.
    The prayers of David, son of Jesse, are finished.

---

12 See Psalm 65:10.

13 A suggested, contextual rendering of an unknown word, *zarziyph*, related in some way to the unused *zaraph*, said to mean 'to drip, flow, irrigate'.

14 A horticultural term: like all creation the righteous were inhibited while sin and injustice prevailed; the advent of the king releases them from pent up bondage (compare Romans 8:19–21).

15 This section is enclosed in references to sun and moon (verses 5, 7). Jeremiah 33:19–26 (compare Jeremiah 31:35–36) links the Davidic covenant with the ordinances of day and night, etc.; the psalm's emphasis on sun and moon may reflect some special emphasis (a link between the king and creation) in the Davidic Cult. Compare Psalm 110:3 where morning and dawn figure in the royal Melchizedek priesthood.

16 Compare Exodus 23:31; 1 Kings 4:21–24. But possibly 'from sea to sea' is a way of saying 'wherever there is land'.

17 'The River' is the Euphrates – 'the river' par excellence! We would be mistaken to emphasise the idea of limits. The psalm wants to stress extent.

18 Those who inhabit dry places. Probably a reference is intended to the fierce independence of desert tribes – even they will submit.

19 Usually thought to be Tartessos in S. Spain – right at the other end of the Mediterranean. Sheba in S. Arabia; Seba, N. Africa – uncertain location. Verse 10a indicates two sea journeys; verse 10b two land journeys, i.e. everywhere without exception – the idiom of totality by means of contrast. Compare 1 Kings 4:21, 34; 10:24–25.

20 *'iyyiym*, distant places reached by water, islands, land masses.

21 The word deserves to be singled out since it offers the reason for international submission: the kings and nations are won by the quality of mercy in the king.

22 Verses 12–13 express the values of the God of the Exodus: Exodus 2:23–25; 3:7, 9; 6:5–6; 22:21–22; Deuteronomy 16:11–12; 27:19.

23 *ga'al*, to redeem as next of kin (*go'el*), i.e. by accepting their needs, problems, etc., as his own. For this use of *ga'al* referring to earthly tribulations and hazards, compare Genesis 48:16.

24 The traditional, formal, acclamation: 'Let the king live!' 1 Samuel 10:24; 2 Samuel 16:16; 1 Kings 1:25; etc.

25 The king is hailed with gifts of devotion and personal acts of devotion. 'Pray', seek his welfare, because upon him everything else in the way of prosperity and peace depends. The verbs 'give ... pray ... bless' are third-person-singular indefinite; Hebrew uses the indefinite 'he' where the equivalent English usage is 'they'. It would be equally accurate to represent the verbs as passives, 'he will be given ... prayed for .... blessed ...' It is at this point we realize that the Old Testament was still waiting for the divine Messiah yet to come.

26 See on verse 3.

27 The mountain tops are in contrast to the city, totality by means of contrast, all people and places alike.

28 *ra'ash,* used of the earth 'quaking', here, given a contextual rendering of the surface of a field of corn undulating in the wind.

29 Lebanon traditionally associated with perpetual, spontaneous growth and beauty (Isaiah 35:2; 60:13; Hosea 14:5–6).

30 In addition to the contrast between mountain top and city, here is the contrast between earth's fruitfulness and fruitful people. Another idiom of totality.

31 Lit. 'be'.

32 See verse 5.

33 An allusion to the Abrahamic blessing (Genesis 22:18; 26:4).

34 The verb, *'ashar,* whence *'ashrey,* 'Blessed', etc. See Psalm 1:1.

35 These verses act as a postscript to Book 2 of Psalms (compare 41:13; 106:48). Whether they also started life as the conclusion of Psalm 72 it is not possible to say, except to note that as a conclusion to the psalm they fit its structure and needs perfectly. The notion of 'glory' unites the two themes of the verses.

Pause for Thought

Here is an attempt to summarise the portrait of the messianic king in the Psalms. If you have time to look up the references, all the better; if not, just gather an impression of a king larger than life, awaiting fulfillment in Jesus. Against world opposition (Psalm 2:1–3; 110:1) he is victorious (45:3–5; 89:22ff.); through the LORD (18:46) he establishes world rule (2:8–12; 45:17; 72:8–11; 89:25), based on Zion (2:6), marked by moral integrity (45:4, 6; 72:2–4, 7). His rule is everlasting (21:4; 72:5), prosperous (72:7, 16), loyal to the LORD (72:18–19), pre-eminent in dignity (45:2–7), friend of the poor and enemy of the oppressor (72:2, 4, 12–14). The righteous flourish (72:7). He is remembered for ever (45:17): his name is everlasting (72:17); he is the object of unending thanks (72:15) and everlasting blessing (45:2). He is heir to David's covenant (89:28–37; 132:11) and Melchizedek's priesthood (110:4). He belongs to the LORD (89:18) and is devoted to him (21:7; 63:1–8, 11). He is his son (2:7), seated at his right hand (110:1), and is himself God (45:6). Much of this portrait stems from Nathan's ministry in 2 Samuel 7, but the steps by which incipient monarchical hopes became the expectation of a perfect, righteous, human, divine, everlasting and universal king cannot be traced. It is still urged that it was the collapse of monarchy at the time of the Babylonian exile that prompted the development of hope of the royal Messiah. This, of course, requires arbitrary re-dating, in contradiction of the clear evidence of the Old Testament. But, in fact, if it is at all true that the seed bed of hope is failure, we do not need to look beyond David himself to find enough failure to give rise to hope that something better lies ahead.

Day 33   Read Psalm 73

Psalm 73.
But is God Good? Faith under Fire

A Song; Asaph's.[1]

A.1. Faith professed: what the Creed says

1.   Yes indeed,
       God is good to Israel,
       to the pure in heart.[2]

B.1. Faith questioned: But Surely! Look at the facts[3]

2.   But as for me,
       a little more and my feet had turned,[4]
       by almost nothing my steps would have been washed
       away,[5]
3.   because I became jealous of the arrogantly self-confident,[6]
       the well-being of the wicked was what I kept seeing.

(Right to the end of life)
4.   Because there are no pains[7] associated with their death;
       and their bodies are fat-fleshed.[8]

(Their reactions to easy abundance)
5.   In the troubles of mortal man[9] they are not,
       and along with mankind[10] they are not plagued.
6.   Therefore
       pride is their necklace;[11]
       they each wrap themselves up in violence as a garment.

(Luxuriousness, indulgence, assumed superiority)
7.   Their eyes bulge with fatness;

1   Psalm 50, heading.

2   The truth the psalm asserts is not that
     of the general benevolence of God
     (Matthew 5:45), but of his particular
     goodness to the 'church within the
     church', the 'pure in heart' among the
     company of mere professors.

3   This section is bracketed by an
     inclusion: verses 2–3, personal
     awareness of the severe problem of
     life's unfairness; verses 13–14, personal
     questioning of the worthwhileness of
     godly disciplines.

4   i.e. from the right way, turned aside.

5   Lit. 'been poured out'. An unusual use
     of the verb here given a contextually
     suitable sense.

6   'The boasters', self-confident, brooking
     no contradiction.

7   Or 'fetters', none of the limitations
     associated with life's last days.

8   Healthy to the last.

9   *'enosh*. Compare Psalm 8:4.

10 *'adham*, the generality of humankind.

11 Something other people see
     prominently in them, and which
     they themselves have no hesitation in
     displaying.

12 There is no heavenly issue on which
     they cannot make a pronouncement,
     and no earthly situation or question
     beyond their range.

13 'His' must refer to Yahweh. Even his
     professed adherents are drawn away.
     The well-being that is a problem to
     Asaph is a magnet to others.

they go beyond anything the heart can imagine;
8. they mock,
   and speak with evil intent of oppression;
   from a superior position they speak;
9. they have set their mouth in the heavens,
   and their tongue walks the earth.[12]

(Getting a following; their practical atheism)
10. Therefore his people[13] turn away hither,
    and waters in full[14] are drained out by them.

(Spiritual complacency)
11. And they keep saying:
    'How does the transcendent God know?'
    And 'Is there knowledge in the Most High?'[15]

(Comment and Reaction)
12. Behold!
    These are the wicked!
    Eternally at ease,
    they have gained great resources.
13. Yes indeed,
    for nothing[16] I have purified my heart,
    and in innocence washed my hands[17] –
14. I was plagued all day,
    and my correction every morning.

C. Faith refocused: Finding a new perspective

(Caring for Yahweh's people: living responsibly)
15. If I said: 'I will recount it like this,'
    behold!
    I would have acted treacherously to the generation of
    your sons.[18]

(Taking it to the Lord)
16. When I gave my mind to know this,
    it was troublesome in my eyes,

14 Lit. 'waters of a full one'. The imagery of a full cup (e.g. Psalm 23:5) indicative of plentiful living.

15 If this is intended to be an accurate report of what they said, they were drawing a wrong conclusion from 'transcendence' (*'el*) and 'exaltedness' – that such a God is too remote to bother with earthly matters. The true conclusion is that such a God inevitably knows everything and is inescapable. On the other hand it may be that Asaph is putting words in their mouth in order to show the absurdity of their position: they would more likely simply have spoken of 'God'.

16 In contrast to the 'gain' referred to in verse 12.

17 A very compressed statement: 'I have pursued a life of innocence, and also made use of the provision God has made for cleansing.' Note the balance in verse 13 of 'heart' and 'hand' – the inward disposition and the outward act. Here is totality expressed by means of contrast: the whole person dedicated to living as God would have it. 'Hand' here is specifically *kaph*, the 'grip' of the hand, the hand in action.

18 'The generation of your sons' is emphatic in the Hebrew. The principle is the same as that in Romans 14:13, 15, 21; 1 Corinthians 8:11–13.

19 In 'transcendent God' there is a subtle backward glance to verse 11: the very God they dismissed from their reckoning is the one who knows and understands all and is the arbiter of their destiny.

20 The word (*'achariyth*) can simply mean 'end', but usually 'end' in the sense of 'outcome/result', even 'destiny'. Jeremiah 29:11.

21 This word of emphasis forms a chain-link in this psalm (1, 11,18).

17. until I went into the sanctuary of the transcendent God:[19]
    I discerned their future.[20]

(The eternal perspective)

18. Yes indeed,[21]
    you set them in slippery places;
    you have determined to make them fall into gross deception.[22]
19. How they come to destruction in a moment!
    They are to be totally swept away by terrors.[23]
20. Like a dream on awakening,
    O Sovereign One,
    when you rouse up,[24]
    you scorn[25] their image.[26]

B.2. Faith unquestioned: self-awareness and future confidence

21. Indeed my heart was embittered,
    and in my kidneys I was pierced through,[27]
22. but as for me,[28]
    I was a brute beast and knew nothing,
    a very animal was I in your presence.
23. But as for me,
    continually I am with you;[29]
    you have gripped my right hand;
24.[30] by your counsel you will guide me;
    and in the future[31] to glory you will take me.
25. Who is on my side in heaven?
    And along with you, I have no desire on earth.
26. When my flesh and my heart are finished,[32]
    God is the rock of my heart and my portion for ever.

A.2. Faith affirmed: the certainties of personal conviction

27. Because – behold! –
    those far from you will perish.

22 'Deceptions', a plural of amplitude. The meaning here is that the proudly self-confident were all the time living in the deceptive world of their own imagination. A small alteration of vowel points would yield the meaning 'complete destruction'.

23 Or, plural of amplitude, 'the great terror'. Job 18:14.

24 As the text stands, the word here means 'in the city'. Could we understand this to mean – in the place where they achieved their 'successes', and heaped up their resources, and attracted their following, they were in reality as solid as a dream? If we understand the word as a contracted form of the verb *ba'iyr* for *beha'iyr*, then 'when you rouse up'.

25 Compare Daniel 12:2; Matthew 7:23; 25:12.

26 'Image' here in the sense 'a shape and nothing more than a shape', a cardboard cut-out with no solidity.

27 The reference is to verses 2–3. In contrast to 'kidneys' which represent the 'feelings/emotions', 'heart' stands for 'thoughts'.

28 Note the contrast of these two 'but as for me' verses. The word translated 'brute beast' (*ba'ar*) is used to describe 'the natural man', man untouched by special grace, unilluminated by the Spirit of God; e.g. Psalm 49:12; 92:6 (NKJV, 'senseless'); Proverbs 30:2 (NKJV, 'stupid'). 'A very animal' translated *behemoth*, the beast of beasts in Job 40:15–24, sheer animal life.

29 'You are continually with me' would express the presence of God; 'I am continually with you' means peace with God, acceptance in his presence. 'I have gripped your hand' speaks of commitment; 'you have gripped' is security.

You are sure to bring to an end all who go whoring[33] away from you.

28. But as for me,

approaching near to God is good[34] for me.

I have established my refuge in the Sovereign One, Yahweh,

so as to recount all your activities.

-----

30 Verse 24 steps into the future: the immediate and ongoing future is already planned out by God, it is 'his counsel'. The ultimate future, the coming future, is glory. The meaning 'to glory' is established by the virtually technical use of the verb 'to take' of being taken from earth into God's presence: Genesis 5:24; 2 Kings 2:1, 3, 5, 9, 10. It is this reference to eternal glory that prepares for the thought of heaven in the next verse.

31 Compare verse 17.

32 In verse 14 daily grief created unanswerable problems; now he is ready to contemplate with equanimity his whole being terminated if only he retain his 'portion'. On 'portion', compare Numbers 18:20; Deuteronomy 10:9; Joshua 13:14, 33; 18:7. Asaph was Levite (1 Chronicles 25:2) to whom the idea of Yahweh as his portion would have been specially prized.

33 *zanah*, 'to be/act as a prostitute'. Arising from the basic use of marriage to define the relationship of the LORD with his people (Isaiah 54:5; Jeremiah 2:2; Ezekiel 16:8; Hosea 2:7), apostasy is regularly spoken of a whoredom, going as a prostitute.

34 Compare 'good' in verse 1, an inclusion to the whole psalm.

Pause for Thought

Psalm 73 contains one of the most rhapsodic and uplifting passages in the whole Psalter, and, indeed, there is hardly need for anything beyond letting their rhythms and sentiments sink into our souls. But, hoping to help and not hinder this process, look at some of the detail of these verses. They are the heart of the message of the psalms. Asaph is weighing things in the balance: what can he reckon in his favour as compared with the 'wellbeing' of the ungodly which so troubled him. There are, indeed, things which we find in our heavenly 'balance sheet' – and which we should constantly prize. First and foremost is peace with God (23a), that we are constantly accepted, welcomed, retained in his presence. 'Peace with God', the firstfruits of Calvary (John 20:19), our unchangeable inheritance in Jesus –

> I know that while in heaven he stands,
> No tongue can bid me thence depart.

Then there is security in his keeping – he who has gripped us by our hands (23b). Recall Matthew 14:31 and John 10:28–29. Thirdly, there is the problem of 'the future all unknown'. To us who cannot foresee what the end of this morning will bring, there is the comfort that everything that happens does so in conformity to and by direction of his 'counsel' (24a). What is impenetrable to us (the future) is an already drawn map lying before him (Eph. 1:3–4; 2:10; Phil. 1:29–30). We can never over-exalt the sovereignty of God: he is truly God – the God in charge. And we need to remind ourselves that this is even especially so when things turn out either other than we expect or would wish. He is always on our side; always implementing his 'counsel'. All this is a store of pure gold entered in our account; yet the finest gold is yet to come. There is that which even the life-assurance man dare not mention by name when he delicately suggests 'if anything should happen'. But the Bible has no such hesitations. It knows all about 'afterwards', the future; it calls it the 'glory' (24b). Our gracious God is not only for earth; he is our guarantee of heaven (25–26).

Day 34 Read Psalms 74–75

Psalm 74.
Appearance and Reality[1]

A teaching poem; Asaph's.

A.1. Prayer: God and his people; is he concerned?

1. Why, O God, have you cast us off in perpetuity?
    Why does your exasperation fume against the sheep[2] of
    your pasture?
2. Remember your assembly which you purchased of old,
    which you redeemed[3] as the tribe of your inheritance;
    Mount Zion where you made your dwelling.

B.1. Prayer: enemies; God's sanctuary and his people

3. Raise your steps[4] to the perpetual ruins:
    the enemy has ruined[5] everything – everything! – in the
    sanctuary.
4. Your adversaries have roared like lions[6]
    in the middle of your appointed place;[7]
    they have set up their signs as signs.[8]
5. Each[9] has made himself known
    as one bringing up high an axe on a thicket of trees.
6. And now the carvings, altogether,
    with chopper and hatchet they keep smashing.
7. They have consigned your sanctuary to the fire;
    to the ground they have defiled the dwelling-place of your
    name.[10]
8. They have said in their hearts:
    'We will oppress them[11] altogether.'
    They have set fire to all the appointed places of God in
    the land.

1   The title for Psalm 74 arises from the fact that 'in perpetuity' appears three times (2, 10, 19), 'perpetual' once (3), and 'continually' once (23). The appearance of things is that disaster seems to have gone on for ever, and seems likely to last for ever. The reality of the situation is that the royal God is truly there for ever (12–17); ever working salvation (12b), overcoming (13–14), transforming (15), in charge of life's regularities and apportionments (16–17).

2   The title used seems to survey the LORD's history with his people: 'sheep' for the Exodus/wilderness period of providential care; 'assembly' for Israel considered as a religious gathering, as at Sinai; 'tribe' for organization in Canaan; Mount Zion for David and the monarchy. The Babylonian conquest and captivity seemed to spell a perpetual end to all this. Compare Lamentations 2:5–9.

3   *ga'al*, redemption by the 'kinsman-redeemer'. See Psalm 19:14.

4   What does this literal rendering mean? It sounds like 'pick your way'. Or does it mean 'pick up your feet', i.e. 'move quickly'? Or is it a colloquial expression used here and not elsewhere, 'Come and survey'?

5   I have understood the perfect tenses of the verbs in verses 3–8 as giving an eye-witness' view of what happened. Considered this way, the pathos of the scene comes home vividly. Note the forcefulness of 'now' in verse 6.

6   The verb used (*sha'ag*) is the pouncing roar of a lion leaping on its prey (Judges 14:5). It is legitimate, therefore, to introduce the word 'like lions'.

9. Our own signs we have not seen;
    no longer is there a prophet,
    nor, in our company,[12] one who knows how long.
10. How long, O God, will the adversary reproach,
    the enemy scorn your name in perpetuity?
11. Why do you keep holding back your hand,
    your right hand from within your bosom?
    Make an end!

C. The saving king: saying the creed in a time of trouble[13]

12. And[14] God is my king from of old,
    accomplishing full salvation[15] in the middle of the earth[16].
13. It was you who by your strength divided the sea,[17]
    broke the heads of the sea monsters[18] on the waters;
14. it was you who crushed the heads of Leviathan,[19]
    gave him as food to the desert folk.[20]
15. It was you who cleft open spring and river;
    it was you who dried up permanent streams;
16. yours is the day;
    indeed yours is the night;
    it was you who established the light-bearer, the sun;
17. it was you set in place all the boundaries of the earth:
    as for summer and winter,
    it was you who fashioned them.

B.2. Prayer: enemies: God's name and his people

18. Remember this:
    there is an enemy who has reproached,
    Yahweh.
    People devoid of moral sensibility have scorned your name.
19. Do not give over to a beast the soul of your dove;
    the life of your downtrodden ones do not forget in perpetuity.

7   'Place' is generally accepted here and in verse 8 (compare Joshua 8:14, but with ESV note.), but the word (*moe'dh*) is used in the Bible for an appointed time, of an occasion of meeting, a festival, or the assembly gathered at such a time. The formation of the word (with its prefaced 'm') ought, however, to allow the meaning of 'place'.

8   Flags or other insignia raised in token of conquest.

9   The verb here is unexpectedly singular, presumably individualising.

10 Deuteronomy 12:5; 16:2; etc.

11 Or, as an exclamation: 'Their heirs and successors all together!' i.e. a root and branch extermination.

12 Lit. 'with us'.

13 Verse 11 has prepared for this great affirmation of faith. The LORD's hand is still there, concealed in his bosom. It is perplexing that he has not acted, but equally he has not changed. Just as verse 11 affirms his unchanged power to act ('hand ... right hand'), so verses 2–17 reaffirm his position as Creator, the one who can transform any situation, the unchanged God of Israel's past. See also note 1 above. In verses 13–17 the emphatic singular pronoun 'you' comes seven times: the first four express divine dominance over the 'forces' of nature (all that would threaten or stand in the way of his people); the last three express sovereignty over the ordering of creation (the world we live in is his world).

14 The conjunction 'and' is full of significance here: in every situation, good or ill, there is always an additional factor: the divine king.

15 'Full salvation', plural of amplitude.

20. Look to the covenant!
    For dark places of the earth are full of habitations of
    violence.
21. Do not let the crushed return disheartened.
    The downtrodden and the vulnerable,
    let them praise your name.

A.2. Prayer: God and his reputation – is he concerned?

22. Rise, O God,
    defend your case.
    Remember your reproach from the morally insensible all
    the day.
23. Do not forget the voice of your adversaries:
    the uproar of those rising against you goes up continually.

Psalm 75.
Four Voices in Harmony:
The All-Ruling God

Belonging to the worship-leader; set to 'Do not Destroy';
a Song belonging to Asaph;
A hymn.

A. The voice of the community: praise for wonderful works

1. We give thanks to you, O God,
    we give thanks:
    your name is near[21] –
    your awe-inspiring works have recounted.[22]

16 So to say, right here on earth. He is the heavenly God but his sphere is not limited to heaven. He is the active agent on earth.

17 Allusion to the Red Sea crossing (Exodus 14). The subjugation of creation is the Bible's reply to pagan myths of a pre-creation combat in which the 'creator god' subdued other 'gods' who would have resisted such an ordering of affairs. The God of the Bible performed his wonders in history and before witnesses.

18 Asaph now calls on mythology to contribute to his credo of the greatness of God: sea monsters and Leviathan, the stuff of pagan myths, all alike – were such ever to exist – are totally subservient to the one real God.

19 See Psalm 104:26.

20 Lit. 'the people, the desert dwellers'. The sense is – what is the famed Leviathan but animal fodder?

21 Shorthand for 'In all that your name reveals about you, you have proved to be our next-of-kin' (i.e. the one who has the right to take, bear and discharge our burdens as though his own).

22 We do not know what circumstance lies behind this psalm, but it must have been some such as the Sennacherib incident (2 Kings 18:13–19:37). We can imagine a national gathering of thanksgiving following just such an experience.

B. The voice of God: the world's Governor and Judge[23]

2. When I seize[24] the appointed time,
   it is I who judge[25] with fairness.

3. When the earth and all its inhabitants are melting
   it is I who have settled its pillars in place.[26] (*Selah*)

4. I say to the arrogantly self-confident,[27]
   'Do not be so sure of yourselves,'[28]
   and to the wicked,
   'Do not exalt your horn;[29]

5. do not exalt your horn on high,
   nor speak with neck stuck out!'[30]

C. The voice of a teacher; lessons learned; world government[31]

6. Because exaltation[32] is not from the east,
   nor from the west,
   nor from the south.

7. because God is the judge[33] –
   one he brings low;
   another he raises up.

8. Because the cup[34] is in Yahweh's hand,
   and the wine has fermented;[35]
   the mixture is full;
   and he pours out some of it;
   yes indeed,
   its dregs all the wicked of the earth
   will drink to the last drop.[36]

D. The voice of the king: ordering society by divine example[37]

9. And as for me,
   I will declare for ever –
   I will make music to the God of Jacob.

23 Passages like 2 Chronicles 20:13–17 show that on national occasions a prophet could intervene and speak as from Yahweh himself. This is the simplest understanding of verses 2–5. Against the background of his solving of the Sennacherib crisis, Yahweh speaks through a prophet explaining how he waits till his chosen moment has come, then acts as world-ruler (2); that though everything seems to be collapsing, the world's stability is his business. not at the mercy of earthly rulers such as Sennacherib (3); and that he rules the world in righteousness (4–5).

24 Lit. 'take' (*laqach*), not elsewhere used with *mo'edh* (see Psalm 74:4, note 7).

25 In the broad sense, as generally, of 'putting things to rights'.

26 'Settled in place' translates *takan* 'to adjust something so that it exactly fits in its place, is adapted for its function'.

27 Often translated 'boasters'. The meaning is arrogant self-confidence.

28 Lit. 'be so arrogantly self-confident', the same verb as note 25. This sort of repetition of the same word 'works' in Hebrew in a way that grates in English.

29 'Horn' symbolises confident prowess, assurance of being 'top dog'.

30 Lit. 'with a forward neck', an 'in your face' attitude.

31 In Nehemiah 8:7 we read the names of those who 'helped the people to understand the law', presumably by being given the opportunity to interrupt the reading with explanations. Such a voice seems to speak here, drawing out the lessons from what the LORD has said in verses 2–5 through his prophet.

10. All the horns[38] of the wicked I will cut off;
    the horns of the righteous will be raised up.

32 The lesson drawn concerns world rule: who gets the top jobs. This is not a matter of being in the right place – east, west, south – at the right time. 'East' etc. are interpretative representations of, respectively (lit.), 'the going forth place', 'the evening place' and 'the wilderness'. The absence of a reference to the 'north' could suggest that it is not the Sennacherib incident but some other that lies behind this psalm.

33 'Judge' in the basic sense that it is God who makes the decision, as Romans 13:1.

34 The 'cup' of destiny in which Yahweh has mixed the ingredients making up the experiences of every one. Compare Psalm 11:6; 60:3; Isaiah 51:17; Mark 10:38; 14:36.

35 Equivalent to 'the time is ripe': i.e. the right decision at the exact time.

36 The familiar idiom of two verbs without intervening conjunction: 'will-drain-will-drink', 'will drink drainingly'. Compare NKJV with ESV.

37 Who but a king could speak, verse 10? Compare Psalm 101:5–8.

38 Compare verse 4.

Pause for Thought

How well Psalms 74 and 75 belong together! In principle Psalm 75 tackles the same situation as 74, but from a different perspective. In Psalm 74 the people are still in the soup, a situation of dreadful calamity and destruction is still unresolved, whereas Psalm 75 looks back on some wonderful work of God which has solved the problem. But within this altered perspective, the message is the same – and it is a message of immense importance for us who live in the same hazardous world as the psalms. At the heart of each psalm (74:12–17; 75:5–7) lies a 'credal' statement: in 74, affirmed by the writer, Asaph; in 75, spoken by God himself about himself. What is this telling us? we should ask. Not, in the first instance, what is its content, but why are we faced, twice over, with the unheralded introduction of truth about God into a situation of trouble? And the answer is plain, is it not? That at the centre of our trouble, danger, loss, sorrow – when hostile forces are on top, rampant, triumphalist – our course is to remind ourselves what we believe about our God. We are to tell ourselves not how horrible life is, how unfairly I have been treated, how insupportable my sorrow is, but how kingly, saving, powerful (74:12–14); how provident (74:15); how totally in charge (74:16-17) God is; how fully in command of history (75:2); how secure is his world (75:3); how subservient to him are earth's arrogant powers (75:4–5). These are the bread and butter truths of the scriptural revelation of God. They speak of a God in charge, a God who makes all the decisions, a God fully and truly God – a God worth trusting. When, in the light of these basic truths, we 'turn our eyes on Jesus', the 'things of earth' do 'grow strangely dim' – that is to say, they take on their proper size and proportions 'in the light of his glory and grace'.

Day 35   Read Psalms 76–77

Psalm 76.
To Know is to Fear

Belonging to the worship-leader; set for strings; a song belonging to Asaph; a hymn.

A. Knowing God: his word is power

1. In Judah God has made himself known.
   In Israel his name is great.
2. In Salem is his lair,[1]
   and his dwelling place in Zion.[2]
3. It was there that he shattered the flames of the bow,[3]
   shield and sword and battle.[4] (*Selah*)
4. You are radiant with light,[5]
   majestic,
   back from[6] the mountains of prey:
5. the potent of heart yield themselves as spoil;
   they have succumbed to deep sleep,
   and none of the men of prowess have deployed their skill.[7]
6. By your rebuke,[8] God of Jacob,[9]
   each lapsed into a coma[10] –
   chariot and horse alike.

B. Fearing God: his word is law

7. As for you,
   you are to be feared.[11]
   And who can stand before you
   in the time of your exasperation?[12]
8. From heaven you pronounced[13] your judicial decision:

1   The word (*sok*) is specifically lion's lair: Psalm 10:9; Jeremiah 25:38.

2   The list of place-names lays huge stress on location: 'Judah', the area with which the psalm is concerned; 'Israel', the name of privilege: the people Israel to whom the revelation of God has been granted; 'Salem', the chosen city, the place of his name (Deuteronomy 12:5), also the place where the first great victory over the forces of the world was acknowledged and hallowed (Genesis 14:18–20); 'Zion', David's royal city (2 Samuel 5:7). It is against this background we feel the force of verse 3, 'It was there ...'. Psalm 76 thus belongs to the same background as Psalm 75: some signal victory of God over forces threatening Jerusalem. Again the typical biblical illustration is the overthrow of the Assyrian forces under Sennacherib.

3   Possibly arrows set alight as incendiaries; maybe, however, just the flashing of arrows in sunlight.

4   i.e. the outcome of the battle itself is God's (2 Chronicles 20:15).

5   I toyed with the idea of translating 'radiant with light' as 'spot-lighted'. God allowed the spot-light to focus on himself so that he was seen in all his radiant glory. Each of the two sections of verses 1–6 opens with a passive participle: verse 1, 'Made known/self-revealed', verse 4, 'illuminated, spot-lighted'.

6   'More than' is an equally possible translation (NKJV, ESV). 'Mountains of prey', the fastnesses where the enemy had to be sought out and defeated. The victorious LORD returns luminous with majesty. Or translate 'On the mountains ...'

the earth feared and became still,[14]

9.   when God rose for judgment,[15]
     to save all the downtrodden of the earth. (*Selah*)

10. Because the wrath of mankind will give you thanks,[16]
     all that remains of total wrath[17] you will bind on.[18]

11. Vow and fulfil it
     to Yahweh, your God;
     let all around him bring a homage gift to The Fear.[19]

12. He will cut off the spirit of leaders;
     to be feared by the kings of the earth.

Psalm 77.
Memories in a Time of Trouble

Belonging to the worship-leader; set to Jeduthun;[20] As-aph's; a song.

A. When prayer, remembering 'God', does not help[21]

1.   With my voice[22] to God,
     how I kept screaming!
     With my voice, to God –
     and he kept his ear open to me.

2.   In the day of my adversity,
     it was the Sovereign One I sought;
     in the night my hand went out[23] and did not relax;
     my soul refused to be comforted.

3.   How I kept remembering God,
     and remained agitated!
     I kept musing and my spirit fainted away.[24] (*Selah*)

B. When recalling personal experiences does not help, only prompt questions

4.   You have gripped my eyelids;
     I am under pressure and I cannot speak!

7   'Deployed their skill' interprets (lit.) 'found their hands' (Compare NKJV, ESV), treating 'hand' as symbolic of personal skill/ability to achieve.

8   Asaph has carefully detailed the enemy armament: arrows, shield, sword, chariot, horse, trained warriors of proven ability – but all God needed to do was speak the word! His word is powerful beyond all the massed contrivances of human power. Compare Revelation 19:13, 15, 21.

9   The title could be used as a deliberate irony: the well-armed foes doubtless thought they were dealing with some local nonenity of a god, little realising that the 'God of Jacob' is the LORD God omnipotent!

10   *radham*, for the sense see the cognate noun, *tardhema*, an unconsciousness induced by act of God (1 Samuel 26:12).

11   Like section **A** (verse 1), section **B** opens with a passive participle, announcing the theme of the second half, 'to be feared'. With the same word (12) the psalm ends, forming an inclusion.

12   Related to the word for 'nose', *'aph* is the snort of anger that announces that patience has run out.

13   Lit. 'cause (people) to hear'.

14   Or 'fell silent'. But meanings refer back to the noise of war brought to an end by the voice of God.

15   To set the affairs of the world to rights.

16   Think of the thanksgiving that arose to God because Sennacherib attacked and was overthrown.

17   'Total wrath' is a plural of amplitude.

18   Either as an ornament or decoration to be worn, or as a weapon to be used.

5. I busied myself thinking of earlier days,
    years from long ago.
6. I keep remembering my song in the night;
    with my heart I muse,
    and my spirit searches thoroughly.
7. Can it be that for ever the Sovereign One casts away,
    and will never again be favourable?
8. Can his committed love cease in perpetuity?
    The word come to an end throughout the generations?
9. Has the transcendent God forgotten to be gracious?
    Or has he closed up his compassion in exasperation?[25]
    (*Selah*)

C. Memories that bring confident assurance

10. And I said:
    'This is my entreating:
    the years of the right hand of the Most High.'[26]

(Works and wonders)

11. I will keep remembering the acts of Yah –
    indeed, how I will remember wonderfulness of old!
12. I will meditate on all that is wonderful[27] about you,
    and on your activities I will muse.[28]

(Holiness and redemption)

13. O God,
    your way is in holiness.[29]
14. You are the transcendent God who does wonders;
    Among the peoples, you have made them know your
    strength.[30]
15. By arm[31] you redeemed[32] your people,
    the sons of Jacob and Joseph. (*Selah*)

(Mastery over and use of the 'forces' of Creation)[33]

16. The waters saw you, O God,
    the waters saw you:

19 For 'Fear' as a title or synonym for God, Genesis 31:53; Isaiah 8:13. He is so worthy of reverential fear that he can be called 'Fear'.

20 See Psalm 62, heading.

21 This heading sounds almost blasphemous, but it is what verses 1–3 say plainly: trouble drove Asaph to unceasing prayer, with his thoughts focused on God (mentioned three times, and 'the Sovereign One' once) but the pressure of trouble was not eased. This is a piece of down-to-earth realism.

22 The words 'with my voice' are never tautologous. They stress the verbalising of our prayers, going into the detail of our need.

23 Lit. 'was poured out', an unusual use of the verb but a vivid image of ceaselessly reaching out to God in prayer.

24 Rather than being offended at the brutal frankness of the psalm we must be sure to learn its lesson. There can be a trouble so dire that even prolonged, earnest prayer (2), even the assurance of prayer being heard (1), even thoughts centred on 'God' bring no relief.

25 The implication of verses 4–9 is that purely personal experience is too insecure a foundation on which to build a doctrine of God. We 'feel' one way one day, another way another day. On a calm, trouble-free day, the answer to the questions in verses 7–9 would be obvious, but, in this apparently prolonged period of soul-destroying adversity, the psalmist can ask the questions but, on the basis of experience, cannot venture a sure answer.

they began to writhe!

Yes indeed! The depths were trembling!

17. The clouds poured out water in floods;

the skies[34] gave voice;

indeed, your arrows went this way and that.

18. The voice of your thunder was in the whirlwind;

lightning flashes illuminated the inhabited world;

the earth trembled and shook.

(Dominion over circumstantial barriers)

19. Your way was in the sea;

and your wake in the abundant waters;

and your footprints were not known.

(Providential, pastoral care)

20. You guided your people like sheep

by the hand of Moses and Aaron.

26 Whatever way this verse is translated there is a measure of uncertainty. The main possibility, other than the above, is; 'This is my wounding' (looking back over the previous verses, the way he has been 'wounded' by adversity); then, abruptly as something which has just come to mind, a new thought is announced – 'The years of the right hand of the Most High' – which leads into the list that follows. In this case, 'wounding' is Infinitive Construct (gerund) of *chalal*, to pierce, wound. In the rendering above, 'entreating' is Infinitive Construct (gerund) of *chalah*, to entreat. In either case, verse 10 marks a transition from the inadequacy of subjective experience (4–9) to dwelling on the objective acts of God for his people. What he has done is a sure foundation on which to build an assured grasp of who and what he is, and therefore a confident basis for entreaty.

27 'Wonder/wonderful', the *pal'a* group of words – compare Isaiah 9:6; Genesis 18:14 (NKJV 'hard'; Jeremiah 32:17, 27) – always contains the note of the 'supernatural', what can only be attributed to God, not man.

28 Contrast the fruitless 'musing' of verse 3. Now there is a secure basis in what Yahweh has himself done.

29 Or (which amounts to the same thing) 'in the sanctuary'. His holiness is his 'otherness' – not just that he is 'different from' (a comparative matter) but that he is 'Other'. In the Bible his 'otherness' is his moral purity, ethical holiness (as Isaiah 6:3). According to verse 15 (see note there) this God of holy Otherness chooses to be the next-of-kin to his people.

30 A reference to the Exodus as divine revelation to the world; compare Exodus 9:16; Joshua 2:10–11.

31 Symbol of personal power to act and achieve (e.g. Isaiah 52:10). In the present verse there is no possessive pronoun. Lit. 'by an arm'. This is probably an example of the idiom of 'indefiniteness for the sake of emphasis' ('by an arm – you know whose!!' Compare Hebrews 1:2 (lit. 'by a Son'), or else it is shorthand for 'by personal strength and agency'.

32 On *ga'al* see Psalm 19:14.

33 If we take verse 15 as a clue, then verses 16–20 trace the history of Israel from Egypt to Canaan. The Red Sea at the start of the journey (16), the storm theme at Sinai (17–18), crossing Jordan at the end of the wilderness days (19) and, throughout, shepherding care (20).

34 A synonymous word for 'clouds'.

Pause for Thought

If the Psalms tell us – directly or by implication – that there is a time to stop praying, we need to sit up and take notice! The overall theme of the collection surely is 'take it to the LORD in prayer'. Nothing else so adequately summarizes what the Psalms are all about. But, says Psalm 77, 'I tried it and it didn't work'. Here is a psalmist in deep trouble; he drives himself to prayer, past the point of exhaustion, and gets no relief. His soul still refuses to be comforted. But eventually – and surely by wonderfully tender divine grace – the solution dawns on his poor battered consciousness: 'the years of the right hand of the Most High' (77:10). Now, the point is this: the solution to every problem is the way of simple faith. It may not prove to be a simple thing to place faith, and to hold on to the way of faith, but faith itself is essentially simple – childlike trust. It was in this way that the eternal problem of getting right with God was solved, was it not – simple faith in Jesus? If the greatest problem yielded to faith, how much more lesser problems, however testing? It is the way to greet each new day, to face every new problem, rise to every new challenge – 'Father, I trust you!' But – and how important this is – faith must rest on a sure foundation. Faith is not a leap in the dark; it is a leap from light into light. Faith is conviction leading to action on the basis of evidence – and the only sufficient evidence is what God has done, objectively, historically. That's why the psalm stops so abruptly. It does not draw a conclusion but demonstrates a solution: the mind stored with, assured of, resting on the great facts of God's salvation is a mind at rest.

Day 36   Read Psalm 78

Psalm 78.
Remembering and Obeying

An instructive poem belonging to Asaph.

Introduction

1. Give ear, my people, to my teaching;
    turn your ear to the words of my mouth.
2. I will open my mouth with an interpretation;[1]
    I will overflow in enigmas[2] from earlier times,
3. which we have heard and known,
    and our fathers have recounted to us.
4. We will not conceal them from their sons,
    as we go on recounting to the following generation
    Yahweh's praises and his mightiness,
    and his wonders which he has done:
5. He implemented a testimony[3] in Jacob,
    and he placed teaching in Israel,
    which he commanded our fathers to make known to their
    sons,
6. in order that the following generation, sons to be born,
    might know,
    might get up and recount it to their sons,
7. and they would put their confidence[4] in God,
    and not forget the acts of the transcendent God,
    but preserve his commandments,
8. and not become like their fathers
    a generation stubborn and mutinous,[5]
    a generation that did not make its heart resolute,
    nor was its spirit reliable with God.

1   *mashal*, a 'proverb, parable, metaphor' – a single saying or an extended statement which brings out the meaning of something otherwise obscure. We discover from the rest of the psalm that what Asaph has in mind is a review of Israel's history told in such a way as to bring out its fundamental principle. The facts have been recounted from past times, and are essential to pass on (3–4), but Asaph wants to do more than simply recount the past. He is aware that history as such is an enigma – why have things happened as they have? He believes he is in a position to explain its hidden meaning.

2   In the context of the psalm, the 'enigmas' or 'riddles' from the past are the inherited stories of Israel's history. These, as such, must be preserved and handed on to succeeding generations (4) as well as the 'testimony' and 'teaching' (5) given at the same time, but what does it all mean? Asaph insists he can elucidate this inner meaning.

3   'Testimony', i.e. what God has 'testified to' as his truth or the truth about himself. This too is a sacred deposit to be held and handed on (6).

4   *kesel* means both 'stupidity, folly' (compare *kesiyl*, the 'fathead') and 'confidence, hope'. The link is the meaning 'simplicity': the 'simple' person can be a 'simpleton' or a person of 'simple trust'.

5   Both these words mean 'rebellious'. If a distinction is intended the first (*sorer*) is the rebel who digs his heels in, pig-headed; the second (*moreh*) the rebel who acts out of personal spite or spleen.

A.1. The first survey of the acts of God (9–39)[6]

(Preface: How did the well-equipped Ephraimites come to be defeated? The deadly sin of forgetting God's wonders)

9. The sons of Ephraim,
    equipped, skilled bowmen,[7]
    turned back in the day of battle.

10. They did not keep the covenant of God,
    and in his teaching they refused to walk –

11. they forgot his activities,
    and the wonderful things which he showed them.[8]

(The acts of God: 1. Redemption completed)

12. In front of their fathers[9] he had done wonders,
    in the land of Egypt, the field of Zoan.[10]

13. He divided the sea[11] and made them go through,
    and he stood the waters up like a heap![12]

(2. Care and provision)

14. And he conducted them by the cloud by day,
    and all night by the light of fire.[13]

15. He split rocks in the wilderness
    and provided drink[14] –
    like the very depth itself[15] – in abundance!

16. And he brought streams out of the rock,
    and made waters come down like rivers.[16]

(3. Wrath)

17. And they went on to sin further against him,
    to mutiny[17] against the Most High in the dry lands:

18. they tested out[18] the transcendent God[19] in their heart,
    asking him food for their desire.

19. And they spoke against God –
    they said:
    'Is the transcendent God able to lay a table in the wilderness?[20]

20. Behold! He struck the rock,

---

6 Verses 40–72 are a second survey. Each of the surveys deals with the same four aspects of God's acts in the same order. The first survey emphasizes wonders in the realm of the natural creation, the second survey, the acts of God in history. This is the enigma of history viewed from the divine point of view: the persevering God who never gives up. Each survey has a 'preface' (verses 9–11, 40–42) stating the fundamental principle which Asaph wishes to bring out. It is not possible to say what defeat the psalm refers to. Joshua was an Ephraimite (Numbers 13:8), and in the early days the Tabernacle was pitched at Shiloh (Judges 21:19; 1 Samuel 1:3) which was also a national centre (e.g. Joshua 18:1). In verse 67 the psalm records how Ephraim forfeited leadership among the tribes and the torch passed to the house of David. The reference therefore in verses 9–11 may be general rather than specific: early Ephraimite leadership led to the spiritually and morally disastrous days of the Judges, etc, and proved its inadequacy.

7 A slightly insecure translation in detail: 'handlers of shooters of the bow'.

8 Behind their defeat (9) lay disobedience (10) and behind their disobedience lay forgetfulness (11). This is the deadly fault – to forget what God has done. This, in a nutshell, is Asaph's explanation of the enigma of history considered from the human point of view. Humanly speaking the defeat was unexpected: they had all the human resources for victory. The defect lay elsewhere than in armaments and skills.

9 A characteristic Old Testament emphasis: the LORD's 'wonders' were performed in history and before witnesses. They are not myth or hearsay but attested fact.

and waters flowed,

and streams came flooding out.[21]

Is he able also to give bread?

Or can he prepare flesh for the people?'

21. Therefore Yahweh heard and became furious,

and fire was kindled[22] against Jacob,

and also exasperation rose against Israel,

22. because they did not believe in God,

and did not trust his salvation.

23. And he had[23] commanded the skies above,

and the doors of the heavens he had opened,

24. and he had rained manna on them to eat,

and the corn of the heavens he had given to them.

25. The bread of the mighty ones[24] people[25] ate.

He sent provisions to them to the full.

26. He brought on an east wind in the heavens,

and led out by his might a south wind,

27. and rained flesh on them like dust,

and, like the sand of the seas, winged birds –

28. they fell into the middle of their[26] camp,

all round their dwellings.

29. And they ate and were very satisfied –

he kept bringing to them their desire.

30. While they were not dissociated[27] from their desire

– their food was still in their mouth! –

31. God's exasperation rose against them,

and he killed their fittest[28] ones,

and brought low the chosen[29] men of Israel.

32. In spite of all this they sinned more,[30]

and did not believe in[31] his wonderful works,

33. and he finished their days in pointlessness,[32]

and their years in terror.[33]

(4. Mercy)

34. If and when he killed them

they would seek him,

and used again turn early[34] to the transcendent God:

10 An ancient capital of Egypt, situated in the Delta, used here as a synonym for the whole land.

11 The reference is to Exodus 14. The incident at the Red Sea was the consummation of Yahweh's work of redemption: see Exodus 14:13, 30–31.

12 Exodus 15:8.

13 Exodus 13:21–22, compare Exodus 14:19–20.

14 Exodus 17.

15 Plural of amplitude, 'the depths'.

16 Or (plural) 'like the great river'.

17 See verse 8.

18 'Testing God out' is abandoning the way of simple trust (compare verse 22). It is requiring God to prove himself before putting trust in him (Matthew 27:42) even though there has already been ample evidence on which to base trust. 'Let's see if he can. Then we'll trust him.'

19 The noun (*'el*) is used seriously here (the utter folly of questioning the ability of such a God!) and ironically in verse 19. They would not have used *'el* because it would make their questioning an absurdity. But the psalmist puts the word into their mouths for the same reason. Unbelief is a nonsense.

20 Exodus 16; Numbers 11.

21 An excellent example of the contrast between Hebrew perfect and imperfect 'tenses'. The perfect of the immediate result ('flowed'), the imperfect of the ongoing abundance ('came flooding …')

22 Numbers 11:1–3.

23 Hebrew does not have a pluperfect tense as such. It is often (as here) a matter of interpretation what past tense best suits the context.

35. they remembered that God was their rock,
   and the transcendent God Most High their redeemer[35] –
36. they deceived him with their mouth,
   and were lying to him with their tongue,
37. and their heart was not fixed on him,
   nor were they reliable in his covenant.
38. And he, compassionate, used to atone[36] for iniquity,
   and used not act to destroy:
   many times he turned back his exasperation,
   and used not give full effect to[37] his rage –
39. he remembered that they were flesh,
   spirit going and not coming back.

A.2. The second survey of the acts of God (40–72)[38]

(Preface: The deadly sin of not remembering God's power)
40. How often they mutinied[39] against him in the wilderness,
   and vexed him in the waste-land:
41. they tested out the transcendent God again:
   and the Holy One of Israel they wounded[40] –
   they were not remembering his hand,[41]
   the day when he ransomed[42] them from the adversary –

(The acts of God: 1. Redemption completed)
43. he who set up in Egypt his signs,
   and his wonders[43] in the field of Zoan:[44]
44. he turned their watercourses[45] into blood,
   and they could not drink their streams;
45. he sent among them the swarm,[46]
   and they ate them;
   and frogs![47]
   And they destroyed them.
46. And he gave their produce to the cockroach,[48]
   and their toil to the locust swarm;[49]
47. He killed their vines with hail,[50]
   and their sycamores with frost;[51]
48. he consigned their livestock to the hail,[52]

24 *'abiyriym*, 'mighty, potent'. LXX interprets as 'angels' (cf., NKJV). In context the 'mighty' are heavenly beings.

25 Lit. 'a man' (*'ish*); the sense is 'ordinary folk'.

26 Strictly 'his camp' but if the reference is to 'Israel', then our idiom requires 'their'. It could of course, refer to Yahweh's camp, the place where his tent was pitched, in which case the plural 'dwellings' means Yahweh's 'great dwelling place'.

27 Lit. 'no strangers to'.

28 Lit. 'fattest', but 'fat' is used (not as 'obese' but) in the sense 'well-favoured, fit and strong'. Isaiah 10:16.

29 In the sense, those who would be picked out for fitness.

30 Following the previously mentioned sins, this reference to 'further' sin could point to the refusal to enter Canaan, and the years of frustration in the wilderness, Numbers 13–14.

31 Or 'in spite of'.

32 *hebhel*, 'vanity/vapour': first what is insubstantial, then what lacks reality or 'substance'; the futile, without meaning or sense; what 'does not add up'.

33 The desert years were lived under the conscious sense of the wrath of God, and with nothing to look forward to but death. Compare the same word (*behalah*), Leviticus 26:16.

34 *shachar*, related to the noun meaning 'dawn', therefore 'to seek early/diligently', Proverbs 7:15; 8:17.

35 *ga'al*; compare Psalm 19:14. Their next-of-kin.

36 See Psalm 65:3, note 21.

37 Lit. 'rouse up'.

and their cattle to the flames.[53]

49. He sent against them the hot anger of his exasperation,
    outburst and indignation, and adversity,
    a mission of messengers of evils.

50. He levelled a path for his exasperation.[54]
    He did not spare their soul from death,
    and consigned their life to the pestilence.

51. He struck all the firstborn in Egypt,
    the first element[55] of virility in the tents of Ham.

52. And he moved his people on like sheep,
    and led them like a flock in the wilderness.

53. And he conducted them in safety,
    and they were not afraid,
    and their enemies the sea covered.[56]

(2. Provision)[57]

54. And he brought them to the territory[58] of his holiness,
    the mountain[59] which his right hand acquired.

55. And he drove out nations from before them
    and he allocated them an inheritance by line.[60]

(3. Provocation and anger)

56. And they tested out, and mutinied against God, the Most High,
    and they did not keep his testimonies:[61]

57. they allowed themselves to backslide,
    and acted treacherously like their fathers;
    they turned themselves aside like a deceitful bow,

58. and they provoked him by their high places,
    and made him jealous by their graven images.

59. God heard and became furious,
    and he spurned Israel exceedingly,

60. and he abandoned the dwelling at Shiloh,[62]
    the tent which he set as a dwelling[63] among mankind.

61. And he gave over his strength[64] to captivity,
    and his beauty into the hand of the adversary,

62. and he consigned his people to the sword,

38 Compare verse 9 above. N.B. note 6.

39 It is important always to remember that though it is possible to analyse psalms, every psalm is a continuous whole. So here, from the point of view of analysis, we are setting out on a parallel review to that already covered in verses 9–39 (a preface followed by four matching aspects of the work of God). Yet see how verse 40 presupposes and moves on from what has gone before.

40 A verb only used here (*tawah*), but obviously a strong meaning. God is wounded/pained by our failure to trust.

41 The symbol of personal intervention in action. Compare our expression, 'Can you give me a hand?'

42 *padhah*. A companion verb to *ga'al* (verse 35). Where *ga'al* stresses the person (next-of-kinship) of the redeemer, *pahah* stresses the price paid. The two verbs have a considerable overlap of meaning in actual use, specially in their shared insistence on price-paying.

43 A 'wonder' excites interest and attention; a 'sign' points to a meaning beyond itself. The first plagues in Egypt were seen as 'wonders' and the Egyptian magicians replicated them (e.g. Exodus 7:11), but the time came when the 'sign' element was recognised (e.g. Exodus 8:18–19).

44 See verse 12.

45 The reference may be to the system of irrigation channels which carried Nile water over the cultivated land of Egypt, or it may be a plural of amplitude, 'the great Nile itself'.

46 *'arobh*, Exodus 8:20–30; Psalm 105:31. Only used of the plague of flies.

47 Exodus 8:1ff.

and with his inheritance he was furious.

63. [65] Fire devoured his chosen men,
and his young women were not celebrated. [66]

64. His priests fell by the sword, [67]
and his widows were not crying.

(4. Mercy)

65. And the Sovereign One woke up like a sleeper,
like a warrior stimulated by wine,

66. and he beat his foes back;
he gave them an everlasting reproach.

67. And he spurned the tent of Joseph
and the tribe of Ephraim he did not choose,

68. and he chose the tribe of Judah,
Mount Zion which he loved,

69. and as the heights he built [68] his sanctuary;
like the earth he founded it for ever.

70. And he chose David his servant,
and took him from the sheep-pens.

71. From after the ewes he brought him
to shepherd Jacob, his people,
and Israel, his inheritance,

72. and he shepherded them as with the integrity of his heart,
and with the full discernment of his hands he guided
them.

---

48 A possible meaning: 1 Kings 8:37; Isaiah 33:4; Joel 1:4; 2:25. Maybe a particular form of locust, or a stage in the development of a locust.

49 Exodus 10:1ff.

50 Exodus 9:13ff.

51 Unknown meaning. 'Frost' comes from LXX and is only a guess. Or 'devastating flood'.

52 Exodus 9:17–22, 25.

53 Exodus 9:24.

54 Verses 50–51 are devoted to the climactic, tenth plague (Exodus 11–12).

55 Compare Genesis 49:3; Deuteronomy 21:17; Psalm 105:36.

56 Like the corresponding section of the first survey (verse 13), the crossing of the Red Sea is the climax, the event which completed the redemption from Egypt.

57 This second review bypasses the wilderness experience (with its emphasis on the wonders of God in 'nature') to the single fact of conquest and inheritance, wonders in history. The verses are bracketed by the inclusion, his territory ... their inheritance.

58 *gebhul* means, first, a border or boundary, then the land enclosed within that boundary.

59 Joshua 6–9. The central hill-country of Canaan was the first to be conquered.

60 'By line' refers to the dividing up of the land under Joshua, compare Joshua 17:5 where 'portions' (NKJV) is the same word 'line'.

61 *'eduth*, from the verb 'to bear witness'. 'Testimonies' are what God has himself witnessed to as his nature, his truth and his ways.

62 e.g. 1 Samuel 1:3; Jeremiah 7:14.

63 A slightly developed translation. Lit. 'the tent which he made to dwell'. Shiloh was the religious centre during the Ephraimite supremacy. The psalm returns here to its starting point in verse 9, the defeat of Ephraim.

64 Referring to Yahweh's people (62). We are meant to be earthly evidence of the strength and beauty of the LORD. Alternatively, the reference to strength and beauty could refer to the capture of the ark (compare Psalm 132:8; 1 Samuel 4).

65 In verses 63–64 'his' could refer either to Yahweh or to Israel. In the latter case (compare NKJV) we should render it 'their'.

66 Understood as 'celebrated in (a marriage) song.'

67 1 Samuel 4:17.

68 While God's tabernacle dwelling can be called his 'house' (1 Samuel 1:7), the verb 'to build' is only used of stone structures. This would date the psalm during the reign of Solomon. This is further indicated by the fact that the psalm indicates a Judahite/Davidic leadership of the people parallel to the earlier Ephraimite leadership. It would not have been possible to leave it at that after the schism of the northern tribes (1 Kings 12).

Pause for Thought

The 'open question' and the 'not-open question'. In Psalm 78 Asaph offered an answer to the riddle of history: what is its fundamental principle and explanation? Why are things as they are, and what next? In the event he indicated a double answer, depending on which point of view we take: looking at history with a human eye or looking at it as God sees it. God's point of view can be summed up in one word: perseverance. He never gives up. At Passover (vv. 12, 43) he put his hand to the plough of our redemption and he refused to turn back. There is a rhythm to history: when redemption is followed by disobedience, this incurs wrath, but wrath does not have the last word. Our misery (even when it is caused by his righteous anger) brings misery in heaven (Judges 2:18b), and compassion prompts mercy. But recall that the second sequence of the same four elements was deliberately linked with the first sequence (40). In other words, the sequence of the four was an ongoing rhythm: it is how things are. For our comfort and reassurance, then, we may take it for granted: God never gives up. He has determined on our salvation with eternal security and he will see to it, amid all the fluctuations and riddles of daily experience. He is the 'faithful God' of 1 Corinthians 1:7–9. We await the revelation of our Lord Jesus Christ and he will confirm us to the end so that we are blameless in that day. Yes, we can take comfort, but we must not lapse into complacency, for, as Asaph saw history from the human viewpoint, the key factors were a sharply focused mind and a keenly retentive memory as the prerequisites to an obedient life. It is there right at the start of our long psalm (9–11): they did not keep his covenant, they forgot his works and thus they refused to walk in his law – and thereby hung the whole tale of their woe.

Day 37   Read Psalms 79–80

Psalm 79.
Plight and Promise[1]

A Song belonging to Asaph.

1. Plight. Loss and shame

('They': Havoc)

1. O God,

    the nations have come into your inheritance;

    they have defiled the temple of your holiness.

    They have made Jerusalem into heaps of ruins.

2. They have given the corpses of your servants

    as food for the birds of the heavens,

    the flesh of your beloved ones to the beasts of the earth.

3. They have poured out their blood like water,

    around Jerusalem,

    and there is no one burying them.

('We': Mockery)

4. We have become a reproach to our neighbours,

    mockery and derision to those around us.

2. Plea. Sin and atonement

('They': Delayed reward)

5. How long, Yahweh,

    will you be exasperated in perpetuity,

    will your jealousy[2] burn like fire?

6. Pour out your rage on the nations

    who did[3] not know you,

    and on the kingdoms

1 The structure of this psalm is dictated by the way *they*-sections, addressed to the destroying nations (1–3, 5–7, 10–12) alternate with *we*-sections, referring to Yahweh's defeated people (4, 8–9, 13).

2 'Jealousy' is part of the divine nature. Compare Exodus 34:14. 'Jealousy' can, of course, be an unattractive and even evil thing, but, in its essence, it is inseparable from true love. Yahweh's pure jealousy is roused when his people defect to other gods or to sin.

3 The reference is back to a specific act: the savage destruction of city and temple (2 Kings 24–25). The implication is that, had they known and called, they could not have behaved as they did. Their doom is sought not because they did not know Yahweh but because of what they did to his place and people. The plea here is not that penalty be deflected from 'us' to the nations, but for even-handed justice: Israel admits its own sin (9) but recognizes another area of just and justifiable divine wrath.

4 This is the biblical view of moral inheritance. No generation is punished for sins committed by someone else, but each generation stands before God in a position of mounting guiltiness. The past cannot be appealed to as an excuse. The generation inheriting guilt is not thereby less guilty but more guilty. Matthew 23:29–36. Because of this inevitability of moral inheritance (the price of being human) the sins are not just those of forefathers but ours also.

5 The passionate, emotional love of God. See Psalm 40:11 (note 16); 51:1 (note 3).

which have not called on your name –

7. because they devoured Jacob,
   and his homestead they have devastated.

('We': Atonement sought)

8. Do not remember against us iniquities of former times;[4]
   may your compassion[5] speedily anticipate our need
   because we are very low.

9. Help us, O God of our salvation,
   because of[6] the glory of your name,
   and deliver us,
   and make atonement[7] for our sins,
   for your name's sake.

3. Promise. Recompense and response

('They': Sevenfold retribution)

10. Why should the nations say:
    'Where is their God?'
    Let there be known among the nations before our eyes
    the avenging of the blood of your servants
    which has been shed.

11. Let the groaning of the prisoner come before you;
    according to the greatness of your arm
    leave a remnant of the sons of[8] dying.

12. And bring back to our neighbours,
    sevenfold[9] into their bosom,
    their reproach with which they reproached you,[10]
    O Sovereign One.

('We': Praise)

13. And as for us,
    your people and the sheep of your pasture,[11]
    we will give you thanks;
    for ever, generation after generation,
    we will recount your praises.

6 'Because of' could be translated 'for the sake of', synonymous with 'for the sake' (9). The translation 'because of' offers a distinct meaning: 'because of what you have revealed yourself to be', whereas 'for the sake of' means in order to uphold the truth of what you have revealed in your name. There is a great emphasis here on the fact that forgiveness can only be sought on the ground of what God is.

7 *kaphar*, see Psalms 49:7; 65:3. Note that there can be no deliverance without atonement.

8 'Sons of' as idiomatic expression describing the condition of those described. Here, those sentenced/doomed to death.

9 'Seven' in its metaphorical sense of 'complete'. 'Into their bosom': the application of wrath exactly where it is deserved.

10 Throughout the psalm the offence to Yahweh has been an emphasis. Not just our plight but your name.

11 Under a wrath of God that seems endless (5), there is still certainty of an unchanged status before him.

Psalm 80.
The Lost Smile[12]

Belonging to the worship-leader; set to 'Lilies'; a testimony; Asaph's; a song.

The endangered flock

1. O Shepherd of Israel,
    open your ear,
    leading Joseph like a flock,[13]
    sitting enthroned above the cherubim,
    shine out!
2. In front of[14] Ephraim, and Benjamin, and Manasseh
    rouse up your prowess,[15]
    and come for our salvation.
3. O God,
    bring us back;[16]
    and light up your face,[17]
    and we will be saved.
4. Yahweh,
    God who is Hosts,[18]
    how long do you intend to fume against the prayers of
    your people?
5. You have made them eat the bread of tears;
    and you have made them drink tears by the pint![19]
6. You make us a matter of contention to our neighbours,
    and our enemies keep mocking us.
7. O God who is Hosts,
    bring us back,
    and light up your face,
    and we will be saved.

Past and present in tension

8. You bring[20] a vine out of Egypt;
    you drive out nations –
    and you planted it.

12 The heart of Psalm 80 is that divine favour has been forfeited, resulting in a double picture of loss: the endangered flock (1–7) and the shattered vine (8–19). Nothing can be remedied except by a restoration of favour, hence the threefold refrain (3, 7, 19). The three tribes mentioned in verse 2 are the ancient 'camp of Ephraim' in the marching order of Yahweh's desert people (Numbers 2:18–24). For this reason we may assume that the psalm is concerned with the tragedy in the north, most likely the fall of Samaria and the end of the northern, Ephraimitish, kingdom in captivity (2 Kings 17), and since the psalm lacks any recognition of sin as the reason for forfeiting divine favour, we may assume it reflects the thoughts of some faithful remnant in the north, bewildered that they have been caught up in such a tragedy. Seen in this light, Psalm 80 matches the parallel Judahite (southern kingdom) focus of Psalm 79.

13 Circumstances do not alter truth. God is still the shepherd of his people even when alienated from them. Compare the stress in Psalm 77 on the persevering God.

14 Numbers 10:33. The request is for a renewal of the halcyon days in the wilderness when the LORD went before his people.

15 The word is specifically heroic or warrior prowess.

16 The psalm makes it clear that they want to come back, but a return is not a mere matter of choice; it is a matter of divine sovereign determination. The key factor, so to say, is a change in God's mind.

17 As the only needful thing: a restoration to divine favour.

9. You cleared a space[21] for it,
    and it put down roots,
    and filled the land.
10. The mountains were covered with its shadow,
    and with its branches the cedars of the transcendent God.[22]
11. It sends out its boughs to the sea,
    and to the River[23] its tendrils.
12. Why[24] have you broken through its fences,[25]
    and all who pass by on the road pluck it?
13. A boar out of the forest tears at it,
    and what moves in the field pastures on it.

The future. Plea and pledge

14. God who is Hosts,
    please come back.
    Look from the heavens and see,
    and attend to this vine,
15. and the root-stock which your right hand planted,
    and to the son[26] you made strong for yourself.
16. Burned with fire, cut down!
    By the rebuke of your face they have perished.
17. Let your hand be on the man[27] of your right hand,[28]
    on the son of man[29] you made strong for yourself.
18. And we will not backslide from you.[30]
    Give us life and we will call on your name.
19. Yahweh,
    God who is Hosts,
    bring us back;
    light up your face,
    and we will be saved

18 'God' and 'Hosts' are nouns in apposition. The translation 'God of Hosts' is erroneous and impossible here. But, very likely, this plain case of apposition is also a clue how we are to understand the frequent 'Yahweh of hosts', i.e. 'Yahweh is Hosts', containing within himself a 'host' of powers. Not a bare unit but a multiplex unit.

19 Lit. a 'third', a measure of a now forgotten amount; compare Isaiah 40:12. The implication is 'tears by the bucketful'.

20 The present tenses from here to the end of the psalm reflect Hebrew Imperfects by which the author imparts vividness to his narrative, as if he were actually watching events unfold.

21 This is the meaning rather than a translation of a somewhat unusual use of *panah*, 'to turn'.

22 This may be an adjectival use of *'el*, in the sense of 'very great'. Compare Genesis 10:9; Jonah 3:3. On the other hand, Psalm 104:16: Lebanon was the work of God, not man.

23 Sea and River, Mediterranean and Euphrates, express expansion in all directions.

24 The question 'why?' (*lammah*) asks after the purpose of what has happened. The other way of asking 'why?' (*maddu'a*, e.g. 2 Samuel 3:7, not used in Psalms) asks on what ground something has happened or been done.

25 Isaiah 5:5.

26 'Son' is used of vine shoot, Genesis 49:22 (where 'bough' [NKJV] is 'son'): this is in the Joseph-section of Jacob's blessing. Used here both in the metaphorical sense, and to prepare for the Benjamin reference of verse 17.

27 *'ish*, referring to an expected individual.

28 In Genesis 35:16–18 Rachel, as she died in childbirth, called her newborn 'son of my sorrow' (*benoni*), but his father, Jacob, welcomed the child of the beloved Rachel by changing his name to Benjamin, son of the right hand. The psalm is confident that Yahweh somehow has a 'son of his right hand' who will put everything to rights. The reference must be messianic.

29 *'adham*, the expected one in his humanity, 'son of Adam'.

30 Expectation includes transformation (verse 18a, a new constancy) and reconciliation (18b), restoration to oneness with Yahweh.

Pause for Thought

Together Psalms 79 and 80 paint a picture of the whole people of God – Israel to the north, Psalm 80, Judah to the south, Psalm 79, in deep trouble. Each section crying out 'How long?' (79:5; 80:4) in their protracted trials. Behind the psalms we can see and feel the trauma and agonizing loss when first Samaria and then Jerusalem fall to the enemy. But they are also complementary in another way. Psalm 79 emphasises that Yahweh's people, under the rod of his wrath, are still his people. In the first two verses the possessive 'your' comes four times: no matter what, it is still 'your inheritance', 'your temple', 'your servants', and, most wonderful of all, 'your beloved'. And at the end of the psalm (79:13), 'your people', 'the sheep of your pasture'. The matching truth in Psalm 80 is that even when our sins alienate him Yahweh does not change: he is still (80:1) 'the Shepherd', still the Sovereign enthroned over the Mercy Seat (Exod. 25:17–22). In a word, our status has not changed, nor has his saving mercy. Press the complementary theme further: in Psalm 79 we learn that we can plead our miseries before him (8, 11). He is still just as he was in Exodus 3:7, feeling our sorrows, and in Judges 2:18, moved to pity and action by our groaning. Psalm 80 matches this by pointing to Yahweh: he is 'Hosts' (4, 7, 14, 19). Whatever we may at any time need, it is there in the plenitude of the divine nature and powers. And he always has his 'secret weapon' – the Man at his right hand (80:17) by whom we can be restored and renewed.

And He is at the Father's side,
The Man of love, the Crucified.

Day 38   Read Psalms 81–83

Psalm 81.
The sad 'might have been'

Belonging to the worship-leader; set to Gittith;[1] Asaph's.

1. Dominion and enactment: The listening God

(Festal joy)

1. Cry out aloud to God, our strength;[2]
    shout to the God of Jacob.[3]

2. Raise a song,
    and sound the tambourine,
    the pleasing lyre and the harp.

3. Blow the trumpet at the new moon,
    at the full moon,[4]
    on the day of our festival.

(Obligation)

4. Because that is a statute[5] for Israel,
    a judgment of the God of Jacob,

5. a testimony he placed in Joseph,[6]
    when he went out over the land of Egypt.[7]
    'A language I had not known I kept hearing.'[8]

2. Response and enrichment: The promising God

(Yahweh's acts)[9]

6. I took his shoulder away from the burden;
    his hands moved on from the basket.

7. In adversity you called and I set you free;
    I went on answering you in the hiding place of thunder;
    I was testing you at the waters of Meribah.[10] *(Selah)*

1   See Psalm 8, heading.

2   A suitable ascription since the psalm is going to look back to Yahweh's domination of Egypt (5). His strength displayed on his people's behalf.

3   A swelling tide of acclamation – the congregation (1), choir (2a), orchestra (2b), trumpeters (3). Old Testament religion was nothing if not exuberant!

4   'New moon' ... 'full moon'. There is much discussion what festival the psalm refers to, the major choice lying between Passover (Exodus 12) or Tabernacles (Leviticus 23:39ff.). Since the psalm calls for celebration on two separate times of the month it is more probable that it is a celebratory meditation on the keeping of the Exodus-based festivals as such. What it records and implies is true of all.

5   'Statute' (*choq*) from *chaqaq*, 'to engrave', hence a fixed requirement, engraved in the rock: 'judgment', and authoritative pronouncement; settling an issue, something Yahweh has decided and promulgated; 'testimony', what Yahweh has 'witnessed to' as truth, as a rule to be followed, as a revelation of himself. The words stress respectively, therefore, perpetuity, authority and revelation.

6   In Egypt the Hebrews were Joseph's family (Genesis 45:16), hence the name here.

7   The very words of Genesis 41:45, describing Joseph actually taking the command over Egypt which Pharaoh had given him. Here used of Yahweh's domination of Egypt at the Exodus.

(Yahweh's requirement)

8.   Hear, my people,
     and I will testify to you,
     Israel, if you will hear[11] me,

9.   there shall not be an alien god among you,
     and you are not to bow in worship to a foreign god.

10.   I am Yahweh, your God,
     who brought you up from the land of Egypt.

(Yahweh's promise)

     Open your mouth wide and I will fill it.[12]

3. Refusal and deprivation: The frustrated God

(Abandoned)

11.   And my people would not hear my voice,
     and it was Israel that did not want me.

12.   And I sent them away to the stubbornness of their heart,[13]
     that they should walk in their own counsels.

(Forfeiture)

13.   Oh that my people were hearing me,
     that Israel were walking in my ways!

14.   Very easily[14] I would bring their enemies down,
     and against their adversaries I would turn my hand.

15.   Those who hate Yahweh would cringe before him,
     and their time[15] would be for ever.

16.   And he would feed them with the cream of wheat.
     And from the rock, with honey, I would satisfy you.[16]

8   Or 'I did not know … I kept hearing'. 'Language', lit. 'lip' (e.g. Genesis 11:1, 6, 7; Isaiah 28:11). All through the psalm the first person singular is Yahweh, but why should he say this and what would it mean? It has been suggested that it is a reference to the change from groaning to the cry for help noted in Exodus 2:23 (see ESV) – but why should this be a unknown 'language'. Possibly, then, we should represent 'lip' by 'a form of speech'. Whatever we do, the verse remains an enigma. Some attribute the words to Israel – but even then what do they mean?

9   Verses 6–10 track the course of Israel from Egyptian bondage (6) to the cry for help and Yahweh's response from the Cloud at the Red Sea (verse 7ab; Exodus 14:10, 19) to a typical wilderness event (verse 7c; Exodus17:1–7) and so to Yahweh speaking at Sinai (8–10a; Exodus 20:1), the fundamental requirement (to hear God's Word, verse 8), the basic law (9), and its foundation in Yahweh's redeeming acts (10a).

10 Meribah gave the name to two 'testings'; Exodus 17:2; Numbers 20:13. At the start and again at the end of their pilgrimage Israel was subjected to a test of faith, and failed each time.

11 Here and in verses 11 and 13 a more accurate translation would be 'listen to' but I felt it right to preserve in English the importance to the psalm of the idea of 'hearing'. The hall-mark of the Lord's people is hearing God's Word.

12 In the structure of the psalm this corresponds to the Yahweh-statement at the end of verse 5. Within the covenant obedience brings blessing.

13 This use of 'to send' is exemplified in Job 8:4. The Lord's punishment is to confirm upon the sinner what he has chosen for himself.

Psalm 82.
Praying for a World Led Astray[17]

A Song belonging to Asaph.

A1 (v.1). The Divine Judge opens the Court

1. God himself has taken his position,[18]
    in the congregation of the transcendent God;
    in the midst of the gods[19] he acts as Judge.

B. The case is heard

(The charge read out)

2. How long will you go on judging deviantly,
    and go on lifting up the faces of the wicked?[20]

(The case for the prosecution: duties; the ideal)

3. Judge[21] the poor and the orphan;
    defend the rights of the downtrodden and those in want;
4. Rescue the poor and the vulnerable;
    Deliver them from the hand of the wicked.

(The witnesses)[22]

5. They do not know and they do not discern;
    they walk around in darkness;
    all the foundations of the earth are tottering.

C. The sentencing

6. For my part, I said,[23] you are gods,
    and all of you the sons of the Most High,
7. but yet like human[24] you will die,
    and like any one of the princes you will fall.

D. A prayer for a tottering world

8. Rise up, O God;
    judge[25] the earth;
    because[26] you are the one who will inherit all the nations.

14 Lit. 'just a little'.

15 For this use of time, compare our expression 'having a bad time'; the sort of experiences that are due to them, their destiny.

16 A third Yahweh-statement, matching verses 5c and 10c.

17 Apart from the fact that it is a court-scene, Psalm 82 gives us little indication how we are to fit the internal divisions together. The following is one attempt to do so.

18 Compare Isaiah 3:13 (NKJV 'stands up'): uses this verb of Yahweh as Judge opening proceedings.

19 In John 10:34–36 Jesus settled the question how we are to understand 'gods' in Psalm 82, namely that it is used of those to whom the Word of God came, in this case, the appointed judges of Israel. Compare verses 2–4 with Exodus 22:22–24; 23:6–9; Deuteronomy 1:16–17; 10:17–19; 16:18–20; 27:19; Isaiah 10:1–3; Jeremiah 22:1–9. Human judges were to execute 'the LORD's judgment' (Deuteronomy 1:17). To bring a case 'before God' and 'before the priests/ judges' are interchangeable (Exodus 21:6; 22:8–9; Deuteronomy 17:8–13). In the light of all this the psalm's application of 'god' to judges is fully understandable. The 'congregation' here is either the people of Israel in solemn assembly, or the judges assembled for their trial.

20 The double accusation of deviating from the legal norm, and malpractice in sentencing.

21 i.e. 'set things to rights for'.

22 This seems to be the best way to understand verse 5. A threefold charge: (a) lack of moral discernment; (b) the distressed left unremedied; (c) the fundamental insecurity of society.

Psalm 83.
Lessons from History

A hymn; a song belonging to Asaph.

A.1. Conspiracy: countered by prayer

(Your enemies)

1.   O God,

    do not keep still,

    and do not remain silent,

    and do not be inactive,[27]

    O transcendent God.

2.   Because – behold! –

    your enemies[28] are making uproar,

    and those who hate you have raised their head.

(Your people)

3.   Against your people they act shrewdly in concert,

    and take common counsel against your hidden ones.[29]

4.   They have said:[30]

    'Come, let us efface them from being a nation,'

    and 'Let the name of Israel not be remembered ever again.'

B.1. Conspirators all around: against Yahweh

5.   Because, with united heart, they take council together;

    against you they are inaugurating a covenant –

6.[31] the tents of Edom, and the Ishmaelites,[32]

    Moab, and the Hagarites,

7.   Gebal,[33] and Ammon, and Amalek,

    Philistia with the inhabitants of Tyre.[34]

8.   Assyria, too, has joined with them;

    they have been an arm[35] for the children of Lot.[36]

23 See David's 'I have said', 2 Samuel 19:29. The formula for pronouncing a royal decision.

24 Or 'like Adam', in consequence of his rebellion.

25 See verse 3, 'put everything to rights'.

26 A prayer that God will do now what will be in fact ultimately his position. 'You will have all the nations as your inheritance.' An Old Testament plea equivalent to 'Come, Lord Jesus' (Revelation 22:20).

27 The thought of these three lines could be considered largely synonymous, but more probably we see, in turn, (negatively stated) a plea for alertness, speech and action.

28 The enemies of God's people are his enemies – so throughout this psalm. It is this truth that gives the psalm its pervasive air of confidence in the face of threat.

29 See Psalm 27:5; 31:20. Keep the thought of hidden treasure in mind.

30 See Psalm 82:6, 'said', as an official decision. Also verse 12 below.

31 On verses 6–8, see 2 Chronicles 20. Some of the names occurring in Psalm 83 are said to have been involved in the confederation of nations in 2 Chronicles – enough to make that incident a suitable background to the Psalm (note 2 Chronicles 22:11; and in verse 2 Chronicles 20:14 an Asaphite Levite was involved), and, if not background, a suitable illustration of the situation.

32 Ishmael was the son of Hagar (Genesis 16). The Hagarites were located in east Gilead (1 Chronicles 5:10, 18–22), and may or may not have a link with Hagar. Ishmaelites appear in Genesis 37:25–28, 36 as travelling traders, linked with Midianites.

B.2. Conspirators past: an identical threat

9. Do with them like Midian,[37]
  like Sisera,
  like Jabin at the River Kishon;
10. they were destroyed at En Dor;[38]
  they became dung on the ground.
11. Make their leaders like Oreb and like Zeeb,[39]
  and like Zebah and like Zalmunna[40]
  all their grandees:[41]
12. who said,
  'Let us take possession for ourselves the pastures of God.'

A.2. Conspiracy countered by prayer

(Your storm)
13. O my God,
  make them like thistledown,
  like chaff before the wind,
14. like fire burns a forest,
  and like flame sets mountains ablaze.
15. So may you pursue them with your tempest,
  and with your whirlwind terrify them.

(Your name)
16. Fill their faces with ignominy,
  and may they seek your name,
  Yahweh.
17. May they reap shame and be terrified for evermore,
  and be abashed and perish,
18. that they may know that you –
  your name is Yahweh – you alone –
  are the Most High over all the earth.

33 A mountainous region in Transjordan, Joshua 13:5.

34 The names in verses 6–7a are to the east, in verse 7b to the west and north, in verse 8 to the north. The picture is of a nation surrounded by foes.

35 The symbol of effective strength. Here equivalent to our colloquialism 'to lend a hand'.

36 Moab and Ammon (Genesis 19: 30–38; Deuteronomy 2:9, 19).

37 Numbers 31, but the reference in verse 9b to Sisera, Jabin and Kishon (Judges 4–5) makes Gideon's defeat of the Midianites (Judges 6ff.) more likely.

38 Below Mount Tabor where Barak won his victory.

39 Judges 7:24–25.

40 Judges 8:4–21.

41 Depending on its derivation, *nasik* means either someone consecrated to an office, like a prince, or installed in an office.

Pause for Thought

According to today's psalms there are three distinct things that threaten personal, social and national stability. Psalm 83 calls attention to international unrest, threatening Israel's life and continuance. Psalm 82 swings the spotlight internally: the insidious threat of the corruption of a sound legal system, the skewing of due process of law to make it serve some in individual or powerful 'interest' and, in particular, the failure of the 'system' to protect the vulnerable and serve the needs of those in want. The notable sense of solemnity in Psalm 82 and the seriousness of the application of historical lessons drawn in Psalm 83 call on us to bring a like sense of urgency to the obviously parallel situations in which we find ourselves today – and to learn the psalmist's lesson of how to respond to these circumstances: namely the exercise of assured prayer (82:8; 83:13–18). The answer does not lie in militarism or alliances; it will not be found in politics or legislation; only God can deal with it, and prayer should be our first, last and on-going remedy. The spotlight points in yet a different direction again in Psalm 81. By his work of redemption (81:6–7) the LORD established dominion over his redeemed (Rom. 14:9), and his authoritative command to them (do you recall?) was 'hear … hear … hear … hear!' The greatest threat to the redeemed is if they fail to listen to the Word of God, and their primary obligation to their Redeemer-God is to hear his holy Word. In their early, wilderness days they had the patriarchal traditions and the living voice of Moses; in our case we have the completed Bible. Amos charged the nations (1:3–2:3) with sins against humanity, against the voice of conscience; but when it came to Judah the cardinal sin was failure to hear the law of the LORD (Amos 2:4).

A carefully balanced statement of restoration: verse 1, the need to be dealt with, restoration; verse 2, its direct cause dealt with, iniquity and sin; verse 3, the ultimate problem solved, divine anger.

Day 39   Read Psalms 84–86

Psalm 84.
Pervasive Blessedness

Belonging to the worship-leader; set to Gittith;[1] belonging to the sons of Korah; a song.

A. The blessedness of the pilgrim's goal

(Fulfilment)

1. How beloved your supreme[2] dwelling place,
    Yahweh of Hosts!
2. My soul[3] has yearned – even reached its end –
    for Yahweh's courts.
    My heart and my flesh are crying out aloud
    to the living, transcendent God.[4]

(Safety)

3. The sparrow, too, has found a house,
    and the swallow a nest for herself
    where she has put her chicks[5] –
    your great[6] altar,
    Yahweh of Hosts, my king and my God.

(Praise)

4. Blessed[7] are they who live in[8] your house.
    Continually they will praise you. (*Selah*)

B. The blessedness of the pilgrim's journey

(On the way)

5. Blessed[9] is the human[10] who finds his strength in you –
    highways are in his heart![11]

1   See Psalm 8, heading.

2   'dwelling place' is plural of amplitude, hence 'supreme'.

3   The psalmist's whole being is caught up in longing to reach Yahweh's courts: the 'soul' is the person at the very centre of his essential being; 'heart' and 'flesh', the inner and outer – the total realities of the person. No part is free of the consuming longing for the fulfilment of personality that only Yahweh's house can bring.

4   The longing can be expressed as for the house but the house is desired only for the Occupant's sake. So, throughout the psalm: the goal of the journey is 'God in Zion' (7); it is not door keeping that is such a delight (10) but Yahweh in grace (11).

5   A daring and telling image. Such is the safety to be found in Yahweh's altar that birds would dare to nest there and expose their young to the undying flame!

6   Another plural of amplitude – 'Your wonderful altar'.

7   *'ashrey*, see Psalm 1:1. All three meanings of the word would suit here! 'Happy' well suits the tone of the whole psalm.

8   Of course, 'living in' Yahweh's house was impossible. But we too use 'live in' of a person constantly found somewhere.

9   'Blessedness' is not only the end result (4) but also the experience on the journey.

10 *'adham* used generically: 'blessed is whoever ...'

6. Going through the valley of balsam[12]
   they keep making it a spring![13]
   Indeed, the early rain[14] wraps it in blessings![15]
7. They keep going from strength to strength.[16]
   Each[17] appears to God[18] in Zion.

(At the End)[19]
8. Yahweh,
   God who is Hosts,
   Hear my prayer.
   Turn your ear, God of Jacob. (*Selah*)
9. See our shield,[20] O God;
   look at the face of your anointed one.

C. The blessedness of the pilgrim's God

(His house)
10.[21] Because better a day in your courts than a thousand!
    I choose door-keeping[22] in the house of my God
    rather than dwelling in the tents of wickedness.

(His grace)
11. Because Yahweh, God, is sun and shield.
    Grace and glory Yahweh will give.
    He will not withhold good to those who walk with
    integrity.

(His blessing)
12. Yahweh of Hosts,
    blessed is whoever is trusting in you.

11 A unique – but wonderfully vivid – expression.

12 'Balsam' (or 'mulberry', 2 Samuel 5:23, NKJV) is said to grow in arid places. It is not known if there was an actual place, 'the Valley of Balsam'. In any case it is used here in illustration of a particular aspect of the pilgrim way. Also *bak'a* may be intended as a pun on *bakah*, 'weeping'.

13 The pilgrim faces every hazard with an habitual eye of faith. The sense is 'treats it as a spring', faces every hazard in the assurance of supply.

14 Usually *yoreh*, but here (compare Joel 2:23) *moreh*. This, too, may be a pun because *moreh* means 'teacher': compare Isaiah 30:20 (where it translates 'your great Teacher'). Combining the two senses, 'God's early rain'.

15 Minimal vowel changes would give the meaning 'pools' – 'early rain envelopes it with the pools'. Many follow this. But it is more stylish to think of another pun: 'blessed pools'.

16 i.e. when difficulties are met in a spirit of faith, strength for the pilgrimage follows.

17 'Appears' is an individualizing singular verb.

18 e.g. Exodus 23:17, appearing before God was a technical term for keeping the pilgrim feasts. Here 'appearing to God' is a 'pregnant' construction, meaning 'appear before God when one attains to God in Zion'.

19 Verses 8–9 allow us to see the pilgrim enjoying the presence of God, as indicated in verse 7: (a) he is in the presence of Yahweh himself in all his fullness; (b) he is engaged in the fellowship of prayer; (c) his typical prayer is for the Davidic king whose continuance guarantees the endurance of the House.

Psalm 85.
Times Change; God Unchanged

Belonging to the worship-leader; belonging to the sons of Korah; a Song.

A. The past: favour granted, anger withdrawn[23]

1. You accepted your land[24] with favour, Yahweh;
   you restored the captivity[25] of Jacob;

2. you bore away[26] the iniquity of your people;
   you covered[27] all their sin;

3. you gathered away all your outbursting anger;
   you turned back from the rage of your exasperation.

B. The present: history repeats itself; will forgiveness?[28]

4. Return[29] us, God of our salvation,
   and annul your indignation with us.

5. For ever will you be exasperated with us,
   will you prolong your exasperation to generation after generation?

6. Will you not, yourself, give us life again? –
   and your people will rejoice in you.

7. Yahweh, make us see your committed love,
   and oh give us your salvation!

C. The future: Yahweh is on his way[30]

(The word of the Lord)

8. Let me hear what the transcendent God, Yahweh, will speak,
   because he will speak peace to his people and to his beloved –
   and let them not turn back to flippancy.

9. Yes indeed, his salvation is near for those who fear him,
   so that glory may dwell in our land.

20 See Psalm 89:18.

21 Verse 10 explains verse 9, and verse 11 explains verse 10. The prayer for the king is explained by the fact that the house is so precious. The house is precious because Yahweh is sun (the giver – what he is towards his people); shield (the protector – what he is for his people); grace (the covenant Redeemer – what he is in relation to his people); and glory (the eternal home – what he holds before his people). Nowhere else is Yahweh called 'sun'. Verse 10 implies the abandonment of wickedness; verse 11, the development of character; and verse 12 the on-going attitude of trust.

22 The 'sons of Korah' (see heading) were gate-keepers, 1 Chronicles 26:1–19.

23 A carefully balanced statement of restoration: verse 1, the need to be dealt with, restoration; verse 2, its direct cause dealt with, iniquity and sin; verse 3, the ultimate problem solved, divine anger.

24 The reference to the land is explained in verses 9, 12: the restoration of fertility. Divine anger manifested in crop failure. Compare Genesis 3:17–19; creation reflects whatever relationship exists between God and man. The return of God's goodwill involved the return of harvests.

25 This is the most direct translation of the words *shub shebhuth*, which occur many times in the Bible (e.g, Psalm 126:4). Often translated 'restored the fortunes'.

26 The idea of bearing sin away, as a metaphor for forgiving, is rooted in Leviticus 16:21–22.

(Even so, come!)

10. Committed love and truth[31] will surely[32] meet together;
    righteousness and peace are bound to kiss each other.
11. Out of the earth truth will sprout,
    and from the heavens righteousness will certainly look down.
12. Yahweh also will give the good,
    and our land will give its produce.[33]
13. Righteousness will go ahead of him[34] –
    and oh may he set his steps on the road![35]

Psalm 86.
Sovereignty in Perfection[36]

A prayer belonging to David.

A. 'To you, O Sovereign One': he hears prayer[37]

1. Turn your ear, Yahweh.
   Answer me.
   Because I am downtrodden and vulnerable.
2. Keep my soul,
   because I am beloved.
   Save your servant – you are my God[38] –
   who is trusting in you!
3. Grant me grace,
   because to you I keep crying out all the day.
4. Gladden the soul of your servant,
   because to you, O Sovereign One, I lift up my soul.
5. Because you, O Sovereign One, are good and all-forgiving,[39]
   and abundant in committed love to all calling out to you.
6. Open your ear, Yahweh, to my prayer,
   and pay attention to the voice of my plea for grace.

27 The verb here is *kasah*, 'to cover over'. The full idea of 'covering' is more frequently expressed by *kaphar*, which includes the fundamental idea of paying the price which covers the debt, see Psalm 49:7.

28 Will the experience of the past be replicated? Once more there is need of restoration (4), withdrawal of anger (5), life and joy (6); all that 'salvation' means (7).

29 The verb 'return' would be classed in English as intransitive – incapable of governing a direct object – and so it is usually in Hebrew. But the distinction transitive/intransitive does not apply in Hebrew as in English, and this is an example (like the same verb in verse 1) of 'return' with a direct object. In verse 1 the verb 'to favour', which usually governs an indirect object in Hebrew, takes a direct object.

30 A prophetic interjection along the lines of 2 Chronicles 20:14. We do not know what situation lay behind Psalm 85, but it is easy to assume a national gathering in a time of duress, when divine favour has been withdrawn, and is being sought. Now a prophet speaks a word of reassurance in the name of Yahweh, coupled immediately with a counsel of seriousness, and the avoidance of 'foolishness' in the form of superficiality. Salvation is near and Yahweh's glory will return to them (9). Following this introduction, the actual 'oracle', the full word of God, follows in verses 10–13.

31 Love and truth, righteousness and peace, are Yahweh's, the divine nature satisfied regarding his people. The harmony of the divine attributes in the work of salvation.

B. 'None like you, O Sovereign One': He is the only God[40]

7. In the day of my adversity I keep calling out to you,
    because you will answer me.
8. There is none like you among the gods,[41]
    O Sovereign One,
    and there is nothing like your works.
9. All the nations which you made will come,
    and they will bow in worship before you,
    O Sovereign One,
    And they will give glory to your name,
10. because you are great,
    and doing wonderful things.
    You are God, you alone.
11. Teach me, Yahweh, your way;
    I will walk intently in your truth;
    Unify my heart[42] to fear your name.
12. I will thank you,
    O Sovereign One, my God
    with all my heart,
    and glorify your name for ever,
13. because your committed love is great for me,
    and you will deliver my soul from the lowest Sheol.

C. 'But you, O Sovereign One': he is sufficient

14. O God,
    conceited[43] people have risen against me,
    and a crowd of terrrifying people have sought my soul,
    and they have not put you in front of them.
15. And you, O Sovereign One, are a transcendent God,
    of compassion and grace,[44]
    long-deferring exasperation,
    and abundant in committed love and truth.

32 The verbs 'have met ... have kissed ... has looked down' are treated as 'prophetic perfects' – future actions so sure that they can be described as having happened.

33 With the restoration of right relations with Yahweh, creation returns to its proper fertility.

34 Like a herald before a king. According to verse 9b, the objective is the return of Yahweh in all his glory; verse 13 therefore looks forward to his coming. Righteousness as a gift from God (compare Isaiah 54:17), and responsive righteousness of life.

35 An excited plea that this advent of righteousness, heralding the advent of Yahweh, may begin at once!

36 In Psalm 86 'the Sovereign One' is mentioned seven times (verses 3, 4, 5, 8, 9, 12, 15), suggesting this title. Another feature of the psalm is the number of explanations it gives, using 'because', nine in total (verses 1, 2, 3, 4, 5, 7, 10, 13, 17). Every one of these is worth studying. Each of the three sections opens by indicating the situation: personal frailty (1), circumstantial threat (7), human enmity (14). Each contains a reference to committed divine love (verses 5, 13, 15). The focus on God as Sovereign is enriched by four references to 'Yahweh' (verses 1, 6, 11, 17).

37 The six petitions in this section are balanced: The first and sixth ask for a hearing; the second and fifth (verses 2a and 4), the preservation and joy of the soul; the third and fourth (verses 2b and 3) seek salvation and grace. The 'because' clauses give reasons for praying.

38 To be read and understood as an urgent aside.

16. Turn to me and grant me your grace.[45]
    Give your strength to your servant,
    and your salvation to the son of your handmaid.
17. Show me a sign for good,[46]
    so that those who hate me may see and reap shame,
    because you, Yahweh,
    have yourself helped me and comforted me.

---

39 This adjective is in an intensive form, justifying the introduction of 'all'.

40 In section **B** (verses 7–10), confidence in the only God is balanced by verses 11–13, consecration to the God known for his love and greatness. David sees himself doing now what all nations will yet do (see verses 9, 12), because he now knows what they will some day know.

41 Biblical monotheism (compare 1 Corinthians 8:5–6) recognizes that there are other objects of worship besides the one and only God. The nations worship such – and they can become a snare to God's Israel. Even though without substance or reality (Psalm 115:4–7) they have the menacing power to make their worshippers like themselves (Psalm 115:8). Yahweh's uniqueness is (a) in heaven ('among the gods'); (b) in his creation ('works'), on earth (all will acknowledge); and in events ('wonderful things').

42 Romans 7:15ff. reveals the tension within our natures; our mixed-up motives and characters; our lack of single-mindedness.

43 From *zudh*, to seethe, boil up. Of people 'puffed up'; full of their own importance; verse 14a, what they are in themselves; verse 14b, what they are capable of.

44 God as he has made himself known in his Exodus self-revelation; Exodus 34:6. As we would say – and as should be true of us – David rests his case on Scripture.

45 There are three dimensions to David's crisis-praying: first, he seek 'grace', unmerited, undeserved divine favour; secondly, deliverance in his specific need; and thirdly, a public benefit – visible divine intervention, bringing conviction to the onlooker.

46 Compare Judges 6:36ff. In cases of great need a sign is sought that all will be well.

Pause for Thought

There is a golden thread running through today's three psalms: the thread of 'glory'. In the wonderful Psalm 84 it is the glory that lies ahead at the end of pilgrimage (84:11); in Psalm 85 it is glory dwelling in the land (85:9) when Yahweh steps on to the scene (13); in Psalm 86 it is the glory of his name, now (86:12) and to come (9). When we arrive in the courts of the LORD (Psalm 84), all will be glory – glory such as is now unimaginable. As soon as we see the face of Jesus we shall know as never before how much we are loved, how fully we have been forgiven, how great and endless is our security in his presence. It is, says Psalm 84:11, the glory of grace and the glory of good. And in that delightful psalm, though glory awaits the end of the road, yet the sense conveyed throughout is that every step of our pilgrim path is touched with his glory – the safety that we find at Calvary (84:3), the sustenance that comes when the pilgrim road is tough (6). Secondly, the glory we desire to see publicly in our land is the glory of Yahweh's personal presence, which comes in response to our prayers for restoration and new life, through his undying love (86:4–7). When we are what we ought to be, he will come and dwell among us in manifest glory. Fundamentally, however, this too is Calvary-based (85:10), where every divine attribute and requirement was satisfied, and a kiss of love resounded through the divine heart. So we come to Psalm 86 and the glory due to his name. The ultimate glory (86:9) is largely his business (Phil. 2:9–11), but 'I will glorify' (86:12) places the responsibility firmly on me – and you. It is a by-product of learning his truth (86:11a), walking in his way (11b), single-mindedly reverencing his name (11c), and all in response to his undying love and salvation (13).

Day 40 Read Psalms 87–88

Psalm 87.
'Zion's Children'[1]

Belonging to the sons of Korah; a song; a hymn.

A.1. What he has founded

1.   His foundation[2] is in the mountains of holiness.[3]

B.1. The beloved city

2.   Yahweh truly loves[4] the gates of Zion
     more than all the dwelling places of Jacob.

C.1. The city of true glory

3.   Deservedly great glory is spoken[5] about you,
     City of God. (*Selah*)

D. Knowledge of God and birth in Zion

4.   I bring to remembrance Rahab[6] and Babylon,
     as those who know me.
     Behold!
     Philistia and Tyre along with Cush –
     even this one was born[7] there!

C.2. The city of true citizenship and divine care

5.   And regarding Zion it will be said:
     each and every one[8] was born in it,
     and the Most High[9] will himself establish it for ever.

1   From John Newton's hymn, 'Glorious things of thee are spoken'. This is the most allusive of the psalms. Throughout it expresses its thoughts in staccato form and is best left like that and not modulated into a more smooth grammar and syntax. Newton's hymn is true to the meaning of the psalm which starts with the historical Zion (1–2) but goes on to speak in a way that can only be understood in terms of the heavenly or eternal Zion, which begins in the Old Testament (e.g. Isaiah 2:1–4) and comes into full view in the New (e.g. Hebrews 12:22; Revelation 21–22), the city in which everyone who knows Yahweh (4) will be able to claim birthright (6). Nehemiah 7:5 is a reflection of the same truth. The psalm is a glorious expression of universal hope, to be realised in the messianic day.

2   The city Yahweh has founded: 2 Samuel 5:6–10; compare Deuteronomy 12:5. 'His foundation' in verse 1 is balanced by 'my springs' in verse 7, forming a contrasting inclusion: Yahweh's will and his people's enjoyment.

3   Psalm 2:6.

4   Psalm 78:68. In verse 2 the participle 'loves' is given the emphatic position, hence 'truly'.

B.2. The privileged city

6. Yahweh will himself recount,
    when he writes down[10] the peoples:
    even this one was born there. (*Selah*)

A.2. What I enjoy

7.[11] Singers and flautists alike –
    'All my springs are in you.'

Psalm 88.
Darkness without Light;
Trust without Hope[12]

A hymn, a song, belonging to the sons of Korah; belonging to the worship-leader; set to Mahalath Leannoth; a teaching poem belonging to Heman the Ezrahite.[13]

A.1. ('I.') Persistent prayer when life ends without hope

1. Yahweh, God of my salvation,[14]
    by day I have screamed,[15]
    by night, in front of you!
2. May my prayer come before you!
    Turn your ear to my loud shout!
3.[16] Because my soul has been sated with evil,
    and my life has come near to Sheol.
4. I have been accounted along with those going down to
    the pit;
    I have become like a person without strength.
5. Among the dead a free man![17] –
    like the fatally wounded,[18] lying in the grave! –
    those whom you do not remember any more;
    those who have been cut off from your hand.

5   The apparent anomaly here of a plural subject ('glorious things') with a singular participle ('spoken') is explained by treating the plural as expressing amplitude, and therefore in effect a singular. Or we could find here an 'impersonal passive' – 'there is spoken glorious things'. As a passive participle ('to be gloried at'), the thought of deserving or worthiness is inherent in the form. Hebrew passive participles have the same force as Latin gerundives. The deserving glories of Zion are expressed in verse 4: it is the world-city of a world-people, individually enrolled by Yahweh himself, and retained in his memory.

6   i.e. Egypt (Isaiah 51:9–11), intended as a mockery (Isaiah 30:7): 'arrogant boasting'/'big mouth'; making large promises but guaranteed to do nothing about them. Coupled with Babylon, the psalm brings together the first enslaver and the current captor in a daring vision that they will be included in Yahweh's worldwide people, along with the ever-hostile Philistia, and along with Tyre to the north and Cush in the far south; completing what we would call a global impression. Philistia and Tyre also contrast the military with the commercial: people of every place and every kind are enrolled.

7   Nehemiah was concerned that everyone resident in his new city had a birth-right to be there (note 1, above). The psalm expresses the daring idea of a spiritual, supernal city where a worldwide people of Yahweh each hold citizenship by birth. Isaiah called this the exalted city of the nations (2:1–4), the strong city of salvation (26:1), the new Jerusalem (65:17–25). It is the Jerusalem of Hebrews 12:22, and Revelation 21–22.

B.1. ('You.') Friendless, under wrath

6. You have put me into the lowest pit,[19]
   into dark places, into the depths.
7. Upon me your wrath has rested,
   and with all your breakers you have brought me down.
   (*Selah*)
8. You have distanced my acquaintances from me;
   you have made me a sheer abomination to them.
   I am shut in and I cannot get out.
9. My eye has languished through affliction.[20]

A.2. ('I.') Persistent prayer facing death without hope

I have called out to you, Yahweh, all the day,
spread out my hands to you.
10. For the dead will you perform a wonder?[21]
    Or will the shadowy ones[22] themselves rise to give you thanks? (*Selah*)
11. Will your committed love be recounted in the grave,
    your truthfulness in Ruination?[23]
12. Will your wonder be known in the dark,
    and your righteousness in the land of forgetting?[24]

B.2. ('You.') Friendless, under wrath

13. And as for me,
    to you, Yahweh, I cry for help.
    And in the morning my prayer is there to meet you.
14. Why, Yahweh, are you rejecting my soul,
    hiding your face from me?
15. I am troubled,
    and about to expire – from youth![25]
    I have borne your terrors!
    I am helpless![26]
16. Over me your bursts of rage have passed!

8 The idiom *'ish 'ish*, an emphatic way of saying 'everyone', is reasonably common (e.g. Exodus 36:4; Leviticus 15:2; Numbers 1:4). The psalm is unique in inserting a conjunction, *'ish we'ish*. This seems to have been done for emphasis, 'each and every one'.

9 Or 'and he will himself establish it as most high'; compare Deuteronomy 28:1.

10 Verse 6 explains verses 4 and 5 by answering the question, 'In what sense born there?' By inclusion in the roll of citizens drawn up by Yahweh himself. On Yahweh's 'book', compare Exodus 32:32; Psalms 56:8; 69:28; 139:16; Isaiah 4:3; Ezekiel 13:9; Luke 10:20; Philippians 4:3; Hebrews 12:23; Revelation 3:5; 20:12.

11 Abruptness like verse 7 is not unknown in the Hebrew Bible. Compare in Isaiah 5:9 where there is no verb 'said' (compare NKJV) but two abrupt exclamations: 'In my ears! Yahweh of Hosts!' So here, choirs and musicians are summoned to respond, and their song is 'All my springs …' For this latter thought: Isaiah 12:3; Joel 3:18. Just as each is enrolled individually, so each has access as by right to the refreshment of the city.

Your alarms have annihilated me![27]

17. They have surrounded me like water all the day,
    encircled me altogether!

18. You have distanced lover and companion from me;
    darkness is my best friend![28]

---

12 This is well-known as the Psalm without a note of hope. Heman does not actually say that he was suffering any illness; he bemoans life-long trouble (15) in which he discerns the wrath of God (5, 7, 14). This leaves him in a state of terror (15–16), especially as the trouble has eroded his strength (4, 9), and has had the effect of alienating his friends (8, 18). The psalm ends without relief coming, but with prayer continuing. Like the old hymn says, 'I'll trust where I cannot see.' The psalm can be read in four sections: the **A**-sections are predominantly first-person singular, Heman sharing his thoughts; the **B**-sections predominantly second-person singular, what Yahweh has done or not done.

13 1 Chronicles 6:33–37.

14 In the light of what we know lies ahead in this 'psalm without hope', how remarkable is the opening line! When there is no hope, the only hope lies in seeking God; when there is no sign of saving action, the only recourse is to cry to the saving God.

15 Not an elegant translation! But an accurate rendering of *tsa'aq*, indicating urgency and determination in prayer. Faith maintained against hope: Romans 4:18–19.

16 We need to handle with care what verses 3–5 and subsequent verses in this psalm, say about life after death. Every verse in every psalm belongs, in the first instance, within the context of that psalm. For example, David's assertion of sinlessness (e.g. Psalm 18:20) is not a claim to 'sinless perfection' but of innocence as charged in that situation. In Psalm 88, the sufferer feels himself to be dying under the wrath of God (7, 16); he has been cast off and Yahweh has hidden his face (13), etc. To die in such circumstance is to die without conscious hope.

17 Set free from earthly suffering only at the expense of dying without hope!

18 We are not told in what circumstance they were 'slain' and we need to be careful to keep the words in context: they were the sort of 'slain' whose death cut them off from Yahweh. That is all we are told.

19 'The pit of nether things', 'the lowest pit'.

20 The lacklustre 'eye' may be meant literally: the failure of bodily powers as a fourth element in 'depression' (v.6), along with a sense of alienation from God (7) and people (8a), and a feeling of inescapable imprisonment (8b). Equally 'eye' can be taken metaphorically as the organ of purpose (what am I aiming at?), and the fifth element in depression is a sense of purposelessness (what's it all about?).

21 The sort of supernatural marvel that only God can achieve. See 9:1. On what these verses say about the dead, see note 16 above.

22 *repha'iym*, the 'shades' or 'ghosts' of the dead, what lives on when body and soul are separated at death: e.g. Proverbs 2:18; 9:18; Isaiah 14:9; 26:19. The word reflects the fact that when body and soul divide wholeness of life has gone, and only a half life continues in Sheol. The Old Testament looks forward to a life beyond Sheol (e.g. Psalm 49:15; 73:24) but awaits the revelation of life and immortality in Jesus (2 Timothy 1:10) and the truth of the resurrection of the body.

23 Possibly 'Abaddon' is meant as a proper name for the 'place'. It comes from *'abadh*, to perish, be ruined.

24 While the psalm is not describing the state of all the dead but only of those dying under wrath, it correctly portrays the decisiveness of death as such. A line has been crossed and a finality has been reached. There is no further outreaching of Yahweh's committed love, and no doctrine of a 'second chance'. Destiny is settled.

25 A climax of hopelessness suitable to the psalm: looking back (15); looking up (16); looking around (17); looking forward (18).

26 An otherwise unused word of uncertain meaning. Some emend to a word meaning 'to grow numb'.

27 A strange, intensive form of the familiar *tsamath*, to bring to an end.

28 Or 'my acquaintances are darkness' – a daring but effective apposition. But I have chosen to understand the plural noun as plural of amplitude.

Pause for Thought

The Bible never hides its head in the sand when it comes to life's troubles! And like all the rest, Psalm 88 is written for our learning. Here is trouble without explanation: lasting as far back as the eye can see; seemingly stretching ahead without relief; and likely to be overtaken, still unsolved, by death. Should such an experience be ours, how is it to be faced? Start where the psalm starts: by affirming what is known about our God – that he, and only he – is the 'God of my salvation', or, as we could translate it, 'My saving God', a God whose very nature it is to save his dear ones. This is the purpose of a creed – scaffolding to hold us upright when the storm comes. When everything in us cries out to moan about our lot, cry out rather that he is Father, Son and Holy Spirit, he is

> … the love that drew salvation's plan!
> … the grace that brought it down to man!

– the God of all grace. Then, like this lovely psalmist, don't hesitate to see your trials as coming from the hand of God. Don't bother your head with problems arising, or thought to arise, from seeing things this way. This is the truth of the matter: if we are in the soup it is he who has decided what sort of soup it is, and at what temperature, and how long, and why! He is God. Jesus has assured us that we cannot be plucked out of his and the Father's hand (John 10:28–29). Where were we when the trouble came? Why, where we always are – in his hand! Did the trial 'get in' because he let go of us? Certainly not; the trial only means that he grips us more tightly! And thirdly, give yourself constantly to urgent prayer (1, 9, 13). To abandon prayer is to embrace atheism. Prayer does change things – and its transformative work is ever and also in the person who is praying. 'Who walks in darkness and has no light, let him trust in the name of the LORD, and lean upon his God' (Isa. 50:10).

Day 41   Read Psalm 89¹

Psalm 89.
'All the promises of God in him are "Yes"'²

A teaching poem belonging to Ethan the Ezrahite.

A.1. Confident singing

1. For ever the committed loves³ of Yahweh I will surely sing.⁴
   Generation after generation I will make to know your faithfulness,
2. because I have said:⁵
   'For ever committed love will be built up.
   It is in the heavens⁶ that you establish your faithfulness.'

B.1. Expectations⁷

(Yahweh's oath)

3. I inaugurated a covenant for⁸ my chosen one;
   I swore to David my servant:
4. 'For ever I will establish your seed,
   and I will build your throne for generation after generation.' (*Selah*)

*(Yahweh's sovereign power: in the spiritual realm)*⁹

5. And the heavens will give thanks for your wonder, Yahweh;
   yes indeed, for your faithfulness,
   in the assembly of the holy ones,¹⁰
6. because,
   who in the sky¹¹ is comparable to Yahweh,

1. Read 2 Samuel 7 as background to this psalm.

2. 2 Corinthians 1:20.

3. This is the great word *chesedh* (see Psalm 51:1, note 3) in the plural. The plural comes again in verse 49, and thus is the 'bracket' or 'inclusion' in which the psalm lives. In the intervening verses the singular comes five times (2, 14, 24, 28, 33) with the intention of spelling out what the plural includes.

4. The verb 'sing' is in the cohortative form here, expressing, as often, personal commitment or resolve. The sense could be expressed by italicizing *will*. In the Old Testament, song is often used as a metaphor for entering with joy into a benefit secured on our behalf without our contribution. Thus in Exodus 15:1, Moses 'sang' in enjoyment of Yahweh's victory at the Red Sea. Compare Psalms 96:1–2; 98:1. Much of the rest of Psalm 89 will describe how Yahweh's love seems to be far from committed, how his promises seem to have been contradicted by events. The song of verse 1 is therefore a telling example of exuberant faith that all will yet be right. At the end of the psalm this singing faith is matched by prayer in the face of unanswered questions.

5. In the sense 'I have decided/I have made up my mind', explaining the faith which provoked the song of verse 1.

6. Therefore God's faithfulness is part of the fixed fabric of life, above the rise and fall of transient things.

resembles Yahweh among the sons of the transcendent gods?[12]

7. A transcendent God, held greatly in terror
   in the fellowship of the holy ones,
   and to be feared above all who are around him.

8. Yahweh, God of Hosts,
   who is like you,
   mighty as Yah?[13]
   And your faithfulness is all around you.

(In nature and history)

9. You are ruling over the swelling of the sea;
   when its waves rise up it is you who soothes them!

10. It is you who crush, like one slain, Rahab;[14]
    by the arm of your strength you scattered your enemies.

(God over all in mightiness)

11. Yours is the heavens;
    indeed, yours the earth;
    the world of people and everything in it –
    you founded them –

12. north and south, it was you created them;
    Tabor and Hermon[15] – in your name they shout aloud!

(Power and moral stature)

13. You have an arm equipped with prowess;
    your hand is mighty;
    your right hand is high.

14. Righteousness and judgment are the foundation of your throne;
    committed love and faithfulness[16] wait[17] before your face.

C. The great 'might have been'.[18]

(The blessed people)

15. Blessed[19] are the people who know the shout of acclamation,[20]
    who walk around, Yahweh, in the light of your face.[21]

7 Still supplying evidence on which singing faith can rest, the psalm now recalls first that the promises are backed by a divine oath, and are to be implemented by sovereign divine power.

8 In the vocabulary of covenant-making, 'for' means 'in the interests of/to the advantage of'.

9 Yahweh's omnipotence guarantees his ability to keep his promises; his faithfulness is a pledge of his will to do so.

10 Taken with verses 6–8 – including 'in the clouds' (6) – reference in a general sense to heavenly or supernal beings. Not to attempt to probe in detail or fashion some sort of pattern of things above, but a broad statement that Yahweh is superior to anything that can be worshipped or called 'god' (2 Thessalonians 2:4). In verse 6, 'sons of' has its idiomatic sense of 'those in the class/category/condition of'.

11 *shachaq* from *shachaq*, to pulverise. The noun, occuring in verse 6 and 37, really means 'dust', used of misty cloud formations (18:11; 36:5; 57:10; 68:34). In verses 6 and 37 translated 'sky' for variation.

12 Is 'transcendent gods' used ironically here, a deliberate (and telling) contrast to its true use in the next line? Or are we to understand it to refer to heavenly, supernal 'principalities and powers' (compare Ephesians 6:12)?

13 An affectionate diminutive of 'Yahweh', e.g. Isaiah 12:2.

14 A mocking nickname for Egypt: Psalm 87:4; Isaiah 30:7; 51:9–11. Reference here to Exodus overthrow.

16. In your name they exult all the day,
    and in your righteousness they are exalted,
17. because you, yourself, are the beauty of their strength,[22]
    and it is in your favour that our horn[23] is exalted,
18. because[24] to Yahweh belongs our shield,
    and to the Holy One of Israel our king.

(The secure king)
19. At that time you spoke in vision to your dearly loved one[25]
    and you said:
    'I have bestowed help[26] on a mighty one;[27]
    I have exalted one chosen from the people.[28]
20. I have found David, my servant;
    with the oil of my holiness I have anointed him.[29]
21. The one with whom my hand is established,
    much more my arm itself will fortify him.[30]
22. An enemy will not get the better of him,
    nor the son of deviancy tread him down.
23. And I will beat in pieces his adversaries before him,
    and those who hate him I will strike down.

(Clear promises: 1. Universal reign)[31]
24. And my faithfulness and my committed love are with
    him,
    and in my name his horn will be exalted.
25. And I will set his hand on the sea,
    and his right hand on the rivers.[32]
26. He will himself call out to me:
    You are my father,
    my transcendent God,
    and the rock[33] of my salvation.
27. Yes indeed, I will myself appoint him the firstborn,[34]
    the Most High of the king of the earth.

(Clear promises: 2. Endless reign)
28. For ever I will keep for him my committed love,
    and my covenant will be faithful for his good.[35]

15 The two chief mountains of north Palestine, Tabor (Judges 4:6; 588m, west of Jordan), Hermon (Psalm 133:3; 2,814m, in Transjordan). Possibly used here to represent respectively west and east, matching the south and north of the preceding line, but maybe simply because they are outstanding physical features.

16 The first pair of words declare Yahweh's absolute justice, respectively in principle and practice; the second describe his modes of action. In perfect righteousness, etc. he deals in unchanging love and fidelity with his people.

17 Like attendants waiting to do his bidding.

18 Actually as well as thematically, these verses are the centrepiece of the psalm: the people that might have been (15–18), the king that was intended (19–23) and the great promises on which all this hope was based (24–26, 27–29, 30–37).

19 *'ashrey,* see Psalm 1:1.

20 The word (*teru'ah*) simply means a 'loud shout' (Joshua 6:5, 20) but is specifically used of a shout of acclamation of a king (Numbers 23:21). Understood in this way in verse 15 it makes an inclusion with the king-reference in verse 18. *teru'ah* is also used of a trumpet-call (Numbers 10:5–6; 29:1; 25:9). This would refer to Israel's privilege in being summoned to Yahweh's feasts. The royal reference is more suitable to this paragraph.

21 i.e. in your favour, compare Numbers 6:25.

22 i.e. it is your presence that makes their strength (their national standing and ability) the beautiful thing it is.

23 Symbol of power to conquer.

29. And I will appoint his seed for ever,
    and his throne like the days of the heavens.[36]

(Clear promises: 3. Guaranteed reign)[37]

30. If his sons forsake my teaching,
    and do not go on walking in my judgments;[38]

31. if they pollute my statutes,
    and do not keep my commands,

32. I will visit their rebellion with a rod,
    and their iniquity with blows.

33. And[39] my committed love I will not annul from him,
    nor will I prove false in my faithfulness.

34. I will not pollute my covenant,
    nor change the utterance of my lips.

35. Once for all, I have sworn by my holiness.
    I swear not to tell a lie to David.

36. For ever his seed will be,
    and his throne like the sun in front of me.

37. Like the moon it will be established for ever –
    the trustworthy witness in the skies.[40]

B.2. Disappointment[41]

(The king)

38. And it is you yourself who have rejected and spurned;
    you have burst out in anger with your anointed.

39. You have abhorred the covenant of your servant.
    You have polluted his crown of consecration[42] to the
    ground.

(The kingdom)

40. You have broken through all his fences.
    You have made his fortified places a desolation.

41. All who pass along the road have plundered him.
    He has become an object of reproach to his neighbours.

42. You have exalted the right hand of his adversaries,
    made all his enemies rejoice.

24 Note the double 'because': the second
   offers the ultimate explanation – a
   matter being traced to its root. So (16),
   there is an exalted people: because
   (17), Yahweh's presence makes their
   strength what it is, and because (18)
   their king is Yahweh's appointed king.
   Thus kingship takes its place as the
   centrepiece of this psalm.

25 I have chosen here to treat the plural
   ('your beloved ones') as a plural of
   amplitude, in effect, therefore, a
   singular, but with reference to Yahweh's
   special love for David.

26 This means either 'I have given him
   the capacity to be a help' or 'I have
   given him my help' (or means both).
   Or, again, 'I have given help against a
   warrior' (perhaps Goliath?). There is
   no other example in the Bible of the
   noun 'help' followed by the preposition
   'upon'. The verb (*'azar*), 'to help',
   with 'upon', means 'to help against': 1
   Chronicles 12:21; 2 Chronicles 26:13.

27 *gibbor*, the same word as in 'mighty
   God', Isaiah 9:6, specifically heroic
   or warrior ability. As of David when
   first chosen, the youthful conqueror of
   Goliath, 1 Samuel 17.

28 2 Samuel 7:8.

29 1 Samuel 16:13.

30 The 'hand' of personal intervention,
   picking David out and putting him
   on the throne; the 'arm' of personal
   strength and ability, girding David for
   the task.

31 The promises are marked off by the
   occurrence of the singular word *chesedh*
   (verses 24, 28, 33) which, in this way,
   spell out the contents of the plural
   word bracketing the whole psalm (note
   2, above).

32 The contrasting water-systems, sea/
   rivers, are the idiom of totality
   expressed by means of contrast.

43. What's more, you kept turning back the edge of his sword,
    and you have not raised him up in battle.

(The throne)

44. You have made his lustre cease,[43]
    and to the ground you have hurled his throne.
45. You cut short the days of his youthful vigour
    wrapped him round with disappointment.[44]

A.2. Puzzled but praying[45]

(Longing for restoration)

46. How long, Yahweh, will you hide yourself in perpetuity,
    will your rage burn like fire?
47. Remember!
    I ... what duration![46]
    For what deceptiveness you created all the sons of
    humankind!
48. Who is the individual who lives and will not see death,
    whose soul escapes from the hand of Sheol?[47] (Selah)

(Pleading the promises)

49. Where are your former committed loves,[48]
    Sovereign One,
    you swore to David in faithfulness?
50. Remember,
    Sovereign One,
    the reproach of your servants,[49]
    my carrying in my bosom all the many peoples![50]
51. How your enemies have reproached,
    Yahweh;
    how they have reproached the heels[51] of your anointed!

(Editorial conclusion to Psalms, Book Three)[52]

52. Blessed be Yahweh for ever.
    Amen and Amen.

33 'Rock' presumably a figure of unchanging constancy, reliability, etc., but also – and always – the smitten, life-supplying rock of Exodus 17:5–6.

34 Compare Psalm 2:7; Acts 13:33; Hebrews 1:5; 5:5.

35 Lit. simply 'for him', a 'dative of advantage', which, in covenanting terminology means that the covenant was drawn up in someone's interest.

36 i.e. in divinely guaranteed order, cf. Jeremiah 31:35–37.

37 This is the best heading I can think of. The psalm replicated 2 Samuel 7:14 on the larger scale of what has transpired in the House of David. Promises are made in relation to a David-like faithful kingship. What if kings are unfaithful? The answer is that the promises still stand. 'If we are unfaithful, he remains faithful. He is not able to deny himself' (2 Timothy 2:13; compare Romans 3:3).

38 What I have authoritatively pronounced to be my will in truth and conduct.

39 'And': could be translated 'But' here, of course. 'And', however, has its own truth to affirm – in every circumstance there is always another factor to take into account.

40 On 'skies' see verse 6. We could translate verse 37, 'and the witness in the skies is trustworthy', i.e. God himself. Or possibly a reference to the rainbow as a covenant sign and pledge (Genesis 9:12).

41 The current state of the Davidic king makes nonsense of the confident hopes grounded in Yahweh's oath, his power, and his promises. The verses treat in turn of the king (38–39), his kingdom (40–43) and his throne (44–45). A comprehensive collapse. The psalm could well reflect on 2 Kings 24–25, the final fall to the Babylonians. No earlier downturn of fortune seems severe enough to account for Psalm 89.

42 *nezer* first means 'consecration' and then whatever constitutes the outward mark of the consecrated person – in the case of the Nazirite, his hair (Numbers 6:9), or the 'holy' crown which marks the king.

43 Probably, more literally, 'you have made him cease from his lustre'.

44 'Diappointment' is, lit. 'shame', but as so frequently of 'reaping shame', being disappointed of what was hoped for.

45 Balancing the confident singing of **A.1.** verses 1–2. The prayer is frank in its puzzlement but urgent and believing.

46 This is exactly what we have in the Hebrew. Hebrew uses nominative pronouns (here 'I') to emphasise possessive pronouns attached to nouns (1 Kings 21:19; Haggai 1:3). If we had here 'my duration', the 'I' would be for emphasis: What meagre duration is mine!'. Maybe we are to understand this, expressed with the allusiveness of the poet. Possibly it is what anyone would understand from the literal rendering above!

47 This is not a considered theological statement about Sheol! It is just the realism which sees that if the king is not restored in this life, then he is not restored to his earthly 'lustre'.

48 The plural, 'committed loves', see verse 1 above.

49 Or, as plural of amplitude, 'your chief servant/your anointed servant'. If the plural is retained, the Davidic king is reminding Yahweh that he is the object of the reproach of all who are Yahweh's servants – his is the king who could not hold off his foes. Like poor George III and the American Colonies!

50 It would be possible to understand 'the reproach of' from the previous line. All the attacking nations have witnessed the defeat of the Davidic king and joined in the mockery. Alternatively, taking verse 50b as a statement in its own right, the Davidic king was promised world dominion, and in his heart he cherishes the hope of ruling the nations.

51 Likely a 'pregnant' form of word: 'have followed on my heels with reproaches'. Some derivatives from *'aqebh,* 'to follow at the heel', have the meaning of 'consequence', what comes after. If that is possible in connection with the noun here, 'they have poured scorn on the outcome for your anointed'.

52 But not an unsuitable comment on Psalm 89 as well. The promises seem to have lapsed but all will yet surely be well.

Pause for Thought

Have you a recipe for the day when everything falls apart? In a time like ours when so many voices are preaching a spurious 'prosperity gospel' it is so essential to remind ourselves how much of the Bible we must consign to the rubbish heap if they are true! Anything that speaks of warfare or the conflict of being a Christian, of striving unto blood in our fight against sin, anything about 'thorns in the flesh' – anything like Psalm 89. But there it stands, right at the heart of God's inspired Word! There are days when everything falls apart – and the Lord Jesus himself warned that 'in the world you will have tribulation' (John 16:33, ESV, NKJV). Being a Christian can be like being a woman in labour (John 16:20–22). So the question presses on us: Have we a recipe? Yes, if we let Psalm 89 be our teacher. The recipe is to sing and to pray – where the psalm begins (1–2) and ends (46–51). What we need are not songs of 'feeling' (though how good some of them can be!) but songs of affirmation, the great hymns which declare fundamental truth about God. That's what Ethan the Ezrahite sang – God in creation (5) and redemption (10), God in his messianic purposes (18). Newton's masterpiece – 'How sweet the name of Jesus sounds' – has emotion enough and truth enough to last us all our days, and light and life for the direst darkness. Then there is praying. In our songs we affirm how true God's truth is; in our prayers we bring our bewilderment into his presence, and believingly ask him to hasten his promises (46–51). We know from scripture that what seems like delay is full of mercy (2 Peter 3:1–9); we also know that he never fails to hear our prayer, and to run to our help. He knows our weakness and remembers that we are but dust (Ps. 103:14). Our prayers may not prompt the Second Coming before a noon deadline, but they will bring the Lord Jesus into our lives, needs and circumstances.

Day 42   Read Psalms 90–92

Psalm 90.
Living with Mortality[1]

A prayer belonging to Moses[2], the man of God.

A.1. Generations past; our home[3]

1. Sovereign One,
    our dwelling place[4] you yourself have proved to be
    in generation after generation.[5]
2. Before even mountains were brought to birth,
    and you travailed[6] with the earth and the world of people,
    from eternity to eternity you are the transcendent God.

B. Present experience: transience and wrath

(Transience by divine appointment)
3. Oh how you bring back[7] mere man[8] to dust[9] –
    you said:[10]
    'Go back, sons of Adam!'[11]'
4. Indeed,[12] a thousand years, in your eyes, are like
    yesterday[13]
    because it passes,
    and like a watch in the night.
5. You flood[14] them away –
    they are mere sleep!
    In the morning, like green grass, which sprouts freshly –
6. in the morning it shoots and grows afresh;
    by evening it wilts and is dried up.

(Divine wrath, human sin)[15]
7.[16] Because

---

1   In Psalm 89 the king lamented his mortality (89:47), pleading for divine intervention (so to speak) before it was too late. Psalm 90 explores this situation further. Both psalms face the question of how to react when bright expectations fail – in Psalm 89 the expectations of the Davidic king; in Psalm 90, the 'morning' expectations of every mortal, blighted by evening (6–7)! Moses had an answer to share. Psalm 89 recommended dealing with life's challenges by singing and praying (89:1, 46–51). Moses went deeper. We can reply to our transiency, fragility (5–7) – and indeed sinfulness (vv.8–9) – by making the eternal God our home (1), and by looking to him (16–17) to give lasting effect to our sojourn and work on earth.

2   There is no serious difficulty in the way of ascribing this psalm (and Psalm 91) to Moses. It is only the unexpectedness of his appearance here (plus the inexplicable enthusiasm of so many commentators to make the psalms of late origin in the history of Israel). Who better than Moses could marvel at finding a home in God throughout generations of homelessness – i.e. the centuries of sojourn in Egypt plus the desert years – during which he watched a whole generation die out without fulfilment? The air of wistfulness in the psalm matches Moses' own sense of loss at being denied entrance to the promised land (Deuteronomy 4:21–22).

3   Psalm 90 opens with a statement of faith (1–2), goes on to expose the difficulties in holding it, and ends (13–17) by indicating the basis on which it rests.

we are brought to an end by your exasperation,
and by your rage we are terrified.

8. You have set our iniquities in front of you,
our hidden things[17] in the lamp of your face,[18]

9. because
all our days turn[19] in your outbursting anger;
we bring our years to an end like a sigh!

10. The days of our years –
what are they but seventy years?
And if, by heroic strength, eighty years,
their boastfulness[20] is toil and trouble,
because it has passed quickly,
and we have flown!

11. Who knows the strength of your exasperation,
and your outbursting anger
in proportion to the fear you deserve?[21]

12. To number our days make us know in such a way
that we may gather in[22] a heart of wisdom.

A.2. Generations to come: contentment and security[23]

(Satisfaction)

13. Oh do return, Yahweh!
How long!
And pity[24] your servants.

14. Satisfy us in the morning[25] with your committed love,
so that we may shout aloud and rejoice all our days.

(Gladness)

15. Make us rejoice according to the days you humbled us,
the years we have seen evil.

(Establishment)

16. Let your activity be seen by your servants,
and your splendour by their sons.

17. And may the loveliness of the Sovereign One,

4 Feel the force of this word in relation to verses 7–8, 11. People who know themselves to be under wrath have no other sheltering place than the God whose wrath they have provoked – and he is there to welcome them in!

5 'Generation after generation' (1) is balanced with 'eternity to eternity' (2). The former is human experience – the disappearing generations; the latter, God's changeless eternity.

6 *chiyl*, to writhe (in giving birth); to have labour pains. Here the metaphor must not be taken beyond the fact that creation was a 'painstaking' work of God.

7 The verb here is in the jussive form, and I am interpreting this in an exclamatory sense.

8 *'enosh*, see Psalm 8:4.

9 Not the word used in Genesis 3:19 (*'aphar*), but *dakh'a*, 'crushing/pulverising'. Genesis states the fact of return to dust; Psalm 90 notes that this happens through divine judgmental action.

10 Some prefer 'You say' (perfect of invariable experience). 'Come back, [A.Q. "Go back" in your trans] sons …' i.e. one generation goes and another is called into being.

11 Or, of course, 'sons of man(kind)'. A reference to Adam seemed particularly suited to this context.

12 *kiy* most often means 'because', but this translation here would make God's eternity (4) the cause of man's transiency (3), which is nonsense. The purpose of verse 4 is to expose human transiency by contrast to the eternal God.

our God,
be on us,
and the work of our hands,
oh establish it for us.

Psalm 91.
The Protected Species[26]

A.1. Affirmation of protection

1. Whoever makes his home in the covering of the Most
    High
    in the shadow of Shaddai[27] finds his lodging.[28]

B.1. Testimony: protection found

2. Saying[29] about Yahweh:
    'My refuge and my stronghold,
    my God, in whom I ever trust.'[30]

C.1. From life's threats: 'He will cover'

3. Because[31] he will himself overshadow you,
    from the trapper's snare,
    from the destructive epidemic.
4. By his feathers he will screen you,
    and under his wings you will find refuge.
    Body-shield and encircling shield,[32] his truth.
5. You will not be afraid of a dread by night,
    of the arrow which flies by day;
6. of the epidemic which goes around in the gloom;
    of the destruction which despoils at noon.
7. A thousand may fall beside you,
    and ten thousand at your right hand;[33]
    to you it will not approach.
8. Only, with your eyes you will watch,

13 Lit. 'like the day, yesterday', a regular Hebrew idiom in which a noun can be followed by another noun more closely defining it (Joshua 2:1, 'men, (namely) spies … a woman, (namely) a harlot'). But 'yesterday' is nowhere else preceded by 'day'. The unique expression seems to be used here so that God's years and days (4) can balance the matching verse 15 with its reference to the days and years of man.

14 The imagery of flood points to helplessness before an overwhelming force; 'sleep' points to intrinsic fragility, something easily ended and gone; and grass to the dominance of internal conditions of withering.

15 How is it that the eternal God visits man with death? These verses have the answer: verses 7, 9, 11 assert wrath; verses 8, 10 balance iniquity and transiency. Verse 11 is an ironical climax. Wrath (7) finds its just target in sin (8); it is wrath (9) which blights life with its terminus in death; yet (11) wrath is the unrecognized factor – who realizes it is there, and, of those who do realize it, how many see it in its full reality?

16 Verse 7 notes the vigour of God's wrath; verse 8, its justice. We are without resource (as to verse 7), and without excuse (as to verse 8).

17 This word may possibly be a singular: our hidden reality.

18 1 John 1:5.

19 Compare the use of this verb (*panah*) in Jeremiah 6:4 ('the day is on the turn') – the only other example of this meaning in the Bible. The sense in the psalm is 'decline/move to their end.'

20 Probably just a reference to the artless way in which some elderly folk insist on telling how old they are.

and you will see the recompense of the wicked.[34]

B.2. Testimony: protection found[35]

9. Assuredly, you, Yahweh, are my refuge!

C.2. On life's pathway: 'He will command'

It is the Most High you have made your dwelling place:

10. Evil will not befall you,
    nor will a blow come near your tent,

11. because
    he will command his angels about you,
    to keep you in all your ways.

12. By hand[36] they will lift you up,
    in case you strike your foot on a stone.

13. On lion and cobra you may walk,
    trample on the prime lion[37] and the serpent.

A.2. Affirmation of salvation[38]

14. Because he is deeply in love with me[39] I will rescue him;
    I will give him top-security because he knows my name;

15. he will call me, and I will answer[40] him;
    I am with him in adversity;
    I will set him free and honour him;

16. with length of days I will satisfy him,
    and I will show him[41] my salvation.

21 A contextual interpretation of 'according to your fear'.

22 Lit. 'bring in', but compare 2 Samuel 9:10; Haggai 1:6, where 'to bring in' refers to bringing in the harvest.

23 In the structure of the psalm, verses 13–14 balance verses 7–10 (divine love in the place of divine wrath); verse 15 balances verses 3–6 (days and years of gladness in the place of years and days of decline and disappointment); verses 16–17 balance verses 1–2 ('establishment' matching 'dwelling place').

24 Or 'and change your mind about/relent about'.

25 There is a 'false dawn' which verse 6 noted: the new generation will be different! We have turned over a new leaf! The failure of mere human promise. But there is a true dawn, a new day which God can bring in. Compare Psalms 30:5; 46:5.

26 Different voices speak in Psalm 91, and those commentators are not to be followed who 'iron out' the differences. It is a short liturgy of some sort. Either the author (Moses?) found this the best idiom to express his theme, or it was devised for some public occasion with the different 'voices' taking part.

27 See Psalm 68:14, note 28. 'Most High' and 'Shaddai' are rooted in Genesis 14. God Most High was Melchizedek's God, identified by Abram with Yahweh, but, like all the patriarchs, Abraham 'knew' Yahweh as El Shaddai (compare Genesis 17:1).

28 Note the balance between 'makes his home' and 'finds lodging'. The former suggests being welcomed into the family; the latter acknowledged that we have no natural right to this: we are stateless refugees looking for lodging.

29 Participle expressing what is unvarying.

Psalm 92.
The Most High: Undeviating in Righteousness

A song. A hymn for the Sabbath day.[42]

A.1. Unfailing praise, declaring love

1. How good[43] to give[44] thanks to Yahweh!
   And to make music to your name, O Most High.
2. To declare your committed love[45] in the morning,
   and your faithfulness every night.[46]
3. On the ten strings[47] and on the lute,
   on soft melodies[48] with the harp.

B.1. The glad people

4. Because you have made me rejoice, Yahweh, in your activity;
   on account of the works of your hands[49] I shout aloud.
5. How great are your works,[50] Yahweh!
   How exceedingly deep your thoughts!
6. The unspiritual[51] man does not know,
   and the superficial[52] does not discern this.

C.1. The wrongdoers destroyed

7. When the wicked one sprouts like grass,
   and all the wrongdoers[53] have blossomed,
   the purpose is that they be destroyed for ever.[54]

D. The eternally exalted Lord

8. And you are on high for ever, Yahweh.[55]

30 Imperfect tense, repeated, or characteristic action.

31 Or 'Certainly'.

32 Two forms of total bodily coverage. Totality expressed by contrast (compare 'bag and baggage'). Complete protection. The unused *tsanan* (whence *tsinnah*, body shield) is thought to mean 'to protect'. 'Encircling shield' comes from *sachar*, 'to encircle'. It could refer rather to an encircling wall, a 'bulwark'. This would still express 'totality by contrast'.

33 Not even an epidemic which claims lives by the myriad can touch the believer's security in God.

34 What is expressed here is not gleeful gloating but one of the facts of God's moral world.

35 This half verse is the physical and thematic centre of the psalm. The initial *kiy* (compare 90:4, note 12) is not an explanation ('because') but an affirmation ('assuredly').

36 'Hand' here is *kaph*, the 'grip' of the hand. The word is plural, 'in their firm grip'.

37 See Psalm 58:6. The heaping up of animal names here is deliberate: whatever danger from whatever quarter, in whatever strength. In verse 13a 'lion' (*shahal*) is translated by some as 'leopard', by others 'panther'. *shachal* is said to mean 'to call out', which helps not at all. If anything it might suggest 'the roaring lion' as distinct from the other word (13b, *kephiyr*) the pouncing lion.

38 This section contains seven distinct verbs of care: rescue, top-security, answer, free, honour, satisfy, show. There are three items to which Yahweh is responding: love, knowledge and prayer – the emotional, the mental and the spiritual.

C.2. The wrongdoers perishing

9. For, behold, your enemies, Yahweh –
    for, behold, it is your enemies will perish;
    all evildoers will separate from each other.[56]

B.2. The exalted people

10. And you have exalted my horn like a wild ox;
    I have been anointed[57] with fresh oil.
11. And my eye has looked[58] upon my foes;[59]
    about those rising against me – evildoers – my ear keeps
    hearing.

A.2. Unfailing vigour: declaring uprightness

12. Like a palm tree the righteous keeps sprouting,
    keeps growing up like a cedar[60] in Lebanon.
13. Transplanted[61] in Yahweh's house,
    in the courts of our God they keep sprouting out.[62]
14. They go on being fruitful in old age;[63]
    vigorous and flourishing they will be:
15. to declare that Yahweh is upright –
    my rock –
    and there is no deviancy whatever[64] in him.

39 This seems to be the significance of *chashaq* with preposition *be* (Genesis 34:8; Deuteronomy 21:11). The illustrations are dubious but the meaning plain!

40 The formation here is a co-ordinate imperfect, stressing the certain connection between prayer and response.

41 Or 'let him see', i.e. experience.

42 It is not at all obvious why Psalm 92 was so specially linked with the Sabbath. The Sabbath, as marking the completion of the works of Creation, forges a link with the stress on the activity and works of Yahweh in the psalm; likewise the holiness of the seventh day could be celebrated by the emphasis on moral rule, the joy of the righteous and the downfall of the wicked. Ancient interpretation understood the 'Sabbath' to refer to the eschatological 'Sabbath rest of the people of God', but this solves nothing, only adding another layer of imaginative possibility.

43 All senses of 'good' (*tobh*) suit: fitting the situation, right in itself, feeling good.

44 The Hebrew is simply 'Good to give …' To bring in the exclamatory 'How!' avoided the harshness of the literal.

45 Note the matching phrase 'to declare that Yahweh is upright' in the concluding section (verses 12–16).

46 'In the nights', a plural of distribution, 'each and every night'; or intensification, 'when night is darkest'; or extension, 'throughout the night'.

47 Lit. 'on the ten'. See Psalms 33:2; 144:9.

48 *higgayon*. See Psalm 9:17, note 33. As a musical term, usually understood as 'resounding music' but there is no reason (or evidence) for this. *hagah* means 'to muse, murmur' and this points to 'meditative' or 'soft' music in the background.

49 Evidence of use does not allow us to make a neat distinction between 'activity' as his works of salvation, and 'work of your hands' as creation. If there is a distinction then 'hands' makes a more direct link between the work and the agent.

50 If we are to treat the parallel section **B.2.** (verses 10–11) as interpreting **B.1.** (verses 4–6), the 'activities' and 'works' mentioned here are the ways in which Yahweh has intervened for the benefit of the psalmist.

51 See Psalm 49:10 (note 15); 73:22 (note 28). It is questionable whether we should link verse 6 back to verses 4–5 or forward to verse 7. It makes sense either way. Without the illumination of God's Spirit, God at work (4–5) remains unnoticed – whether the works are those of creation or individually applied works of salvation. Equally certainly there is blind insensitivity to coming judgment.

52 See Psalm 49:10 (Note 14). The *kesiyl* may very well be extremely clever and intelligent in other matters but spiritually and religiously he is on another planet.

53 'The workers of *'awen'*. Always needs contextual rendering, because in itself *'awen'* is non-specific – extending from mischief, to idolatry, to moral iniquity. In the present verse the parallelism with 'the wicked ones' fixes the meaning, as 'wrongdoers'.

54 This is the Spirit-given perception: that wickedness and destruction cannot be separated. To such an extent it is the case that even prosperity and fresh vigour of life are but stepping stones to doom.

55 Or 'You are exaltedness itself', a noun in apposition. You are the norm by which exaltedness can be judged. This credal statement is the exact centre of the psalm, made all the more emphatic by the three-line stanzas (verses 7, 9) on each side, contrasting with the two-line formation in the rest of the psalm.

56 *paradh*, 'to separate'. The form in verse 9 is Hithpael, which can be translated (NKJV, ESV) 'to be scattered', but it is better to retain the reflexive force of Hithpael, expressing here the inherent divisiveness of sin.

57 Uncertain, contextual translation. *balal* means 'to mix, mingle, moisten (meal ready for offering)'; not elsewhere in the meaning required here. Could 'I have been mingled with fresh oil', be a metaphor for 'I have been consecrated/made ready for Yahweh's service'?

58 Not with unholy glee at their downfall. In use it is like our expression, 'see the last of'. Compare Psalm 91:8. Likewise, of the ear – an expression only found here. Contextually the complement to 'has seen ... keeps hearing' is 'what Yahweh has done'.

59 *shur*, only found here. Presumably related to *shorer*, a (hostile) watcher, one 'keeping an eye on' someone else. See Psalm 5:8, note 45.

60 Contrast the fragility of the grass and blossom of verse 7 with the stateliness and stability of palm and cedar. The majestic with the tiny; the durable with the transient.

61 Compare Psalm 1:3. It is not by nature but by grace they are what they are: Yahweh's transplants!

62 A different form of the verb in verse 12, slightly more emphatic – 'sprouting ... sending out sprouting branches'.

63 The world's ambition is to 'stay young'; the Bible's, to grow old fruitfully. Deuteronomy 34:7.

64 The word for 'deviancy' (*awelah*) here has its extended form (*awelathah*), suggesting the emphasis 'whatever'. 'Deviancy' is a perfect contrast with 'upright/straight'.

Pause for Thought

'Taking up residence' is the thought that runs through these three psalms. In 90:1, Moses, who has been a resident alien for forty years in Midian, links himself with Israel which has seen four hundred immigrant years in Egypt. He notes that nevertheless they have had a permanent address, a dwelling place in generation after generation, the covering of the Most High (91:1). Psalm 92:13 is careful to remind us that this is all of grace: we are Yahweh's transplants. Our residency is by his will and deed: as Colossians 1:13 puts it in kingdom terms, he 'rescued us from the power of the darkness, and moved our house into the kingdom of the son of his love'; or James 1:18, in family terms, 'Having made up his mind to do so, he gave us birth by the word of truth' (compare 1 Peter 1:23). This is something that is all of God (Eph. 1:4; 2:8–9) – from the thought to the deed to the regenerating word. It is where we are; the fundamental, unchangeable truth about us in Christ. But there is another aspect to all this which we can call 'claiming our residence'. Paul put it this way. When he had reminded Timothy that the last days would include 'menacing times' (2 Tim. 3:1), seductive people (3:6), and increasing wickedness (3:13), he gave this directive (3:14), 'but as for you, abide in the things you have learned.' You have a permanent address; make sure you are living there. Make sure you can always be found 'care of' The Word of God. How did our psalms make this point? On the one hand Yahweh is our dwelling place; on the other, I keep 'Saying about Yahweh: "My refuge and my stronghold, my God, in whom I ever trust"' (91:2) … 'you, Yahweh are my refuge' (91:9). The dwelling place is mine, by divine appointment; let it also be mine by constant choice, deliberate personal reminder, personal affirmation of what is the 'real truth' about me. I live with the Holy One (90:7), so let me be holy; I live with the unfailingly loving God (92:2), so let me set my love on him (91:14). This is a great part of what the New Testament words 'in Christ' mean.

Day 43   Read Psalms 93–94[1]

Psalm 93.
A Vision Kingship:[2] Two Voices

Voice 1. Affirmation: Yahweh reigning

1.   Yahweh is king;[3]
     with exaltation he is clothed;
     Yahweh is clothed[4] –
     With strength he has girded himself.[5]
     What's more, the peopled-world is established;[6]
     it will not be shaken.

Voice 2. Testimony to Yahweh's reign, through all history, from everlasting

2.   Established is your throne from time past;[7]
     you are from eternity.

Voice 1. Affirmation: Yahweh ruling

3.   The rivers[8] have lifted up, Yahweh –
     the rivers have lifted up their voice –
     how the rivers lift up their pounding![9]
4   More than the voices of abundant waters –
     those mighty ones, the breakers of the sea –
     mighty in the height is Yahweh!

Voice 2. Testimony: Yahweh indwelling, in word and holiness

5.   Your testimonies[10] are exceedingly to be trusted;
     for your house[11] holiness is fitting,[12]
     Yahweh,
     for length of days.[13]

1   With Psalm 93 we begin a set of psalms dealing with Yahweh's kingship. Psalms 93–100 (or indeed Psalms 90–106) may be an originally separate collection inserted in its totality into the final psalter. We shall note as we go along how the psalms belong together in pairs.

2   Psalm 93 asserts and then pictures Yahweh's worldwide kingship, the turbulent world seen as the restless sea with its breakers; Psalm 94 sees Yahweh as 'Judge of the earth' (verse 2) and deals with the 'real' threats against his people.

3   Or 'reigns', a perfect tense of fixed reality: he is king because he always has been and always will be.

4   'Clothing' is used in the Old Testament with symbolic significance: depicting what a person is and what he has set himself to be and do (Joshua 5:13–14; Isaiah 59:16–18). Wearing royal robes because he is king and intends to reign as king.

5   Often in preparation for war, but also in general, readiness for action.

6   The psalm leaves us to draw the conclusion that it is the stability of Yahweh's throne that guarantees and secures the stability of the 'world of people'. The passive verb points to the fact that stability is not inherent in the world but is something achieved on its behalf.

7   Lit. 'from then', used as an indefinite reference to 'formerly', leaving it to the context to suggest how long in the past 'formerly' is.

Psalm 94.
The Judge of all the Earth:[14]
Living in Yahweh's World[15]

A.1. Appeal: to Yahweh to put the world to rights

1. Transcendent God of perfect requital,
   transcendent God of perfect requital,[16]
   shine out!
2. Lift yourself up, Judge of the earth,[17]
   return full payment upon the proud.

B.1. Wickedness defiant; against Yahweh and his people

3. How long will the wicked, Yahweh –
   how long will the wicked go on celebrating?
4. In torrents they speak arrogantly;[18]
   all the wrongdoers[19] put themselves forward.
5. Your people, Yahweh, they keep crushing,
   and your inheritance they keep humiliating.
6. Widow and refugee[20] they would kill,
   and orphans they would murder.
7. And they have said:
   Yah does not see,
   nor does the God of Jacob[21] discern!

C.1. Divine knowledge

8. Discern![22]
   You unspiritual ones[23] among the people;
   and, you dunderheads,[24] when will you be sensible?[25]
9. He who plants the ear,
   will he not hear?
   Or he who forms the eye, will he not see?
10. Does he admonish[26] nations?

8 'Rivers', seen in connection with 'pounding' waves, must refer to ocean tides or currents. (As we refer to the 'Gulf "Stream"').

9 The first two verbs are perfect tenses: the 'forces' in creation, symbolising the fixed attitude of opposition to Yahweh. The third is imperfect, used to impart liveliness to the description – expressed here by making it an exclamation!

10 See Psalm 19:7, note 8; 25:10, note 25. 'Testimony' is Yahweh himself as witness vouching for Scripture's statements, promises, warnings, truths.

11 Compare e.g. Joshua 24:15. 'House' goes beyond meaning 'temple' to mean 'household'.

12 The implication is that Yahweh, indwelling his people, in his house, is a speaking God, requiring a listening people, a holy God looking for a holy people. As in Genesis 2:3, passages dealing with Creation naturally terminate on the note of holiness: Psalms 104:35; 139:19–24.

13 As Psalm 23:6, note 49. Intended as equivalent to 'eternally', as long as days last.

14 In Psalm 93 we sat, so to speak, beside the King and looked at the world – noting that, for all its display of power, it was beneath him. In Psalm 94 we descend into the arena of the world and look at the King.

15 Compare Psalms 91:9; 92:8. Psalm 94 centres on verse 12, blessedness/happiness in Yahweh's world arises from learning his word. The judge of the earth is the teacher of his people. It is the theme of universal rule that gives Psalm 94 its place in this set of psalms.

Will he not rebuke? –
he who teaches humans knowledge!

11. Yahweh – of course[27] – knows the thoughts of
    humankind,[28]
    that they are vacuous!

D. Blessedness/happiness in Yahweh's world

12. Blessed is the individual whom you, Yah, admonish,
    and instruct out of your teaching.

C.2. Divine intentions

13. The intention is to give him rest from the days of evil,
    until a pit is dug for the wicked.
14. Because Yahweh will not abandon his people,
    nor will he forsake his inheritance;
15. because to righteousness judgment[29] will return,
    and after it[30] will go all the upright in heart.

B.2. Wickedness countered: Yahweh and his people[31]

16. Who will rise up for me against the evil doers?
    Who will take his stand for me against the wrongdoers?
17. Only that Yahweh had been my help – what a help! – and
    mine too! –
    almost my soul would have made its dwelling in silence![32]
18. If I had said,
    'My foot has slipped',
    it was your unfailing love, Yahweh, that kept upholding
    me.
19. In the abundance of my perplexing thoughts within me,
    your comforts soothe[33] me.
20. Will the throne of destruction enjoy fellowship with you
    – shaping trouble by statute?
21. They crowd together against the soul of the righteous,
    and innocent blood they pronounce guilty.

16 If distinction can be drawn between 'requital' (*neqamah*) and payment (*gemul*); the former possibly deals with the situation – doing what it requires; the latter dealing with people. But this distinction cannot be pressed. 'Perfect requital' is plural of amplitude. 'Full payment' has the 'good' meaning of 'deal bountifully with', and the 'hostile' meaning of full retribution. This prayer expresses the faith that such retribution must and can be left to Yahweh. Leviticus 19:18; Proverbs 20:22; Deuteronomy 32:35; Romans 12:19.

17 Genesis 18:25. 'Judge' is (as often) the kingly office in its functional role of making those decisions which 'set things to rights'.

18 That sins of speech precede even offences against Yahweh's people reflects the biblical sense of their seriousness. Psalm 34:12–13; Isaiah 6:5.

19 Psalm 92:7–9.

20 *ger* is a person without rights seeking protection, political asylum.

21 verse 7 puts into the mouths of the oppressors not necessarily what they said but words chosen to expose the irrationality of their position. 'Yah', the loving diminutive of Yahweh, the Exodus God who identified with his 'resident aliens' in Egypt, and who made strangers, widows and orphans his special care (compare Deuteronomy 16:11; 24:21–22). Likewise 'the God of Jacob' is the God of the homeless man without a settled future (Genesis 28:10–22). How then can they hope to maltreat the helpless and vulnerable with impunity?

22 The call to discernment is followed by allusions to God in creation (9–11); in redemption (compare 'people', 'inheritance', 13–15); in care (16–19), in judgment (20–23). God is all around if only they would see!

A.2. Affirmation: Yahweh's rule asserted

22. And Yahweh has been on my side, top-security,
    and my God the rock of my refuge.
23. And he has determined to bring back on them their mischief,
    and in payment for their evil he will cut them down.
    Yahweh, our God, will cut them down.

---

23 See psalms 49:10 (note15); 73:22 (note 28). 'Animal man', man untouched by the regenerating work of God's Spirit. 1 Corinthians 2:14.

24 *kesiyl*, cf. 49:10, note 14, the 'thickhead'.

25 See psalms 14:2; 64:9;106:7, referring to an intelligent understanding of God's working.

26 'Admonish' (*yasar*) and 'rebuke' (*yakach*) are pretty well synonymous.

27 'Of course' is intended to give 'Yahweh' the emphasis it has in the Hebrew here.

28 The relation of Creator to creature is not simply the external (so to speak) one of bringing faculties into existence. He also knows his creatures in their inward and secret reality.

29 When 'righteousness' and 'judgment' occur together, the former stands for right principles and the latter for right decisions and actions. Verse 15 sums up the perfection that is yet to be, a perfect social framework: right decisions resting on right principles, and perfected people devoted to righteousness.

30 Hebrew uses the preposition 'after' as a quasi-verb 'to follow/go after'.

31 The final settlement of things is on its way, but (15) not yet. Meantime there is need to take sides (16). Yahweh's people need his constant care (17–19), and Yahweh himself stands aloof from the scheme of things ('throne') which uses legal forms to bring about illegality (20). Questions (16, 20) bracket this section.

32 Not, of course, describing how the dead actually are but how it seems to the onlooker. Compare 'When this poor lisping, stammering tongue lies silent in the grave' (from Cowper's fine hymn, 'There is a fountain filled with blood').

33 *sha'a*, compare Isaiah 66:12, of a child being petted and cuddled.

Pause for Thought

When we look around at the world we are living in what should we see? Psalm 94:20 refers to a 'throne of destruction' – in other words governments doing or planning something we know to be a disaster, and even backing it up by fresh laws to give it a colour of rightness. What should we see? Or suppose we ourselves are 'up against it' through bad or ill-minded employers? What should we see? Psalm 93 replies, we should see a God of unimpaired sovereign rule, far, far superior in power to any, every or all forces on earth. The 'breakers' pounding us may seem invincible, but Yahweh on high is mightier. Psalm 94 replies, we should see a call to prayer, to cry out to the God to whom requital belongs (94:1–2). Are we to say, then, that we are to live 'looking two ways'? Yes, provided we understand what this means. Our first, before-all-else, look is to the real throne where real power resides. 'God is still on the throne' we used to sing – and the thoughtless accused us of being simplistic! No, not simplistic, just holding to a simple truth, the greatest and most reassuring truth that ever was. Our God is king. This is the statement of faith with which to begin every day, and of which to remind ourselves over and over as the day develops: Our God Reigns! Look into the face of disaster or ill-mindedness and affirm the truth. And let the truth hold you firm. There is no greater resource for the troubled day than 'I believe in God the Father Almighty'. Nor is there a more practical rejoinder to challenges at whatever level – governmental, civic, personal – than that to 'leave it' (Rom. 12:19) to the God to whom vengeance belongs. Leave it to him in the exercise of constant, urgent, trusting prayer. He is over all powers, he is the Creator (94:9), redeemer (14), carer (17), the God who is on our side (18–19), who knows how to dig pits and place them suitably (94:13). The God of top-security (94:22).

Day 44 Read Psalms 95–96[1]

Psalm 95.
Shout out, Bow down, Listen up!

A. The worship of God

(The Creator)

1. Come
    let us shout loudly to Yahweh.
    Let us acclaim the Rock[2] of our salvation.
2. Let us approach his face with thanksgiving.
    With songs let us acclaim him.
3. Because Yahweh is a great transcendent God,
    and a great king over all gods.[3]
4. In his hands are the deep places[4] of the earth,[5]
    and the tops of the mountains are his.
5. The sea is his, and it was he who made it,
    and as to the dry land, it was his hands shaped it.

(The Shepherd)

6. Come in,[6]
    let us worship and bow down.
    Let us kneel[7]
    before Yahweh, our Maker.[8]
7. Because he is our God,[9]
    and we the people of his pasture,[10]
    and the sheep of his hand.

B. The Word of God

Today,
if only you would listen to his voice!

1   Two psalms of singing and rejoicing. Psalm 95 lies within the fellowship of the church, those who know Yahweh as the Rock of their salvation, and are called to obedience; Psalm 96 moves out into testimony to the world of the only God, coming to put the world to rights. 'Glad tidings of Salvation' covers both psalms. Psalms 93–94 bring Yahweh's kingship into relationship with the turbulent world (93:4; 94:4–7); Psalms 95–96 bring him into relationship with 'other gods' (95:3; 96:4–5). The former pair guard us against being *blown* off course, the latter against being *enticed* off course.

2   'Rock' carries with it the obvious symbolic significance of stability, permanence, etc., but also, always in the Bible, the life-giving, smitten rock of Exodus17:6, and much more here where it introduces the theme of Massah/Meribah (Exodus 17:7) in preparation for verse 8.

3   Not that other gods 'exist' as supernal beings, but they do exist and exert a malign attraction as objects of worship – as in 1 Corinthians 8:5; compare 1 John 5:21. And we become like what we worship, Psalm 115:8.

8. Do not harden your heart,
   like Meribah,
   like the day at Massah in the wilderness
9. when your fathers put me to the test,[11]
   tried me out,
   yes – and they had seen[12] my action!
10. For forty years I loathed a generation,
    and said:
    'They are people going astray in their heart.
    They (of all people!) do not know my ways!'
11. To whom I swore in my exasperation,
    'I swear they will not come into[13] my rest.'

Psalm 96.
Joy to the World

A.1. Command to sing

1. Sing to Yahweh a new[14] song.
   Sing to Yahweh, all the earth.
2. Sing to Yahweh;
   bless[15] his name.

B.1. Command to tell (of salvation)

Tell the good news[16] of his salvation from day to day.
3. Recount his glory among the nations;
   among all the peoples his wonders.

C.1. Explanation: Yahweh the Creator[17]

4. Because
   Yahweh is great and exceedingly worthy to be praised
   he is to be reverenced above all gods.[18]
5. Because all the gods of the nations are godlets[19]
   and as for Yahweh, the very heavens are what he has
   made!

4 Lit. 'places of search', needing exploration, research sites. But in context, to contrast with 'mountain tops', 'depths'. In mythology the depths belonged to Molech, demon-worship, the god of fiendish cruelty and human sacrifice by fire (2 Kings 21:6). The mountain-tops were the domain of Baal who was worshipped on 'high places' (2 Kings 23:15 etc.), and Tiamat/ Rahab ruled the waves. To the psalmist, all alike belonged to Yahweh, the Creator and only God. Note totality by contrast: depths/tops; sea/dry land; the vertical (depth/tops) and the horizontal (sea/land); Molech and Baal were 'gods' of Canaan, Tiamat of Babylon. Hence: all creation, all gods.

5 The work of creation is evidence of genuine Godhead, Psalm 96:5.

6 More specific than 'come' (*halak*) in verse 1. *bo'* here underlines access, 'come in' (Romans 5:1–2; Ephesians 2:18). If Psalm 95 is a 'processional', verse 1 invites people to join the procession; verse 6 invites them actually to enter the temple precincts.

7 The psalm moves from Creation, the realm of the general grace of God, to redemption, his care of his flock, the realm of special grace. Creation excites the voice of praise; redemption, the bowed knee of worship.

8 Referring to Israel, the redeemed people, to 'make' signifies 'made us what we are' – by election, redemption, revelation, etc.

9 Following 'made us' (note 8), he is 'our God' not by our choice of him but his choice of us!

10 'Pasture' points the general work of the shepherd, leading his flock from place to place; 'hand' is his particular care of the individual sheep, as each passes under his hand each night into the safety of the fold.

6. Splendour and majesty are before him;
    strength and beauty in his sanctuary.

A.2. Command to worship

7. Give to Yahweh,
    families of the earth,
    give to Yahweh glory and strength.
8. Give to Yahweh the glory of his name.
    Bring a gift-offering,[20]
    and come in to his courts.
9. Bow in worship to Yahweh in the majesty of holiness.[21]
    Writhe[22] before him, all the earth!

B.2. Command to tell (of security)

10. Say among the nations;
    'Yahweh is king!
    Yes, indeed, the world of people will be established;
    It will not be shaken.
    He will decide the case of the people with fairness.'

C.2. Explanation: Yahweh the Judge[23]

11. Let the heavens rejoice,
    and the earth exult.[24]
    Let the sea and its fullness thunder;[25]
12. let the field and all that is in it celebrate.
    Oh then all the trees of the forest will shout aloud! –
13. Before Yahweh! When he comes!
    Because
    he is coming to judge the world.
    He will judge the world of people with righteousness,
    and the peoples with his truth.

---

11 'Test' and 'Try' are synonyms. To 'put Yahweh to the test' (Exodus 17:2) is to withhold trust until he provides fresh proof – instead of believing on the basis of what he has already done. As though to say, 'Can he do it again? We'll believe him if he does!' The psalm looks back to Exodus 17; Numbers 14:22; Numbers 20:13. They turned an occasion on which they could prove that they were believers into a chance for God to prove that he was among them!

12 Or 'saw', i.e. Yahweh's reaction in mercy and judgment throughout the wilderness years. 'Had seen' exposes the unbelievable nature of their refusal to trust after all he had done in Egypt and at the Red Sea, etc. This seems to me the preferable understanding.

13 Matching 'come in' in verse 6, an inclusion which binds the two sections of the psalm together.'They' may not enter, but the door is still open! See Hebrews 3:7–4:11.

14 The idea is 'a fresh song', responding to truth freshly received, fresh experience. Just as 'compassion' is 'new every morning' (Lamentations 3:22–23) so is the responsive song.

15 See Psalm 26:12.

16 The unceasing message (day after day) is the core truth of salvation; God's glory is who and what he is in himself – the revelation summarised by his name. His wonders are how he has done what he has done.

17 Yahweh's position as Creator gives him the right to address all the earth.

18 On 'all gods' see Psalm 95:3, note 3.

19 A punning effect in Hebrew: 'the elohim are elilim' – 'nothings', pale imitations of the real thing.

20　This is addressed to all the earth: there is an offering which admits them to the 'courts' and then to the very presence of Yahweh, 'before him'.

21　In the full reality of his holy nature.

22　'Writhe' as though in pain. A very strong expression, here, of a deep sense of the holy God. Some understand the verb to be 'to whirl', i.e. of ritual dance.

23　How can the coming of a judge be a call to rejoicing? Because 'judge' basically refers not to condemnation but to making those decisions which will put everything to rights. The whole world at last under the perfect king!

24　Human sin brought the earth itself into 'the bondage of corruption' (Genesis 3:17–19; Romans 8:19–22). When Yahweh comes to reign, the curse will be lifted from creation, liberating it into its true exuberance. Compare the stones crying out, Luke 19:40.

25　Contrast the sea in Psalm 93:3–4. 'Its fullness' – everything in it – is important. The sea was mythologically the sphere of Tiamat/Rahab. 'All that is in it' leaves no room for continuing alien powers of any sort. Philippians 2:9–11.

Pause for Thought

When John commands his readers to 'keep yourselves from idols' (1 John 5:21) he is looking beyond the mere outward fact of physical representations of 'gods' in wood and stone to the supposed reality behind them. In this sense, the ancient 'gods' which the psalms inveigh against are extraordinarily relevant today. Baal makes the most obvious connection. Mountain tops belonged to him (Ps. 95:4) because his worship required visibility. It had to be performed where he could see it. You see, Baal was not a person but a force, the force that guaranteed fertility – for humans, animals and land. The only way to try to make this important force operate was to do, visibly, on earth what you wanted Baal to do from heaven – hence Baal sanctuaries concentrated on the sexual acts of human fertility hoping that Baal would see and copy. It was called imitative magic. If Baal took the hint, the economy prospered. And there, indeed, is the point: wherever nothing is more important than 'the economy'; where 'market forces' are the primary factors; where the 'gross national product' is what really matters – Baal is still worshipped. Should we also say that where sex is exalted out of all proportion, Baal is worshipped? Where materialism reigns supreme? Or we trust our bank balances for security? Tiamat ruled the sea (95:5) – the sea with its constant, powerful battering against the defences of the habitable land. Tiamat was the god of success by power. So then wherever physical prowess is the priority, where problems are to be solved by militarism and domination, Tiamat is still on the throne. At a local level Tiamat is the god of the bully, the ruthless pursuit of the 'rat race', the business empire which trampled on its competitors. Molech, with his dreadful rituals in the depths of the earth (95:4), is the god of things done in darkess or in hiding – wherever the occult is 'god' – or there is a secret life under whatever cover (Eph. 5:8–12). May we see to it that for us the deep places are in 'his hand; the heights belong to him, and the sea is his!'

Day 45 Read Psalms 97–98[1]

Psalm 97.
'Oh, the joy to see Thee reigning!'[2]

A.1. Reigning God: rejoicing world

1. Yahweh is king:
    let the earth exult;[3]
    let the abundance of coastlands[4] rejoice.

B.1. The world-rule of the righteous God

(His throne)

2. Clouds and darkness[5] surround him;
    righteousness and judgment[6] are the basis of his throne.

(His enemies)

3. Before him, what a fire[7] goes!
    And it consumes his adversaries all round.

(His presence)

4. His lightning[8] illuminates the world of people;
    the world of people sees and writhes.

5. Even mountains melt like wax because of Yahweh's
    presence –
    because of the presence of the Sovereign of all the earth.

(Cosmic revelation)

6. The heavens have declared[9] his righteousness,
    and all the people will see his glory.

C.1. The shaming of idolaters; the submission of
their gods

7. All those who serve an idol will reap shame –

1 So far these psalms have established
the link between kingship and holiness
(93:5; 94:15, 20; 96:9, 13). In Psalms
97–98 this rises to a climax: the
throne of righteousness (97:2); the
declaration of righteousness (97:6); the
call to righteousness (97:10–12); the
righteousness of God (98:2); coming
righteousness (98:9); Yahweh as the
God of the holy name (97:12); and
the holy arm (98:1). Note also the link
with joy (97:1; 98:8).

2 From F.R. Havergal's hymn, 'Thou art
coming, O my Saviour!'

3 Note how 'exult … rejoice' open the
first half of the psalm, and 'rejoice …
exult' open the second half (8).

4 'Islands', but in usage, with the general
meaning of 'coasts' or simply 'regions',
'iyiym is used of what we might call 'far
flung' places; in Isaiah 40:15 it would
be better represented as 'land-masses'.
Places only reached by water.

5 Pictorial features drawn from
Sinai: Exodus 19:9, 16, 18; 20:21;
Deuteronomy 4:11; 5:22.

6 As ever, when paired, righteous
principles matched by just practice.
Both are aspects of holiness (Isaiah
5:16).

7 The symbol of divine holiness in its
active aspect as hostile to and a danger
to sin and sinners. Exod. 3:2, 5; 19:18,
21; Deut. 5:24–26; Isa. 33:14.

8 On natural 'forces' as evidence of the
presence of God, Psalm 18:7–15.

who are making their boast in the godlets.[10]
Bow in worship to him, all you gods!

A.2. Revealing God: rejoicing church

8. Zion has heard and rejoiced,
    and the daughters of Judah have exulted
    because of your judgments,[11] Yahweh,

B.2. The supernatural rule of the Most High God

9. because you, Yahweh, are Most High over all the earth.
    Exceedingly you are exalted over all gods.

C.2. The joy of the righteous in a God of salvation

(Moral commitment)
10. O you who love Yahweh, hate evil.

(Guaranteed care and enrichment)
    He simply[12] keeps the souls of his beloved;
    from the hand of the wicked he delivers them.
11. Light is sown[13] for the righteous,
    and for the upright in heart rejoicing.

(Joy in a revealed God)
12. Rejoice, you righteous ones in Yahweh,
    and give thanks to the memorial[14] of his holiness.

Psalm 98.
One God, One World, One Shout![15]

A Song.

A. Yahweh the Saviour (of all the earth)

(Salvation accomplished)
1. Sing to Yahweh a new song

9   As in Psalm 19:1–4, the creation has always 'spoken' of the Creator, hence the contrast between past and future tenses here.

10 See Psalm 96:5. Significantly, the church (Zion, Yahweh's people) is depicted as rejoicing over what he has revealed. See next note.

11 e.g. Deuteronomy 5:1, 'judgments' is used as a comprehensive word for what Yahweh has decided upon as truth and requirement, his revealed truth.

12 I have introduced the word 'simply' to reflect the emphasis on 'keeps' in the Hebrew.

13 An unusual association of ideas. It signifies that 'light' is always available and bearing fruit for Yahweh's beloved who walk in his way.

14 Compare Exodus 3:15. Yahweh's name is his memorial, how he is to be remembered.

15 Psalm 98 makes clear what earlier psalms in this series implied: the world is saved in Israel's salvation. What Yahweh does for Israel he does for all.

16 'For him' stresses that salvation is Yahweh's plan: he has achieved what he set out to achieve.

17 i.e. not only is salvation Yahweh's personal work, but also it has been done in such a way as to satisfy the claims of his holiness. See verse 2, where 'righteousness' and 'salvation' are parallel terms.

18 It is because of his commitment in love and truth to Israel that his salvation is available to all.

19 On the restoration of creation to its true state, see Psalm 96:11–13.

20 Set everything to rights.

because of the wonderful things he has done.
His right hand has achieved salvation for him,[16]
and the arm of his holiness.[17]

(Salvation revealed)
2.   Yahweh has made known his salvation:
    in the sight of the nations
    he has revealed his righteousness.

(Salvation explained)[18]
3.   He has remembered his committed love and his truth
    for the house of Israel.
    All the ends of the earth have seen
    The salvation of our God.

B. Yahweh the king (of all the earth)

4.   Shout aloud to Yahweh, all the earth;
    burst forth, and shout out, and make music.
5.   Make music to Yahweh with the lute and the voice of
    melody.
6.   With trumpets and the voice of the horn,
    Shout aloud before Yahweh, the king.

C. Yahweh the judge (of all the earth)

7.   Let the sea[19] thunder, and all it contains,
    the peopled-world and those living in it.
8.   Rivers – let them clap hands.
    Together let mountains too shout out,
9.   before Yahweh
    because he is coming to judge[20] the earth:
    he will judge the world of people with righteousness,
    and peoples with fairness.

Pause for Thought

There can be no salvation until God declares himself satisfied. Put like that, it makes sense, does it not? If God were indifferent to our sin, we would not need saving. Rather, he would say, 'Oh, what does it matter? Let's not bother!' But his holiness (97:12) will not let him take that view. Our sin does matter – simply because he is what he is. Right, then, salvation has to satisfy holiness or it is not salvation. Psalm 97 focuses in on Yahweh's own and terrible righteousness: it is the foundation of what he is (2), inherent in the very nature of things (6), and drastically dangerous to his enemies (3–4). Salvation must – if it is real salvation – satisfy that righteousness. Psalm 98 says that it does. Salvation itself is a work of holiness (98:1); when Yahweh makes known his salvation, he is revealing his righteousness (2). To such a complete extent does his salvation meet his righteous requirements that 'salvation' and 'righteousness' are parallel terms – different words describing the same thing. We can therefore confidently say that the holy God is satisfied to look on him (Jesus) and pardon me – satisfied, the very heart of salvation! Look at Hebrews 12:22–24 (NKJV). We are called 'just' and 'made perfect', and the proof of this is that we live, without fear, in the presence of 'God the judge of all'. The supreme Judge himself is content to have us! Satisfied! Now we can feel the rightness and force of Psalm 97:10–12. We are called 'the righteous' because that is our status in his presence – in New Testament terms,

> Clothed in His righteousness alone,
> Faultless to stand before the throne.

Isn't it very obvious, then, that we are called on to 'hate evil' and to rejoice in that which brings the holiness of our God to mind?

Day 46   Read Psalms 99–100[1]

Psalm 99.
The quadrilateral of the reigning king[2]

A. Exaltation

1. Yahweh is king.
   The peoples tremble.
   He sits enthroned upon the Cherubim.[3]
   The earth shakes.
2. In Zion Yahweh is great,
   and he is high over all the peoples.
3. Give thanks to his name.
   Great and to be feared.
   He is holy.

B. Atonement

4. And it is judgment that the strength of the king loves.[4]
   You have yourself established fairness.
   Judgment and righteousness[5] in Jacob
   you have yourself done.
5. Exalt Yahweh our God,
   and bow in worship at his footstool:[6]
   he is holy.

C. Revelation[7]

6. Moses and Aaron were among[8] his priests,
   and Samuel among those calling on his name.
   They were calling to Yahweh,
   and he himself used to hear them.

1   Psalms 96 and 98 looked forward to the coming reign of the king. Psalms 99–100 depict what it will be like when he does reign, with his worldwide rule and the whole world coming singing into his presence.

2   The poetic formation of this psalm dictates its division into four parts: verses 3, 5, 7, 9 are all composed of three lines, compared with the two-line form of the rest of the psalm.

3   The Cherubim here denote the awesome exaltation of Yahweh. They are the guardians of his holiness (Genesis 3:24), the supporters of God enthroned over all creation (Ezekiel 1:10 with 10:15; 1:22, 25–28).

4   This wording is unusual but perfectly understandable. Those who would emend the text lack imagination. Poetry is poetry. With all his strength the king backs the decisions ('judgment') he has made; he is devoted to his truth.

5   On this pair, see 97:2, note 5.

6   Yahweh is enthroned on the Cherubim (1), so what is his footstool? The Cherubim were part of the 'mercy-seat'/the 'atonement cover' of the Ark (Exodus 25:17–21). The feet of the enthroned God rested on the 'mercy seat'; the transcendently holy God 'touched earth' at the place where the atoning blood was sprinkled (Leviticus 16:15), and the 'mercy seat' was over the tablets of the law whose breach constituted our sin (Exodus 40:20).

7. In the pillar of cloud he used to speak to them.
   They kept his testimonies,[9]
   and the statute[10] he gave them.

D. Forgiveness and discipline

8. Yahweh our God,
   you answered them yourself.
   Transcendent God, bearing sin away,[11] you were to them,
   and one avenging their actions.[12]
9. Exalt Yahweh our God,
   and bow in worship at the mountain of his holiness,
   because Yahweh our God is holy.

Psalm 100.
The Worshipping World[13]

A song for thanksgiving.

A. Come in because he is God

(The threefold call)
1. Shout aloud to Yahweh, all the earth.[14]
2. Serve Yahweh with joy.
   Come in to his presence with loud shouting.

(Explanation)
3. Know that Yahweh is God:[15]
   he made us himself,[16]
   and we are his[17] –
   his people,
   and the sheep of his pasture.

B. Come in because he is good

(The threefold call)
4. Come in within his gates with thanksgiving,[18]

7 Verse 6 describes the reality of the holy God living among his people. There was a true fellowship with him; calling out and being answered. Verse 7: this fellowship rests on the revealed truth – Yahweh's personal voice speaking (Exodus 29:42–46; 33:9–11), testifying to his truth, and embodying his truth in his statutes as a way of life.

8 The three named individuals are noted as 'among'– i.e. not chosen for their speciality but as typical of fellowship with Yahweh. Did Yahweh speak to Samuel in the cloud? Only if (as may have been the case) the cloud remained on the Tabernacle during its days in Shiloh (1 Samuel 1:3).

9 Psalms 19:7, note 8; 25:10, note 25.

10 See Psalm 81:4, note 5.

11 The verb 'to bear/carry away' is used as an ellipsis for 'bearing sin away', based on the reality seen in Leviticus 16:20–22. The psalm either (daringly) sees Yahweh as the sin-bearer or as providing the sacrifice which bears sin.

12 Compare Exodus 34:7.

13 Compare Psalm 95:6–7 with 100:2–3. What the former says about Yahweh's people the latter says about a worldwide people. Psalm 100 is the incoming of a world-Israel into Yahweh's presence in worship. This is its place as the climax of a series which has repeatedly proclaimed Yahweh as the universal king.

14 Progressive nearness: the homage shout leads to worship in religious 'service', and then to enjoyment of Yahweh's presence.

15 From the centre outwards: what Yahweh is in his own nature; what he has done; and what he now and always is to his people.

his courts with praise.
Give thanks to him.
Bless his name

(Explanation)
5.   because Yahweh is good.[19]
    For ever is his committed love,
    and to generation after generation his truth.

---

16 Not the work of creation but of making his people what they are. See Psalm 95:6; Isaiah 43:1.

17 Or 'and not we ourselves'. This is a case where we choose between *lo'* ('not') and *lo* '(belonging) to him' – or accept both! Both make sense in context.

18 Increasing nearness: from the gate to the court to the intimate reality of the name. On 'Blessing Yahweh', see Psalm 26:12.

19 From the centre outwards: his essential goodness, the committed love that reaches out to his people, the extension of fidelity or dependability through time.

Pause for Thought

From earth's wide bounds, from ocean's furthest coast,
Through gates of pearl streams in the countless host,
Singing to Father, Son and Holy Ghost,
Allelujah! Allelujah!

That is what Psalm 100 celebrates. Isaiah (24:14–16a) heard the pilgrims sing as they picked their way through a broken earth to their home of bliss, and he caught more than a glimpse of what awaited them (Isa. 25:6-10a). Paul foresaw the gathering from a different and altogether more wonderful perspective – the union of all Jesus' people at his blessed Return (1 Thess. 4:15–17). John was actually allowed to see the eternal reality of the innumerable company, their white robes, their palm branches of welcome; to hear their shouts of acclamation and acknowledgement of their God-wrought salvation; to marvel at the blood that cleansed their robes, and to learn of the Lamb who was their Shepherd (Rev. 7:9–17); and finally to see the heavenly Zion itself (Rev. 21:2, 27),

a city bright;
Closed are its gates to sin;
Naught that defileth …
Can ever enter in.

Today's 'thought' is not to be '*lost* in wonder, love and praise' as Wesley puts it, but to be '*found* in wonder, love and praise', reminding ourselves that though as pilgrims we are still en route, nevertheless it is our privilege, even now, to savour our citizenship (Phil. 3:20) – to live in the night as if in The Day (Rom. 13:12), and in our resident alienship here as at home in the eternal Zion (Heb. 12:22). Two elderly friends of mine had the privilege of an invitation to Her Majesty's garden party at the palace. A kindly parking attendant, noting their age, pointed them to a gate off the car-park. 'Go in that way. It will save you a long walk.' 'What!' said they. 'What!! Do you think that with the Queen's invitation in our hands we are going in by a back gate!!!' Revelation 22:14.

Day 47 Read Psalms 101–102

Psalm 101.
Ideals for a King[1]

Belonging to David. A song.

A. Beginning with God[2]

1. Of committed love and judgment do let me sing.
   To you, Yahweh, let me make music.
2. Let me act prudently in a way of integrity.
   When will you come to me?

B. Home and heart

   I will go around[3] with integrity of heart within my house.
3. I will not place before my eyes[4] a thing of worthlessness.[5]
   The doing of compromise[6] I determine to hate;
   it will not cling to me.
4. A crooked heart will go away from me;
   evil I will not know.

C. Society

5. One covertly slandering his associate[7] –
   him I will exterminate.
   Haughtiness of eyes and arrogance of heart –
   him I will not put up with![8]

D. At court[9]

6. My eyes are on the trustworthy ones of the land
   that they may live with me.
   Whoever walks in the way of integrity –

1 The psalm sounds like David's meditation on the standards and practices that should mark the ideal king. Compare the psalm with the beginning of his advice to Solomon when he passed on the throne (1 Kings 2:2–4). But (like his advice to Solomon) the ideals were somewhat lost in transit! Nevertheless what David failed to achieve remains as a testament to true kingship, and a forecast of the True King. The analysis of the psalm into subject matter is tentative. A psalm for every leader to ponder.

2 The starting point for the ideal king: pondering what is true about Yahweh (1a); joyful worship (1b), commitment to consistency backed by longing for the divine presence.

3 Lit. 'walk about, go here and there', his life-style.

4 'Eyes' symbolise what one is 'looking for' in life, aims and objectives.

5 'A matter of Belial' see Psalms 18:4, note 8; 41:8, note 30. The king's priorities, positive values, nothing that is a 'waste of time'.

6 Very uncertain translation. The verb seems to be a participle, possibly 'those who fall away'. Maybe to backslide, compromise. The point here is not the company of such people but 'the doing of/the activity of'; the behaviour they exemplify.

7 A very non-specific word. Contextually it can mean 'friend' etc. but often, as here, simply 'somebody else': 'his contemporary', 'his fellow man'.

he is the one who will be my minister.

7. There will not live within my house anyone who works deceit.
   Whoever speaks lies will not be established in front of my eyes.

E. Administration of justice

8. Morning after morning[10] I will exterminate
   all the wicked of the land,
   so as to cut down from Yahweh's city all wrongdoers.

Psalm 102.
Messiah: hesitations and assurances[11]

A prayer belonging to the downcast when he is fainting, and pours out his musing before Yahweh.

A. Fleeting days[12]

1. Yahweh, do hear my prayer,
   and my cry for help – let it come to you.

2. Do not hide your face from me,
   on the day I am in adversity.
   Turn your ear to me;
   on the day I keep calling, answer me with speed.

3. Because my days end in smoke,[13]
   and my bones are scorched like a hearth,[14]

4. my heart has been struck like grass and has dried up.
   Indeed, I have been forgetful of eating my bread.

5. Through the voice of my groaning my bones[15] have stuck to my flesh.

6. I resemble a pelican[16] in the wilderness;
   I have become like an owl in the wasteland;

7. I am wakeful, and have become

8. Lit. 'be able for'. In situations of conflicts, 'to overcome, have strength to deal with'. Here 'cannot stand'.

9. 'Live with me', 'my minister', 'my house' suggest that we are dealing with the 'court' David gathered round him to run things.

10. Compare Exodus 18:13 and (sadly) 2 Samuel 15:2–4.

11. Hebrews 1:10–12 authoritatively points to the interpretation of Psalm 102 when it uses verses 25–27 to assert the eternal deity of Jesus. In these verses, says Hebrews, the God himself is addressing God incarnate, the Father speaks to the Son. Understood like this Psalm 102 is very holy ground where we must step hesitantly. It is not only concerning the pains of Messiah that 'we may not know, we cannot tell'. Did the Lord Jesus Christ experience the hesitations of verses 3–11, for example? In the reality of his incarnation, when he was tested in all points as we are (Hebrews 4:15), the answer, in principle, must be yes, and there are biblical passages to be consulted in confirmation, passages prompting reverence but not encouraging probing: Isaiah 49:4; Mark 9:19; John 12:24–28; Hebrews 5:7. In Psalm 102 we stand beside our incarnate Lord Jesus, and walk with him through a dark valley into the light of assurance with which the psalm ends. As with Psalms 22 and 40 we assume here some earthly experience of the Davidic king modulated by inspiration to speak of the promised king to come.

12. These verses are carefully crafted. Following the opening prayer to be heard (verses 1 and 2): verses 3 and 11 – the brevity of life; verses 4–5 with verses 9 and 10 – listlessness and its explanation; verses 6 to 8 – isolation, opposition and mockery.

13. Like the expression to 'go up in smoke', vanish utterly.

like a sparrow perched alone on a roof.

8. All day long my enemies reproach me;
    those who view me with arrogance swear.[17]

9. Indeed, ashes[18] like bread I have eaten,
    and my drink with weeping I have blended,

10. because of your indignation and impatience,[19]
    because you lifted me up and threw me down.

11. My days like a shadow have declined,
    and as for me, like grass I dry up.

B. The basis of assurance[20]

12. And as for you, Yahweh,
    for ever you will sit enthroned.
    And your remembrance[21] is for generation after
    generation.

13. You will yourself actively[22] have compassion to Zion,
    because there is an appropriate time for showing grace,
    because the appointed time is coming,

14. because your servants take pleasure in its stones,
    and even its dust they view with favour.

15. And the nations will fear the name of Yahweh,
    and all the kings of the earth his glory,

16. because Yahweh has determined to build Zion,
    to display himself in his glory.

17. He is sure to turn to the prayer of the resourceless,[23]
    and not to despise their prayer.

18. This is put in writing about a future generation;
    and a people to be created will praise Yah.

19. Because Yahweh will certainly look down from the height
    of his holiness;[24]
    will certainly gaze from heaven to earth –

20. to hear the sighing of the prisoner,
    to release the sons of dying,

21. to recount in Zion the name of Yahweh,
    and his praise in Jerusalem,

22. when the peoples are gathering together,

14 'Like a hearth' is a tentative rendering involving a fresh division of the Hebrew consonants. As the test stands it uses an unknown word.

15 The Hebrew here is singular, 'my bone'; this is in order to achieve a rhyming effect which cannot be carried over into English, but is extremely effective in achieving pathos in the Hebrew.

16 These animal identifications are customary but uncertain.

17 Possibly 'those who are mad at me', lit. 'my madmen'. The basic meaning (*halal*) is 'to be boastful', arrogantly confident. Maybe, 'make a fool of me.' 'Swear', *shabh'a* followed by preposition *be*, regularly points to the basis on which an ought is sworn, 'to swear by'. Here, uniquely, it either means 'to swear at' (heap curses on), or 'use me as a swear word'.

18 A sign of humiliation (2 Samuel 13:19), mourning (Esther 4:1).

19 Two of Hebrews words for 'anger', 'indignation', *za'am*, the hostility of anger; and 'impatience', *qatsaph,* the 'snappishness' of anger.

20 Like verses 1–11, this section also consists of matching portions, centring on verse 17, Yahweh's guarantee to hear and answer the prayer of the resourceless: verses 12, 22, the enduring Lord and coming kingdom; verses 13, 21, Zion's guaranteed future; verses 14, 20, present and future citizens of Zion; verses 15, 19, the kings of earth and the Lord of heaven; verses 16, 18, the coming city and its people.

21 Exodus 3:15. That by which Yahweh wishes to be remembered in his name, as 'shorthand' for what he revealed of himself at the Exodus: the God who redeems his people and overthrows his foes.

and the kingdoms, to serve Yahweh.

C. Full assurance[25]

23. He humbled my strength along the way,
    cut short my days.
    I kept saying:
24. 'O my transcendent God,
    do not take me up at the halfway mark of my days.'

(Yahweh's reply!)
    Throughout generation after generation are your years.
25. Earlier on you founded the earth itself,
    and the heavens are the work of your own hands.
26. It is they which will perish,
    and it is you who will stand –
    all of them, like a garment will grow old,[26]
    like clothing you will change them,
    and they will change.
27. And you are the same,
    and your years will not reach completion.
28. The sons of your servants will take up residence,
    and in your presence[27] their seed will be established.

22 Two verbs without conjunction: the second being the main idea and the first equivalent to an adverb. So 'you will arise have compassion', 'you will actively/effectively …' etc.

23 From *'arar*, to strip oneself, an intensive noun, 'stripped, laid bare', metaphorical for 'destitute'.

24 Not just the place ('his holy height') but the essential reality of God himself in his holiness.

25 In verses 23–24a Messiah speaks, seeking to be saved from death; in verses 24b–28 God replies. The heavenly Father and the Incarnate Son in holy conversation. Messiah is the Eternal and the Creator, passing on eternal life to his 'children'.

26 These three lines speak in turn of intrinsic obsolescence, divine action in making change, and permanency of result.

27 i.e. and you will be there to see it!

Pause for Thought

Nowadays Psalm 101 would be called 'David's Mission Statement'. We can picture him at the start of his monarchy setting out the sort of king he intends to be, the 'court' he will assemble, and with what objectives he will rule his people. The fact that – in the Bible's honest way – we know how he failed, does not take away from the fact that this is a noble statement, and one from which every one of us, whether in leadership or simply in the course of influence, can draw lessons. We cannot, of course, set about purging society as David vowed (101:8), but we can pray that our leaders will do so: like the old prayer says, 'the punishment of wickedness and vice and the maintenance of godly living and virtue'. We are, though, often in a position to determine who our close associates will be – or our marriage partners (6–7). One thing, however, is vital – to start where David started. How often have we heard it said today that what a person is and does in private is his business, and does not effect his public duties? David would not agree! See how he began with the 'private man', his life of praise with God (1), his domestic and personal ideals (2–4). David knew that what he was in secret and in private and at home shaped the man he hoped to be in public. And this is the main way in which his 'Mission Statement' speaks to each and every one of us. It is what Jesus put in his perfect way when he said, 'Cleanse the inside of the cup and dish, that the outside of them may be clean also' (Matt. 23:26, NKJV) – not, in fact, a good policy for the washing up, but an essential truth about holy living: everything starts on the inside. It is exactly as Proverbs 4:23 says!

Day 48 Read Psalm 103

Psalm 103

David's.

A.1. Personal responses: Yahweh's benefits

1. My soul, bless Yahweh,
    and all my inward being, the name of his holiness.[1]
2. My soul, bless Yahweh,
    and do not forget all[2] his sufficiencies.[3]
3. He is forgiving to all your iniquities,
    he is the healer of all your illnesses,
4. he redeems your life from the pit,
    he crowns you with committed love and compassion,[4]
5. he satisfies your ongoing life[5] with good,
    so that your youth is renewed to be like an eagle.[6]

B. Yahweh's benefits explored

6. Yahweh is ever working total righteousness,[7]
    and exact judgment for all the oppressed.
7. He kept making known his ways to Moses,[8]
    to the sons of Israel his activities.
8. Compassionate and gracious is Yahweh,
    patient, and abundant in committed love.
9. Not in perpetuity does he find fault,[9]
    nor for ever does he keep on.
10. Not according to our sins[10] has he acted towards us,
    nor according to our iniquities has he paid us in full.
11.[11] Because like the height of the heavens over the earth
    his committed love is mighty[12] over those who fear him;
12. like the distance of the east from the west[13]
    he has distanced our rebellions[14] from us;

1 Rather than reducing this full expression to 'his holy name', I prefer the literal rendering – the name encapsulated his holiness.

2 Note how the word 'all' comes four times and is balanced by the four 'alls' in verses 19–22.

3 Lit. 'his (full or exact) requitals'. The word often refers to Yahweh's apportionment of exact justice, but here the thought is his full sufficiency for every need.

4 The two sides of divine love: 'compassion' is his passionate love, love in all its emotional content and excitement – compare 1 Kings 3:26. 'Committed love' is love expressed by a determined act of the will, fixed, committed, 'till death do us part'.

5 A translation dependent on a slight alteration of the Hebrew text, ever uncertain.

6 i.e. in its natural vitality. The supposition that an eagle can 'renew' itself is unfounded.

7 Plural of amplitude, so also 'exact judgment'. The former, Yahweh's consistent fidelity to righteous principles, the latter his undeviating correctness of decision in each case. Note his righteousness in verse 6 is balanced by righteousness in verses 17–18.

13. like a father has compassion[15] for his sons
    Yahweh has compassion for those who fear him.
14. Because he himself knows our form,[16]
    he is reminded that we are dust.
15. Mortal man – his days are like grass,
    like the blossom in the field, so he blossoms,
16. because a wind has passed over it and it is not,
    and its place does not recognize it any longer.
17. And Yahweh's committed love[17] is from eternity to
    eternity
    for those who fear him,
    and his righteousness to the sons of sons,
18. to those who keep his covenant,
    and to those who remember his precepts[18] so as to do
    them.

A.2. Cosmic responses: Yahweh's universal dominion

19. Yahweh has established his throne in heaven,
    and his kingliness rules over all.
20. Bless Yahweh, you his angels,
    mighty in power, doing his word.
21. Bless Yahweh, all his hosts,
    ministering to him, doing his will.
22. Bless Yahweh, all his works,
    in all places of his rule.
    My soul, bless Yahweh.

8   The Exodus, as ever, the classical story of human unworthiness and divine grace. Verses 7–8 are matched by verses 14–16, the revelation of God in characteristic action (his ways); specific deeds (his activities); and intrinsic character – concern for the undeserving (grace), committed love, knowledge of humanity in its frailty, patience, love.

9   *riybh*, technically of bringing a case to law, pursuing a suit. Verse 9 matches verses 12–13: the double 'not' ('not/nor') of verse 9 and the double comparison, 'as' ('like'), of verses 12–13.

10 'Sins' are actual commissions and omissions, specific misdemeanours. Iniquities points to the hidden warp or defect in human nature giving rise to sins.

11 The central verse of the section.

12 Prevails or dominates like a warrior (*gabhar*) in prowess. Compare Genesis 7:18–20 where the flood 'prevailed', covered, dominated.

13 i.e. immeasurable.

14 The third word in the 'sin' group, the wilful rebellion which says 'no' to the will of God

15 Passionate, maternal love, as 1 Kings 3:26.

16 Referring to the 'shaping' of man in Genesis 2:7.

17 *chesedh*, love as an act and determination of the will.

18 The word is *piqqudh*, suggesting detailed application of law to life.

Pause for Thought

Psalm 103 is not unique in the psalms of David but like, for example, Psalm 145, it is an exercise in sheer concentration on Yahweh, without mention of circumstances good or bad, no reference to enemies. Just Yahweh, his benefits and sufficiencies. The three wonderful comparisons in verses 11–13 tell us everything. The first concerns height, the second distance and the third parenthood. Just as the heavens overarch the whole earth, so Yahweh's unfailing, committed love *prevails*. The same verb is used of the floodwaters (Gen. 7:18–20) irresistibly covering the earth and swamping every opposition. Just so his love is always there (overarching) and is an active force fighting like an armed man on our side, irresistibly sufficient for every opposition and eventuality. 'East is East and West is West, and never the twain shall meet.' I don't know what the poet meant, but geographically the words are correct. Micah (7:19) saw all our sins in the depths of the sea (like atomic waste sunk where it can do no more harm). David went one better: the distance is infinite, never ending; our sins are gone without trace, irrecoverable, never to be located. Verse 13 is best of all: 'like a father has a mother's passionate love for his sons'. The word 'compassion' (*rachamim*) belongs to the same word-group as *rechem*, a womb, and we see it in action in 1 Kings 3:26. Here is perfect parenthood, father and mother all in one, Joseph as well as Mary. Yahweh's love is thus an overarching, constant, powerful, active love; it is a saving love, taking our sins from us, bearing them away to such a place as is ever infinitely beyond reach. And it is a fullness of love, a love that lacks nothing that makes true, perfect love what it is, a love of welcome, protection, warmth and strength; passion and steadfastness is equal proportions. 'There is no love like the love of Jesus.'

Day 49   Read Psalm 104[1]

Psalm 104.
The Rhapsody of Creation

A.1. Prologue: Creator God, worthy of blessing

('You' are great, majestic, LORD of Creation)

1. My soul, bless Yahweh!
    Yahweh, my God, you are exceedingly great!
    With splendour and majesty you are clothed[2] –

2. wrapping yourself in light[3] like a cloak,
    stretching out the heavens[4] like a curtain:

('He' is present in his Creation)

3. who lays the beams of his upper rooms in the waters;[5]
    who makes clouds his chariotry;
    who walks on the wings of the wind;

4. making winds his messengers,
    a fire of flame his ministers.

5. He founded the earth on its firm base,
    not to be moved for ever and ever.

B. The songs of Creation

('You' sovereignly imposed your will on what you created)

6. With the deep,[6] as with a garment, you covered[7] it;
    the waters were standing above the mountains.

7. By your rebuke they were fleeing;
    by the voice of your thunder they went hurrying off in
    alarm.

8. Up they went to the mountains,
    down they went to the valleys –
    to the place which you founded for them.

9. You set the border they were not to overpass,
    they were not to come back to cover the earth.

---

1   Ps.104 is a poetical meditation on Genesis 1. It alternates 'You' passages and 'He' passages. The latter look objectively at God the Creator; the former express personal praise for the Creator and joy in the creation. The various passages are so unequal in length it is hard to see them as 'antiphonal'. Maybe the psalm was a sort of cooperative effort like Judges 5:1, with two voices alternating.

2   The verbs in this section (as throughout the psalm) are perfects (i.e. permanent, fixed realities), imperfects (ongoing, customary acts, etc.), participles (unchanging situations). 'Clothed' (1) and 'founded' (5) are perfects; the remaining verbs are participles. Yahweh is both outside his creation (1, 5) and immanent in its forces and constituents (2–4).

3   Genesis 1:3–5.

4   Genesis 1:6–8.

5   Probably referring to the upper waters of Genesis 1:7. At what dizzying height, then, are his upper rooms.

6   Genesis 1:9–10.

7   'Covered' (6), 'founded' (8), 'set' (9) are perfect tense. This is the way things always are. The remaining verbs are imperfect, with the vividness of 'See them flee' or 'How they flee!' etc., as if we were watching it happening while the Creator commanded and creation obeyed.

8   An unusual use, in the Bible, of the verb 'to break', but compare our expression, 'to break one's thirst'.

('He' orders creation so as to provide for its creatures)
10. He who sends the springs into the river-valleys.
    Between the mountains they keep going.
11. They provide drink for all the living things of the field;
    wild donkeys break[8] their thirst.
12. Beside them the birds of heaven make their dwellings;
    in between the thick foliage they give voice.
13. Watering[9] the mountains from his upper rooms.

('You' have created a fully fashioned world)
    With the fruit of your works the earth is satisfied.

('He' has produced an integrated creation; everything satisfied)
14. Making grass shoot[10] for the beasts,
    and greenery for the service of humankind –
    to bring out bread from the earth,
15. and wine which gladdens the heart of mortal man;
    to make his face shine with oil,
    and bread which sustains the heart of mortal man.
16. Yahweh's trees are kept satisfied:
    the cedars of Lebanon which he planted
17. where the little birds make their nests.
    The stork – the fir trees are her house.
18. Mountains – the high ones – for the goats;
    crags, a refuge for the rock-badgers.
19. He has made the moon for appointed times;
    the sun knows its entrance.

('You' appoint times and seasons, spheres of life, provide food, satisfy your world, life and bread are alike his to apportion)
20. You appoint darkness, and it becomes night.[11]
    In it all the living things of the forest creep.
21. The prime lions[12] are roaring at their prey,
    and in order to seek their food from the transcendent God.[13]

9   Note how this section is enclosed between two participles (10, 13a). The rest of the verbs are imperfects (see note 7).

10 Genesis 1:11–13.

11 Genesis 1:14–19.

12 Often translated 'young lions' but it does not mean 'cubs' but lions in the prime of their youthful strength.

13 Typically of Psalm 104 it is God in his supreme greatness who concerns himself with animal feed!

14 Compare Job 3:8; 41:1; Psalm 74:14; Isaiah 27:1. In Isaiah Leviathan seems to be a supernatural foe whom Yahweh defeats at the eschaton. In Job 40, Leviathan is a mighty sea monster parallel to Behemoth as a fearsome land monster, both subject only to their Creator. Likewise here: even the most awesome creatures are but part of his creation; Leviathan a mere plaything. Genesis 1:21–31.

15 cf. Ps. 93:5. Like Gen.2:3, the thought of holiness is never far from the work of creation.

22. The sun rises; they remove themselves,
    and at their habitations they lie down.
23. Man goes out to his activity,
    and to his service until evening.
24. How many are your works, Yahweh!
    All of them in wisdom you have made;
    the earth is full of your possessions.
25. Here is the sea, great and wide;
    there, creeping things, innumerable,
    living things, the small with the great.
26. There the ships go about.
    Leviathan[14] which you formed to make merry in it.
27. All these wait confidently for you
    to give their food at the right time.
28. You give to them; they gather;
    you open your hand; they are satisfied with good;
29. you hide your face; they are terrified;
    you remove their spirit; they expire,
    and go back to their dust.
30. You send out your Spirit; they are created,
    and you renew the face of the earth.

A.2. Epilogue: Adoration of a glorious, awesome, holy God, worthy of blessing and praise

31. May Yahweh's glory be for ever;
    may Yahweh rejoice in his works –
32. he who looks at the earth and it trembles,
    touches the mountains and they smoke.
33. Let me sing to Yahweh throughout my life.
    Let me make music to my God as long as I last.
34. Let my musing be sweet to him.
    As for me, I will rejoice in Yahweh.
35. May sinners[15] be completely gone from the earth,
    and wicked ones – no more of them at all.
    My soul, bless Yahweh!
    Praise Yah!

Pause for Thought

Everywhere we look in the world around we should see God. This is very likely contrary to the way we were taught at school. Mechanism reigned supreme! What caused rainfall: why rain bearing clouds were driven higher by mountains – or was it that they dropped lower as the land fell away? I can't remember, but it was all a matter of cause and effect. River valleys were the result of the movement of glaciers, weren't they? Or was it water-erosion? Well, Psalm 104 has lovely news for us: whatever 'tools' he may or may not have used, God the Creator did it all. Mechanistic explanations of rainfall may well be clever, and speak to us of the wisdom and art of the Creator, but how much more splendidly marvellous it is to say that 'he waters the hills from his high rooms'! Talk about the food chain? Who set it up but the transcendent God who cares whether lions get their meat? Look at the dark clouds massing and approaching. The Creator is walking towards us. Sentiment tells us we are 'nearer God's heart in a garden' – how true, for the garden of Eden shows us he loves horticulture – but his heart is also in sunrise, seed time and harvest, wind, storm, earthquake, thunder. No aspect of 'nature' is without the immanent God, just as no part of nature is big enough to contain him who is exceedingly great, clothed with splendour and majesty, the giver of life and the giver of death, controller of oceans and tides, providing crags for wild goats and foliage for little birds. It is because it is his world that we can live in it with easy minds. We cannot see what may come over the hills tomorrow, but we do know that whatever happens will happen in his world where he rules and reigns (Ps. 121:1–2), and where nothing happens without his say-so. Learn it, my friends; learn it! Learn to look out of your window and see your God.

Day 50 Read Psalm 105

Psalm 105.
A God's Eye View of
History – Obey![1]

A.1. Abraham's Seed: thanking, sharing, thinking, seeking, remembering

1. Give thanks to Yahweh!
    Call on his name!
    Among the peoples[2] make them know his activities!

2. Sing to him!
    Make music to him!
    Muse on all his wonderful works.

3. Make your boast[3] in the name of his holiness!
    May the heart of those who seek[4] Yahweh rejoice!

4. Seek Yahweh and his strength!
    Seek his face constantly!

5. Remember his wonderful works which he did,
    his wonders and the judgments[5] of his mouth!

6. O seed of Abraham his servant,
    sons of Jacob, his chosen ones.

B.1. Yahweh's wonders: Abraham, Isaac and Jacob[6]

(The Abrahamic Covenant)

7. He is Yahweh our God;
    his judgments are in all the earth.[7]

8. He determined to remember[8] for ever his covenant,
    the word he commanded for a thousands generations,

9. which he inaugurated with Abraham,
    and his oath to Isaac;

1   Throughout Psalm 105 there is no reference to human response to Yahweh's activities. We are permitted to look at history as from the throne of God: what he did for his people. All history – what we would call the 'good' bits and what we would call the 'bad' bits – in his hands.

2   This psalm opens and closes (6, 42) with Abraham, the founding father (compare Galatians 3:7, 14). It also strikes the note of universalism: all nations were to find their blessing in Abraham (Genesis 12:3; 22:18).

3   Not 'arrogant boastfulness' but 'confident pride'.

4   Not looking for something that has been lost, but frequenting where he is known to be found. Two different verbs are used meaning 'to seek' in verses 3–4 (*baqash* and *darash*). They are precisely synonymous. The change is simply for variation.

5   The authoritative decisions he has made about truth and conduct – decisions then spoken to his people in direct, verbal revelation.

6   Covering Genesis 12–50, the promise made first to Abraham (7–11); Jacob's nomadic period in Canaan (12–15); Joseph and the basis of the sojourn in Egypt (16–22).

7   On 'judgments' and universalism, see notes 2 and 5.

8   I have taken the perfect tense ('he remembered') as perfect of determination, as being more suited to a context which is looking back over the centuries.

10. and he set it up for Jacob as a statute,
    for Israel, an everlasting covenant,
11. saying:
    'To you I will give the land of Canaan,
    the line[9] of your inheritance.'

(Nomads in Canaan)
12. When they were numerable individuals[10] –
    just a few –
    and resident aliens in it,
13. and they went to and fro from nation to nation,
    from a kingdom to a different people,
14. he did not permit anyone to oppress them –
    he rebuked kings on their account:
15. 'Do not touch my anointed ones,
    and do not harm my prophets.'[11]

(Joseph and Egypt)
16. And he[12] summoned a famine over the land:
    the whole staff of bread he broke.
17. He sent ahead of them a man,[13]
    sold as a slave, Joseph.
18. They afflicted his feet with fetters;
    his neck came into iron.[14]
19. Until, at the right time,[15]
    his word[16] came about,
    the word of Yahweh refined him.
20. The king himself[17] sent and set him free;
    the ruler of the peoples released him.
21. He appointed him sovereign over his house,
    and ruler over all his property[18] –
22. to bind his princes at his desire,
    and to make his elders wise.

9   Land was apportioned and measured
     out by line; Amos 7:17; Zechariah 2:1.

10   Lit. 'men of number', capable of being
     numbered, i.e. 'few'.

11   'Anointed', those set apart and
     endowed for a particular purpose;
     'prophets', those entrusted with, and
     guardians of, Yahweh's word.

12   i.e. Yahweh. Every event and
     eventuality is by his will.

13   Genesis 37:28, compare Genesis 50:20.

14   Or 'iron entered his soul'.

15   *'eth,* time, season, does not mark a date
     but a time distinguished by event. e.g.
     'May' is a date on the calendar; 'spring'
     is the same period known by event and
     content.

16   Two different Hebrew words are
     translated 'word' here. It is not possible
     to distinguish them in meaning. The
     former is from the verb 'to speak', the
     latter from 'to say'.

17   Lit. simply 'a king', the idiom of
     indefiniteness for the sake of emphasis
     – 'a king (would you believe?)'.

18   Genesis 41:38–46.

19   Genesis 46:1–5.

20   Exodus 1:9.

21   *haphak,* to overturn, turn right over.
     Typically used of what God did to
     Sodom.

22   Exodus 1:10ff.

23   Exodus 3–4.

24   Exod. 5-12

25   Here and in verse 34, *'amar,* which
     means 'to say'. Obviously English
     usage requires that it be translated
     here, 'spoke'.

B.2. Yahweh's wonders: Egypt, Moses, the Exodus, the wilderness

23. And Israel came into Egypt,[19]
    and Jacob was a resident alien in the land of Ham.

24. And he made his people exceedingly fruitful,
    and he made them tougher than their adversaries.[20]

25. He turned[21] their heart round to hate his people,
    to act cunningly with his servants.[22]

26. He sent Moses, his servant;
    Aaron whom he chose.[23]

27. They placed among them the words of his signs,
    and wonders in the land of Ham.[24]

28. He sent darkness, and made it dark,
    and they did not revolt against his word.

29. He turned their waters into blood,
    and put their fish to death.

30. Their land swarmed with frogs –
    in the inner rooms of their kings!

31. He said,[25] and swarms came –
    gnats in all their territory.

32. He gave their rain-showers as hail,
    fire with flames in their land.

33. And he struck their vines and their fig trees,
    and shattered the trees in their territory.

34. He said, and the locusts came –
    creeping locusts – and without number,

35. and they ate all the greenery in their land:
    they ate the fruit of their earth!

36. And he struck every firstborn in their land,
    the foremost of all their power.

37. And he brought them out, with silver and gold,[26]
    and in their tribes there was none who stumbled.

38. Egypt rejoiced when they went out,[27]
    because dread of them had fallen on them.

39. He spread a cloud as a screen,[28]
    and fire to give them light by night.[29]

26 Exodus 3:21–22; 12:35–36.

27 Exodus 12:33.

28 Exodus 14:19–20.

29 Exodus 13:21–22.

30 The verb is singular, 'he asked', but 'he' could refer to Israel as a people, justifying the translation 'they'.

31 Quails and Manna, Exodus 16.

32 Exodus 17:1–7.

33 Note the abruptness of the ending. Throughout Psalm 105 there has been no reference to human response to Yahweh's wonders. It reviews Israel's history, Abraham to Canaan, as seen from the Throne: what Yahweh planned and did. The sudden introduction of the thought of obedience is remarkably dramatic.

40. One asked[30] and he brought quails,[31]
    and with the bread of heaven he satisfied them.
41. He opened the rock and waters flowed out:
    they went, a river, in the dry lands.[32]

A.2. Abraham's people: inheriting in order to obey

42. Because he remembered the word of his holiness,
    Abraham his servant,
43. he brought his people out with gladness
    with loud shouts, his chosen ones.
44. And he gave them the lands of the nations,
    and they were possessing the toil of states,
45. on this account that[33]
    they should keep his statutes,
    and preserve his teachings.
    Praise Yah!

Pause for Thought

Psalm 105 sees the whole history of Israel to that date as embraced by Abraham. That is where it found its characteristic origin (6), and at the contemporary end Israel is still the people of Abraham (42–43). But more: Matthew insists that if we are to understand Jesus and the gospel we must start with Abraham (Matt. 1:1–2); John sees Jesus as the fulfilment of Abraham's hopes (John 8:56); for Paul, Abraham is the father of all who belong to Jesus (Gal. 3:7). Paul (Rom. 4:16–25), the writer of Hebrews (11:8–12, 17–19) and James (2:21–23) all look to Abraham as the exemplar of the life of faith. The psalm does not go into any details of Abraham's walk with God. It tells us just the cardinal fact that God made a covenant with Abraham (8), bringing five truths together – covenant, word, oath, statute and inheritance. God's 'covenant' is not a two-way 'bargain': you do this for me and I will do that for you. No, in Genesis 15 Abram was an immobilised spectator (Genesis 15:12) while God alone undertook the burden of the covenant (15:17). In Genesis 17:1–7 God alone spoke the word of multiple promise, the divine 'oath' which spelled out the covenant blessings, and pledged the coming inheritance (17:8). The call to Abraham was to embrace God's covenant in a life of obedience – God's 'statute', starting with circumcision (17:9–10). Obedience is not the way Abraham entered the covenant but the way of life in which he embraced and made his own the blessings sovereignly pledged to him by God's freely spoken word. The word of God explained the covenant to him; obedience to the word of God was the hallmark of the covenant man. Now think again about that abrupt reference to obeying with which the psalm ends. Abraham's people were in the covenant of God not by effort or merit, but by gift and inheritance. Very well, then, let them show it by obeying the word God has spoken. So, for us too: Acts 5:32.

Day 51 Read Psalm 106

Psalm 106.
Israel's Sad Failures
throughout History[1]

A.1. Responses: thanksgiving and righteousness

1. Praise Yah!
   Give thanks to Yahweh, because he is good,
   because his committed love is for ever!
2. Who will utter the total prowess[2] of Yahweh,
   publicise[3] all his praise?
3. Blessed are they who keep judgement,
   each who does righteousness[4] at every time.
4. Remember me, Yahweh, with favour for[5] your people;
   visit me with your salvation –
5. that I may see the goodness of your chosen ones,
   rejoice in the joy of your nation,
   make my boast[6] along with your inheritance.

B. Constant failure, unfailing constancy

(Egypt to the Red Sea)
6.[7] We, with our fathers,[8] sinned;
   we acted iniquitously with wickedness.[9]
7. Our fathers in Egypt
   did not respond wisely to your wonderful works;
   they did not remember the abundance of your committed love,
   and they rebelled contentiously at the sea,
   at the Red Sea.
8. And he saved them for his name's sake,

1 Psalm 105 reviews the course of Israel's history from Abraham to Canaan as seen from Yahweh's Throne: a glorious record of his wonderful works. Psalm106 covers the period from Egypt to Canaan, recognizing the wonders and mercies of Yahweh (1–2, 7, 21), but turning throughout to the grim reality of defection, rebellion and apostasy.

2 *gebhurah* means 'prowess', with military overtones. 'Power'/'might' are not quite accurate enough. See verse 8.

3 More lit. 'cause (people) to hear'.

4 'Judgment' and 'righteousness' refer here to aspects of divine revelation: what Yahweh has revealed of his truth, its application to life, and the righteous principles on which it is based. Compare the use of 'judgments' e.g. in Deuteronomy 5:1 (KJV, RV, NKJV).

5 'For ... of ... of', i.e. typically experienced by.

6 See Psalm 105:3.

7 Verses 6–12, human forgetfulness, Yahweh's salvation: matching verses 39–46, human rebellion, Yahweh's remembrance.

8 The solidarity of succeeding generations; compare Matthew 23:32–36.

9 Two verbs without conjunction: We committed iniquity, we acted wickedly.

10 Exodus 15:1, 20–21.

11 Discontent with divine arrangements (13–18), matches discontent with divine worship (34–38).

to make known his prowess:

9. he rebuked the Red Sea and it dried up!
   And he made them walk through the depths as through a
   wilderness!

10. And he saved them from the hand of him who hated,
    and redeemed them from the hand of the enemy.

11. And the waters covered their adversaries –
    not even one of them was left!

12. And they believed his words,
    were singing his praise.[10]

(The wilderness)[11]

13. Quickly they forgot his works,
    did not wait for his counsel:[12]

14. They gave themselves to desire[13] in the wilderness,
    and tested the transcendent God in the wasteland.

15. And he gave them their request,
    and he sent emaciation into their souls.

16. And they were jealous of Moses[14] in the camp,
    of Aaron, Yahweh's holy one.

17. The earth opened and swallowed Dathan,
    and covered the company of Abiram.[15]

18. And fire burned[16] in their company,
    flame was burning up the wicked.

(Sinai, the Golden Calf)[17]

19. They made a calf in Horeb!
    And bowed in worship to a molten image!

20. And they changed their glory
    for the construction of an ox[18] eating grass!

21. They forgot the transcendent God, their saviour,
    the doer of great things in Egypt,

22. wonderful things in the land of Ham,
    awe-inspiring things at the Red Sea.

23. And he said he would destroy them,[19]
    had not Moses his chosen one
    stood in the breach[20] before him

12 This section ranges widely over the wilderness periods (not just the time between Egypt and Sinai). The reference here could be to Exodus 32:1; impatience when Moses seemed to delay returning from Sinai. They failed to use the consultative arrangement Moses left with them (Exodus 24:14).

13 Numbers 11:4–5.

14 Numbers 16:1ff.

15 Numbers 16:28–33.

16 Numbers 11:1, 4 with 31–34.

17 Exodus 32; Psalm 106:19–23 (false religion) match verses 106:28–33, same subject.

18 Exodus 32:8, 22–24.

19 Exodus 32:10.

20 Exodus 32:11–14, 31–32.

21 In the structure of verses 6-46, these verses (24–27) are central: the cardinal sin of refusing to obey the word of God and to listen to his voice.

22 Numbers 13:31–14:38.

23 The gesture of making an oath.

24 Numbers 14:32–37.

25 The threats of verse 27 are not recorded in the wilderness records.

26 See note 17 above.

27 Numbers 25:1–9.

28 Numbers 25:2.

29 i.e. offered provocation to Yahweh.

30 Numbers 25:8b–9.

31 Numbers 20:2–13; Deuteronomy 3:26.

to turn back his rage from destroying.

(Refusal to enter Canaan; refusal to obey, to listen)[21]

24.   And they spurned the land[22] of desire –
     they did not believe his word.

25.   And they grumbled in their tents –
     they did not listen to the voice of Yahweh.

26.   And he lifted up his hand[23] to them
     that he would make them fall in the wilderness,[24]

27.   and that he would make their seed fall among the
     nations,
     and scatter them in the lands.[25]

(Further wilderness rebellions)[26]

28.   And they yoked themselves to Baal Peor,[27]
     and they ate the sacrifices of the dead.[28]

29.   And they provoked[29] through their actions,
     and plague[30] burst out among them,

30.   and Phineas stood up and interposed,
     and the plague was restrained.

31.   And it was accounted to him for righteousness,
     for generation after generation for ever.

32.   And they provoked at the waters of Meribah,
     and it went badly for Moses on their account,[31]

33.   because they rebelled contentiously against his Spirit,[32]
     and he spoke out thoughtlessly with his lips.

(In Canaan. Compromise)[33]

34.   They did not destroy the peoples,
     as Yahweh said to them –

35.   they mingled themselves among the nations,
     and learned their works[34] –

36.   they served their images,
     and they became a snare to them.

37.   They sacrificed their sons,
     and their daughters to demons,[35]

38.   and they shed innocent blood –

32   Possibly, but less likely, 'they made his spirit rebel' – i.e. Moses' spirit. The next line, of course, refers to Moses.

33   Note 11, above.

34   Deuteronomy 7:2–4; Judges 1:21, 27–33; 2:12; etc.

35   Compare 1 Corinthians 10:28.

36   In the Bible the environment is morally sensitive, reflecting the relationship between humans and their Creator. Sin brought a curse on the soil (Genesis 3:19), and it ceased to cooperate and became resistant. Leviticus 18:25 speaks of the land 'vomiting out' its inhabitants, itself defiled and revolted by their sin. Compare Isaiah 24:5; etc.

37   Since marriage and its covenant symbolize the relationship of Yahweh and his people, their turning to false gods is called 'harlotry'.

38   e.g. Judges 3:7–8; 4:1–2.

39   This could, of course, be translated 'holy name', but the idea is not simply that the name itself is a holy thing, but that it encapsulates and expresses the holiness of the one who bears it.

the blood of their sons and their daughters
whom they sacrificed to the carved idols of Canaan,
and the land was polluted[36] by blood-guiltiness.

39. And they were defiled by their works,
committed harlotry[37] by their actions,

40. and Yahweh's exasperation was kindled against his people,
and he abhorred his inheritance;

41. and he gave them into the hand of nations,
and those who hated them ruled over them,

42. and their enemies oppressed them,
and they were subdued under their hand.[38]

43. On abundant occasions he used to deliver them,
and they, for their part, kept rebelling by their counsel,
and they collapsed through their iniquity.

44. And he looked at the adversity they had,
when he was hearing their outcry,

45. and he remembered his covenant in their interest,
and he was moved to pity,
according to the abundance of his committed love,

46. and he consigned them to compassion
before all their captors.

A.2. Responses: pleading and praising

47. Save us, Yahweh our God!
Gather us from the nations!
So that we may give thanks to the name of your
holiness,[39]
and make our boast in your praise.

(Conclusion to the fourth Book of Psalms)
48. Blessed be Yahweh, God of Israel,
from eternity to eternity.
And let all the people say, Amen.
Praise Yah!

Pause for Thought

In effect verse 15 says, 'Take care what you pray – you might get it!' – like the frightful island in *The Voyage of the Dawn Treader* where people always get what they dream! This is what happened in Numbers 11:33. Desire developed into the sin of covetousness – the 'can't-do-without-always-want-more' mind-set which the New Testament calls idolatry (Eph. 5:5) – and provoked divine wrath (compare James 1:14–15). The only sure way forward is to safeguard all our prayers with a fervent and heart-felt 'May your will be done!' People often say (and think), Do I have to say this every time? And behind that question lies a misunderstanding. Walk through a graveyard and you will find – is it specially on gravestones recording a particularly sad death? – 'Thy will be done'. Is there a thought lying behind this that since God is in charge I can only accept life as he orders it, but if I were in charge I would arrange things better? I fear it sometimes is just like that. What an understandable but terribly mistaken reaction! Tell me: what makes heaven heaven? Why is it the utterly perfect place it is? Answer: because the will of God is perfectly done there. When we obey Jesus and pray, 'Your will be done on earth as it is in heaven', what are we asking? We are asking for heaven on earth, for the utterly perfect. And when we safeguard our prayers by adding 'your will, not mine be done', what are we doing? We are saying, Don't give me what I am asking, give me what you know to be perfect. To say 'your will, not mine' does not bring our prayers down from the heights of what we would generously give ourselves; it lifts our prayers up to the heights of the best and most generous and totally perfect thing our heavenly Father has at his disposal. It removes all limitation from our praying, the limits of our wisdom, our feebleness in asking (Rom. 8:26), our sheer boneheaded blindness. It lifts our prayers up to heaven and asks for heaven on earth.

Day 52   Read Psalm 107

Psalm 107.
'Lo, from the North we come, From East, and West, and South'[1]

A.1. Yahweh's committed love (on a worldwide scale)

1. Give thanks to Yahweh,
    because he is good,
    because his committed love is for ever.
2. Let Yahweh's redeemed[2] ones say so,
    whom he redeemed from the hand of adversity,[3]
3. and assembled from the lands:[4]
    from the east and from the west,
    from the north and from the sea.[5]

B. Four pictures of Yahweh's love[6] in action[7]

(Love leading the wanderers home) [8]

4. They wandered in the wilderness, in the wasteland;
    the way to a city of habitation they did not find.
5. Hungry, thirsty too,
    their very soul in them was fainting.
6. And they screamed out[9] to Yahweh in their adversity.
    From their distresses how well he delivered them,[10]
7. and he led them along a straight road
    to come to a city of habitation.
8. Let them give thanks to Yahweh for his committed love,
    and for his wonderful works for the sons of man,[11]
9. because he satisfies the frantic[12] soul,
    and is certain to fill[13] the hungry soul with good.

1   The title (from C.E. Oakley's hymn, 'Hills of the North') reflects the worldwide emphasis of the psalm (3) which is a meditation on the international promise to Abraham (Genesis 12:3; 22:18). To link the psalm with the return from Babylonian exile – simply an Israel/Judah gathering – overlooks the psalm's own specification of its theme. Maybe it is a worshipper at one of the pre-exilic pilgrim-feasts envisaging the worldwide gathering yet to be – as we might look forward (Revelation 7).

2   On 'redeemed', Isaiah 35:9.

3   Hebrew uses 'hand of' in a versatile way: 'the hand of the sword' (Job 5:20, KJV); 'the hand of the flame' (Isaiah 47:14); 'from the hand of the trap' (Psalm 141:9). So here, the power of adversity to hurt.

4   Thematically linked with the prayer of Psalm 106:47.

5   We would expect 'and from the south' and many make the fairly easy (and very obvious) adjustment to the Hebrew text to make it conform to expectation. The text means 'and from overseas', giving huge emphasis to the thought of universal gathering.

6   The psalm opens and closes on the note of Yahweh's 'committed love' (*chesedh*, verses 1, 43). For this reason it is justifiable to see the psalm as recording love in action. Compare verses 8, 15, 21, 31.

(Love releases the prisoner from the bondage of sin)[14]

10. Those living in darkness and deadly shadow,
    prisoners of humiliation and iron[15] –
11. because they rebelled against the sayings[16] of the
    transcendent God,
    and spurned the counsel of the Most High –
12. he bowed down their heart with trouble;
    they stumbled, without any to help.
13. And they shrieked to Yahweh in their adversity;
    from their distresses how well he saved them!
14. How well he brought them out from darkness and deadly
    shadow,
    and snapped open their bonds!
15. Let them give thanks to Yahweh for his committed love,
    and for his wonderful works for the sons of man.
16. Because he has shattered the doors of bronze,
    and cut the iron bars in pieces.

(Love heals and ransoms the sinner: the sickness of sin)[17]

17. Fools,[18] through the way[19] of their rebellion,[20]
    and through their iniquities, humiliate themselves.
18. Their soul abhors all food,[21]
    and they reached the gates of death.
19. And they shrieked to Yahweh in their adversity,
    from their distresses; how well he saved them!
20. He sends his word and heals them
    and rescues them from certain destruction.[22]
21. Let them give thanks to Yahweh for his committed love,
    and for his wonderful works for the sons of man,
22. and let them sacrifice[23] sacrifices of thanksgiving,
    and recount his works with loud shouting.

(Love rescues in life's storms and calms the storm itself)[24]

23. Those who go down to the sea in ships,
    doing work in the abundant waters –
24. they are the ones who see Yahweh's works,
    and his wonders in the deep.

7 Do not think of four separate groups of people – compare NIV interpretation, 'some … some … some … others' (verses 4, 10, 17, 23). The four are, rather, four typical situations from which Yahweh rescues his people, four ways of looking at the same reality – how Yahweh deals with sinners in their plight.

8 The four pictures are chosen and worded so as to suggest wholeness. The **a**-pictures are completeness by contrast – land-travellers and sea-travellers; the **b**-pictures are the two sides of sin, bondage and infection.

9 There are two synonymous verbs which I have translated 'scream' (verses 6, 28) and 'shriek' (13, 19). Note how one (*tsa'aq*) occurs in **a.1** and **a.2**, and the other (*za'aq*) in **b.1.** and **b.2**. This is typical of the carefully balanced writing of this psalm.

10 Treating the imperfect tense here as used for vividness, hence 'How well!'. See verses 13, 14, 19, 29.

11 Adam, so also verses 15, 21, 31.

12 The verb (*shaqaq*) means 'to rush about' (e.g. Isaiah 33:4). Here and in Isaiah 29:8 the context is craving for a drink, hence the contextual translation, 'parched'. 'Frantic' seems to suit the verb and the present situation.

13 Perfect tense expressing what is certain to be.

14 See note 8 above.

15 The two sides of the effect of sin: subjectively, 'degradation', the conviction and shame of sin; objectively, 'iron', the bondage of sin.

16 The cardinal sin of the LORD's people, to flout his word.

25. He speaks,[25]
    and sets the stormy wind in place,[26]
    and it raises up its waves.
26. They go up to the heavens;
    they go down to the depths.
    Their soul melts through trouble.
27. They tack this way and that,[27]
    and reel about like a drunkard,
    and all their wisdom scuppers itself![28]
28. And they screamed out to Yahweh in their adversity,
    and from their distresses how well he brought them out!
29. He causes the storm to issue in calm,[29]
    and their waves[30] are silent,
30. and they rejoice because they are quiet,
    and he leads them to the haven of their desire.
31. Let them give thanks to Yahweh for his committed love,
    and for his wonderful works for the sons of man:
32. Let them lift him high in the assembly of the people,
    and praise him in the session of the elders.

C. A meditation: God's marvellous transformations[31]

(Places and things)

33. He makes rivers into a wilderness,
    and outflowings of water into thirsty land
34. (a land of fruitfulness) into a salt waste
    (through the evil of those who live in it).
35. He makes a wilderness into pools of water,
    and a dry land into outflowings of water.
36. And he settles the hungry there,
    and they establish a city of habitation.
37. And they sow fields and plant vineyards,
    and produce a fruitful yield.
38. And he blesses them and they multiply exceedingly,
    and their cattle too he never diminishes!

17 See note 8 above. On sin as an infection and 'sickness' of the human heart, Isaiah 53:4, 'our sicknesses'.

18 This variety of 'fool' (*'ewiyl*) is the 'fathead'. The verb *'ul* may mean 'to be fat'. Typically he treats everything as a joke; 'flippant'; very often he thinks he knows just that bit better than everyone else present, little realizing that he is a tiresome bore.

19 'Way' is the sense 'as is characteristic of rebels'.

20 *pesh'a* is conscious, wilful rebellion against the known will of an overlord.

21 What we may call the 'boomerang' effect of sin, striking back against the sinner. In verse 12 this is the direct act of God.

22 'Destruction' is plural, so, here, 'certain destruction' or 'complete destruction'.

23 Only in this section dealing with sin is sacrifice mentioned.

24 See note 8 above.

25 The verb (*'amar*) usually 'to say'.

26 'sets in place', lit. 'makes to stand'.

27 A contextual translation. *chagag* is thought to mean 'to leap, dance'.

28 *bal'a* 'to swallow'. Here 'swallows itself/ is swallowed up', used in the sense 'to disappear from view/come to a complete end'; contextually 'to scupper itself'.

(People and experiences)

39. And[32] they are diminished and brought low –
    through oppression, evil and grief.

40. He is the one who pours out contempt on nobles[33]
    and makes them go astray meaninglessly[34] without a road.

41. And he gives top-security to the vulnerable, away from affliction,
    and makes a family[35] like a flock.

42. The upright see and rejoice,
    and all deviancy shuts its mouth.

A.2. Understanding Yahweh's committed love

43. Who is the wise one?
    He will keep these things.
    They will discern Yahweh's committed love in all its
    fullness.[36]

29 Note in every case how precisely prayer is answered, verses 7, 14, 20, 29–30. Here the LORD who causes the storm (25) stills it! He is sovereignly in charge of the whole range of our experiences. The rendering 'causes … issue' is the best I can do with a somewhat unusual use of the verb *qum* 'to rise up', here in the Hiphil mode, 'to make to rise up'. The Hiphil is used of fulfilling a prediction: making it stand up. This gave me the thought of 'issuing in', as if the purpose of the storm was the calm that was intended to follow. This is the only case of *qum* in this context. The form of the verb in verse 29 (jussive, Hiphil), it is suggested, was intended to add vivacity to the description – 'See him stilling the storm!'

30 i.e. the waves that so troubled them.

31 The four pictures have described transformations which Yahweh has brought about in answer to prayer. The meditation offers general observations about the God of transformations. Notice that each section includes the truth of the moral undergirding of the work of transformation (verses 34, 42), one reference in each section, at the beginning of the first and the end of the second, thus bracketing the whole meditation and teaching that all God's transforming work lies within the framework of his moral rule. The first reference illustrates judgment on the wicked (34), and the second (42) benefit for the upright.

32 The force of the conjunction here is plainly 'When' or 'If' or 'Should they be …'

33 *nadhiybh,* 'willing (hearted)' (Exodus 35:5); a general word for 'princes/leaders' (Psalm 47:9). Usually in a 'good' or neutral sense, but here requiring the thought of the tyrant, the oppressive ruler.

34 Lit. 'on *tohu*': compare Genesis 1:2, 'without form', i.e. expressing no meaningful shape or purpose; compare Jeremiah 4:23–26. It is equivalent to our intention when we say something 'does not add up'.

35 Understand 'for them'.

36 Plural of amplitude, 'his committed loves'.

Pause for Thought

David, of course, was 'the sweet singer of Israel' (2 Samuel 23:1), but he was not the only singer! No, not by a long chalk! Singers hardly come any 'sweeter' than the poet who wrote Psalm 107, do they? This gracious author, so full of confidence in Yahweh, and obviously intent to bring us to a similar confidence! He has confidence in the greatness of Yahweh's love. His first thought is to respond gratefully to such committed, unchanging love (1) but by the end of the psalm it has becomes 'loves' (43), a spring tide of love rising, flooding, full. It is the love which caters for every need and eventuality (8, 15, 21, 31). Do we realize, then, how greatly we are loved, that under no circumstances – whether externally in our situation, or internally in our sinfulness – will that love either let us go or fail to be sufficient. When tempted to think otherwise, hold fast to and discern the meaning of the four pictures in this psalm, as verse 43 commands. It is the love which hears and answers prayer. We noticed in the psalm that God's answers exactly correspond to the need described. So it always is. The psalm, wisely, does not go into how the need was met: how did he lead the ones who had gone astray (7)? We are not told – but he did! How did he bring the prisoners out to liberty? We are not told but he did (14)! How did he send his healing word (20)? We are not told – but he did! There is an almighty power that raises storms – and stills them (25, 29, compare Mark 4:37, 39), and it is on our side. The importance of the meditation with which the psalm ends comes into its own at this point, because it teaches that the four pictures are not just transformations God happened to make for some people in the past: transforming power is part of the nature of God himself. It is what he is like!

Day 53   Read Psalms 108–109

Psalm 108.
Offended but still loving[1]

A hymn. A song of David's.

A. Praise responding to a loving God

1. My heart, O God, is truly established.[2]
    I will sing and make music –
    yes indeed, and with my glory![3]
2. Wake up, lute and harp!
    I will wake the dawn up!
3. I will give thanks to you among the peoples, Yahweh,
    and I will make music to you among the states,
4. because great, above the heavens, is your committed love,
    and, above the clouds, your faithfulness.[4]

B. Prayer resting on the promise of God

(Prayer)
5. Be high, above the heavens, O God,
    and over all the earth, your glory!
6. In order that your loved one may be set free,
    Oh save with your right hand, and answer me!

(Promise)
7. God himself has spoken in his holiness:
    with celebration I will divide Shechem,
    and measure out the valley of Succoth.
8. Mine is Gilead, and mine is Manasseh;
    and Ephraim is the protection for my head;
    Judah is my law-giver's staff.

1   With verses 1–5 compare Psalm 57:7–11; with verses 6–13 compare Psalm 60:5–12. But Psalm 108 is no mere repetition. David draws on previous psalms to meet a new crisis. Some fresh threat has arisen from the ever hostile Edomites (compare Amos. 1:11), while, at the same time, David also feels that he has offended Yahweh. Beyond this we cannot surmise the circumstances of this psalm of praise and prayer. The wonder of Psalm 108, and its message, is that even when we have offended him, Yahweh's love and faithfulness are still available to stimulate praise, and his ear is open to our prayer. In this sense Psalm 108 links with the theme of the two middle pictures in Psalm 107 (107:10–16, 17–22).

2   i.e. steadfastly determined, after whatever has given the offence implied in verse 11.

3   Every part of me that is worthy to rise up in praise of God.

4   Notwithstanding whatever offence has been caused, the great overarching reality of divine love and fidelity remains unchanged.

5   See Psalm 60, notes 35–39.

6   We only know what we can 'read between the lines'. David obviously senses a divine alienation (11), yet in whatever crisis he is now facing he is confident that God will be his helper and give him victory (12–13).

9. Moab is my wash-basin;
   on Edom I throw my shoe;
   over Philistia, I will shout in acclamation.[5]

C. Confidence in an offended God[6]

10. Who will conduct me into the fortified city?
    Who is ready to lead me into Edom?
11. Is it not you, O God, who have rejected us,
    and who are not going out with our armies?
12. Give us help from the adversary,
    for human salvation is falsehood!
13. By God we will act valiantly –
    he it is who will trample on our adversaries.

Psalm 109.
Anger – Human and Divine[7]

Belonging to the worship-leader; David's, a song.

A.1. This is where I am, Lord

1. O God of my praise, do not be silent
2. because a wicked person's mouth and a deceitful mouth
   have opened against me.
   They have spoken of[8] me with a lying tongue,
3. and with words of hatred they have surrounded me,
   and gone to war with me without cause.[9]
4. In place of my love keep opposing me,
   and I, for my part, am simply prayer![10]
5. They have appointed against me evil in place of good,
   and hatred in place of love.

B. Let divine justice have its way

6. Appoint a wicked man over him,[11]
   and let an opponent stand at his right hand.

7 Psalm 109 is possibly the most outspoken and 'violent' of the imprecatory psalms, and for that reason is condemned by commentators as not only lacking but contradicting the spirit of Christ and the Gospel. This is an unthinking reaction. David professes love for his opponents, and his attitude towards them is one of prayer (4). Furthermore, as in all the imprecatory psalms, the response to unmerited (1–3) malignity (16–17) on grand scale, is to take it to the LORD and leave it there (Romans 12:19). No personal counter attack is envisaged – and we are not at liberty even to imagine David harbouring vengeful thoughts, for such would be incompatible with the profession of love and the practice of prayer. The nearest we have as a ground for complaint is the vigour with which David words his requests (e.g. verses 9–13). Compared with today's instruments of revenge – and the spirit in which they are used – this would have to be considered a minor fault (even were it true as stated)! But, in fact, what we find unacceptable is such realism in prayer. Consult Deuteronomy 19:16–19. The LORD required that the false accuser receive what he intended to fall on the one he falsely accused. This is the way divine justice works. David was realistic enough to ask explicitly for it, rather than, as we would have done, pray blandly, 'Please, LORD, will you deal with this situation.' Some suggest that in verses 6–19 David is quoting what his opponents have said. Verse 20 suggests otherwise, but, in any case, I would suggest the 'quotation' theory rests on a misunderstanding of the whole nature of the imprecatory psalms – and it flies in the face of Acts 1:20.

7. When he is judged,
   let him emerge guilty,
   and let even his prayer become a sin.
8. May his days be few,
   his appointment let another take.[12]
9. Let his sons be orphans and his wife a widow.
10. Let his sons ever keep wandering and asking,[13]
    and seeking from[14] their desolations.
11. Let a creditor lay traps for everything he has,
    and strangers plunder his toil.
12. Let there not be anyone extending loving fidelity to him,
    nor anyone being gracious to his orphans.
13. Let his posterity be destined for cutting down.
    In the next generation let their name be wiped away.
14. Let his fathers' iniquity be remembered by Yahweh,
    and his mother's sin not be wiped away.
15. Let them be before Yahweh continually,
    and let him cut off remembrance of them from the earth –
16. because he did not remember showing loving fidelity,
    and he pursued the downtrodden man and the vulnerable
    and the heart-broken to do him to death.
17. And he loved cursing –
    and it is sure to come upon him!
    And he found no pleasure in blessing –
    and it is sure to be far from him!
18. And he dressed himself with cursing as his garment –
    and it is sure to come into his inner being like water,
    and like fatness into his bones!
19. Let it be for him like the garment he wraps around him,
    and like a belt which he fastens on continually.
20. Let this be the wages from Yahweh for my opponents,
    and for those who speak evil against my soul.

C. This is where I want to be, LORD

21. And as for you,
    Yahweh, Sovereign One,

8 Lit. 'spoken with', which some suggest is a legal idiom, of confrontation in court. The implication here would be that false charges were actually laid before a magistrate, thus bringing Deuteronomy 19:16–19 into play.

9 i.e. intent on David's overthrow and death.

10 'I am prayer' is a striking example of the way Hebrew can use words in apposition (cf. Job 5:24, 'your tent is peace'). The intent of apposition is to assert one thing as the exact equivalent of another. In other words, David's entire reaction to his opponents was prayer and prayer only.

11 In the opening section David's opponents were in the plural; the singular either individualises, and is in effect 'each', or else there was a notable and leading opponent who is singled out.

12 See Acts 1:20, where this verse is interpreted as predicting Judas Iscariot. Following this clue and seeing the psalm as messianic, the imprecations represent what Revelation 6:16 calls 'the wrath of the Lamb'.

13 i.e. 'begging'.

14 Either far from the desolations where they live, or begging from desolate places where there is no likelihood of help.

15 i.e. that you have personally interposed for my deliverance.

deal with me for your name's sake;
    because your committed love is good, deliver me!
22. Because I am downtrodden and vulnerable,
    and my heart he has pierced within me.
23. Like a shadow when it lengthens, I am gone!
    Shaken off like a locust!
24. My knees totter through fasting,
    and my flesh grows lean for want of fatness.
25. And as for me, I have become an object of reproach to
    them –
    they see me, they shake their head.
26. Help me, Yahweh, my God!
    Save me, according to your committed love!
27. Let them know that this is your hand;
    it is you, Yahweh, who have done it.[15]
28. Let them – as far as they are concerned – curse,
    while you – for your part – keep blessing,
    and your servant will keep rejoicing.
29. My opponents will be clothed with dishonour
    and wrap themselves with their shame as with a robe.
30. I will give thanks exceedingly to Yahweh with my mouth,
    and among many I will praise him,
31. because he stands at the right hand of the vulnerable,
    to save him from those who judge his soul.

Pause for Thought

Do you feel more than a bit battered after reading Psalm 109? Of course you do! But let it be for the right reason. It is not (as some commentators on the Psalms would suggest) that every reader is properly horrified at finding such unsanctified human rage and spite inside the covers of the Bible. No, it is because in Psalm 109 we are listening to the Holy God stating the consequences of sin and pronouncing the terms of his condemnation and judgment. And if we like to imagine that his eyes are full of tears as he does so, we are correct. The voice of David and the voice of the Holy Spirit are one voice, just as Acts 4:25 (ESV, correctly) says about Psalm 2. This is the biblical realism of David's praying. He asks (without rancour, in a truly sinless anger) for what the Word of God affirms is inevitable in the situation of hatred, opposition, false accusation and malignity he was facing. Sin brings us under the domination of the wicked one (6), ruins everything about us (7), extends its infection to those linked with us (9–10), pauperizes (11), leaves us friendless (12), simply because it brings on us the fruits of our own choices, attitudes and actions (16–20). And (as you readily see) such a survey does no more than scratch the surface of this terrifying psalm. It is a place into which so many streams of biblical revelation and warning flow – the cardinal seriousness of sins of speech, for example, and (a thing that hits and hurts at the family level), if it is true (as Proverbs 20:7 teaches) that the children of the righteous are blessed, it is equally true that the iniquity of fathers passes through the channels of genetic solidarity to those we love most dearly – a moral and spiritual entail that is part of the price of being human. If we recoil on reading the central section of Psalm 109, let us dwell at length and with all our hearts on the great cry to God with which the psalm ends.

Day 54   Read Psalms 110–112

Psalm 110.
'Priestly King, Enthroned for Ever'[1]

David's; a song.

A. The King

(Promise)

1.   The word of Yahweh to my Sovereign One:

(Status)

    'Sit enthroned at my right hand

(Dominion)

    until I make your enemies
    a footstool for your feet.'

2.   The sceptre of your strength
    will Yahweh send out from Zion.
    Dominate[2] among your enemies!

(Headship)

3.   Your people are complete willingness[3]
    in the day of your muster;[4]
    in the splendour of holiness.[5]

(Refreshment)

    From the womb of the dawn[6]
    yours is the dew[7] of your youthfulness.

B. The priest

(Promise)

4.   Yahweh has sworn

---

1   A line from Michael Saward's fine hymn, 'Christ Triumphant'. Psalm 110 meditates on the Messiah as both King (1–3) and Priest (4–7). In doing so it looks back to Melchizedek ('king of righteousness', Genesis 14:18–22) who was 'king of Salem' and 'priest of God Most High'. Centuries later Joshua 10:1 tells us that the king of Jerusalem was Adonizedek ('Sovereign of righteousness'). If we may assume that, having essentially the same name, he too was 'priest of God Most High' (and why not?) then a line of priest-kings survived in Jerusalem. When David, then, took Jerusalem (2 Samuel 5:6–9) he, in turn, became 'king of Salem' and 'priest of God Most High', a priesthood centred in David's line, parallel to the Aaronic priesthood – as indeed Hebrews 7–9 teaches. In Psalm 110 David meditates on his royal priesthood and sees it in relation to his coming greater Son, anticipating the authoritative interpretation given by the Lord Jesus Christ himself (Mark 12:35–37; compare Acts 2:33–35; Hebrews 1:13; 10:11–14).

2   Hebrew uses the imperative to express a future event so certain to happen that it can be commanded. 'Dominate' (*radhah*) is a very strong verb.

3   'Willingness' is plural of amplitude. On words in appositon ('your people are willingnesses'), see Psalm 109:4, as if to say 'your people represent willingness itself'.

and will not change his mind:

(Status)

'You are a priest for ever[8]
in succession to[9] Melchizedek.

(Dominion)

5. The Sovereign One is at your right hand.
    He has determined to shatter kings[10]
    in the day of his exasperation.

(Headship)

6. He will pronounce judgment on the nations.
    Full of corpses!
    He has determined to shatter the head[11]
    over the abundant earth.

(Refreshment)

7. From the wayside brook he will drink;[12]
    therefore he will lift (his) head.[13]

Psalm 111.[14]
Yahweh in character and action[15]

A.1. Praise and thanks

1. Praise Yah!
    I will give thanks to Yahweh with all my heart, (*aleph*)
    In the company of the upright and the assembly.[16] (*beth*)

B. Yahweh's works and character

2. Great are Yahweh's works, (*gimel*)
    sought[17] by those who delight in them (*daleth*)
3. Majesty and splendour, his activities, (*he*)
    and his righteousness[18] stands[19] for ever. (*waw*)

4   *chayil* is a versatile word: 'a man of
    substance' (1 Samuel 9:1); 'valiant' (1
    Samuel 10:26); 'army' (1 Samuel 14:48
    – like our word 'the forces'); 'ability'
    (1 Samuel 14:52). In verse 3, 'the day
    of your (armed) force', the day you
    muster our troops.

5   Compare Isaiah 54:17; but the
    reference could equally be to Messiah's
    holiness, compare 2 Chronicles 20:21.

6   This form of the noun 'dawn' is only
    found here but it is a perfectly formed
    noun with a plain meaning. 'Dawn'
    or morning is the time for fresh
    beginnings (Psalm 30:5).

7   'Dew' has a widespread symbolic
    coverage: wellbeing (Genesis 27:28),
    royal favour (Proverbs 19:12), divine
    blessing (Hosea 14:5). Here, along with
    'dawn' and 'youthfulness', it speaks of
    freshness, refreshment, vigour.

8   A strikingly novel thought in the
    Old Testament, where the ever-
    changing Aaronic priest was the norm.
    Compare Hebrews 7:13–17. David is
    developing, for the Priest-Messiah, the
    promise of an eternal kingship.

9   One of the many possible translations
    of *'al dibhrathiy*. 'Because of/for the
    sake of/on the model of'.

10 The priestly Messiah does not engage
    in war: the example of David rules this
    out (1 Chronicles 28:3). In verse 5
    Yahweh himself is the warrior; in verses
    6–7 the victory campaign seems to pass
    back to the king.

11 i.e. go for the killing blow; achieve a
    total victory leaving no opponent alive.

12 1 Samuel 30:8–10 provides the model
    behind this picture of opportunistic
    refreshment. Note the contrast between
    David and those who were too weary
    to continue the pursuit. The wayside
    brook envigorates the king to carry the
    battle to victory.

4. A memorial for his wonderful works he has made.[20] (*zayin*)

   Gracious and compassionate is Yahweh.[21] (*cheth*)

5. Food[22] he gives to those who fear him. (*teth*)

   He will remember his covenant for ever. (*yodh*)

6. The power[23] of his works he has declared to his people (*kaph*)

   in giving them the inheritance of the nations. (*lamedh*)

7. The works of his hands are truth and judgment;[24] (*mem*)

   trustworthy are all his precepts,[25] (*nun*)

8. maintained for ever and ever, (*samech*)

   done in truth and uprightness. (*ayin*)

9. Redemption he sent his people. (*pe*)

   he has commanded his covenant for ever. (*tsadhe*)

   Holy and awesome is his name.[26] (*qoph*)

A2. Obedience and praise

10. The beginning of wisdom is the fear of Yahweh. (*resh*)

    Good prudence[27] belongs to all who take action.[28] (*sin*)

    His praise stands for ever. (*tau*)

Psalm 112.
The Family Likeness[29]

A.1. The God-fearer and his delight

1. Blessed[30] is the man who fears Yahweh,[31] (*aleph*)

   who delights exceedingly in his commandments. (*beth*)

B. The God-fearer: character and influence

2. Mighty[32] in the land will be his seed: (*gimel*)

   the generation of the upright will be blessed. (*daleth*)

3. Splendour and wealth are in his house (*he*)

   and his righteousness stands for ever.[33] (*waw*)

13 'To lift up the head' as an idiom for 'to continue the fight/to dominate', Judges 8:28.

14 Psalms 111 and 112 belong together. They balance each other: Psalm 111 glories in Yahweh's character and works; Psalms 112 (with a good number of parallel verses and thoughts) describes how in character and conduct Yahweh's people should reflect their God. Both are alphabetical psalms (see Psalms 9–10, 34).

15 Psalm 111 is (in my opinion) best appreciated by being read through without pausing over indications of analysis – beyond the bare indication of content. It is a running rhapsody of Yahweh and his works. Within brackets of praise (1, 10), the topic alternates between Yahweh's works (2–4a, 6–8) and Yahweh's character (4b–5, 9).

16 'Company' (*sodh*) stresses fellowship, enjoyment of each other's company; 'assembly' suggests coming together by agreement and obedience.

17 In such a context as this 'to seek' is not 'to search for something lost' but to frequent diligently the place where something is known to be found. Compare Deuteronomy 12:5. In other words those in the fellowship of Yahweh's assembly delight to keep pondering his works.

18 i.e. his activities always bear the mark of his total integrity and commitment to his own righteous principles and promises.

19 i.e. remains unchanged.

20 The memorial is, as always, his *name* (Exodus 3:15). To ponder his name is to recall, appreciate and understand his works.

21 Exodus terminology, Exodus 34:6.

4. Light has arisen[34] in the darkness for the upright, (*zayin*)
   gracious and compassionate and righteous. (*cheth*)
5. How good is the man who is acts with grace and lends: (*teth*)
   he orders[35] his words[36] in judgment.[37] (*yodh*)
6. Indeed, for ever he will not be shaken. (*kaph*)
   Destined for remembrance for ever is the righteous. (*lamedh*)
7. Of bad news he is not afraid; (*mem*)
   his heart is steadied, trusting in Yahweh; (*nun*)
8. His heart is maintained[38] – he does not fear – (*samech*)
   until he sees the end[39] of his adversaries. (*ayin*)
9. He has given lavishly[40] to the vulnerable; (*pe*)
   his righteousness stands for ever.[41] (*tsadhe*)
   His horn will be raised high in honour. (*qoph*)

A.2. The wicked and his desire

10. The wicked sees and is indignant; (*resh*)
    he grinds his teeth and melts![42] (*shin*)
    The longing of the wicked ones will perish. (*tau*)

---

22 These verses seem to be a general meditation on history from Egypt to Sinai: the revelation of the meaning of 'Yahweh' at one end of the journey and the covenant at the other. 'Food' (5) is lit. 'prey', such as trapped or slaughtered animals. A possible reference to the quails of Exodus 16:13.

23 Yahweh's power displayed in what he has done, here particularly his power displayed in history when he routed the nations and brought Israel in under Joshua.

24 Yahweh's works reveal his reliability/trustworthiness ('truth') and his sound decision-making ('judgment').

25 'Precepts' are his detailed requirements in the lives of his people, but here the contention is that the principles they express are equally seen in what he has done.

26 It is this last line which compels us to include verse 9 under the heading of Yahweh's character. Plainly 'redemption' could otherwise be considered as something he has done, but the reference to his name means that we understand 'redemption' and 'covenant' are revelations of what he is: these are the things his name summarises. He redeems (here, 'pays the redemption price') and makes covenanted promises because he is that sort of God.

27 'Prudence' (*sekel*) is that sort of wise, practical action that is designed to bring good results.

28 Who act in the fear of Yahweh.

29 Like Psalm 111, this is an alphabetic psalm, but the subject now is the character and impact of the God-fearing person: what he is in himself and within his house and what he is to the world around in influence and activity. The psalm is bracketed by a contrasting inclusion: the God-fearer (1) and the wicked (10). Inside this bracket, two topics alternate: influence (2, 5–6, 9), quality (3–4, 7–8). As with Psalm 111, I will set this psalm out as a whole with a minimum intrusion of internal headings.

30 See Psalm 1:1.

31 A 'domino' link with the end of Psalm 111.

32 Mainly of military prowess (*gibbor*), but here in the general sense of 'important', as we might say 'a power in the land'.

33 Identical with 111:3b. Yahweh is unchangeably faithful to his own principles of righteousness; we are to be unchangeably faithful to his righteous requirements. Our characters should reflect his.

34 Or 'He (Yahweh) has arisen as light in the darkness'. In which case verse 4b (identical with 111:4b) also refers to Yahweh. However, to make verse 4b refer to the God-fearing person reflecting Yahweh's character is more suited to the relationship between the two psalms.

35 Imperfect tense of habitual action.

36 Here, his affairs, his word-in-action.

37 The sequence is important: 'grace' is the constituent of his character, his disposition; it makes itself seen outwardly in caring for those he is in a position to help by lending; but everything is done with 'judgment', thoughtful right decision-making. Graciousness and lending has already appeared in Psalm 37:21, 26.

38 The steady heart (7b) is not a passing mood or a 'flash in the pan' but a maintained attitude to life.

39 Lit. simply 'sees/looks at'. The expression must always be detached from any idea of gloating or triumphalism. The idea is that he will outlast his enemies, be still there when they are gone. Not unlike our colloquialism 'see them off'.

40 The familiar construction of two verbs without conjunction between: 'he has scattered he has given'. The second carries the main point, the first acts as an adverbial qualification: 'he has given scatteringly, engaged in widespread giving, given lavishly'.

41 2 Corinthians 9:9.

42 Joshua 2:11.

Pause for Thought

Psalm 111:6–8, recalling Yahweh's works, points to their effectiveness (6), how they reflect his reliability and sound judgment (7), and his truth and righteousness (8). In the middle of this list it remarks, 'all his precepts are trustworthy'. His 'precepts' are things he commands. Does this mean that God obeys his own laws? Well, yes, that's one way of looking at it, but, at a deeper level, it is saying that just as power, truth, judgment, uprightness are aspects of the divine nature, so is his law – the law he has revealed for the obedience of his people. His precepts are not an arbitrary set of random rules that might be otherwise. Every precept of his law represents a principle of his nature. The easiest place to see this is Leviticus 19. It seems a very odd chapter, sweeping together all sorts of rules and regulations in a haphazard sort of way. This is part of its intention. Life itself is haphazard, but whatever turn or twist it takes, the law of God still rules there; there is always a call to obey. But all these diverse laws in Leviticus 19 are held together by the repeated 'I am Yahweh' (vv. 4, 10, 12, 14, 16, 18, 25, 28, 30, 31, 32, 34, 36, 37). And 'Yahweh', you will remember, is an abbreviation of 'I am what I am' (Exod. 3:14). In other words, every precept is commanded because 'I am what I am' – so to speak, 'This rule is not just what I say; it is what I am.' You must keep it in order to fulfill the basic requirement (Lev. 19:2) that 'you shall be holy because I Yahweh your God am holy'. If we are to be like him we must obey the revealed law which expresses who and what he is. When we conform our lives to his law we are living in his likeness. This is exactly how Psalm 112 grows out of Psalm 111. The God-fearer delights in his commandments (112:1), or, as the Lord Jesus Christ put it: 'If you love Me, keep My commandments. ... He who has My commandments and keeps them, it is he who loves Me' (John 14:15, 21, NKJV).

Day 55   Read Psalms 113–116[1]

Psalm 113.
God Descending, Man Ascending

A. Yahweh's universal and eternal name[2]

1.   Praise –
     servants of Yahweh –
     praise Yahweh's name!

2.   May Yahweh's name be blessed,[3]
     now and for ever!

3.   From the sun's rising to its setting!
     Yahweh's name is worthy to be praised.

B. Yahweh's exaltation and self-humbling[4]

4.   High over all the nations is Yahweh,
     over the heavens, his glory!

5.   Who is like Yahweh our God,
     who goes high to sit enthroned,

6.   who comes low to look at
     the heavens and the earth?

C. Yahweh's transformation[5]

7.   Raising the poor from the dust;
     from the ash-heap he ever lifts high the vulnerable

8.   to make him sit enthroned with nobles,
     with the nobles of his people;

9.   giving the barren woman a house to live in,
     a rejoicing mother of sons!
     Praise Yah!

1   It may well be that Psalms 113–118 were part of celebrating the Passover right back to the time of Jesus. If so, he and his upper room company would have sung 113–114 before the Passover meal and 115–118 would have been the 'hymn' mentioned in Matthew 26:30. This makes this group of psalms very special. It is called 'the Egyptian Hallel', an act of praise meditating on the Exodus. Psalm 113 celebrates an act of God; 114 records Yahweh's sovereignty over creation in the Exodus event; 115 and 116 call for praise and trust in respect of rescue from spiritual and physical death; 117 extends the benefits worldwide; and 118 allows us to join the Passover procession through the gates into Yahweh's presence.

2   Everything starts with the *revealed* name (113:1). Praise (like thought and prayer) must start with what God has revealed about himself: here, his name (Exodus 3:14–15), the compendium of who and what he is. Then, the *eternal and universal* name (2, 3a): he was revealed to one nation on earth, but he is no restricted national God. His name is for the whole world and for all time. Finally, the *worthy* name (3b), rightly deserving of the praise indicated in verses 1–3a.

3   On 'blessing' God, see Psalm 26:12.

4   The 'inclusion' (bracketing word) in verses 1–3 was 'name'; in verses 4–6 it is 'heaven' (in verse 4, the height of Yahweh's exaltation; in verse 6, the beginning of his self-humbling). In verse 4 he is *comprehensively* exalted; in verse 5a, *incomparably exalted*. In verses 5b–6, he is the *self-humbling* exalted God; or, in the same verses, *transcendentally* exalted, in that to view even heaven requires self-humbling.

Psalm 114.
The Sufficient God[6]

A. Completed redemption

1. When Israel came out from Egypt,
   the house of Jacob from a people speaking unintelligibly,[7]
2. Judah became his sanctuary,[8]
   Israel his actual realm.[9]
3. The sea saw, and fled!
   The Jordan – it turned itself[10] back![11]
4. The mountains[12] skipped like rams,
   the hills like the sons of the flock.

B. Perfect provision[13]

5. What is the matter with you, Sea, that you are fleeing?
   Jordan, that you are turning yourself back?[14]
6. Mountains, that you are skipping like rams,
   hills like the sons of the flock?
7. Because of the presence[15] of the Sovereign, writhe, O
   earth!
   Because of the presence of the God of Jacob
8. who turns the rock into a pool of water,[16]
   flint-stone into a spring of water.

Psalm 115.
Blessing the God who Blesses

A.1. The heavenly God and his earthly people[17]

1. Not to us, Yahweh, not to us,
   but to your name give glory,
   on account of your committed love,
   on account of your truth.

5 The sequence here is, first, the principle (7), and then two examples – the public and the private (8, 9). Out of the dust (7), on to the throne (8), into fulfillment (9). A condescension of God equally at home in affairs of state (compare 1 Samuel 30:1, 6; 2 Samuel 2:4), and private misery (1 Samuel 1:2, 7, 10–20; 2:21).

6 What Psalm 113 affirms in principle Psalm 114 shows working out in practice in the history of Israel from Egypt to Canaan: identification with the poor, transformation of experience, gifts and benefits bestowed, and an exalted God superior over all powers – human and historical, natural and creational. A poetic rhapsody on the Exodus, marvellously full in implication, totally simple in expression.

7 An allusion to the fact that, even after four hundred years, Israel was still a distinct, unassimilated people, and, to them, the Egyptians still foreigners.

8 Yahweh did not redeem and then desert. Redemption included 'I will take you as my people' (Exodus 6:7), i.e. the establishing of a permanent relationship, described here as the Holy God making Israel his holy dwelling place. Transformation: they had been building cities for Pharaoh (Exodus 1:11), now they are the dwelling place of Yahweh.

9 The formation of this noun makes it mean 'the place of his rule'. Once a landless people, now a kingdom with a divine King. The introduction of 'actual' caters for the fact that 'realm' is plural of amplitude.

10 In this line the subject 'the Jordan' is given the place of emphasis in the sentence, and the verb ('turned back') is an imperfect of vivacity.

2. Why should the nations keep saying:
   'But where is their God?'[18]
3. As for our God, he is in the heavens,
   everything which he desires is what he has done.

B.1. Idols, their uselessness and their baleful influence

4. Their images are silver and gold,[19]
   the work of human hands:
5. they have a mouth – and they do not speak![20]
   They have eyes - and they do not see!
6. they have ears - and they do not hear!
   They have a nose – and they do not smell!
7. Hands – and they do not feel!
   Feet – and they do not walk!
   They do not make a sound in their throats!
8. Like them are those who make them –
   everyone who is trusting in them.

B.2. Yahweh, his effective presence and his blessing[21]

9. Israel, trust in Yahweh!
   Their help and their shield is he!
10. House of Aaron, trust in Yahweh!
    Their help and their shield is he!
11. You who fear Yahweh,[22] trust in Yahweh!
    Their help and their shield is he!
12. Yahweh has remembered us he will bless us.[23]
    He will bless the house of Israel;
    He will bless the house of Aaron.
13. He will bless those who fear Yahweh,
    the small ones with the big ones!
14. Yahweh will add[24] to you –
    to you and to your sons.
15. You are Yahweh's blessed ones,[25]
    maker of heaven and earth!

11 'The sea' is the Red Sea, the barrier to their leaving Egypt (Exodus 14); the Jordan was the barrier to their entering Canaan (Joshua 3, N.B., verse 15). This depicts the completed work of redemption, bringing out and bringing in, compare Deuteronomy 4:37–38.

12 A reference to the inclusion of mountainous terrain in the conquests of Joshua (Joshua 11:16).

13 The theme changes here to Yahweh's care for his pilgrim people, facing, on their journey, the barriers of rivers and the privations of the wilderness. The presence and care of their God dealt with both needs. They walked, dryshod, through the rivers, and ate bread from heaven all their wilderness years.

14 Imperfect tenses give the impression that we are actually watching it happening!

15 The psalm still brings before us the greatness of Yahweh: he does not actually have to do anything: just be there! 'Sovereign' is the noun *'adhon,* compare Joshua 3:11, 13. The noun has no definite article, making it an example of 'indefiniteness or the sake of emphasis' – 'a Sovereign – and who else do you think that might be?'

16 Exodus 17:1–7.

17 Only Yahweh be praised (1) – and why? a mistaken taunt (2); the heavenly and sovereign God (3). We will find substantially these three points in reverse order in verses 16–18, verses 1–3 and 16–18 forming an 'inclusion' around verses 4–15.

18 The occasion behind the psalm is hinted at here, but we have no way of knowing what it was. Possibly we should simply see the psalm as a flight of poetic creative writing, meditating on the possession of the land and the defeat of the nations. What ground have *they* (and their dead gods!) to scorn Yahweh!

A.2. The heavenly God and his earthly people[26]

16. The heavens are Yahweh's heavens;
    and the earth he has given to the sons of man.[27]
17. It is not the dead[28] who praise Yahweh,
    nor all who go down to silence.
18. It is we who will bless Yah
    from now and for ever!
    Praise Yah!

Psalm 116.
Requitals[29]

A.1. Yahweh's full requital: answered prayer

(a. Love and prayer pledged)
1. I love,
    because Yahweh hears my voice,
    my plea for grace,
2. because he has turned his ear to me,
    and throughout my days I will keep calling.

(b. Deadly danger)
3. Cords of death encircled me,
    and the nooses[30] of Sheol found me out.
    I kept finding adversity and depression,
4. and on Yahweh's name I kept calling:
    'Ah, Yahweh,
    rescue my soul!'

(c. Yahweh's recompense)
5. Gracious is Yahweh and righteous:
    our God is compassionate.[31]
6. The keeper of the guileless[32] is Yahweh.
    I was resourceless,
    and to me he kept ministering salvation.[33]

19 A typical Old Testament (and, of course, authoritative) view of idols and idolatry: there is nothing beyond or behind the 'idol'. We may charitably assume that the more sophisticated worshippers looked to some spiritual, supernal, entity represented by the idol, but the Old Testament does not give credence to this. The idol was 'the lot'! Compare Isaiah 40:18–20; 44:6–20. However, dead object in itself, the idol had the dreadful capacity to transform its worshippers into its own image – we become like the 'god' (or the God) we worship.

20 Behind this series of observations lie serious theological accusations: no voice, no revelation; no sight, no moral observation of right and wrong; no ears, no hearing of prayer and response; no sense of smell (Genesis 8:21), no provision of an acceptable sacrifice of atonement; no hands, no 'feeling' of our infirmities (Hebrews 4:15), no touching hand, no care; no feet, no movement, no activity (Isaiah 41:7b); no 'musing' (so, lit.) in their throat, no thought. It is probably intentional that there are seven charges against idols, a comprehensive charge-list.

21 The section on idols and their influence (4–8) starts from their status as 'made' and runs to their power to corrupt those who trust them; the section on Yahweh (9–15) starts with a call to trust him and runs on to his status as Maker of all. The intervening verses contrast the lifelessness of idols (5–7) with Yahweh's active power to bless, and increase (10–14). Verses 9–15 sound like a liturgy. We can imagine two choirs, one singing verses 9a, 10a, 11a, 12a, and the other responding with verses 9b, 10b, 11b, 12b–13. Maybe, around this core, verses 1–3 and 16–18 are the voice of the congregation, and verses 4–8, 14–15 the worship-leader.

7.　Come back, my soul, to your resting place,
　　because Yahweh has fully requited you.

B. Deliverance and renewal

8.　Indeed, you have freed my soul from death,
　　my eye from tears,
　　my foot from stumbling.
9.　I will walk around in Yahweh's presence,
　　in the lands of the living.
10.　I believed,[34]
　　even though I was speaking.
　　For my part, I was brought very low –
11.　for my part, I said in my alarm,
　　'Everybody is telling lies!'

A.2. Responsive recompense

(a. Salvation received, vows paid)
12.　What am I to return to Yahweh
　　for all his full recompense to me?
13.　The cup of full salvation[35] I will take,[36]
　　and on Yahweh's name I will call.
14.　My vows to Yahweh[37] I will pay in full –
　　please, in the presence of[38] all his people!

(b. Deadly danger averted)
15.　Valuable[39] in Yahweh's eyes is the death[40] of his beloved
　　ones.
16.　Ah, Yahweh,
　　indeed[41] I am your servant,
　　I am your servant,
　　the son[42] of your maidservant.
　　You have opened my bonds.[43]

(c. Responsive recompense)
17.　To you I will sacrifice a sacrifice of thanksgiving,

22　In later days 'God-fearers' became a technical term for those of another nation who joined in on the margins of Israel (Acts 13:16). A psalm like this could have been the origin of the title.

23　Two verbs with no conjunction between: 'bless' is the main verb; 'remember' is an adverbial qualification. He will bless us rememberingly; i.e. because he ever remembers us (perfect tense of fixed attitude).

24　In context, will add further blessings.

25　Compare Genesis 26:29.

26　See note 17 above. In verses 16–18, the 'heavens' match verse 3; the silent dead (17) contrast with the taunting nations (2); 'blessing' (16) matches 'praise' (1).

27　The earth is the arena of human experience of Yahweh and his mighty deeds (1). It is here we see him at work, on our behalf, against our taunting foes (2). It is here we must respond in praise (17).

28　Not a comment on the eternal state of the dead as such but a simple observation: earthly blessings can only find a response of praise and blessing from those on earth to tell the tale. The psalm arises from some notable deliverance which left the nations without any credible taunt to make (1–2). Otherwise the taunt would remain and 'we' would have been silenced. Compare the Christian hymn, 'When this poor lisping, stammering tongue/ Lies silent in the grave' (W. Cowper, 'There is a fountain filled with blood').

29　A situation is sketched of deadly danger (3, 8, 15), apparently caused by human unreliability (11), met by faith (10a) and prayer (1–2, 4, 17). Yahweh is found listening (1–2), gracious, righteous, compassionate, bringing salvation (4–6), deliverance (8), provision (7, 12). Vows are made and kept, publicly (14, 18).

and on Yahweh's name I will call.

18. My vows to Yahweh I will pay in full,
    please, in the presence of all his people;[44]
19. in the courts of Yahweh's house,
    in your midst, Jerusalem.
    Praise Yah.

30   Or 'straits'/'distresses'.

31   Unmerited goodness (grace) resting on
     a foundation of inflexible commitment
     and promise-keeping (righteousness),
     issuing from a heart of love
     (compassion).

32   Often translated 'simple', with the
     'bad' sense of 'gullible' and the 'good'
     sense of 'guileless'.

33   The verb 'to save' followed by
     preposition *le* ('to'), compare Joshua
     10:6; Judges 10:14; etc.

34   Verse 10 requires a little reading between the lines. It begins with an assertion of maintained faith. All the way through
     this period of trial he remained a believer. His position of faith was not to be called in question by anything he said 'in
     alarm'. The way one line follows rapidly on another, leaving much unexplained, itself reflects the nervous alarm of the
     situation. But what it amounted to was a frightening sense of isolation and the absence of anyone really trustworthy.

35   Plural of amplitude.

36   A striking reply! Asking what am I to give back, he replies 'I will take'. Our true response always is first to receive what
     Yahweh gives. He fills the cup, we take it.

37   Vows made in time of trouble are not a sort of bargaining counter with God. They evidence a serious attempt to learn
     from and make spiritual progress through the experience – a determination to emerge from it a better, more dedicated
     person.

38   The wording here (repeated in verse 18) – the preposition 'before' followed by the particle of entreaty *n'a* – is
     unexemplified elsewhere. Does it suggest that whatever his trouble was, it included exclusion from the assembly of
     Yahweh's people, so that making public gestures is not something that can be taken for granted?

39   Valuable, like a precious jewel, too valuable to be allowed to be 'squandered' as a result of some human squabble or trial.
     Some prized gift Yahweh reserves to be bestowed in the proper way at the proper time.

40   The 'long' feminine form of the noun, used here to call attention to what is said. As though to say 'death – yes, death! – …'

41   i.e. as has just been proved by the deliverance Yahweh has granted.

42   Doubly your servant, by commitment and by inheritance. The point is to have a double claim to Yahweh's care and
     protection.

43   This could be a reference to the recent deliverance – the opening of the 'cords of death' of verse 3. Or it could sketch an
     imaginary situation in which Yahweh has granted manumission to a servant, who declares he does not want to 'go out
     free', preferring to remain for ever a servant to such a master (Exodus 21:5–6).

44   See notes 37, 38 above.

Pause for Thought

The Bible makes no secret of the fact that life on earth can be a troubled existence, and that life's troubles are no cause for surprise. James calls us to joy in trial (James 1:2–4) because it is God's plan for our spiritual perfecting. Peter (1 Peter 4:12) tells us it is nothing strange: it is the way the Master went; shall not the servant tread it still? And what does Psalm 116 teach? A great deal, indeed! The writer can look back over the whole period of the trial and say without hesitation: 'I believed' (10) – a strong, undeveloped statement, a maintained position of faith. Like Jesus, when he asked his awesome question, 'why?' (Mark. 15:34), was careful to preface it with 'My God, my God', a double affirmation of sustained faith. Not a thing we always do! Yet what a lesson to learn! To look into teeth of the storm and say 'I believe'. Come what may, this is not going to knock me off course. Here I stand! In the psalm the writer's faith found expression in rest: Come back to your rest (7). Don't let the storm drift you from your moorings; come home to God. And inside that enclave of security, give yourself to prayer (4, 13, 17). Please be aware that none of this is easy. It contradicts our fallen nature – which is always to turn from God to ourselves, to rehearse our grievances rather than to pray. But, above all, in Psalm 116, the time of trouble is a time of spiritual determination and commitment, an opportunity to decide to make spiritual progress (look again at the affirmation with which the psalm opens, 'I love'), to come out of the testing loving him more than ever: more aware of his grace, righteousness, compassion (5); more disciplined in walking in his presence (8–9), and keeping our promises to him (14, 18); more public in our testimony (14); closer to Calvary and the one great, all-sufficient sacrifice (17); drinking ever more deeply from the cup of salvation (13).

Day 56 Read Psalms 117–118[1]

Psalm 117.
Our God, Their God[1]

1. Praise Yahweh,
   all nations!
   Acclaim him,
   all clans,

2. because mighty[2] over us is his committed love,
   and Yahweh's truth is for ever.

Psalm 118.
The King's Procession[3]

A. The procession assembles and moves to the Temple Gate

1. Leader: Give thanks to Yahweh, because he is good,
   People: because his unfailing love is for ever.

2. Leader: Oh let Israel say
   People: that his unfailing love is for ever.

3. Leader: Oh let the house of Aaron say
   People: that his unfailing love is for ever.

4. Leader: Oh let those who fear Yahweh say
   People: that his unfailing love is for ever.

5. King: Out of supreme distress[4] I called on Yah.[5]
   Yah answered me, in a broad place.[6]

6. Yahweh is on my side;
   I will not fear;
   what can a human do to me?[7]

7. Yahweh is on my side:
   my sufficient helper;[8]

1 Why should the nations praise God for what he has done 'for us'? The answer to this question uncovers a great Old Testament conviction: what he has done for us is for the world. There is only one way of salvation, one saving God, one saving work. We enter it by faith; it is open to all on the same terms. Exodus 12:48–49; 1 Kings 8:41–43; Acts 15:8, 11. The message of Psalm 117 is one God for all people; one people united in the one God; one way and work of salvation; true religion as a joyous response to what God is and what he has done. Psalm 117 is quoted in Romans 15:11, fulfilled in Revelation 7:9–10.

2 *gabhar*, of the stronger force in a battle (Exodus 17:11); of flood waters dominating the earth (Genesis 7:18–20); of our transgressions (Psalm 65:3); of God's love (Psalm 103:11).

3 The 'Egyptian Hallel' reaches its climax in Psalm 118, which celebrates not the entrance into Canaan but the ultimate objective of the Exodus: the kingdom of David, the people in their own land, with their own 'house of God', gathered around their true king. It would seem that a number of 'voices' contribute to their psalm – and identifying them is something of a guesswork, but surely the individual in verses 10–14 can only be the king. This accords with the New Testament authoritative identification of the psalm as messianic (Matthew 21:42; 23:39; 1 Peter 2:7). I see the psalm as a processional: verses 1–18 bring the procession to the gates of the temple; verses 19–21 is the entrance ceremony; and in verses 22–28 the procession reaches the altar of sacrifice. I surmise that the individual 'voice' throughout is that of the king.

I will myself look on those who hate me.

8. Choir:[9] Better to take refuge in Yahweh

than trusting in humans;

9. better to take refuge in Yahweh

than trusting in nobles.

10. King: All the nations[10] surrounded me.

In Yahweh's name, yes, I kept warding them off!

11. They surrounded me – indeed they surrounded me.

In Yahweh's name, yes, I kept warding them off!

12. They surrounded me like bees;

they were doused like a fire in thorns.[11]

In Yahweh's name, yes, I kept warding them off!

13. How hard you pushed me so that I would fall![12]

And it was Yahweh who helped me.

14. My strength and song is Yah,[13]

and he has proved to be my salvation.

15. Choir: The voice[14] of loud shouting and salvation

in the tents of the righteous.[15]

Yahweh's right hand acts with valour!

16. Yahweh's right hand is exalted!

Yahweh's right hand acts with valour!

B. The entrance ceremony[16]

17. King: I will not die.

Indeed, I will live!

And I will recount the works of Yahweh.

18. Yah has disciplined me thoroughly,

but to death he has not given me.

19. Open for me the gates of righteousness;

I would enter them;

I would give thanks to Yah.

20. Gatekeeper: This is Yahweh's gate;

it is the righteous who may enter it!

21. King: I will give thanks,

because you have answered me,

and have proved to be my salvation.

4 See 116:3, note 30. In 118:5 'distress' has the definite article, making it effectively a superlative.

5 Matching the four occurrences of 'unfailing love' (*chesedh*) in verses 1-4, there are four occurrences of the divine name in verses 5–7. Verses 1–4 are the divine *chesedh*; verses 5–7, Yahweh acting in *chesedh*.

6 i.e. and bought me into a broad place – 'distress' being seen as constriction, being hemmed in, under pressure, etc.

7 The words of David in Psalm 56:11.

8 Or 'among my helpers'. I am treating the preposition *be* as *beth essentiae*, pointing to one whose essential characteristic is that of 'helper', but also, 'helpers' is plural, understood as plural of amplitude, 'sufficient helper'. 'Helper' is a participle, indicating an unchanging situation.

9 Instead of 'choir', neatness would be served here (and in verses 15–16) by supposing an intervention by the worship-leader/people, singing antiphonally as in verses 1–4 (and maybe verses 26–29, certainly verse 29). In this way the king's songs would be bracketed and interspersed by leader/people contributions.

10 Compare Psalms 2:2; Acts 4:27.

11 i.e. fierce but short-lived

12 Some (see ESV) alter the Hebrew vowels here to read third person plural, referring to enemies. As the text stands the king turns suddenly to address his unsuccessful enemies directly – and why not?

13 First sung in Exodus 15:2.

14 The noun 'voice' could be use here in its exclamatory sense: 'Listen! Loud shouting and salvation!'

C. The procession moves on from gate to altar

22. Priest: The very stone the builders spurned
    has become the head of the corner!
23. People: Straight from Yahweh has this happened.
    It is a wonderful thing in our eyes.
24. Priest This is the day Yahweh has made.
    Let us exult and rejoice in it!
25. People: Ah, Yahweh, please grant salvation!
    Ah, Yahweh, please bring prosperity!

D. At the altar

26. Priest: Blessed is he who comes in Yahweh's name!
    We bless you (all)[17] from Yahweh's house!
27. Choir: Yahweh is the transcendent God.
    He has shone on us.
    Priest: Bring[18] the sacrifice[19]
    with ropes,
    up to the horns of the altar.
28. King: You are my transcendent God,
    and I will give you thanks,
    my God, I will exalt you.
29. Leader: Give thanks to Yahweh, because he is good.
    People: Because his unfailing love is for ever.

15 The 'salvation' granted to the king is extended to his people. 'Righteous' as always, those 'right with God'.

16 In verses 17–18, the king reviews his demanding career to date, recalling Yahweh's deliverances and his own preservation from death. In verse 19, he calls on the Gatekeeper for admission, but notes the qualification of 'righteousness' (as note 15). The Gatekeeper (20) repeats the qualification, but the king's song in verse 21 implies that he has passed the test and has been admitted.

17 The inserted 'all' indicates that 'you' here is plural.

18 The verb 'to gird', probably used here in the sense 'make ready' (2 Kings 9:21).

19 'the festival', but Malachi 2:3 identifies 'feast' with one component, and possibly so here. But whatever one does with verse 27b is highly conjectural. It must mean something like the above. There is no evidence for tying the sacrificial animal to the horns of the altar.

Pause for Thought

When the New Testament finds Jesus in something from the Old Testament it is always worthwhile going back to look at the Old Testament context, where we will discover how exactly the Scriptures are being quoted and what a fuller portrait of the coming Messiah emerges. This is richly true, for example, of the list of quotations from the Psalms in Hebrews 1, and notably true of Psalm 118. The notes added above on verse 10, for example, called attention to Psalm 2:2 and Acts 4:27, but when we look at everything Psalm 118 says about the Davidic king, we see what was then 'writ small' of him was finally written in cosmic and eternal letters by the King himself. Follow this nine-fold portrayal through into the New Testament: the king prayed under extreme pressure and was answered (v. 5; Heb. 5:7); he was confident against all comers (vv. 10–14; John 18:3–6); he overcame through the Name (v. 12; John 10:25; 17:12); faced one particular, individual foe (v. 13; John 12:21; 14:30); found Yahweh's help, strength and salvation (vv. 14–16; John 6:57; 8:29); came through deadly danger alive (v. 17; Matt. 28:5–7); endured Yahweh's 'chastening' (v. 18; Isa. 53:10; John 18:11; Heb. 5:8); was qualified to enter the gates of righteousness (vv. 19–21; John 16:8–10; Heb. 5:5; 6:19; 9:24; 10:20); was rejected by human judgment (v. 22a; Matt. 21:42; 1 Peter 2:7); became the chief cornerstone (vv. 22b; Matt. 21:42; Acts 4:11; Eph. 2:20). Was the earlier king aware that his experiences were predictive and anticipatory? Probably not, but we speak, do we not, of 'coming events casting their shadow before them' and this is what happened right through the Old Testament. Historical events and significant persons all took the shape they did within the shadow of the One to come. The whole Bible is about Jesus.

Day 57　Read Psalm 119:1-24[1]

ALEPH (119:1–8).
Longing[2]

(Blessedness: the integrated life)[3]

1. Blessed[4] are those who are integrated[5] in the way,
    who are walking in Yahweh's teaching.[6]
2. Blessed are those who are preserving his testimonies,[7]
    with the whole heart are seeking[8] him.

(Moral conformity)

3. Yes indeed, they have determined not to act with
    deviance,
    determined to walk in his ways.[9]
4. You have yourself commanded your precepts[10] –
    for total keeping![11]

(Longing)

5. Oh would[12] that my ways were established
    to keep your statutes![13]

(Rewards)

6. Then[14] I would not be embarrassed
    when I look at all our commandments.[15]
7. I would give thanks to you with uprightness of heart
    when I learn the judgments[16] of your righteousness.

(Commitment)

8. Your statutes[17] I will keep;
    do not leave me at all.

1　Psalm 119 is the greatest of the alphabetic acrostic psalms: see on Psalms 9–10, 34. In this case the theme is what God has revealed to his people: his teaching, his rules, all thought of as his very words, spoken by himself. Almost every verse contains a reference to this basic fact. Likewise, almost every verse is a prayer: possessing God's word lies within the context of a life ever lived in relationship with him; he speaks in his word, we who possess this word speak to him as we seek to live by what he has spoken. The unknown writer devotes eight verses to each letter of the Hebrew alphabet in turn, but, as ever in Hebrew poetry, form is subordinate to meaning. Part of the fascination of Psalm 119 is to observe how, within the apparent rigidity of making eight verses all begin with the same letter, each letter in turn is pressed into service to express the truths and emphases the writer desires.

2　Four times the idea of 'keeping' God's word is heard – as a means of blessing (verse 2, *natsar*), a command (verse 4), a longing (verse 5), and a determination (verse 8) – all these *shamar*).

3　Both 'walk' (verse 1) – the habitual conduct of life – and 'heart' (verse 2), devotion to revealed truth

4　*'ashrey*, see Psalm 1:1.

5　*tamiym*, of 'completeness in all parts', a task fully done (Joshua 5:8); a whole generation died out, one by one (Deuteronomy 2:16); 'whole-hearted in commitment' (Deuteronomy 18:13).

BETH (119:9–16). Absorption[18]

9. By what means can a young man make his pathway pure?[19]
   By keeping it according to your word.[20]

10. With all my heart I have determined to seek[21] you;
    do not let me err from your commandments.[22]

11. In my heart[23] I have hidden away your word,
    in order that I may not sin against you.

12. Blessed are you, Yahweh!
    Teach me your statutes.[24]

13. With my lips I recount
    all the judgments[25] of your mouth.

14. In the way of your testimonies[26] I am glad,
    like over all richness.

15. On your precepts[27] how[28] I keep musing,
    and how I look at your pathways!

16. In your statutes I find my elation.
    I do not forget your word.

GIMEL (119:17–24). Dependency and Devotion

17. Deal fully[29] with your servant,[30]
    so that I may live and keep your word.[31]

18. Take away the covering[32] from my eyes that I may see
    wonderful things out of your teaching.[33]

19. I am a resident alien[34] in the land:
    do not cover your commandments[35] from me.

20. My soul is crushed with longing
    for your commandments in every situation.[36]

21.[37] You rebuke the arrogant – cursed ones! –
    who err from your commandments.

22. Take away from burdening[38] me reproach and contempt,
    because I preserve your testimonies.[39]

6 *torah* often (but misleadingly) translated 'law'. From *jarah*, to shoot, to direct (information) to, teach. Twenty-five times in Psalm 119 of divine truth imparted.

7 *'edhah*, from *'udh* to bear witness. What God bears witness to about himself, his truth and his requirements. Twenty-two times in this psalm.

8 Frequenting where he is known to be found (e.g. Deuteronomy 12:5).

9 *derek* 'road', but it is impossible to change the traditional 'ways' here (and three other places). The characteristic life-style that matches God's teaching.

10 *piqqudh*. The parent verb contains the idea of enumeration; God's 'precepts' are the detailed application of his truth to life. Twenty-one times.

11 Lit. 'for keeping exceedingly'.

12 The strong and unusual word *'ahalay*.

13 *choq* from *chaqaq*, to engrave. What is carved in the rock for permanence. The permanence of God's teaching. Twenty-two times.

14 'At that time'.

15 *mitswah* (twenty times), a general word, expressing the idea that God's revealed truth is intended for obedience.

16 What God has decided upon as truth or commandment. His authoritative decisions. Here expressive of his inherent righteousness. When 'judgment' and 'righteousness' occur together, the latter points to principles and the former to practices.

17 Note 11.

23. Also[40] princes have taken their seat;
    they talk together against me.
    Your servant[41] is one who muses[42] on your statutes.
24. Also[43] your testimonies are my elation,
    where I look for advice.[44]

18 There is a clear link between *Aleph* and *Beth*, an expansion of the reference to 'integrity' (1) and 'whole-heartedness' (2). *Beth* reviews the whole constitution of a person: mind, emotions and will absorbed in the word of God – concentrated attention (9); heart and feet (10); memorization (11); instruction (12); facility in use (13); values (14); thinking (15); emotions and retentiveness (16).

19 The question concerns the practical issue of the 'path' life takes; the answer (10–16) is directed to the exercise of mind, memory, emotions in relation to God's truth.

20 'Word' (*dabhar*, twenty-three times) forms the inclusion of this section (16) and the synonym, *'imrah* (nineteen times) is used in verse 11. Both words point to revealed truth as personally spoken by Yahweh himself.

21 i.e. 'be where you are known to be found'.

22 Verse 5.

23 Proverbs 4:23. 'Heart' here stands for the entirety of the internal aspects of human nature – mental, emotional, volitional – as the following verses show. The objective of the stored up word is the moral life.

24 Verse 5.

25 A 'judgment' is an authoritative pronouncement: whether of truth or requirement; compare Deuteronomy 5:1.

26 Verse 2.

27 Verse 4.

28 The verbs in verse 15 are cohortatives, expressing personal commitment to the task: 'I *will* …'

29 Often translated 'deal bountifully', but it means 'deal fully', provide everything I need (here, for the life of obedience).

30 Three verses of dependence on God (enabling, 17; illumination, 18; revelation, 19); one verse of devotion (20).

31 Verse 9.

32 I have adopted this awkward translation (instead of 'uncover') as the only way of showing that the same verb occurs in its other meaning ('take away') in verse 22. Note how 'uncover' (18) is balanced by 'do not cover' (19): we need special illumination if we are to understand divine truth, but also divine truth has to be revealed to us before we can see it. Both the scales on our eyes (Acts 9:18) and the veil on the Word (2 Corinthians 3:14–15; 4:4) need to be dealt with – by God.

33 Verse 1.

34 Leviticus 25:23. Even 'refugee', one fleeing for safety, looking for asylum. Accepting dependent status.

35 Verses 6, 10.

36 The word is *'eth* which means 'time', not as a date but as a set of circumstances.

37 One verse of caution (what Yahweh thinks of those who forsake his truth, 21) followed by three verses of responsive commitment (freedom from human criticism in reward for devotion, 22; persistence in God's truth in spite of 'high up' critics, 23; delight in and conformity to what Yahweh has attested, 24).

38 Compound preposition, 'from upon'.

39 Verse 2.

40 'Also' links back to verse 22, indicating that the criticism there came from a human source.

41 'Your servant' is given priority in the sentence, making the word more a definition than simply stating a fact.

42 'Muse … elation … advice', in turn mind, emotion, will – all subservient to the word of God.

43 Alongside this flood of criticism there is always another component of life: his testimonies!

44 Lit. 'the men of my advice/counsel', meaning the place where I look for advice for life.

Pause for Thought

It is easy, in Psalm 119, to pay so much attention to the lines which contain the key-word which describes Yahweh's truth – 'word', 'teaching', commandment', etc. – that we overlook what the parallel line says. Look, for example, at verse 2: line one is hugely important in commending to blessing those who 'preserve Yahweh's testimonies'. Of course we dwell on the word 'testimonies'. What an assertion! God himself has gone into the witness box and has personally born witness to what he affirms to be true and what he looks for in his people by way of obedience: his teaching and his commandments. That's what our Bibles are: God's personal testimony! But then there is the other, accompanying line – a line further describing the testimony-preservers, 'those who seek him with their whole heart'. The verb 'seek' is imperfect tense, describing recurrent, repeated action, a customary feature of life. And what are they doing consistently? They are 'seeking him' – they are regularly, consistently frequenting where he is known to be. They are found 'in' the word of God not for the word's sake (precious though it ever is), but for his sake, because when we are 'in' his word we meet with him. Years ago the Scripture Union annual card used to include helpful 'pointers' for our Bible Reading – is there a promise to believe, an example to follow, a sin to avoid? Things like that. Best of all is 'a truth about Jesus to learn'. In one of his books, Bishop J. C. Ryle warns against the peril of self-satisfaction in just 'moving the book mark on a page'. And it is a peril, to preen ourselves on keeping up the habit. Here is the antidote: has our Bible reading brought us nearer to our Lord? Have we actually spent time with him? Do we know him better than we did thirty minutes ago? 'Preserving his testimonies' is not putting them into the freezer! It is finding them a succulent meal whereby we 'feed on his word'.

Day 58 Read Psalm 119:25-48

DALETH (119:25–32).
Clinging On[1]

A. In depression: revealed truth grasped and pondered

25. My soul clings[2] to the dust.
    Give me life[3] according to[4] your word.[5]
26. My ways I have recounted, and you answered me.
    Teach[6] me your statutes.[7]
27. Give me discernment in the way of your precepts,[8]
    and, oh, I will muse on your wonderful works.

B. In sorrow. Revealed truth chosen and practised

28. My soul is sleepless[9] through sorrow.
    Lift me up[10] according to your word.
29. The way of falsehood remove from me,
    and grace[11] me with your teaching.[12]
30. The way of truth I have determined to choose;[13]
    to your judgments[14] I have given priority.[15]
31. I have determined to cling to your testimonies,[16] Yahweh.
    Do not disappoint me!
32. I will run the way of your commandments,[17]
    because you broaden[18] my heart.

HE (119:33–40).
Initiatives and Responses[19]

(Total commitment)

33. Teach me the way of your statutes,[20]
    and I will preserve it for the future.[21]

---

1 'Clinging' forms an inclusion in this section (25, 31). In depression, the soul clings to the dust; the antidote is to cling to God's attested word. This is the subject of *daleth*. The parallel references to the 'soul' (25, 28) divide the section into two parts, as above.

2 'Cleaves/is stuck to'. What an accurate image of depression!

3 The first of seven prayers in this section, a heavy emphasis on the place of prayer in times of depression and sadness.

4 As our word promises, or, in the way your word does.

5 See verse 9.

6 'Teach … discernment … muse': the part played by the mind in dealing with depression; divine truth received, understood, pondered.

7 See verse 5.

8 See verse 4.

9 Or 'drops/drips', i.e. weeps, Job 16:20.

10 The active mood of the verb 'to rise up'. Sorrow prostrates; the word raises up.

11 i.e. when revealed truth penetrates through our sorrows to the place where it can lift us up, this is a work of grace.

12 See verse 1.

13 In *daleth* part 1, the truth was taught and received; in part two we are proactive. The truth is chosen (30), clung to (31) – we are determined to stick with it – and made a way of life ('run', verse 32).

34. Give me discernment,
    and, oh, I will preserve your teaching,[22]
    and keep it wholeheartedly.[23]
35. Make me walk in the path of your commandments,[24]
    because in it I delight.

(Inner threats)[25]

36. Turn my heart to your testimonies,[26]
    and not to questionable profit.[27]
37. Move my eyes off seeing what is worthless,
    in your way give me life.[28]

(Assurance, forbearance, renewal)

38. Implement your word to your servant,
    something which tends to your fear.[29]
39. Make the reproach which I loathe[30] move on,
    because your judgments are good.
40. Behold!
    I have longed for your precepts.
    In your righteousness give me life.

WAW (41–48).
Things that Belong Together[31]

(Always)

41. And, Yahweh, your committed love will come[32] to me:
    your salvation[33] according to your word.[34]

(The spoken word)

42. And I will answer with a word[35] whoever reproaches[36] me,
    because[37] I have put my trust in your word.
43. And do not at all snatch away the word of truth from my
    mouth,
    because I have put my hope in your judgments.[38]

(Resolutions)[39]

44. And oh I would keep your teaching[40] continually,

14 See verse 13.

15 Lit. 'I have set/placed your judgments',
    presumably 'before me'. Given pride of
    place.

16 See verse 2.

17 See verses 6, 10.

18 See Psalm 118:5, where 'a broad place'
    signifies freedom, liberty of action.
    'Broadening' the heart means setting
    the heart free from the restricting,
    confining parameters of debilitating
    sorrow.

19 These eight verses contain ten prayers
    for divine initiative in blessing,
    enabling understanding, a grasp
    of revealed truth, conformity of
    lifestyle, new motivation and vigour;
    and six responses, affirming either
    commitment or conformity to the
    truth. The heart of the section (verses
    36–37) dwells on the need to be saved
    from false inclinations (heart) and
    objectives (eyes). The last verse (40)
    goes into reverse, putting response
    before request.

20 See verse 5.

21 Or 'to the end' (of my life), or 'to the
    uttermost' (of what is required).

22 See verse 1.

23 When the truth is 'discerned' it must
    be 'preserved' by good trusteeship and
    embraced by total commitment (whole
    heart).

24 See verses 6,10.

25 The truth is always challenged by (a)
    the wayward heart (36), and (b) the
    attraction of alternative objectives –
    the 'eye' signifies what we are keeping
    our eye on, what draws us, holds our
    attention.

26 See verse 2.

for ever and ever.

45. And oh I would walk around at liberty[41]
    because I seek your precepts.[42]

46. And oh I would speak of your testimonies[43]
    before kings and not be embarrassed.[44]

(The loved word)[45]

47. And I will find my elation in your commandments,[46]
    which I love.

48. And I will lift up my hand according to your
    commandments,
    which I love,
    and I will muse on your statutes.

27 *bets'a*, gain by violence – but as much by violence to the truth, to moral or social order (e.g. taking bribes), as violence to the person.

28 The first of two prayers for renewal: renewal for obedience (37); renewal guaranteed by divine, inflexible commitment to what is right (40).

29 Lit. 'which is for your fear', 'for' in the sense 'in favour of', 'tending to'. When we see the LORD implementing his word we grow in proper reverence to him.

30 The whole context deals with our relationship with the God of truth; no reference to human opposition. Therefore the sense is, 'May there be nothing for which you would reproach me; I would loathe that! Besides (verse 39b) everything you have decided upon is good as far as I am concerned.' 'Make … move on' could be translated 'take away', but it is the same verb as in verse 37. The same God can direct my eyes and withhold his disapproval.

31 Every verse in *waw* begins with 'And'. This does not necessarily appear in English versions because translators do not like the repetition, and (legitimately enough) use 'also' instead, or (illegitimately) leave it out altogether. But in Hebrew 'and' is not used insignificantly. It joins together things that belong together. The 'and' introducing the opening verse 41 indicates that in every situation of life there is always this extra component: Yahweh's changeless love, issuing in salvation, backed by his word of promise. Within the basic 'and' structure, verses 44, 45, 46 are bound together by the form of the verb used, and they are flanked by associated pairs, 42–43 and 47–48, as in the outline structure.

32 The construction here is of an intransitive verb with a direct object – impossible in English but not in Hebrew. In the case of 'to come': often used in a hostile sense, but here to stress the actuality of the coming and the objectivity of 'love' and 'salvation' as forces met with.

33 'Love' and 'salvation' express respectively attitude and activity.

34 See verse 11.

35 See verse 9.

36 The assumption is that the committed life attracts criticism, but the one nourished by love and salvation can speak a word in reply.

37 Or 'that I have trusted in your word' – i.e. this is the reply made and the explanation offered.

38 See verse 13.

39 Trusteeship (44); lifestyle (45); ministry (46).

40 See verse 1.

41 'in a broad place', i.e. with liberty of movement.

42 See verse 4.

43 See verse 2.

44 i.e. let down by the word spoken not fulfilling what was promised.

45 The word in the heart (47); the word governing our life with God (48). 'The uplifted hand' is a gesture of prayer. Coming before him, our understanding of who he is and how we should conduct ourselves are things we learn from his word.

46 See verse 6.

Pause for Thought

All the connections of one thing with another in verses 41–48 of Psalm 119 merit our thought, but the most striking thing about the *waw* section is that in essence it only makes one supreme connection. The opening verse (41) is a concise description of a converted person: one who has been confronted by the unfailing, committed love of God, and has benefited from the divine activity of salvation – all as described by the word of God. The 'and' with which the verse begins tells us that this is the additional ingredient at every moment and in every circumstance of our lives. But what are (as Hebrews 6:9 would call them) 'the things which accompany salvation'? In effect, just one: 'the word' (42), the 'word of truth' (43), 'your teaching' (44), 'precepts' (45), 'testimonies' (46), 'commandments' (47, 48), 'statutes' (48). The converted life is life obsessed with revealed truth – an understanding of it which enables us to reply to critics (42) – a personal, confident commitment (43b) which makes us a safe deposit for the word (43a). It enables obedience (44), diligence (45), unafraid testimony (46), elation, love as we open our Bibles (47), and a life with God: with the word of God as its central and controlling factor (48). Picture the great George Muller on his knees before his open Bible, so that he could worship God in the light of his truth, and turn what he was reading into prayer and praise. It is all a far cry from perfunctory daily Bible reading, is it not? But why should it be? And why should you and I not be different? Well, mainly because we love our beds too much to start the day with God or to end it with real time in his presence. This amazing *waw* section of Psalm 119 would prove revolutionary if only we would listen to it.

Day 59 Read Psalm 119:49-72

ZAYIN (119:49–56).
The Resident Alien in an Alien Land[1]

(The comfort of the word)

49. Remember the word[2] to your servant
     upon which you have made me hope.

50. This is my comfort in my humiliation,
     that your word[3] has given me life.

(Life in an alien setting)

51. Arrogant people have treated me with excessive cynicism;[4]
     from your teaching[5] I have not turned.

52. I have remembered your judgments[6] from of old,
     and I have drawn the comfort I need.

53. Raging anger[7] has gripped me because of the wicked,
     those who forsake your teaching.

54. They have become songs for me, your statutes,[8]
     in the house of my sojourning.[9]

(The name and the word)

55. I have remembered your name[10] in the night, Yahweh,
     and I have determined to keep your teaching.

56. This has become mine –
     that[11] I have preserved your precepts.[12]

CHETH (119:57–64).
Reactions[13]

(Living with the God who is our portion)

57. Yahweh is my portion.[14]

1 This title arises directly from the four central verses (51–54): he is under pressure from cynics, vexed by the wicked – the former self-confidently dismissive, the latter abandoning divine truth as irrelevant. A good description of an uncongenial society in which he finds himself 'sojourning' (54), living as a resident alien. On each side of this central block verse 49 is balanced by verse 55 (Yahweh's remembrance and the psalmist's remembrance), and verse 50 by verse 56, both opening with the emphatic 'this', and with the life-giving power of the word balancing the life devoted to the word.

2 See verse 9.

3 See verse 11.

4 'Arrogance' is their estimate of themselves; cynicism, their estimate of spiritual values and realities. On the cynic, see Psalm 1:1.

5 See verse 1.

6 See verse 13.

7 Suggested meanings for this word, which occurs only here, are either 'annoyance' or 'raging heat'.

8 See verse 5.

9 From *gur*, to be a resident alien, a refugee, a person seeking political asylum. 'A place of temporary residence, resident alienship'.

10 In verse 1 Yahweh was asked to remember his word (of truth and promise); the psalmist remembers Yahweh's revealed name, another way of fixing the mind on revealed truth.

I have said[15]
that I will keep your words.[16]

58. I have entreated your favour[17] with all my heart.
Grant me grace according to your word.[18]

59. I have been busy pondering my ways,
and I have brought my feet back to your testimonies.[19]

60. I have hurried, and not hesitated
to keep your commandments.[20]

(Living in a world full of divine love)

61. The cords of the wicked surround me;[21]
I have determined not to forget your teaching.[22]

62. Half way through the night I keep getting up
to thank you for the judgments[23] of your righteousness.

63. I am companion to all who fear you
– to those who keep your precepts.[24]

64. Of your committed love, Yahweh, the earth is full.
Teach me your statutes.[25]

TETH (119:65–72).
Hard Knocks, Good Knocks[26]

(Lessons in the School of Hard Knocks: 1. Good God, good taste, good objectives)

65. You have done good to your servant,
Yahweh,
in accordance with your word.[27]

66. Teach me good discretion[28] and knowledge
because I believe in your commandments.[29]

67. Before I was brought low I was straying,
and now I am determined to keep your word.[30]

68. You are good and ever doing good.
Teach me your statutes.[31]

(Lessons in the School of Hard Knocks: 2. Taking sides)

69. The arrogant have smeared falsehood over me.

11 Or 'because', but the parallelism with verse 50 suggests that 'that' suits best in both cases.

12 See verse 4.

13 The *cheth* section opens by declaring Yahweh's sufficiency as our 'portion' (57), and ends by declaring his ever-available love (64). How do we live with him who is our portion? The answer comes in verses 57b–60. How do we live in a world filled by his love? The answer is in verses 61–64.

14 The idea of the 'portion' goes back to the land-allocation in the time of Joshua. Each tribe had land according to its size (Numbers 33:54). Their 'portion' or 'inheritance' was their livelihood, designed to be their sufficiency. The Levites did not inherit with the other tribes because (Joshua 13:14) they were provided for in other ways (Numbers 18:20; Joshua 18:7). To say 'Yahweh is my portion' is equivalent to saying he is 'my sufficiency'.

15 Verses 57b–60 are a programmatic statement of living within divine sufficiency: (a) a stated commitment to obey (57b); (b) humble prayer for grace (58); (c) thoughtful self-examination and redirection of life (59); (d) urgent obedience (60).

16 See verse 9.

17 Lit. 'I have mollified/softened your face', a daring expression, as if it fell to us to predispose Yahweh to favour us. Notice how any false impression created along these lines is corrected by the immediately following reference to grace.

18 See verse 11.

19 See verse 2.

20 See verse 13.

As for me,
wholeheartedly I preserve your precepts.[32]

70. Their heart is as insensitive as fat.
As for me,
I am elated by your teaching.[33]

71. It is good for me that I was brought low
in order that I might learn your statutes.

72. Good for me is the teaching of your mouth,
more than thousands in gold and silver.

---

21 Another programmatic statement (61–64), this time of living in a world where divine love – Yahweh in all his love – is available everywhere. (a) The writer feels the 'pull' of surrounding wickedness: the antidote lies in the remembering mind (61); (b) regularity in seeking God in praise – even through sacrificing hours of sleep: the thinking mind (62); (c) cultivating a fellowship of the like-minded (63); (d) looking to Yahweh for his teaching – the learning mind (64).

22 See verse 1.

23 See verse 13.

24 See verse 4.

25 See verse 5.

26 In one form or another the word 'good' occurs six times. The Psalmist learned about the good – what it is, how to appreciate it, where to find it, what is its source and its demands – in times when he was 'down' (verses 67, 71). He has come to appreciate the positive 'goodness' of such times, their purposefulness. He does not specify what brought him low: that is not the point. Any downcast experience can prove to be the School of Hard Knocks, with the prospect of graduation to a fuller life.

27 Now, as then, the Word of God is frank that hard times come and do so for a good purpose (Romans 5:3–5; James 1:1–2.

28 *ta'am*, corresponds to *aisthesis* in the New Testament (Philippians 1:9; Hebrews 5:14). In Jonah 3:7 it means making the right 'decree' in a given situation. Sensitive discrimination, proper 'feeling'.

29 See verses 6, 10.

30 See verse 11.

31 See verse 5.

32 See verse 4.

33 See verse 1.

Pause for Thought

It is an association of thought frequent in Psalm 119, but it comes five times in today's reading: the link between seeking God and dwelling on God's word – or, in the reverse order, the link between pondering the word and reaching after God himself. Verse 55 is one of two 'night-time' verses. It feels like an unexpected wakefulness, bringing with it the recollection of Yahweh's name – his work of redemption (Exod. 3:15; 6:6), the Passover and the blood of the Lamb – but pondering the name leads to a fresh commitment to obey Yahweh's truth. Verse 62 seems more like a deliberate setting of the alarm clock for the 'wee small hours', so as to engage in a session of worshipful thanksgiving, but it is driven by a preceding awareness of Yahweh's revealed truth in all its rightness. Then there are three verses which agree how rich and bountiful Yahweh is – his sufficiency as our 'portion (57), the way his unfailing love meets us at every turn of the earthly pathway (64), his sheer goodness (68). But these realisations drive us to commitment to his word (57) and make us long to know more (64, 68), which is only possible if Yahweh himself be our teacher. Each of these verses is important in and of itself, but their united message is the most important of all. It is so desperately easy to read the word of God just as a habit (moving the book-mark forward!), or to satisfy our pleasure in learning more, becoming more familiar with the great book. At one level both of these are praiseworthy, but the LORD's intention is that his word should lead us to himself; that the outcome of every session of Bible reading is that we are now closer to him than we were, and know him more fully that we did. But, equally, the other way round. All our experience of God – every new sense of closeness, every fresh ambition to walk with him – everything must be governed and controlled, dominated by his word of truth, like Jesus said (John 15:7): 'if you abide in me, *and my words abide in you.*'

Day 60   Read Psalm 119:73-96

YODH (119:73–80).
Shaped by God[1]

73. It is your hands that made[2] me, and established me.[3]
    Give me discernment[4] that I may learn your
    commandments.
74. Those who fear you will see me and rejoice,
    because it is for your word that I wait in hope.
75. I know, Yahweh, that your commandments are
    righteousness,[5]
    and that it is in faithfulness that you have brought me
    low.
76. Oh may your committed love[6] be for my comfort
    according to your word to your servant.
77. Let your compassion come upon me so that I may live,
    because your teaching is my delight.
78. May the arrogant ones reap shame,
    because in falsehood they treated me perversely.[7]
    As for me, I will muse on your precepts.
79. May those who fear you return to me,
    those who know your testimonies.
80. May my heart be perfect in your statutes,
    in order that I may not reap shame.

KAPH (119:81–88).
The Art of Waiting[8]

A.1. Beginning at the end: hope and comfort

81. My soul is at an end for your salvation.[9]
    For your word[10] I have determined to hope.[11]

1 The opening line of verse 73 can be taken as setting the scene: a sort of banner headline. The individual believer has been shaped by the LORD's hands, fashioned with the characteristics and capacities he possesses and put where he is, within a certain set of circumstances. What is to be expected in such a life? How is it to be lived? At centre is the committed love (76) and the passionate love (77) of the LORD. On each side of this core, the verses are balanced: human hostility (78) is in the LORD's hand as his afflictions (75); all around (74, 79) are other believers to whom an example must be set. The all-surrounding truth is that the true believer prays for a mind (73b) and heart (80) grasping and holding revealed truth.

2 'Made' as in Genesis 1, the shaping of the original creative act of God to make something fit for his purpose in the place he put it.

3 *kun* in the simple active, to put in place, set up (as on a foundation), make secure. Here (*polel*) 'establishing' the psalmist where he is, putting him amid ill-minded opponents, and before a watching church looking for his example.

4 The prayer is not for learning the truth but for an inward work of God whereby the ability to discern and hold the truth is imparted. Note the 'inward' stress throughout: knowing (75), delighting (77), musing (78), heeding (80).

82. My eyes are at an end for your word,[12]
    saying, 'When will you comfort me?'

B.1. The days of persecution: waiting for vindication

83. Because I have become like a wine-skin in smoke.[13]
    Your statutes[14] I have determined not to forget.[15]
84. How many are your servant's days?[16]
    When will you execute judgment[17] on my persecutors?

B.2. The days of persecution: waiting for help

85. The arrogant have dug[18] pits for me,
    a thing which is not according to your teaching.[19]
86. All your commandments[20] are fidelity itself.
    It is in falsehood that they persecute me.
    Help me!

A.2. Beginning at the end: perseverance and life

87. Just a little more and they had made an end of me on
    earth!
    And as for me, I have not abandoned[21] your precepts![22]
88. According to your committed love, give me life
    so that I may keep the testimony[23] of your mouth.

LAMEDH (89–96).
Eternal Security[24]

A. Stability and continuance

89. For ever, Yahweh,
    your word is firmly fixed[25] in the heavens;
90. for generation after generation, your faithfulness.
    You established the earth, and it stands.[26]
91. According to your judgments[27] they[28] stand today,
    because the whole lot are your servants.

5 The great grounds of our security: knowing that Yahweh's decisions (here, what he has commanded to happen) are totally 'right', and that times of difficulty come, not because he has forgotten, but because he is faithful.

6 As always 'love' and 'compassion' hold the balance between the 'legal' bond in which Yahweh commits himself to love us for ever, his covenanted love, and passionate, surging emotional love (like 1 Kings 3:26). Hence, in verse 76 we read 'according to your word', i.e. as pledged; but in verse 77 'because I delight': obedient response as the key to blessing.

7 The details of this hostility are not given. This is a deliberate ploy so that, should adversity strike us, we may fill in the details of our own need.

8 The verses alternate between telling Yahweh how things are (81, 83, 85, 87) and seeking his action (82, 84, 86, 88). These are the two sides of prayer: telling him what he knows already, and asking for his active intervention. The bracketing thought (82, 88) is that, within the situation, he will 'comfort' and 'give life' to the psalmist, i.e. a prayer for the grace which enables us to sustain the discipline of waiting, until he chooses to deal with our persecutors (84, 86). Within the alternating pattern, pairs of verses belong together: 81–82 and 87–88 are linked by the verb *kalah,* to come to an end/to bring to an end; 83–84 and 85–86 introduce the 'persecutors' and look for Yahweh's action to deal with them. Throughout, the psalmist's attitude is one of waiting – and how best to fill the waiting hours.

9 'Soul' is here one's vital powers, resilience, ability to face life. 'For': i.e. 'while waiting for'.

10 See verse 9.

92. Were your teaching not my delight,
    then I had perished in my lowliness.[29]

B. Security, life and liberty

93. For ever I will not[30] forget your precepts[31]
    because by them you have given me life.
94. To you I belong: save me,
    because I have determined to seek your precepts.
95. It is for me the wicked wait to make me perish;
    I keep exercising discernment on your testimonies.[32]
96. I see that there is a limit[33] to all that is finite;
    your commandment is exceedingly wide.

11 'Hope', as always, to 'wait with confident expectation'. We use 'hope' to express confidence as to timing ('I hope tomorrow will be fine') but uncertainty as to event – i.e. 'tomorrow ' is sure, but 'fine' is uncertain. The Bible uses 'hope' with certainty as to event but uncertainty as to time. 'Jesus is coming again' – the event is certain, the timing is unknown.

12 See verse 11.

13 An unexplained simile. Presumably blackened, dried out by the heat, ready to crack, no longer usable. Well illustrative of 'come to an end'.

14 See verse 5.

15 The one thing that remains when all else is ending.

16 Even though we now have fuller light on the world to come than our Old Testament forebears, we can identify with the desire implied here that earthly issues be settled on earth. It is a logical consequence of the biblical doctrine of Creation that we desire actually to see this world as the arena of the Creator's just and equitable rule.

17 See verse 7.

18 Or 'dig', the perfect tense representing their settled policy.

19 See verse 1.

20 See verse 6.

21 Or 'determined not to abandon'.

22 See verse 4.

23 See verse 2.

24 'For ever' (le'olam) marks out the two parts of this section: 'for ever the word is settled' (89); 'for ever the precepts are unforgotten' (93). Section **A** focuses on the reason why the cosmos – the heavens and the world of the passing generations – is stable (89–91), and verse 92 teaches how we can enter into that stability. Section **B** introduces the dangers inherent in this world – specifically, the life-threatening hostility of the wicked (95).Wherein does safety and liberty consist?

25 On duty as in a military 'post'. Yahweh's word is the ruling factor in heaven and earth.

26 In the sense 'stand firm', 'continue in stability'. So also verse 91.

27 'Judgments' are his decisions and directives. The cosmos is not self-governing or self-perpetuating, nor are its regularities simply those of a well integrated machine. Everything depends all the time on Yahweh's decision that it should be so.

28 Both heaven (89) and the sweep of human generations (90) are alike maintained in continuance by Yahweh's word. Together they are the 'they' of verse 91.

29 What is true of heaven and earth is true also of the human individual. Fragile in lowliness, yet continuing through Yahweh's express will. Only the believer knows this. 'Then' is temporal, 'at that moment/time'; i.e. stability and delighting in the teaching belong together.

30 English style demands that 'for ever … not' become 'never', but as far as *lamedh* is concerned this would destroy the balance with 'for ever' in verse 89 on which the structure of the section depends.

31 See verse 4.

32 See verse 2.

33 *qets* 'an end'. But just as 'wide' is used to describe what affords 'wide-ranging' freedom of movement, so here, by contrast, 'end' means 'finitude, limitation'. 'Finite' here translates *tiklah*, which may derive from either *kul* (comprehend, contain) or *kalah* (be at/come to an end). The ideas therefore of containment, fixity, limitation are prominent in a word not found elsewhere. Contextually, what is 'finite'. Only Yahweh's word is wide enough to secure true freedom (compare verse 45).

Pause for Thought

The opening verse of today's reading (73) links two thoughts together: first he has made us; secondly, may he grant us discernment so as to learn his commandments. He made us, the Bible says, in his own image. Our true life is to express that image; anything else is a falling short of the ideal. Hold that thought in your mind and consider something else: God's law is what it is because he is what he is – this is the teaching of the marvellous Leviticus 19, where all life is assembled and brought under the appropriate commands of God. But each command is enforced by the statement 'I am Yahweh' – in other words 'I am what I am' (Lev. 19:2, 3, 4 etc.; Exod. 3:14–15). The law of God is another way of expressing the image of God. We, by creation, express his image in personal terms; the law expresses his image in terms of commandments. The law says, Do this and you will be like him; obedience to the law is our way of living according to our true nature. Now look at verse 88: In his love he imparts his life to us *in order that* we may do what he says. This is God's highest and best will for us. So often when we say we are seeking God's will we actually mean 'where' we should be or 'what' we should do. But his will is, first and foremost, who we should be, 'what manner of persons' (2 Peter 3:11, NKJV) – i.e. people true to our 'real' nature, those in whom the image of God is made visible. Finally, re-read verse 96 (and recall verse 45). 'Your commandment is exceedingly wide'. It is the 'place' where I can enjoy true freedom, transcending human finitude, living according to what James calls 'the perfect law, the law of liberty' (James 1:25): 'perfect' in that it is perfectly designed to match our true, real nature (Jer. 31:31–34; Heb. 10:15–17), bringing us 'liberty' because obedience triggers the image of God in us so that we are what we were always meant to be.

Day 61 Read Psalm 119:97-120

MEM (119:97–104).
All-sufficient, All-renewing

A. The new and superior mind[1]

97. How I love your teaching![2]
    All the day it is my meditation.
98. More than my enemies you make me wise – your commandments![3] –
    because for ever it is mine.
99. More than all who teach me I act with prudence,[4]
    because your testimonies[5] are my meditation.
100. More than the ancient ones I exercise discernment,
    because I have preserved[6] your precepts.[7]

B. The redirected pathway

101. From every evil pathway I have restrained my feet,
    in order that I may keep your word.[8]
102. From your judgments[9] I have not turned away,
    because you have yourself taught me.

C. Comprehensive renewal[10]

103. How agreeable to my palate is your word,[11]
    more than honey to my mouth.
104. Because of your precepts I act with discernment,
    therefore I hate every pathway of falsehood.

1 A comprehensive survey of what revealed truth can do for our minds. When the mind is lovingly focused on God's teaching (97), it is equipped for the hazards and threats of life (98), possesses a wisdom beyond the merely human (99) and transcending the merely traditional (100).

2 See verse 1. Verse 97 describes subjective pleasure in the truth; it is balanced at the end of the section by verse 103, the truth's inherent sweetness. Personal experience is founded on intrinsic reality.

3 The implication of course is 'by your commandments' but the Hebrew is abrupt and best left like that. The translation 'your commandment makes me wise' (ESV) requires an alteration of the text.

4 *sakal* holds together the ideas of prudent and successful action – the right thing to do in the circumstances and the right thing in order to achieve a desired result.

5 See verse 2.

6 Note the emphasis on sustained attention to the truth: 'meditation' (97, 99) implies extended if not leisurely attention, made explicit by 'all day' (97), 'ever' (98), 'preserve' (100).

7 See verse 4.

8 See verse 9.

9 See verse 7.

10 Verse 103 covers our new *emotions* responding to the truth; verse 104a describes the new *mind*; verse 104b a new moral awareness, the new *will* shunning the false pathway.

NUN (119:105–112).
Truth for Life[12]

A.1. Walking in the truth[13]

105. A lamp for my foot is your word,
and light for my pathway.[14]
106. I have taken an oath and have determined to implement it,[15]
to keep the judgments of your righteousness.[16]

B.1. Life's trials: Yahweh applies his truth[17]

107. I have been brought very exceedingly low.
Yahweh, give me life according to your word.[18]
108. The freewill offerings of my mouth,[19] do accept with favour, Yahweh,
and teach me your judgments.[20]

B.2. Life's trials: Personal devotion to the truth[21]

109. My soul is in my hand constantly,
and your teaching[22] I have not forgotten.
110. The wicked have set a trap for me,
and from your precepts[23] I have not strayed.

A.2. Loving the truth[24]

111. I have gained possession of your precepts[25] for ever –
indeed they are the gladness of my heart.
112. I have directed my heart to do your statutes,[26]
for ever to the end.

11 See verse 11.

12 This very practical section faces seriously the difficulties and challenges of life (107, 109, 110) but affirms that there is a pathway through (105, 112). The LORD's antidote is to apply his truth (107, 108); our calling is to embrace and live out his truth (109, 110).

13 The reference to 'feet' indicates that the topic is practical living in the light of the truth (105). This requires deliberate commitment (106).

14 The contrast between 'foot' and 'pathway' is, in our terms, the contrast between the hand-held torch that indicates where to make the next step, and the car headlight which lights up the road ahead.

15 *qum* is part of covenanting vocabulary. In the Hiphil mode (causative active) it means to implement a previously undertaken covenant obligation (e.g. Genesis 6:18, NKJV 'establish'). Here the intensive active (*piel*), as is customary with stative verbs, has the same meaning. It is a perfect of determination.

16 When 'judgment' and 'righteousness' occur together, the former is the practical decision, the latter the foundational principle from which it arises.

17 The two internal sections (**B.1.**, **B.2.**) face up to the fact that life brings challenges – things which 'bring us low' (107), actual dangers we cannot evade (109) and ill-intentioned people (110) with their concealed menace.

18 See verse 9.

19 The 'freewill offerings of my mouth' refers back to the oath taken in verse 106. Just as we look to Yahweh to keep his promises (verse 107), he expects us to keep ours.

SAMEKH (119:113–120).
On Being Different

A. Distinct[27]

113. Undecided[28] ones I hate
  and your teaching[29] I love.
114. You are my hiding place and my shield.
  For your word[30] I wait expectantly.
115. Go away from me, you evildoers
  so that I may preserve[31] the commands[32] of my God.

B. Supported[33]

116. Uphold me according to your word[34] that I may live
  and not reap shame[35] from[36] my hope.
117. Support me that I may be saved,[37]
  and keep my eyes fixed constantly on your statutes.[38]

C. Fearful[39]

118. You reject all who keep erring from your statutes,[40]
  because their deceitfulness is falsehood.[41]
119. As dross you bring all the wicked of the earth to an end.
  Therefore I love your testimonies.[42]
120. Because of dread of you my flesh creeps,[43]
  and because of your commands I am afraid.

20 In verse 107 Yahweh stands by his truth; in verse 108 he brings his truth home to us. On 'judgments' see verse 7.

21 The two verses of this section deal respectively with the mental retention of Yahweh's truth and practical obedience in daily life.

22 See verse 1.

23 See verse 4.

24 Just as 'foot' was the leading thought in **A.1.** – the outward pathway – so 'heart' is the leading thought in **A.2.**, forming an inclusion by contrast. The two verses balance inward delight with outward action. Gladness without obedience is frivolity; obedience without gladness is conformism.

25 See verse 4.

26 See verse 8.

27 'Distinctiveness' involves (inwardly) what is hated and what is loved (113), (upwardly) taking cover in Yahweh and waiting for his word (114), and (outwardly) living among people in obedience to heavenly truth, taking sides. In each of the three verses 'distinctiveness' is secured by loving, waiting for a preserving revealed truth. It is not just a case of 'being different' (which could be no more than being 'odd'), but the distinctiveness which arises from following a different code, learning from a different source.

28 Related to the word for 'branch', therefore what goes off at a tangent; also of a 'fork', in a road (1 Kings 18:21), therefore uncertainty of the way ahead. Of a 'divided' mind.

29 See verse 1.

30 See verse 9.

31 Two words are used of 'keeping' God's word. Here *natsar*, to preserve, obedience to the whole word, preserved in its wholeness and integrity. The other word, *shamar* (e.g. verse 57) may by contrast refer to obedience by the whole person. We could think of *natsar* as uncompromising obedience, and *shamar* as unstinting obedience.

32 See verse 6.

33 These two verses are linked by the synonyms 'uphold … support'. They are contrasted in that verse 116 asks Yahweh to prove faithful to what he has said, and 117 asks for help that we may be faithful to his truth.

34 See verse 11.

35 The verb 'be ashamed' goes beyond feeling embarrassment to 'reaping shame': being disappointed of what one so confidently hoped for.

36 Possibly implying 'far from …' – very different from what I hoped.

37 Here in the broad sense of being brought safely through the 'changes and chances of this mortal life'.

38 See verse 5.

39 I tried many words to describe these verses but in the end decided it is best to take a lead from verse 120. This is the 'fear' referred to in 1 Peter 1:17. The opposite of taking our salvation casually, presuming on grace. There is a seriousness in God's dealings (verses 118–119) which it is all too easy to forget or discount. These verses continue the emphasis that runs through the whole section: the identity of Yahweh and his word. To love him is to love his word, to shelter in him is to hope in his word, to reject his word is to be rejected by him. Fearing his word and fearing him are two ways of saying the same thing.

40 See verse 5.

41 A very allusive statement, hard to pin down. Possibly 'their deceitfulness reveals how false they are to you'. This meaning best suits the fact that the words are an explanation ('because') of the divine rejection mentioned in the previous line.

42 See verse 2.

43 Or 'my hair stands on end'. See Job 4:15 for another use of this verb, and Jeremiah 51:27 for its noun (NKJV 'bristling locust').

Pause for Thought

Recall that Jesus said 'If you love me, keep [or, you will keep] my commandments' (John 14:15). Was he thinking particularly about Psalm 119:97–120? Probably not, but there is no better summary of the central thrust of these verses. Obedience is the required proof not only of our commitment to the word of God – his revealed truth – but our love for God himself. The psalm says so; Jesus says so. Take then, almost at random, what Psalm 119 says here about relating to God's truth: 'meditation all day' (97); consistency in our 'walk' because his word is his teaching (102); emotional delight (103); the use of revealed truth as light on life's pathway (105) and resource (first port of call, so to say) in life's threats (107, 109); truth memorized (109); concern for the whole truth (115, see note 31); seeking God's upholding so that we may obey – and undeviating concentration on his word (117); devotion to his word as the passport to his favour (119). We possess his revealed truth: his teaching (97); what he has revealed of himself, this truth and his way (99, 111, 119); the very word he has spoken (101); what he designed for our obedience (104); his lamp for the next step, and his light for the way ahead (105). If we feel we need life and renewal, is it because we have neglected his renewing, life-imparting word (107, 116)? Love and respect for the word opens and closes today's reading (97, 120) and lies close to the centre (113). I need to ask, 'How do I stand in the light of all this – and, by the way, how do you stand?' The fact of the matter – calling us all to a reassessment of ourselves and our daily use of our Bibles – is that the Word of God and the God of the Word are inseparables.

Day 62 Read Psalm 119:121-144

AYIN (119:121–128).
A Survival Kit for Hard Times[1]

121. I have acted in judgment and righteousness.[2]
    Do not leave me[3] to my oppressors.
122. Make a pledge of good[4] to your servant.
    Do not let the arrogant oppress me.
123. My eyes have come to an end[5] for your salvation,
    for a word[6] of your righteousness.
124. Act for your servant according to your changeless love
    – teach me your statutes.[7]
125. I am your servant;
    Give me discernment
    in order that I may know[8] your testimonies.[9]
126. It is Yahweh's opportunity to act;
    they have treated your teaching as void of signficance.
127. Therefore I love your commandments[10]
    more than gold, than fine gold.
128. Therefore all the precepts on everything I consider right;[11]
    every path of falsehood I hate.

PE (119:129–136).
Shining Word ... Shining Face

A.1. The light of Yahweh's word

129. Wonderful[12] are your testimonies,[13]
    therefore my soul has resolved to preserve[14] them.
130. The door[15] of your words brings light,
    bringing discernment to the teachable.[16]

1 In two halves, each beginning with a first person singular statement (121,125). In part one 'oppressors' are active (121, 122), Yahweh is silent (123) but confidence in his love remains (124). In part two there has been a general ('they', 126) dismissal of Yahweh's teaching as irrelevant; 'therefore' (127, 128) time to reaffirm my love for his truth and commitment to his path. If we label the verses a-b-c-d-d-c-b-a, the d-verses (bridging the two 'halves') deal with servanthood in a dark day: assured of Yahweh's love, longing for Yahweh's truth. The c-verses express desire for divine action – for me and against them. The a-b-b-a-verses seek divine intervention (121–122) and pledge personal commitment (127–128).

2 Two words describing revealed truth; here the living out of revealed truth by making right decisions based on right principles.

3 *nuach*, to rest, rest down. Here 'to cause to rest', 'to put down, consign', etc.

4 *'arabh*, to give a pledge, undertake a commitment. Here 'make yourself responsible for the welfare of ...'

5 i.e. 'are worn out watching for'.

6 Not a reference to the word as possessed (in the sense that we possess our Bibles), but to some truth brought home to mind and heart in a given situation of need.

7 The implication of verse 124 is that Yahweh expresses his love by teaching his truth. On 'statutes' see verse 5.

B.1. The grace that nourishes

131. My mouth I have opened wide – and how I gasp[17]
     because I long for your commands.[18]
132. Turn to me and grant me your grace
     according to the judgment[19] for those who love your
     name.[20]

B.2. The ransom that liberates[21]

133. Establish my steps in your word,[22]
     and do not cause any wrong thing[23] to lord it over me.
134. Ransom me from human oppression
     so that I may keep[24] your precepts.[25]

A.2. The light of Yahweh's face[26]

135. Make your face shine on your servant –
     teach me your statutes.[27]
136. Channels of water go down from my eyes
     because they do not keep your teaching.[28]

TSADHE (119:137–144).
The Perfect Match[29]

137. You are righteous, Yahweh,
     and your judgments[30] are upright.
138. You have commanded in righteousness[31] your
     testimonies,[32]
     and in faithfulness – exceedingly!
139. My concern has annihilated[33] me,
     because my adversaries have forgotten your words.[34]
140. Your word is purified – exceedingly ! –
     and your servant loves it.
141. I am insignificant and despised.
     I have not forgotten your precepts.[35]

8   The three verbs ('teach …discernment …know') form a progression: the divine teacher accompanies his teaching with inspiration, the gift of 'discernment'. The resultant state is 'knowledge', truth grasped.

9   See verse 2.

10 See verse 6.

11 This form of *yashar*, to be straight, right, usually means 'to make straight'. This seems to be the only place requiring the meaning 'to account straight/right'.

12 From *pal'a,* yielding the significance of 'out of this world', supernatural.

13 See verse 2.

14 See verse 101, note 31. To preserve intact, in its wholeness. We are called to be genuine 'conservators' of God's revealed truth, no addition, no subtraction.

15 i.e. when the 'door' is opened light floods through. The word is never unilluminated or fails to illuminate. Psalm 49:4 offers another possibility: to open up meaning. Hence ESV 'unfolding'. This is the supernatural 'wonder' of the revealed truth.

16 *pethiy* has a 'bad' meaning, 'gullible', but a good meaning, 'open-minded/ ready to learn'. See Psalm 19:7.

17 The voracious chick or the hungry child awaiting the return of the mother bird or the parent.

18 See verse 6.

19 The gift of the word as essential food is the characteristic work of grace. 'Judgment' (see verse 7) describes what Yahweh has decided is the right action in such a situation.

142. Your righteousness is righteousness for ever,
   and your teaching is truth.
143. Adversity and distress have been my lot.
   Your commands are my delight.[36]
144. The righteousness of your testimonies is for ever.
   Give me discernment so that I may live.

20 As ever, longing for the word of truth is a relational matter, inseparable from loving Yahweh's 'name', his revealed character and person.

21 The theme of these verses (133–134) is the removal of obstacles to the practice of the truth: in verse 133, the inward opposition of sin; in verse 134 the outward opposition of hostile people. 'Ransom' (padhah) – paying the price that liberates the captive – buys back the kidnapped, restores liberty. The structure of these verses is a-b-b-a, where A prays for obedience, and B seeks the removal of constraints.

22 See verse 11.

23 'awen, a wide-ranging word, anything from 'mischief' to 'idolatry'!

24 See verse 101, note 31. Here shamar, give myself to keeping.

25 See verse 4.

26 Another insight into the 'supernatural' quality of revealed truth. Where the word shines Yahweh's face shines.

27 The shining face is the teaching of truth. Yahweh's face shines (with delight and favour) as he teaches his truth. On 'statutes' see verse 8.

28 The context is that Yahweh's revealed truth is so 'wonderful' that it is heart-breaking that anyone should fail to keep it.

29 The two halves of the tsadhe section are marked out by the contrasting statements, 'You are righteous' (137) and 'I am insignificant' (141). In each half the four verses pair off with each other: the upright word (137), the unforgotten word (141); righteousness and faithfulness (138), righteousness and truth (142); the loved word (140), the life-giving word (144). Verses 139 and 143 set the scene: life in an uncongenial society (139), life in a trouble world (143). Uncongeniality should drive us all the more passionately to God's truth, which matches his character (137–140); troubles should increase our delight in the word whose life-giving power makes up for our inadequacies.

30 See verse 7.

31 There is a perfect 'match' between what Yahweh is (verse 137) and the truth he has revealed (138). This is another aspect of the insistence that to know him we need his word, and that in his word we meet himself.

32 See verse 2.

33 A very strong statement, to be compared with our feeling when we say that 'we found the news shattering'.

34 The thought is of the absolute tragedy that anyone should sit loose to truth so important and wonderful.

35 i.e. our only 'worth' is our possession of the pure gold of revealed truth.

36 Matching the thought (139) that life's adversities should drive us all the more to our Bibles; here it is life's difficulties.

Pause for Thought

Are you ready to exercise a bit of imagination with me? Each of today's sections of Psalm 119 has its own very telling way of thinking about the Word of God, his revealed truth as they possessed it – in our terms, the Bible. In the *ayin* section (v. 127) it is 'gold ... fine gold', that is to say, inherently precious: not a unique thought in the Bible (e.g. Ps. 19:10) but not to be treated as commonplace – in Her Majesty's Coronation Service, 'the most precious thing this world affords'. The section *pe* (v. 130) prefers the imagery of 'light'. There is this door, and when we open it light floods out as from a gloriously illuminated room – at least that is one way of thinking about the picture involved. Finally, *tsadhe* has a third view: when revealed truth is grasped it is like taking hold of life itself (v. 144). God's teaching is 'truth' (v. 142), and the truth is a life-imparting agency. So far so good, but now we come to the imaginary bit! First of all, gold does not fall into our pockets; it has to be panned from rivers or mined from rocks. It is 'there' but it has to be sought and wrought (Prov. 2:1–4). Superficial, hurried Bible reading will not do; it is like being where treasure is to be found but leaving without any treasure to carry off. Stay and do some panning; take your pick and do some mining. Secondly, stay in the light until your eyes get used to it, and you begin to see clearly. Again it takes time, does it not? Coming out of darkness into light, we come into a situation where at last 'seeing' is possible, yet we can see nothing because the very light blinds our eyes until we acclimatize. Thirdly, truth brings life, vitality, new energy, but again, not without patience. Dare we think of an infra-red ray lamp rather than a reading lamp? It takes time to work its effects, coming back again and again – but the effectiveness is there, waiting to benefit the assiduous and persevering. Now here is a word of encouragement: *ayin* (v. 124), *pe* (v. 135) and *tsadhe* (v. 144) pray that Yahweh himself will be with us to teach us and give us discernment in his truth. When we open our Bibles he is always there, and we have come into his classroom.

Day 63 Read Psalm 119:145-176

QOPH (119:145–152).
The Required Pre-commitment

A. 'Draw near to God …'

145. I call out[1] with my whole heart;
     answer me, Yahweh!
     I will preserve[2] your statutes.[3]
146. I call you![4]
     Save me!
     And I will keep your testimonies.[5]
147. I am there ahead of the half-light,[6]
     and cry for help.
     It is for[7] your words[8] I hope.
148. My eyes are there ahead[9] of the night watches
     to muse on your word.[10]

B. '… and he will draw near to you' (James 4:8)

149. Hear my voice according to your committed love,[11]
     Yahweh.
     According to your judgment[12] give me life.
150. Those who pursue a plan[13] draw near:
     they are far from your teaching.
151. You are near,[14] Yahweh,
     and all your commands are truth.
152. Of old I have known your testimonies –
     that for ever you have founded them.

1. Perfect tense (also in verse 146), expressing fixed habit.

2. See verse 115, note 31.

3. i.e. there is a conscious pre-commitment to obey Yahweh's word (so also verses 146–148) – no waiting to see whether it appeals or not. 'Whatever he says to you, do' (John 2:5). 'Statutes' see verse 5.

4. 'To call out' ordinarily requires an indirect object ('to'). Here it has a direct object, an idiom used to stress the directness of the appeal.

5. See verse 2.

6. *nesheph* ordinarily means 'twilight', but here, apparently, used of the 'twilight' before dawn. See Job 3:9 (NKJV 'dark'); possibly Jeremiah 13:16. In the present context the balance between verses 147 and 148 is that between rising up early and staying up late.

7. Or 'in', i.e. resting on the certainty of Yahweh's promises.

8. See verse 9.

9. *qadham*, to be beforehand, anticipate, be ahead of. Also verse 147.

10. See verse 11.

11. The second half of the section opens with unchanging love (149) and ends with the unchanging word (152).

12. See verse 7. Here, what is known to be what Yahweh has decided to do in such cases.

13. *zimmah*, where context requires, has all the sinister meaning we can attach to 'a secret agenda'.

RESH (119:153-160).
Sure Word: Life-giving God

A.1. The unforgotten word[15]

153. See my humiliation and set me free,
    because I have not forgotten your teaching.[16]
154. Plead my cause[17] and redeem[18] me;
    give me life according to your word.[19]

B.1. The wicked and revealed truth

155. Salvation is far from the wicked,
    because they have decided[20] not to seek[21] your statutes.[22]

C. Abundant hostility, abundant compassion, sustained fidelity

156. Your compassion[23] is abundant, Yahweh.
    Give me life according to your judgments.[24]
157. Abundant are my persecutors and my adversaries.
    I have not turned from your testimonies.[25]

B.2. The unreliable and revealed truth

158. I see the unreliable and I am filled with loathing –
    they have determined not to keep your word.[26]

A.2. The beloved word

159. See how I love your precepts.[27]
    Give me life, Yahweh, according to your committed love.[28]
160. The head[29] of your word is truth:
    every judgment of your righteousness[30] is for ever.

14 *qarobh,* 'near', is used in the 'next-of-kin' family of words, e.g. Ruth 3:12. It can be given that force here: Yahweh is at hand as our next-of-kin to shoulder all our burdens as if his own. Compare Psalm 145:18.

15 Just as the psalmist does not forget Yahweh's teaching (153), so Yahweh is certain to stand by what he has said (154). The pattern of 153-154 is a-b-b-a: plea for divine help (153a), based on sustained commitment to Yahweh's teaching (153b); plea for divine aid (154a), based on certainty that Yahweh will do what he has said (154b).

16 See verse 1.

17 Yahweh is pictured as a lawyer taking a case. This is related to the biblical insistence that deliverance, salvation, setting free, etc. must accord with righteousness and fulfil God's law. Compare Isaiah's question, 'Can the captives of the righteous be delivered?' – i.e. if they are *legally* held captive, they must be *legally* delivered. Legal rights cannot be trampled on but must be satisfied.

18 Matching the 'lawyer' imagery, Yahweh is also the divine 'next-of-kin', taking and shouldering all our needs as his own. Compare on Psalm 19:14.

19 See verse 11.

20 Perfect tense expressing fixed policy.

21 In its customary sense of 'to frequent, to be where they are'.

22 See verse 8.

23 Yahweh's passionate, heartfelt love.

24 See verse 7. This is what he has 'decided' as his settled policy.

25 See verse 2.

26 See verse 11.

SHIN, SIN[31] (119:161–168). The Love of my Life[32]

A. The constant heart[33]

161. Princes[34] persecute me without cause,
      and my heart has determined to stand in awe of your words.[35]
162. I am ever[36] truly[37] glad about your word,[38]
      like someone finding abundant spoil.[39]
163. Falsehood I hate and abhor;
      your teaching[40] I love.

B. The constant life[41]

164. Seven times a day I plan to praise you
      because of the judgments of your righteousness.[42]
165. Abundant[43] peace belongs to those who love your teaching,
      and they have nothing that trips them up.
166. I have fixed my hope on your salvation, Yahweh,
      and your commands[44] I have determined to perform.

C. The constant obedience

167. My soul has determined to keep your testimonies,[45]
      and I have determined to love them exceedingly.
168. I have determined to keep your precepts[46] and your testimonies,
      because all my ways are before you.

27 See verse 4. Matching (**A.1.**): Yahweh's revealed truth held perpetually in memory. Is the love of that truth prompting devotion to it?

28 In **A.1.**, the gift of life was in accordance with what Yahweh has said or promised. Here it is the product of his committed, changeless love, the love that is guaranteed by his will or willing commitment. In this way the section is teaching that what he says and what is in his heart are identical; his word expresses his mind.

29 'Head' is used in the sense of 'leading feature/characteristic', the 'foremost' reality or fact, 'the chief thing about...'

30 It is much better to spell out this expression in full rather than compress it into 'your righteous judgments'. His 'judgments' (what he has decided upon, see verse 7) are each the expression of eternal righteousness.

31 In verses 161, 162, 166 the first word begins with the letter *sin*. In the rest of the verses with *shin*.

32 Love of revealed truth runs through this section: 'heart' (161), love (163, 165, 167) and can be isolated as the main theme, but the structure of the verses is determined by the distribution of Hebrew's two 's-sounds', 's' and 'sh'. Verses 161–163 respectively are led by s-s-sh; 164–166 by sh-sh-s; and 167–168, sh-sh. The middle verses of the first two divisions balance each other with 'abundant spoil' and 'abundant peace'; the two verses of the final division begin with 'keep'. It is a beautifully planned little poem on loving God's word.

33 In turn what it reverences (161), what it treasures (162), what it loves (163).

TAU (119:169–176).
A Fourfold Prayer

A. Hear my prayer[47]

169. Let my loud cry come near before you, Yahweh.
     Give me discernment according to your word.[48]
170. Let my plea for grace come before you.
     Deliver[49] me, according to your word.

B. Let me praise[50]

171. Let my lips pour out praise,
     because you teach me your statutes.[51]
172. Let my tongue sing of our word,[52]
     because all you commands are righteousness.[53]

C. Grant me help[54]

173. Let your hand be prompt to help me,[55]
     because I have chosen your precepts.[56]
174. I long for your salvation, Yahweh,
     and your teaching[57] is my delight.

D. Bring me home

175. Let my soul live, and it will praise you,
     and let your judgments[58] help me.
176. I have strayed like a lost sheep.
     Seek your servant,
     because I have not forgotten your commands.[59]

34 'Princes' is the title used of the people who actually run things. In governmental terms, it is the title of what we call the Civil Service. The situation here, therefore, is that the whole way things are 'going' makes life difficult for one who is committed to revealed truth.

35 See verse 9.

36 'Glad' is a participle which, according to Hebrew usage, describes what is an unchanging state of affairs.

37 'Glad' is given a place of emphasis in this line, meriting the insertion of 'truly' or some such word.

38 See verse 11.

39 The word 'spoil' points to the fruits of victory. Are we meant to take this seriously – that in the constant wear and tear of princely opposition, victory and its rich consequences come to the lover of God's word?

40 See verse 1.

41 In turn, its response in praise (164), its wellbeing and consistency (165), its patient obedience (166).

42 See verse 160, note 30.

43 'Abundant' forces us to understand 'peace' in its total meaning of peace with God, with other people and in our own inner experience – spiritual, social and personal peace and wellbeing.

44 See verse 6.

45 See verse 2.

46 See verse 4.

47 Biblical praying often begins, as here, with a 'prayer to be heard'. Knowing as they did the deeply intimate relationship between Yahweh and his people, nevertheless there is no cocky bursting into his presence (compare Exodus 19:21). These verses are held together by the double 'before you', and the double reference to Yahweh acting as he has said (respectively see verses 9, 11). The confident 'loud cry' of verse 169 is balanced by the 'plea for grace' (170).

48 The section makes it clear that there is need for divine, saving action but the priority request is for discernment in revealed truth.

49 'Discernment' asks for an inward work of God; 'deliverance' seeks his dealing with an outward circumstance.

50 These verses belong together: (a) referring to lips and tongue, (b) both are prayers for making a response – the first 'because', of learning; the second 'because', of recognizing the value of Yahweh's word.

51 See verse 5.

52 See verse 11.

53 Express Yahweh's righteous character and will.

54 The last four verses have a strong element of personal testimony: 'I have chosen … long … my delight … my soul … I have strayed … not forgotten.' The uniting theme of verses 173–174 is response to the word.

55 These verses deal respectively with a predisposition on the part of Yahweh (readiness to act), and a predisposition on the part of the psalmist (longing and delight).

56 See verse 4.

57 See verse 1.

58 See verse 7.

59 See verse 10.

Pause for Thought

Of all ways for Psalm 119 to end could you have guessed a confession of being a lost sheep? Following all the mighty thoughts contained in this Golden Alphabet! 'I am a lost sheep … seek me!' But how realistic! How totally true! When all comes to all what we need to be told is how to deal with the realities of life – and, above all the reality of our own feeble, lost and ever-failing nature. The hymn-writer teaches us to sing: 'Prone to wander, Lord, I feel it,/ Prone to leave the God I love …' then offers a solution: 'Here's my heart, O take and seal it …' Some great act of dedication – and doubtless acts of dedication have their place, but in most cases they leave the basic situation unchanged. And this is where Psalm 119 scores so heavily. The wandering sheep seeks a solution in divine action and human obedience: the searching, rescuing Shepherd and the unforgotten commandments; faithful divine action, never for one moment abandoning the sheep he has made his own, and faithful human continuance in revealed truth. The essentials of the personal testimony in verses 173–176 can be called 'the Wandering Sheep's Charter': the vows and commitments with which we begin our lives in the Shepherd's care; the vows and commitments renewed at the opening of every day; the vows and commitments we repeat at the onset of every temptation to wander – 'I choose … I long for … I delight … I do not forget your commands.' And all of this embraced and filled with prayer: 'Let your hand help … fill my soul with life … let your judgments help … seek your servant.' Four commitments and four appeals.

Day 64 Read Psalms 120–122[1]

Psalm 120.
The Resident Alien[2]

A song of the Great Ascent.

Prayer heard

1. To Yahweh, in the very real[3] adversity[4] I have,
   I called out and he answered me.[5]
2. Yahweh,[6]
   Oh deliver my soul
   from the lip of falsehood, from the tongue of deceit.[7]

Retribution merited

3. What should he[8] give to you,
   and what more, in your case,
   you tongue of deceit?[9] –
4. a warrior's arrows – sharpened –
   along with coals of the broom tree![10]

The problem awaiting solution

5. What distress is mine![11]
   That I am a resident alien in Meshak,
   that I reside among the tents of Kedar.[12]
6. My soul has had enough[13] of residing among those who
   – each and every one - hate peace.
7. I am peace,[14]
   and when I speak, they are for war!

1 Each of Psalms 120–134 is entitled 'A song of ascents'. The simplest explanation of this is also the best: that 'ascents' is a plural of amplification, 'the great ascent', and that it refers to the pilgrim journey to Jerusalem to keep the feasts of the LORD (Exodus 23:14–19; Deuteronomy 16, esp. verse 16). This is the law Joseph and Mary obeyed annually in their Passover pilgrimages (Luke 2:41). Possibly Psalms 120–134, with 135–136 as a conclusion (compare how psalms 105–106 conclude the 'royal' song book [90–104]), formed a Pilgrimage Songbook used annually by the travelling companies as they journeyed, and was eventually formalized and incorporated into the completed collection of the Psalms. Psalms 120–134 fall into five groups of three. In each group the first of the three exposes a situation of difficulty, the second focuses on God's power to keep, and the third security in Zion and its God. The last group (132–134) is wholly one of arrival, and forms an inclusion with the 'far off country' theme of the opening Psalm 120.

2 A resident alien (5) and a nomad at that ('tents') in the uncongenial society of far off Meshech and Kedar, subject to false, hurtful vilification (3–4). Prayer has been made and answered (1–2), but the writer is still awaiting the answer to arrive (3–7). Resorting to prayer as the solution involves patience and trust.

3 The noun 'adversity' here in the extended feminine form, hence needing some emphasis.

Psalm 121.
Security[15]

A song of the Great Ascent.

The question

1. I keep raising my eyes to the mountains.
   Where will my help come from?[16]

The answer (1). Yahweh the Creator

2. My[17] help comes straight[18] from Yahweh,
   Maker of heaven and earth.[19]

The answer (2). Yahweh, God of Israel, the Redeemer

3. He will not allow your foot to slip.
   He who keeps you does not become drowsy.
4. Behold!
   He does not become drowsy and does not sleep,[20]
   the keeper of Israel![21]

The answer (3). Yahweh our companion and protection

5. Yahweh is your keeper!
   Yahweh is your shade in attendance at[22] your right hand.
6. By day the sun will not strike you,
   and the moon by night.[23]

Summary: comprehensive[24] preservation

7. Yahweh will himself keep you from all evil.
   He will keep your soul.[25]
8. Yahweh will himself keep your going and your coming,[26]
   from now and for ever.

4 The 'adversity' was verbal vilification (3); an unceasing contradiction (7) for no other reason, apparently, than that the author was an immigrant.

5 There was certainty that the prayer had been answered, but this was followed by discipline of waiting for the answer to arrive. Prayer is the solution; but it is also a summons to patience.

6 The psalm begins with talking to God (1–2) and ends talking to others (7). There was much to complain about, but the whole 'complaint' was addressed to Yahweh; all that people heard was words of peace.

7 The Hebrew text makes these two words nouns in apposition –'a tongue that is deceit its very self!' i.e. 'inveterately deceitful'. Stylistically this is balanced by the appositional expression 'I am peace' in verse 7.

8 Referring to Yahweh, or a 'third person indefinite' ('one give'), equivalent to a passive, 'be given'.

9 Again, nouns in apposition, see note 7.

10 A double picture: death in battle (arrows), and the post-battle burning of the detritus of war. Together signifying total victory. Why a 'broom tree'?

11 This emphatic form of the word for 'Woe!' is only found here. Equivalent to 'alas and alack!'

Psalm 122.
Arrival

Beginning and ending: fellowship all the way

1. I rejoiced among those who were saying to me:
   'Let us go to Yahweh's house.'
2. Our feet have been actually standing[27]
   in your gates, Jerusalem!

Look around: privileges in abundance[28]

3. Jerusalem which is actually built so as to be a city[29]
   which is designedly integrated together;
4. to which the tribes go up –
   the tribes of Yah –
   the testimony[30] to Israel –
   to give thanks to Yahweh's name.[31]
5. Because[32] there thrones[33] for judgment[34] abide,
   thrones belonging to the House of David.

Long may it be so! The duty of prayer

6. Ask peace for Jerusalem.
   May they be at ease[35] who love you!
7. May there be peace within your perimeter,
   ease in your palaces!
8. For the sake of my brothers and contemporaries
   oh do let me speak!
   'Peace be upon you!'
9. For the sake of the house of Yahweh our God,
   Oh I will seek good for you!

12 Meshek, steppe dwellers in the far north – between the Caspian and Black Seas: Genesis 10:2; Ezekiel 38:2. Kedar (Genesis 25:13) is in the Syro-Arabian Desert, but both may rather refer to Nomadic tribes in widely separated areas. In any event it is impossible to live in both at the same time. The intention, therefore, is rather to amplify the thought of alien, uncongenial social environments. Should we go even further? Meshek could be understood as 'prolongation' (*mashak*, to draw out) and Kedar as 'blackness' – a life shrouded in darkness to which there seems to be no end?

13 The preposition *lecha* occurs here, intensifying the extent to which the subject feels whatever sensation, emotion, etc. is involved. 'My soul has had its fill …'

14 A beautiful example of the way Hebrew uses nouns in apposition: the total identification of one thing with another. 'Totally committed to peace'. See Psalm 109:4.

15 Six times we hear the verb 'to keep'. This marks out the topic of Psalm 121 – very emphatically in that the danger or problem in question is not described.

16 This is as much as the Psalm tells us of the problem faced. It is deliberately left vague so that the message of the psalm is not pinned down to any given situation, but is made applicable to any and every threat as it arises, now as then. The 'looking up to the mountains' suggests some such situation as when a watcher on the walls looked anxiously at the mountains round Jerusalem (125:1) for signs of an attacking force, or, perhaps, a far off pilgrim was thinking of the menacing regions through which he must pass to reach Zion, and specially the mountain lairs of marauding robbers. In either case, how can security be guaranteed? Or maybe a rebuttal of the thought that Zion's safety is to be found in its surrounding mighty hill defences?

17 Verses 1–2 are first person, verses 3–8 are third person. Thus the subjective needs of an individual are met by the objective certainties of the truth.

18 The compound preposition, 'from with'.

19 Behind this seemingly simple statement lies the Old Testament's rounded, fourfold doctrine of God the Creator as the One who begins, maintains, controls and directs everything in his creation. Nothing can happen outside his direction; every situation we face, every danger which threatens, is within his created realm. Nothing can 'pluck us out of his hand' (John 10:28–30).

20 A subtle jibe at Baal. See 1 Kings 18:27.

21 The distinctive feature of verses 3-4 is the introduction, at the end, of the new thought: God of Israel, the God of the Exodus, the God who overthrows his enemies and redeems his people. As Jesus implies in the sequence from John 14:1 to John 14:2, he has not secured our eternal home only to lose us in earth's troubles! The eternal significance of the work of redemption is part of our present security.

22 The preposition 'al, used of a servant 'waiting on' a master (Judges 3:19; compare Genesis 18:8). In Isaiah 6:2, of Seraphim ('in attendance on him').

23 'Round the clock' preservation – from dangers real (sun-stroke) and imaginary (moon-stroke). 'Sun … moon': comprehensiveness expressed by contrast.

24 Every threat, the whole person, in every activity, for all time (starting now).

25 i.e. you in your essential, personal integrity. Everything that in any way makes the individual a unique person.

26 The idiom of comprehensiveness expressed by contrast, every possible movement or journey.

27 An expression of wondering joy – something almost too good to be true!

28 The very appearance and plan of the city speaks of unity (3); this is what we could call a 'churchly' unity: the coming together of the twelve tribes of the redeemed – out of their dispersed locations into united thanksgiving, obedient to what Yahweh had 'testified' was his requirement (4); a monarchical unity, held together and maintained by the Davidic throne (5).

29 The very architecture and town-planning enhance an idea and an ideal: the one city of one people. Thus unity is the unchangeable, 'given' reality at the end of pilgrim road, the chosen locus of the twelve-tribe confederation, waiting for them to enter and enjoy. In Zion the tribes are not an aggregation but a congregation, bound together by the given unity of the one city, the one revealed truth ('testimony'), and the one throne.

30 One of the main words for the revealed truth Yahweh has given to his people (see Psalm 119 passim). The most 'personal' of the words: Yahweh 'giving his testimony' about himself and what he wishes to see in his people. Here, their regular coming together in the pilgrim feasts (Deuteronomy 16).

31 The promise was that he would cause his name to inhabit his Jerusalem 'house' (Deuteronomy 12:5), his 'name', of course, as the summary statement of all he had revealed himself to be.

32 Pilgrimage to Jerusalem is possible because the Davidic Monarchy hold the city secure. Compare Psalm 84:8–10.

33 Maybe a plural of majesty: the 'great throne, David's throne'.

34 The power of the crown to decide issues.

35 This can have the 'bad' meaning of complacency (e.g. Ezekiel 16:49), but here the good meaning of 'unanxious rest/ restfulness'.

Pause for Thought

Coming events cast their shadow before them, says the proverb, and we ought to expect that the New Testament revelation of God as the Holy Trinity prompted some foreshadowings. But think carefully. The revelation of God as 'Father, Son and Holy Spirit' only comes with the New Testament – first at the baptism of Jesus, when he, the sinless one, was 'numbered with the transgressors' (Isa. 53:12) by coming to John the Baptist. No amount of hunting through the Old Testament as such will bring that revelation to us. We may wonder at the 'us' of Genesis 1:26; take note that the Old Testament speaks of a God who 'is Hosts'. Hebrew uses the idiom of repetition to express a superlative or that which is the 'whole truth' about something, consequently the 'Holy, Holy, Holy' of Isaiah 6:3 – the only time a superlative or comprehensive claim needs to be raised to the power of three. As to its significance, however, the Old Testament is silent. But, looking back from the New Testament, we can affirm that the Yahweh of the Old Testament is not to be thought of as 'just' 'God the Father'; he is the Holy Trinity Incognito: Father, Son and Holy Spirit waiting to be revealed; God to the power of three; 'hosts' concentrated into the almighty unity of the Three Persons. The same applies to Psalm 121, with its beautiful meditation on Yahweh as Creator, Redeemer and Companion, a perfect but totally concealed forecast of Father, Son and Holy Spirit – concealed, but one we can grip to ourselves as we venture on pilgrimage in this uncongenial, hostile and threatening world. What a way to start each day! What a way to face every eventuality! St. Patrick knew all about it when he sang his 'breastplate' hymn – and we can do the same as we make his words our own: 'I bind unto myself today, the strong Name of the Trinity … the Three in One, the One in Three.'

Day 65 Read Psalms 123–125[1]

Psalm 123.
Yahweh Desperately Needed

Song of the Great Ascent.

'The upward glancing of an eye …'[2]

1. To you[3] I have lifted up my eyes,
   Enthroned One in the heavens.[4]
2. Behold!
   Like the eyes[5] of servants to the hand of their master;
   like the eyes of a maid-servant[6] to the hand of her mistress –
   so are our eyes to Yahweh our God,
   until he grant us grace.

The downward gift of grace

3. Grant us grace, Yahweh,
   grant us grace
   because we have been more[7] than sated with contempt.
4. Our soul has been more than sated –
   the mockery – the complacently at ease –
   the contempt typical of the proud!

1 The same triadic movement which characterizes this whole collection of Psalms of Ascent: among enemies (123), ready help (124); security in Zion (125).

2 From the hymn, 'Prayer is the soul's sincere desire'; 'Prayer is … /The upward glancing of an eye,/When none but God is near.' Like 120, 123 is a psalm of prayer in a time of stress. Nehemiah 2:19; 4:4 illustrate the situation.

3 Emphatic in the Hebrew just as here. In human terms it is called 'going over someone's head' in a difficult situation. Take your case to the higher court. The foes are earthly, the resource heavenly.

4 Or, simply, 'seated in the heavens': prayer brings us into the place of stillness and rest; 'enthroned' – into the place of authority, direction, rule; 'in the heavens' – the place of resource and sufficiency.

5 The 'eye' is the organ of desire; the 'hand', of personal intervention and action. We are called to patience, presenting our desires to his timetable. Note 'until' (2).

6 The contrast between male and female, and between plural and singular: the idiom of totality by means of contrast. This is the complete way to deal with the problem.

7 See Psalm 120:6.

Psalm 124.
Every Picture tells a Story: Yahweh on Side

A song of the Great Ascent; David's.[8]

A.1. Yahweh all-sufficient

1. 'Had it not been Yahweh who was on our side!'
   Oh let Israel say –
2. 'Had it not been Yahweh who was on our side
   when humans rose against us!'

B.1. Deliverance against the Odds[9]

(Earthquake)

3. Then they would have swallowed us alive.[10]

(Flood)

4. Then the waters would have flooded on us.
   The torrent[11] would have passed over our souls.[12]
5. Then there would have passed over our souls
   the foaming waters.

B.2. Deliverance in totality

(Savage beasts)

6. Blessed be Yahweh
   who did not give us over as prey to their teeth.

(The hunter's trap)[13]

7. Our soul – like a little bird – has escaped
   from the trap of those out hunting.[14]
   The trap has been broken,
   and, as for us, we have escaped!

8. Every situation of the sudden and hidden dangers the psalm mentions can be replicated in the history of David. His authorship is the simplest and most satisfactory explanation of the origin of this skilful poem of danger and escape. e.g. 1 Samuel 18:23–25, 29; 19:10; 21:7; 23:25–26; Psalm 57:4.

9. The first two threats are in the natural realm; the second two in the animal/human realm. The contrast expresses totality.

10. Compare Numbers 16:30, 32, 34; 26:10.

11. Usually 'torrent, stream' is *nachal*. The unique form here (*nachalah*) is said to be the retention of an obsolete accusative ending, compare *layelah*, 'night'. Maybe used for poetic effect, or as a deliberate archaism.

12. *Nephesh* here (and verse 5) could have its other sense of 'throat', i.e. the threat of drowning.

13. Verse 7a stresses the human agency in this danger; verse 7b the total end of the danger in that the trap itself has been broken.

14. The use of a participle here points to this danger as constant whereas all the others were occasional. Looking back, the contrasts teach us that from whatever source a danger arises, and with whatever certainty it exists – whether occasional or permanent – Yahweh is sufficient.

15. See Psalm 121:2.

16. There is a double comparison: in verse 1 we find Mount Zion and its living counterpart: the people of God. The immoveable mountains, the immoveable people. Eternal security experienced by faith. In verse 2 we find the surrounding hills and their spiritual counterpart, the surrounding Yahweh, again with the stress 'for ever'.

A.2. Yahweh all sufficient

8.   Our help is in the name of Yahweh
    Maker of heaven and earth.[15]

Psalm 125.
Yahweh our security:
Security in Zion

A. Secure in Yahweh's care[16]

1.   Those who are trusting in Yahweh are like Mount Zion.
    It will not be shaken.
    For ever it abides.
2.   Jerusalem - the mountains are round about it,
    and Yahweh is round about his people,
    now and for ever!

B. Secure over the course of time

3.   Because[17] the sceptre of the wicked
    will not rest on the lot[18] of the righteous,
    in case the righteous reach out their hands to deviancy.[19]

C. Secure in a moral world[20]

4.   Oh do good, Yahweh, to those who are good,
    and to those who are upright in heart.
5.   And as for those who move off to their crookednesses,
    Yahweh will lead them off along with wrong doers.
    Peace be on Israel!

17   'Because' is slightly unexpected here, where 'therefore' would seem more natural – i.e. Yahweh is the city's guardian deity, therefore unjust rule will only have a limited period of rule. The reasoning, however, is rather that the downfall of oppressive or unacceptable rulers happens because Yahweh rules, and is evidence of it.

18   The promised land was allocated by lot, Numbers 26:55; Joshua 14:2; Judges 1:3; Psalm 16:5.

19   Periods of stress last in relation to the ability of Yahweh's people ('the righteous ones', those 'right with him') to endure them. Further prolongation might lead them to compromises or courses of action which deviate from his will. One can think, for example, of foreign alliances which in essence exchanged trust in Yahweh and his promises for trust in foreign armaments. Hezekiah, in Isaiah 38–39, is a prime example. He had Yahweh's promise (Isaiah 38:6) but chose rather alliance with Babylon (39:1–2). Or compare Nehemiah 4:10, 12; 5:1–5, where the stresses of the day led to defeatism, pursuit of self-interest, and compromise.

20   The psalm ends with an implicit call for living by faith – that the world we live in is ruled by Yahweh so as to enforce moral standards, to reward well-doing and punish evil-doing. In verses 4–5 this is made a matter of prayer – not prayer against the oppressors (or whatever) but prayer that Yahweh will act according to his nature and the revelation of his will. This is the way to keep the ultimate in sight when the immediate is rough.

Pause for Thought

Hezekiah's tunnel was one of the most amazing feats of civil engineering in the ancient world. Jerusalem was in a naturally fortified position with its girdle of high hills (Ps. 125:1–2) but it has an elementary vulnerability in that its water-supply was an overground conduit from the Pool of Gihon into the city. An enemy who could not take the city by assault could deprive it of water – and just wait! To remedy this defect, Hezekiah's engineers dug through 643 metres of rock. Starting from the two ends, they wonderfully met in the middle! The length of the tunnel was almost double that of a direct line from source to reservoir, because the tunnellers turned this way and that to avoid difficulties or to follow natural fissures. But they met in the middle! A cause for joy and pride? So the Jerusalemites thought (Isa. 22:1–2a), but Isaiah, who watched the work in progress (22:8–11), saw the tunnel as the unforgiveable sin (22:14). Now why should that be? Well think of the whole picture: Jerusalem was the city Yahweh had chosen to make his name dwell there. When he made that choice, did he not know all about its vulnerable water-supply? Did he make a mistake? No, he made a promise – straight to Hezekiah too! 'I will deliver … this city from the hand of Assyria, I will defend this city' (Isa. 38:6). Did Hezekiah trust the promise? No, he dug a tunnel! The unforgiveable sin is failure to trust Yahweh's promises.

Day 66 Read Psalms 126–128[1]

Psalm 126.
Tension. Now and Not Yet:
Laughter and Tears

A song of the Great Ascent.

Joy: what Yahweh has done

1.   When Yahweh brought back the banishment[2] of Zion
     we were like people dreaming.[3]
2.   Then our mouth was ever filled with laughter,
     and our tongue with loud shouts.
     Then they kept saying among the nations,[4]
     'Yahweh has done great things for these!'
3.   Yahweh has done great things for us;
     we are rejoicing!

Longing: what Yahweh will yet do – prayer and answer

4.   'Bring back our banishment, Yahweh,
     like water-courses in the Negeb.'[5]
5.   Those sowing in tears,[6]
     with loud shouting will reap.
6.   Whoever persists in going out –
     even weeping –
     carrying a bag[7] of seed,
     will surely come with loud shouts
     carrying his sheaves![8]

1   This third triad of Psalms of the Great Ascent follows the established pattern. In Psalm 126 Yahweh's people long for a further divine work of deliverance and are instructed to 'sow in tears'. Psalm 127 reveals Yahweh as the source of sound building and security, the promoter of rest and happiness. Psalm 128 sings of blessing in Zion. Unlike the first two triads, however, this one is Zion-centred throughout – even starting with the city in 126:1. It is more, then, about the nature of a pilgrim's life in Zion, a sort of pilgrimage of the heart, living with the diverse experiences of Yahweh's people who, in Psalm 126, are both fully saved (1) and not yet saved (4).

2   The word is imprecise – even insecure in spelling. It could refer to any experience of alienation from Yahweh. It may be – as some hold – that we are meant to understand the familiar 'restore the fortunes of Zion' (e.g. Psalms 14:7; 53:6; 85:1). It is easy for us to 'slot ourselves into' Psalm 126: we have been saved (Ephesians 2:5), are being saved (Acts 2:47) and will be saved (Romans 5:9). So, in the psalm, the past tense of verse 1 lies in tension with the implied future of verse 4.

3   i.e. we took no part in it. It was done for us – we woke up to find it was true. So throughout the psalm laughter, singing (2) and rejoicing (3) often (as here) are evidence of a salvation to which the recipients have contributed nothing but subsequent joy.

4   Compare, e.g. Nehemiah 6:15–16.

Psalm 127.
In the Interim:
The Call to Restfulness

A song of the Great Ascent. Solomon's.[9]

(The secret of success)

1. If it is not Yahweh who is building a house[10]
    its builders have toiled for nothing.
    If it is not Yahweh who is keeping a city
    its keeper has stayed awake for nothing.

(The recipe for failure)

2. You gain nothing –
    you who are getting up early,
    delaying to rest,
    eating the bread of pains.

Restfulness (Yahweh's gift)

Exactly so[11] he gives sleep to his beloved one.[12]

Fulfilment[13]

3. Behold![14]
    Sons are an inheritance[15] from Yahweh;
    the fruit of the womb payment.
4. Like arrows in the hand of a warrior
    so are sons of youth.
5. Blessed[16] is the person whose quiver is full of them:
    they will not experience disappointment when they speak
    with enemies in the gate.[17]

5   The prayer is for another sudden work of God: a dry watercourse suddenly foaming with water because there has been rain in the hills. The Negeb is the southern desert.

6   Note the contrast: the prayer (4) is for suddenness; the answer (5–6) directs patient continuance in sowing and reaping, discipline and tears. Compare Hebrews 6:12, 13–15; 10:36.

7   Or a 'line' or 'trail' of seed – seed for sowing in lines, or the sower leaving a trail of seed as he goes along. The word is *meshek* and could have been deliberately chosen for this unusual expression to recall Meshek in Psalm 120:5. While we await final salvation we are still in the uncongenial far country – but call to sow and reap.

8   The metaphor of sowing and reaping is repeated in verses 5 and 6. Doubled for the sake of emphasis. In verse 5 the centre-ground is held by the contrasting 'tears ... shouting', i.e. the disciplined life is often a costly one; in verse 6 the main point is the certainty of sheaves.

9   Most commentators reject the idea of Solomon as author – but do not say why. He was noted for wisdom (1 Kings 4:29–34) – in the wider sense of breadth of knowledge and in the narrower sense of wise sayings, the applied wisdom of Proverbs (1 Kings 4: 32; compare I Kings 3:16–28). It is this wisdom that the psalm exemplifies. He was faced with the daunting task of following David, and rightly feeling inadequate (1 Kings 3:7), with large building enterprises facing him (1 Chronicles 29:1). The emphasis on 'house' in Psalm 127:1 is obviously appropriate to Solomon in reference to Yahweh's house, but even more so if we take into account 2 Samuel 7 and the 'building' of the 'house' or dynasty of David. There could not be a better setting out of which a psalm like this could emerge than Solomon's early reign.

Psalm 128.
Peace at the Last!¹⁸

A song of the Great Ascent.

A.1. The foundation: the blessed individual

1. Blessed[19] is everyone who fears Yahweh,
   who walks in his ways.[20]
2. The toil of your hands you will indeed eat.[21]
   You will be blessed –
   it will be good for you.

B.1. The private/marital community

3. Your wife, like a fruitful[22] vine[23]
   in the privacy[24] of your house;

C.1. The immediate family

   your sons like transplanted[25] olives
   around your table.

A.2. The foundation: the blessed individual

4. Behold!
   Thus indeed the person will be blessed[26] –
   whoever fears Yahweh.
5. Yahweh will bless you from Zion.

B.2. The public community

   And look[27] upon the good of Jerusalem
   all the days of your life.

10 Typically of Hebrew 'Wisdom', Psalm 127 does not deal with abstract questions but with practicalities: the house, the city and the family – in our terms the mortgage, security and education.

11 The word 'so' introduces the second member of a comparison. What is the 'just as' sentence here? To the same extent that nothing is achieved by mere human endeavour, to that extent Yahweh covers the situation with his gift of sleep. His gift of restfulness is the exact antidote to our capacity for anxiety.

12 'Solomon' was the king's regnal or public name; his personal name was Jedidiah, 'Yahweh's Beloved' (2 Samuel 12:24–25).

13 The implication of verses 1–2 could easily seem to be that we should stop worrying, cease from a 24-hour, 7-day working programme and leave it all to God. If we were to accept the suggestion of many that verse 2b means 'he gives to his beloved in sleep' (while they sleep), this meaning would be near irresistible. In the Bible, however, the opposite of rest is not work but restlessness. Hence, the psalm introduces another illustrative situation – children. Babies cannot be conceived and born without the human activity of procreation, but, the Bible insists, it is not sexual intercourse as such that leads to conception. Only God can 'open the womb'. Compare Genesis 29:31; 30:1–2, 16–17. So, says verse 3, children are not our achievement but his gift! The 'call' of Psalm 127 is to engage in all life's activities – its obligations as well as its privileges – in restful reliance on Yahweh and expectation of his effective working.

14 See how important this word is – commanding attention to the key verses of the whole psalm.

C.2. The family of the future

6.   See indeed the sons of your sons,

D. Consummation

      peace upon Israel.

---

15 'Inheritance' is something that comes to us by another's choice; 'payment' is what is considered just in a given circumstance.

16 See Psalm 1:1.

17 Whether negotiating with a would-be attacker, or contending with an adversary at law. That a substantial family gives a man standing in the community is the thought here, not that a posse of well-built sons enables him to sway judicial verdicts!

18 The psalm covers the same ground twice – a biblical way of saying that this is a certain, established truth. The basic essential is the devout individual (1, 4); from him (in the psalm) blessing fans out into home and family and into the community and the future. The psalm requires that the ending is not a prayer ('peace be') but an affirmation ('peace' is something he will see). Psalm 128 is a psalm of finality.

19 In verse 1, *'ashrey* (compare Psalm 1); in verse 5, *barak*, 'to bless'. The verb conveys the sense 'to put in a favoured position'; the adjective, 'to be in a favoured position'.

20 Blessedness results from a dovetailing of attitude ('fear') and action ('walk'). By implication here, there is a heart rightly reverent; a mind that knows God's revealed truth; and a will directing the daily walk.

21 Contrast Judges 6:3–6; Deuteronomy 28:30.

22 Not to be restricted to the bearing of children, but including all the wifely virtues Scripture praises.

23 There is no biblical evidence for taking the vine as such as a symbol of fruitfulness – hence it needs here the idea of fruitfulness expressed separately. Rather (Song of Solomon 7:8) it is a symbol of sexual attractiveness. Other metaphorical uses are prosperity (Genesis 49:11), sweetness (Judges 9:12–13), peace (Malachi 3:11), fragrance (Song of Solomon 2:13). A symbol of Israel (Psalm 80:8, 14). Deuteronomy 8:8 couples vine and olive as symbolic of God's richness in blessing.

24 Lit. the inner parts. Contrast Proverbs 7:11.

25 For the use of *shathal*, 'transplanted', compare Psalm 1:3; 92:13. They are not where they began but have been moved to a new position: i.e. not what they are by nature but what they are by grace, 'born again' (John 1:12–13).

26 'Be blessed' is the explanation of 'blessed' in verse 1. How did this person come into the place of blessing? By the action of Yahweh. The key element in such a person is the state of his heart ('fears'). In verse 1 it was coupled with 'walks', but here it stands by itself as the key ingredient.

27 'Look upon' and 'see' (6) are both imperatives (which can never express a precative, 'may you be …'). It is the Hebrew idiom of 'imperative of certain outcome' – a future event so sure of happening that it may be commanded. Equivalent to 'you will without any possible doubt see …'

Pause for Thought

As young Christians my wife and I were set back in our Christian understanding and growth by some very gifted preachers who came along telling us (in effect) that sanctification was a matter of 'letting go and letting God'. Or as the hymn says, 'sanctified by faith in Jesus, not by effort of my own'. And, accordingly, we presented ourselves as we were told that Romans 12:1–2 required us to do – we sat back and waited for it to happen, which, of course, it did not: not that Jesus is unable to do so, but that it is not the Scriptural way. To want an easy way to perfection is as old as Psalm 126, and is explicitly rebutted there. It is natural to the believing heart to want heaven on earth – and to want it now. So we identify easily with the prayer 'bring back our captivity like watercourses in the Negeb'(4). There they are, at one moment dry as dust, and, next moment, flooded with water. What could be more marvellous, and one glad day it will be so: when we see him we shall be like him (1 John 3:2), but not yet. Now is the time for the disciplined tasks of sowing the word of God, accepting the hardships that move us to tears, looking forward to the day of loud shouts and abundant sheaves. Planting the seed of the word of God includes sharing that word with others – the duty of testimony – but it neither begins nor ends there. James 1:18, 21–22 is our great teacher: verse 18 tells us that we were brought to new birth by God's word (compare John 15:3). This is the creative word which at the beginning said, 'Let there be light, and there was *light*', and in the individual case of each believer, 'shone in our hearts to give the light of the knowledge of the glory of God in the face of Jesus Christ' (2 Cor. 4:6). Now then, teaches James 1:21, be decisive and 'receive the implanted word' – yes, consciously take on board that which you already have. If you like, feed on what God has already said, and then (James 1:22) 'be doers … not hearers only'. You have the word in your heart, make sure there is a crop to be reaped. When James wrote, he was living in the spirit and reality of Psalm 125 – and so should we.

Day 67   Read Psalms 129–131[1]

Psalm 129.
'Help in Ages Past, Hope for Years to Come'

A song of the Great Ascent.

(The past)

1. 'More than enough[2] have they troubled me from my youth
    Israel may now keep saying;

2. 'More than enough have they troubled me from my youth[3] –
    also they have not been able for[4] me!'

(Agricultural metaphor: determination on a crop)

3. On my back[5] ploughmen have ploughed.
    They extended their ploughlands.

(Double statement: Yahweh's opposition)

4. Yahweh the righteous!
    He has severed the cords of the wicked![6]

(The future)

5. They will reap[7] shame and be turned away back,
    all who hate Zion.

(Agricultural metaphor: no crop)

6. They will be like grass on a roof[8]
    which, as soon as it produces a blade,[9] withers;

7. with which a reaper would not fill his hand,
    nor the binder of sheaves his bosom,

---

1   In its general movement this triad is the same as the rest: it opens (Psalm 129) with a situation of hostility, moves (Psalm 130) to crying out to Yahweh, waiting for him with sure hope though morning is slow to come, and ends (Psalm 131) with a beautiful picture of calm contentment in his presence. On the other hand, Zion is only mentioned in the opening psalm (129:5) – even then referring to its opponents – and not again. The problem besetting the psalmist in 130 is not external, but his own iniquities. In other words, we are again involved not with a pilgrimage to Zion (as in 120–122, 123–125) but a pilgrimage of the heart (as in 126–128), the personal battle to walk with God.

2   The same idiom as 120:6; 123:4.

3   Compare Jeremiah 2:2; Ezekiel 23:3; Hosea 11:1. The psalm offers a general and non-specific review of a troubled history.

4   Hebrew uses the verb 'to be able' in the sense 'able to overcome'.

5   Combining a picture of humiliation (Isaiah 51:23; compare Micah 3:12) with one of cruel suffering. The word translated 'back' has that meaning but is not the usual word. This word also means 'bulwarks, fortifications' and the context may hint at that meaning here.

6   Up to verse 4 the rhythm of the lines has been 3:2 (i.e. three significant or stressed words followed by two). In verse 4 the rhythm is reversed, 2:3. In the most subtle way possible the truth is inculcated that the presence of Yahweh turns the tables on enemies.

(Double statement: no blessing from Yahweh)

8. nor will those passing say,[10]
    'The blessing of Yahweh on you!
    We bless you in Yahweh's name.'

Psalm 130.
The Voice of Paul in the
Old Testament[11]

A song of the Great Ascent.

(Appeal)

1. Out of the depths[12] I have called[13] you, Yahweh.
2. Sovereign One, do hear my voice!
    Let your ears ever be attentive
    to the voice of my plea for grace.

(Danger and solution)

3. If you should keep[14] iniquities, Yah,[15]
    Sovereign One, who could stand?
4. But indeed with you there is real[16] forgiveness,
    in order that you may be feared.[17]

(Confident hope)

5. I have waited,[18] Yahweh.
    My soul[19] has waited.
    And for his word[20] I have tarried.
6. My soul – for the Sovereign One!
    More than watchmen for the morning!
    Watchmen for the morning![21]

(Reasoned appeal)

7. Tarry, Israel, for Yahweh,
    because, with Yahweh[22] there is real committed love,
    and in abundance, with him, there is power to ransom.[23]

7   Or 'May they reap' (so throughout verses 5–7). It is impossible to be certain which is right. If a prayer, this is how to deal with life; if prediction, this is how to face the future.

8   Isaiah 37:27. The sort of wispy growth that can come up between tiles or in a gutter – easy to pluck but amounting to nothing.

9   *shalaph*, to draw a sword. Not elsewhere used in this vegetative sense.

10 Compare Ruth 2:4.

11 Martin Luther called Psalm 130 a 'Pauline Psalm' because it strikes the typically 'Pauline' notes of humankind naturally under condemnation: free mercy, redemption as the sole act of God, human total dependence on mercy. Suitable to its place as the second psalm in its triad, a psalm of divine sufficiency. Psalm 129 sees Zion endangered by inveterate hostility; Psalm 130 finds the real danger to Zion in unforgiven sin.

12 Maybe initially the depths of misery to which enmity and hurt (Psalm 129) have driven him, but with a sudden realization of the more serious pit of sin. Coming to God with one problem may easily (and blessedly) expose the 'real' problem that needs to be solved. Compare Mark 2:3–5.

13 The perfect tense signifying a past situation continuing into the present (so also verse 5). Or a perfect of fixed intention: 'I have set myself to …'

14 In the sense 'keep an account of/keep endlessly in mind', reserve for future treatment.

15 The use of the diminutive of endearment is especially significant here. Yahweh is at his most loving and most loved when the sinner comes for forgiveness.

8. And he it is who will ransom Israel from all its
iniquities.[24]

Psalm 131.
Utter Contentment[25]

A song of the Great Ascent. David's.

1. Yahweh, my heart[26] is not arrogant,
nor my eyes haughty.[27]
I have not been occupied with great matters,
nor with things too wonderful for me.

2. I affirm[28] that I have composed and stilled my soul
like a weaned[29] child beside its mother.
Like a weaned child alongside me is my soul!

3. Tarry, Israel, for Yahweh,
now and for ever.

16 Lit. 'the forgiveness' (compare verse 7,
'the committed love'), meaning 'the
real thing/the genuine article', or 'the
only forgiveness'.

17 Not fear in any servile sense, but
(compare 1 Peter 1:17) fear of
offending one so loving and caring; the
reverence with which his fellowship
is enjoyed on the basis of forgiveness
– and in which his word is obeyed by
forgiven sinners. Nowhere is the full,
awesome reality of the divine nature
more present than in the bestowal of
forgiveness.

18 'Waited... tarried' (qawah... yachal) are
synonyms. Both combine the thoughts
of patience, hope and confidence. They
also signify that there is nothing we
can do about our sinful state and its
consequences. Exodus 14:13.

19 i.e. no superficial or formal 'waiting',
but one that has absorbed my whole
being and commitment.

20 In context, waiting for Yahweh to
speak the word of forgiveness.

21 Illustrative of the combination of patience, hope and confidence. Morning is sure to come but at its appointed time. All
the watchman can do is wait, but that is enough and it is fruitful. A hope that will not fail.

22 'With Yahweh' – as his ever-present companions. Where he is, they are.

23 From padhah, to pay the ransom price; the noun here is peduth. Nouns ending in -uth tend to be equivalent to English
nouns ending -ness. We have no noun; 'redemptiveness' – all that is involved in desiring, undertaking and performing
the work of redemption.

24 The root of our salvation is Yahweh, the God of committed love (Ephesians 2:4); its means the payment of a sufficient
ransom-price (Mark 10:45); its agent, Yahweh – 'he it is' (Hebrews 9:14; 10:10–14). The accomplishment is total: 'all ...
iniquities' (John 19:28, 30; Hebrews 10:12).

25 Three parts. (i) Error disclaimed (1), the restlessness to be something else. The heart at ease with itself; eyes (the organ
of target, aim, ambition) at rest. (ii) Contentment professed (2). (iii) Waiting, hoping, trusting recommended (3), a
permanent focus on Yahweh. The heart of the matter is the picture in verse 2. We remember it in our tiny children,
and some of us see it a second time round in our grandchildren: the total relaxation, unquestioning contentment, the
absence of fretfulness of a five year old holding its mother's hand. All's well; the world is safe; what more could anyone
want? Psalm 131 is a psalm of final contentment, at home with Yahweh, all attention fixed on him. The way Psalm 131:3
repeats 130:7 not only links the psalms but means that those who have waited patiently on Yahweh for redemption must
go on replicating that attitude in perpetuity. The key to redemption is the key to life. At the end of our pilgrimage rest
is not in Zion's city but in Zion's God. In Psalm 130 'waiting' was a means to an end – redemption; in Psalm 131 it is a
life-style.

26 'Heart', the inner person; 'eyes', ambitions, objectives, desires, aims, longings. 'Occupied with' (lit. 'walked in'), the outward life of daily business; 'great matters'; over-ambitious plans; unrealistic projects. Not a call to the trivial but to the manageable; 'wonderful', learning to live with unanswerable questions.

27 The idea here is caught by the expression 'to look down on'.

28 More properly 'I swear that'. The psalm uses the oath formula.

29 A child who has gone beyond the stage of seeing its mother as a source of supply and has entered the stage of simple contentment to be where she is.

Pause for Thought

Yahweh has three companions. They never leave his side; he never comes without them. First mentioned is 'forgiveness' (Ps. 130:4), a word always used of sin and divine forgiveness – a word, therefore, of relationship. Yahweh has been offended by our actions, but has pardoned the offence and restored the broken relationship. Then there is the personal word, 'committed love' (130:7). Unlike its companion word, *rachamiym*, 'compassion', which refers to 'being in love', *chesedh*, committed and unchanging love, is the love which makes a promise for life, the love which stays the same 'for better, for worse, for richer for poorer'. Yahweh's third companion is 'ransom' (130:7), the sufficient price which covers the need, buys back the kidnapped one, satisfies any lawful claim. We can call it, for convenience, the legal word. Of course, when we call these Yahweh's companions, we really mean that they are part and parcel of Yahweh himself; they declare what he is. When we come to him in all our sin and unworthiness, we enter a rich company. When he comes to us in our sin, he comes not to condemn but to love, ransom and forgive – and that is the proper 'order' of the words: the personal (love), the legal (ransom) and the relational (forgiveness). Everything else flows from the inexplicable basis: he loves us (Deut. 7:7–8); and because he loves us he himself provides and pays the ransom price, so that forgiveness full and free floods over our guilty souls. If it occurred to you to wonder how we could ever rest, unworried, calm, content, in his presence, as in Psalm 131, ask his three companions.

Day 68   Read Psalms 132–134[1]

Psalm 132.
Chosen King, Chosen City[2]

A. David, his oath and his commitment

(Prayer)

1. Yahweh, remember for[3] David
   all his submissive toil:[4]

(Oath)

2. how he made an oath to Yahweh,
   vowed to the Mighty One[5] of Jacob –

3. 'I will not go into the tent of my house;
   I will not go up to the couch of my bed;

4. I will not grant sleep to my eyes,
   slumber to my glances,[6]

5. until I find a place[7] for Yahweh,
   a dwelling place for the Mighty One of Jacob.

(Searching, finding, establishing)

6. Behold!
   We heard it in Ephrathah![8]
   We found it in the Fields of Jaar.[9]

7. Let us go to his chief dwelling place![10]
   Let us bow in worship at the footstool[11] of his feet!

(Prayer)

8. Rise up,[12] Yahweh, to your place of rest –
   you and the ark of your strength!

9. May your priests be clothed[13] with righteousness,
   and your beloved ones[14] shout aloud!

1   This final triad of psalms of the Great Ascent is unlike most of the preceding groups in that all three psalms are centred in Zion. There is no Zionward movement as in the first two triads, nor a 'nearer my God to thee' movement as in the third and fourth. These are psalms of 'home at last'! There is, however, movement: from the establishment, the distinctive city (Psalm 132), to the heaven-blessed fellowship of the gathered family (133), to the ultimate reality of worshippers in Yahweh's presence (134).

2   Psalm 132 should be read in conjunction with 2 Samuel 7, on which it is a poetic meditation. Just as David purposed a house for Yahweh (2 Samuel 7:1–3) and Yahweh promised a house to David (2 Samuel 7:10–17), so the psalm balances David's oath with Yahweh's oath.

3   To 'remember for' is to credit to someone's account. Nehemiah 13:31, 'remember for me …', compare Psalm 137:7.

4   This noun could be paraphrased 'all the trouble he took'. Self-submission to what God required.

5   Compare Genesis 49:24; Isaiah 1:24; 49:26; 60:16. The title stresses sheer power.

6   See Psalm 11:4. Here 'my eyes … my peepers'!

7   'Place' (*maqom*) has a technical sense; a religious site, a sacred place of worship. Compare Genesis 12:6. The additional 'dwelling place' is therefore important: in the case of this 'place' the deity was really in residence.

B. Yahweh, his oath and his commitment[15]

(Prayer for/of the current Davidic king)

10. For the sake of David your servant
    do not turn back the face of your Anointed One.

(Oath)

11. Yahweh has made an oath[16] to David,
    the truth,
    he will not go back on it.
    'One who is of the fruit of your body
    I will put on your throne.

12. If your sons keep my covenant,
    and my testimony[17] which I will teach them,
    their sons, too, for ever and ever,
    will reign on your throne.'[18]

(City)

13. Because Yahweh has chosen Zion.
    He has longed for it as a habitation for himself.

14. This is my place of rest for ever.
    Here I will sit enthroned,
    because I have longed for it.

15. Its provision I will truly bless.
    Its vulnerable ones I will satisfy with bread.

16. And its priests I will clothe[19] with salvation,
    and its beloved ones will shout out loud.

(Monarchy: the Davidic promises)

17. There I will make a horn[20] sprout out for David;
    I have determined to tend a lamp[21] for my Anointed.

18. His enemies I will clothe with shame,
    and on him his consecrated crown[22] will blossom.

8 On 'Ephrathah' compare Genesis 35:16, 19; 48:7; Ruth 4:11, where it seems to be a parallel name for Bethlehem. But in Ruth 1:2; 1 Samuel 17:12, it is rather a description of a class of person. Some say Ephrathite is equivalent to Ephraimite. Uncertain.

9 See 1 Samuel 7:1–2; 2 Samuel 6:10–12; 1 Chronicles 13:2-3. The Ark had been side-lined in Israel. Psalm 132 depicts the importance of its return of its central position by sketching a sort of national treasure hunt.

10 The motivation is not simply the restoration of a religious 'icon' but the reconstitution of Exodus 29:42–46, to make sure Yahweh is dwelling at the heart of his people. 'Dwelling place' here is a plural of majesty, meriting the introduction of 'chief'.

11 Compare 1 Chronicles 28:2; Psalm 99:5; Isaiah 66:1; Lamentations 2:1. In relation to the Ark, Yahweh was enthroned above the cherubim. His 'footstool', therefore, was the 'mercy-seat' or 'atonement cover' where the blood was sprinkled (Leviticus 16:11–16).

12 Compare Numbers 10:35. The restoration of the Ark was seen as a return to the first and normative days of Israel.

13 'Clothing' is symbolic of what a person is and what a person is for. It points here to the ideal of Old Testament priesthood.

14 *Chasiydh* is a passive noun related to *chesedh*, Yahweh's committed, unchanging love. The *chasiydhiym* are those who have been graced with that love, the 'beloved'.

Psalm 133.
Blessed City; United People

A song of the Great Ascent. David's.[23]

(Situation)
1. Behold!
    How good and how delightful[24] –
    when brothers dwell – also at one![25]

(Illustration)[26]
2. Like oil – the best – on the head,
    going down on the beard –
    Aaron's[27] beard –
    going down on the opening[28] of his robe.[29]
3. Like the dew of Hermon going down on the mountains
    of Zion.

(Explanation)
4. Because there[30] Yahweh commanded the blessing,
    life for ever.[31]

Psalm 134.
The City, the House and
the Worshippers[32]

A song of the Great Ascent.

(Yahweh, the object of blessing)
1. Behold![33]
    Bless[34] Yahweh,
    all you servants of Yahweh,
    who are standing[35] in the house of Yahweh by night.[36]
2. Lift up your hands to the Holy One[37]
    and bless Yahweh.

15 We move here into the second half of the psalm: 'For the sake of' matches 'for David' (verse 1); Yahweh's oath matches David's (verse 2). The prayer for the Davidic king is characteristic of Zion-psalms (compare Psalm 84:9): delight in the sanctuary and prayer for the king belong together in that he was the 'guardian' of the shrine, its continuance depended on his power.

16 2 Samuel 7:8–17.

17 Compare Psalm 119:2.

18 The possessive 'your' is not, here, the simple possessive pronoun but the rather more emphatic, 'the throne that belongs to you' or 'is specifically yours'. Subsequent kings held the throne not by personal right but by Davidic right, by reason of Yahweh's undertaking to David personally.

19 See verse 9. The 'clothing' – which symbolises character, function, mission – in verse 9 points inwardly to the character of the priest; here outwardly to the ministry of grace dispensed to the people.

20 The symbol of conquering strength.

21 Compare 2 Samuel 21:17; 1 Kings 11:36. The 'horn' is victorious strength; the 'lamp' personal continuance.

22 *nezer'* means both 'crown' and 'consecration' (specifically of Nazirite, Numbers 6).

23 David experienced the unity of the people – around himself, the Ark and his new capital city of Jerusalem – in 2 Samuel 6. Such an occasion could well have prompted this psalm.

24 The tendency of 'delightful' is to emphasize the subjective experience of delight – rather than the objective possession of delightfulness. We should probably see this balance here: 'good' in itself, 'delightful' in experience.

(Yahweh, the source of blessing)

3.   May Yahweh bless you, each one,[38] from Zion –
  the Maker of heaven and earth.

---

25 'Brothers' necessarily implies belonging together, family oneness, but 'unity' is another thing altogether! It is good to see the family together, but if there is true unity that is a bonus and a huge additional blessing. Oneness by blood advances to oneness of heart.

26 Two distinct illustrations: first, the oil of consecration, pointing to unity as a sacred blessing from God, creating the priestly people Israel was meant to be (Exodus 19:6). The second deals with a miracle – Hermon's dew falling on Zion's hill. Hermon was the chief mountain of the north; Zion the chief mountain of the south. That they should be united in this way could only be an act of God: such, then, said David, is the unity of the family of God's people, a God-wrought miracle.

27 Exodus 29:7.

28 Lit. 'the mouth of', the opening in a robe to allow it to go over the head.

29 The only use of *middah* ('measure') in this meaning.

30 'There' reaches back past the illustrations to the opening of the psalm: where there is unity, there blessing falls by Yahweh's command.

31 Not that eternal life is earned by unity, but that Yahweh shares his sort of life with those who cherish unity. This is the obvious understanding of the words, though we could link 'for ever' with 'commanded'. This is a perpetual certainty. Essentially the meaning would be the same because we would still have ask what 'life' is intended – and the reply would be 'Yahweh's life'.

32 A true psalm of homecoming. First, it completes the final triad of psalms: blessing for Zion (132); blessing in Zion (133); blessing from Zion (134). But also it forms an inclusion with the opening psalm 120. The psalmist was then spiritually in the far country (Meshek, Kedar); now he is home in the House in Zion. As a word, Kedar means 'black, dark', and in Psalm 120 reflected the darkness of uncongenial circumstances. How very different is the darkness of night-time worship in the house (134:1)!

33 This could be the voice of a worship-leader addressing priestly company on duty (possibly as they came on duty); or is he addressing a congregation gathering for a night service?

34 The word 'bless' occurs in each verse. It sounds the keynote of the psalm. To 'bless' Yahweh is to review gratefully what he is and to respond in worship. See Psalm 26:12.

35 In a context like this, 'to stand' means to 'stand in attendance on' – a servant's position.

36 Lit. 'by nights' – every night or all night. Compare 1 Chronicles 9:33; 23:30; Isaiah 30:29. Passover was by nature a night festival.

37 Or 'in holiness', or 'to the holy place'. A reference to Yahweh is more consistent with the general content of the psalm.

38 'You' here is singular, in contrast with the second person plural throughout the psalm. It is an 'individualizing' singular. Compare the singular in Numbers 6:24.

Pause for Thought

The striking simplicity and simple beauty of Psalm 134 make it a supremely wonderful conclusion to the Songs of the Great Ascent. How easy it is to picture a family group reaching the city in the evening of their pilgrim journey, with the youngsters clamouring to go straight to the Temple. Father is adamant, 'You've had a long enough day. Tomorrow will be soon enough.' But the youngsters are too canny for that, and know that mother will be a softer touch! 'Of course they want to see the Temple. Another late night won't hurt them.' And they arrive in time to see the entrance of the night-priests, to join in the greeting for their blessing, and they stay late enough to hear the blessing pronounced on each one of them – and all in the dark security of the city which has been their goal all along their pilgrim way. Would they not indeed feel that all the blessings and securities of the Maker of heaven and earth were indeed enfolding them in that sacred enclosure and in the soft darkness of that night? All his irresistible will as Creator, all his sovereign power, all his resources – and (coming out of Zion as its source) all the mercy and grace of his great salvation. All worship should be like that: a 'blessing' of Yahweh, a review of his character, his grace, his saving power, his providential care, the blood of the sacrifice he has provided and ordained; the rest he gives to his beloved as he welcomes us into his house and home. 'To behold the fair beauty of the LORD' (Ps. 27:4). Look again at Revelation 1. There were seven lamps. What were they illuminating with their complete light? The light was directed inward, to reveal the beauty and glories of the One 'in the midst of the lamp-stands'.

Day 69   Read Psalms 135–136[1]

Psalm 135.
Irresistible in Power

A.1. Praise

1. Praise Yah![2]
    Praise the name of Yahweh!
    Praise, you servants[3] of Yahweh!
2. You who stand in the house of Yahweh,
    in the courts of the house of our God!
3. Praise Yah,
    because Yahweh is good,[4]
    make music to his name because it is delightful,
4. because it was Jacob that Yah chose – for himself!
    Israel for his personal possession.[5]

B.1. Yahweh in his greatness[6]

5. Because I myself know that Yahweh is great –
    our Sovereign more than all gods.[7]
6.[8] Everything which Yahweh desires he has done
    in heaven and on earth;
    in the seas and all depths.[9]
7. He brings up rising clouds[10] from the end of the earth;
    lightning flashes as well as[11] rain he has made;
    he brings out the wind from his stores.

C. Yahweh and his people

(Deliverance)

8. He who struck down the firstborn of Egypt,
    humans and beasts alike.[12]
9. He sent signs and wonders[13] right into you, Egypt –
    against Pharaoh and all his servants.[14]

1   These two psalms are 'orphans' in that
    no authorship or other attribution is
    made. The only reason for attaching
    them to the songs of the Great Ascent
    is suitability: both psalms sketch the
    great pilgrimage of Yahweh's people
    from Egypt to the promised land
    (135:8–14; 136:10–22), and it is
    easy to imagine their use by festival
    pilgrims. Did they possibly think of
    themselves as replicating the story of
    their nation? Why not? They too were
    'marching to Zion' from the darkness
    of an alien world into the city, security
    and fellowship of their God. Psalm
    135 is bracketed by calls to 'praise'
    and 'bless' Yahweh: his dominance
    over creation (5–7), history (8–14)
    and other 'gods' (15–18) allows us to
    review his excellencies and respond.
    Psalm 136, covering much the
    same ground in creation (6–9) and
    history (10–22), traces every single
    item to Yahweh's unfailing love. It is
    therefore suitably bracketed by calls to
    thanksgiving (1–3, 26).

2   Yah or Yahweh occurs seven times in
    this sub-section.

3   Servants 'who stand' is a link
    (deliberately?) with 134:1, suggesting
    that we are to think of Psalm 135 as
    the pilgrim's homecoming song.

4   'Good … delightful', see Psalm 133:1.

5   See the 'secular' use of *segullah* in 1
    Chronicles 29:3; Ecclesiastes 2:8.
    Of Yahweh and Israel, Exodus 19:5;
    Deuteronomy 7:6, etc.; Malachi 2:8.

6   Depending on how we reckon verse 6,
    there may be seven facts of Yahweh's
    greatness here, matching the seven
    impotencies of the 'gods' in verses
    15–18.

(Inheritance)

10. He who struck down many nations,
    and killed mighty kings –

11. Sihon[15] king of the Amorites,
    and Og king of Bashan –
    all the kingdoms of Canaan.

12. And he gave their land as an inheritance,
    an inheritance for Israel his people.

(Care)

13. Yahweh is your name for ever.[16]
    Yahweh is your remembrance[17] for generation after
    generation.

14. Indeed, Yahweh will plead the cause[18] of his people,
    and for his servants he will show his pity.

B.2. The 'gods' in their impotence[19]

15. The images[20] of the nations are silver and gold,[21]
    the work of human hands.

16. They have a mouth – and do not speak!
    They have eyes – and do not see!

17. They have ears – and do not give ear!
    Why! There is absolutely no spirit in their mouths!

18. Like them[22] are those who make them –
    everyone who is trusting in them.

A.2. Blessing[23]

19. House of Israel, bless Yahweh!
    House of Aaron, bless Yahweh!

20. House of Levi, bless Yahweh!
    You who fear Yahweh, bless Yahweh!

21. Blessed be Yahweh out of Zion – he who dwells in
    Jerusalem!
    Praise Yah!

7   Expressions like this do not imply the existence of such 'gods' but merely that they are features of current life, believed in by others, constituting a temptation to Yahweh's people. Compare 1 Corinthians 8:4–6.

8   In verses 6–7 the verbs are alternating participles (desires … brings up … brings out) and perfect tenses (has done … has made). The distinction is between the on-going activities of the Creator and the unchanging determination which underlies the work of creation. In effect, however, an English present tense is the best way to understand all the verbs. In this way present (5–7) contrasts with past (8–12) and future (13–14).

9   The ground for treating 'seas … depths' as a distinct work of Yahweh is that the ever-restless sea was thought of as typifying the hostility of spiritual forces to Yahweh's ordering hand as Creator; the 'depths' were the special abode of the monster Tiamat.

10 A somewhat uncertain rendering. Proverbs 25:14 (NKJV 'clouds').

11 Lit. 'lightning … for rain' (NKJV, ESV). What does this mean? NIV 'with'. I have not found another example of the preposition *le* used exactly as here. There seems no reason in principle why it should not be able to mean 'in addition to/as well as'.

12 Exodus 12:29.

13 A wonder commands attention; a sign points to a significance.

14 'Against Pharaoh' etc. is not a needless elaboration. It calls attention to the fact that Yahweh really took on his peoples' enemies face to face. Not just entering the land but facing the centre of power itself, a 'super-power' of the day.

Psalm 136.[24]

A.1. Thanksgiving

1. Give thanks to Yahweh because he is good
   Because for ever is his committed love.
2. Give thanks to the God of gods[25]
   because for ever is his unchanging love.
3. Give thanks to the Sovereign of sovereigns,
   because for ever is his unchanging love.

B.1. Creation[26] ordered for life

4. To him who does great wonders – he alone!
   Because for ever is his committed love.
5. To him who with discernment makes the heavens
   because for ever is his committed love.
6. To him who extends the earth upon the waters,
   because for ever is his committed love.
7. To him who makes the great lights –
   because for ever is his committed love –
8. the sun for dominion by day,
   because for ever is his committed love,
9. the moon and stars for dominion by night,
   because for ever is his committed love.

C. Conquest, deliverance and inheritance

(Overthrow and escape)
10. To him who struck down Egypt through their firstborn,[27]
    because for ever is his committed love,
11. and brought out Israel from among them,
    because for ever is his committed love:
12. by a strong hand and an outstretched arm,
    because for ever is his committed love.

(Full salvation)[28]
13. To him who cut the Red Sea in pieces,

15 In the Hebrew here Sihon, Og and all the kingdoms are prefixed with *le,* which some treat as a particle of emphasis – 'even Sihon, even Og, even all'. It is more likely the appositional use of *le.* The war against Sihon and Og was both the last act of Moses and the first act of the conquest (Deuteronomy 2:26–3:22).

16 'Forever' means duration throughout time; 'generation after generation' means duration in human experience.

17 i.e. how you wish to be remembered. Exodus 3:13–15.

18 In the immediate context, make sure that his people have a full legal right to their inheritance; in general, look after his people in every situation as it arises.

19 Seven facets of the folly of images. Compare **B.1.** (verses 5–7).

20 Derived from *'atsabh,* to form, shape. Hence 'images' rather than 'idols'.

21 Doubtless the more sophisticated worshipper thought of the spiritual reality supposedly behind and represented by the image, but the steady testimony of the Old Testament is that there is nothing but what can be seen and touched, what human hands have fashioned.

22 Dead and lifeless they are but nevertheless they have a deadly power – to make their worshippers in their own image!

23 Matching **A.1.** with seven references to Yahweh; balancing four 'praise' plus one 'sing praise' with four 'bless' and one 'praise'. On 'blessing Yahweh', Psalm 26:12.

because for ever is his committed love,

14. and brought Israel over in the middle of it,
    because for ever is his committed love,

15. and shook off Pharaoh and his force into the Red Sea,
    because for ever is his committed love.

(Providential care)

16. To him who brought his people through the desert,
    because for ever is his committed love.

(Conquest and inheritance)

17. To him who struck down great kings –
    because for ever is his committed love –

18. and killed mighty kings,
    because for ever is his committed love:

19. Sihon[29] king of the Amorites,
    because for ever is his committed love,

20. and Og king of Bashan,
    because for ever is his committed love,

21. and he gave their land as an inheritance,
    because for ever is his committed love,

22. an inheritance to Israel his servant,
    because for ever is his committed love.

B.2. Providential care

23. Who, in our lowliness,[30] remembered us –
    because for ever is his committed love –

24. and snatched us like prey[31] from our adversaries,
    because for ever is his committed love.

25. One who gives bread to all flesh,[32]
    because for ever is his committed love.

A.2. Thanksgiving

26. Give thanks to the transcendent God of heaven,
    because for ever is his committed love.

24 Covering much the same ground as Psalm 135, Psalm 136 is distinctive in its repeated insistence (twenty-six times) that everything in Yahweh's work of creation, redemption, conquest and care arises from his committed, unchanging love. This is the greatest truth about him. No 'wonder' exceeds the wonder of his love.

25 See Psalm 135:5.

26 The main verbs throughout this section are participles, and could, of course, be translated 'the Maker of', and this justifies NKJV, ESV in a past tense 'who made', looking back to the initiating divine act. But the participle as such bears witness to an ongoing relationship, the creatorial work whereby the creation is sustained.

27 Compare Exodus 11:1.

28 See Exodus 14:13, 30–31. The Red Sea events were the final acts of God, completing the liberation of Israel from Egyptian bondage.

29 See Psalm 135:11.

30 Very emphatic in the Hebrew. His changeless love is also condescension.

31 *paraq*, compare Genesis 27:40 (tearing off yoke); Psalm 7:2 (snatching prey); Lamentations 5:8 (rescue from bondage). 'He snatched us as his prey from being their prey!'

32 It is particularly this note of universality that links back to **B.1.** and Creation.

Pause for Thought

Let's face it – our immediate reaction to twenty-six statements that Yahweh's love is eternal, committed and changeless is 'boring'. We tire of the repeated refrain, but it ought not to be so. His love for us is one of the high points of the Bible, and, by rights, we should be progressively and increasingly thrilled. Try it again. Read the psalm, revel in the refrain – not like a repetitive, parrotted ritual but as a wondering and exciting affirmation. It is the abiding grounding of the whole work of God, creation to new creation; it is the reason for every single thing he has ever done. It is the comforting, reassuring truth for the difficult day, when we walk through the wilderness (136:16); it is the inexplicable reason for the great day when our particular Sihons and Ogs fall (19–20), or we experience a bit more of our eternal inheritance (21–22). In two ways Psalm 136 goes beyond Psalm 135. Whereas Psalm 135 is restricted to Zion, and the rest of the world consigned to useless 'gods', 136:25 extends Yahweh's benevolent love to 'all flesh'. The thought is not elaborated, but it is there, and some day the Bread of Life will be on offer to a whole loved world (John 3:16; 6:35). Verse 23 puts its finger on a different issue – 'our lowliness'. If ever we sing in our hymn, 'Jesus, what didst Thou find in me/That Thou hast dealt so lovingly?' the answer is as early as Deuteronomy 7:7–8: he 'set his love on you' … 'because [he] loves you'. The answer is as total as Psalm 136. Love to the power of 26! Not in our greatness, worthiness, importance, significance – whatever – did he love us, but in our negligibility, when we were 'without strength … sinners … enemies' (Rom. 5:6–10). 'Love to the loveless shown,/That they might lovely be'– becoming like the God we worship.

Day 70   Read Psalms 137–139

Psalm 137.
Our Past, God's Future

We remember: the sorrows of memory[1]

1. Beside the streams[2] of Babylon –
    there we sat;
    we cried, too,
    when we remembered Zion!
2. On the willows in it we hung up our lyres,
3. because there our captors asked us for the words of a
    song,
    and our tormentors[3] for joy:
    'Sing to us some song of Zion.'
4. How are we to sing Yahweh's song in a foreign land?
5. If I should forget you, Jerusalem,
    may my right hand forget!
6. May my tongue stick to my palate
    if I do not remember you!
    If I do not raise Jerusalem up above the summit of my
    joy!

Yahweh remembers: the pure justice of memory

7. Remember, Yahweh, for[4] the sons of Edom[5]
    the day of Jerusalem –
    who were saying:
    'Strip it bare, strip it bare,
    to the foundation in it!'
8. Daughter of Babylon,
    destined to be destroyed!

1   Life in Babylon was not arduous, as we gather from Jeremiah 29, and from the fact that when opportunity came so comparatively few elected to return to Judah. But there were those who could not settle but (as this psalm shows) were beset by the restless longing of true devotion.

2   The waters of Tigris and Euphrates were fed across the plain of Babylon by an extensive system of irrigation canals.

3   Uncertain meaning. Many emendations suggested, which are no more than guesses put into Hebrew! Some such meaning as 'those teasing us'.

4   To 'remember for' is to remember to put to the account of (for recompense, good or bad). Compare Psalm 132:1.

5   See Obadiah 1:10–14.

How right[6] he will be who pays in full to you
what you requited fully to us!

9.   How right he will be who seizes and shatters
     your children against a rock!

Psalm 138.
A Royal testimony:
the Past and the Future[7]

David's.

(Need, prayer, answer, worship)

1.   I will give you thanks with my whole heart;
     before the gods[8] I will make music to you.

2.   I will bow in worship towards the temple[9] of your
     holiness,
     and I will give thanks to your name
     for your committed love and for your truth,
     because you have magnified your word above all your
     name.[10]

3.   In the day I called out you answered me.
     You invigorate me with strength in my soul.

(Expectation: worldwide recognition)

4.   All the kings[11] of the earth will give you thanks, Yahweh,
     when they have heard[12] the words of your mouth,

5.   and they will sing of Yahweh's ways,
     because Yahweh's glory is great!

(Confidence: unchanging love)

6.   Though Yahweh is high,
     it is the lowly that he sees,
     and the haughty he knows at a distance.[13]

7.   If I should walk in the middle of adversity
     you will give me life;
     against the exasperation of my enemies

6   The word *'ashrey* (compare Psalm 1:1)
    must always be translated according
    to context. The translations 'blessed'
    (i.e. under God's blessing, compare
    Psalm 32:1) and 'happy' (e.g. 1:1;
    etc.) are clearly wrong here, but the
    third meaning (in line with the basic
    meaning of the word 'straight') is
    'right' – doing the right thing in a
    given circumstance (e.g. Psalm 106:3;
    Proverbs 14:21; Isaiah 30:18). This is
    what this psalm requires here and in
    verse 9. When Babylon is treated as
    Babylon treated Jerusalem it will be,
    in the same way, a just requital. The
    ruins of Jerusalem which the returned
    community see all around them reveal
    that the world is ruled by a holy and
    just God, and a like justice will be
    Babylon's portion. Does the psalmist
    say that he wishes it to be so? No.
    Neither does he personally intend to do
    anything about it. But he knows that
    it will be so, because that is the sort of
    world we live in. And it will be 'right'.

7   The 'occasion' prompting this poem
    is not recorded but something like 2
    Samuel 5:17–25 suits: David's infant
    kingdom and early monarchy was
    faced with a mortal threat. In answer
    to prayer, Yahweh granted victory
    and deliverance. The main themes of
    the psalm are evident: Yahweh's king
    threatened by earthly rulers; David as
    a mere beginner in monarchy finds
    Yahweh on his side; his throne is
    established, the kings are routed, a
    portent for the future submission of
    earth's kings to Yahweh. It is the lowly
    and needy that he 'regards'. He has
    brought David to the throne and will
    not desert him.

8   2 Samuel 5:21 specially notes the
    defeat of the 'gods'.

9   Note that the tent at Shiloh is called
    a 'temple' (1 Samuel 1:9; 3:3 – NKJV
    'tabernacle' in each case; see ESV at
    3:3). There is nothing anachronistic in
    referring to a temple in David's day.

you will stretch out your hand,
and your right hand will save me.

8. Yahweh will himself act fully on my behalf.
Yahweh, your committed love is for ever.
Do not let down the works of your hands!

Psalm 139.
No Escape ... No Regrets ...
No Hiding Place[14]

Belonging to the worship-leader. David's.[15] A song.

No hiding place:[16] God all-knowing[17]

1. Yahweh, you have searched[18] me,
and you know!

2. It is you who knows
when I sit down and when I get up!
You discern my intentions at a distance.

3. My path and my lying down[19] you sift through,
and all my ways you take account of.

4. Indeed, there is not a word in my tongue[20]
behold!
Yahweh, you know all about it!

5. Behind and in front, you encircle[21] me.
And you place your hand[22] over me.

6. The knowledge[23] is too marvellous for me;
it is up high;
I am not able for it.

(No escape: God ever-present)

7. Where am I to go from your Spirit?[24]
And where[25] am I to flee from your face?

8. If I should ascend to heaven,[26]
you are there!

10. 'Name' is shorthand for all that Yahweh has revealed about himself and his ways. David feels that recent experience has gone even beyond all that.

11. This could indicate that from the start of his reign David was aware of Yahweh's intention to make his monarchy worldwide. On the other hand, all he says is that the truth about Yahweh when it is heard will provoke acceptance. Compare Joshua 2:9-11.

12. Or 'because they are sure to hear'.

13. i.e. he knows all about them but distances himself from them.

14. Typically of the Old Testament great theoretical notions of God – omnipotence, omniscience, omnipresence, etc. – are seen in the light of practical morality and personal moral responsibility. The psalm is a combination of high spirituality, serious theological thought and strict moral application.

15. The psalm could belong to any period of David's life. The often noted Aramaic presence in the Hebrew here is not (as is now recognized) proof of lateness or of the post-exile.

16. Many commentators pose the question 'Why would David want to flee from God?' and propose the answer, 'Because of sin.' This sets our thinking about Psalm 139 off in the wrong direction. The thought of the psalm rather is: 'We can't ever escape from our God. Isn't it wonderful!' No escape ... no regrets! He is everywhere, so we are safe! We cannot escape from him – who would want to?

17. Omniscience, not formulated as a doctrine, but confessed in adoration. Eight references to divine knowledge in verses 1–6: 'know ... knows ... discern ... sift ... take account ... know ... encircle ... knowledge'.

And should I spread my bed in Sheol,[27]
behold! You!

9. Should I lift up[28] the wings of the dawn,
make my dwelling on the west of the sea –

10. there too it is your hand that will guide me,
and your right hand grip me!

11. And should I say,
'The darkness, of course, will crush[29] me,'
night is light around me.

12. Indeed even the darkness does not make things too dark for you;
like darkness like light![30]

(No Evasion: God all-creating)[31]

13. Because[32] it is you who possess full rights[33] over my kidneys,
protected[34] me in my mother's body.[35]

14. I give you thanks because I am awesomely wonderful;
your works are wonderful –
my soul knows it very well indeed!

15. My structure was not hidden from you
when I was made under cover,
woven in the lower places of the earth.[36]

16. My embryo your eyes saw,
and in your book all of them were written up,
days which were to be formed,
when there was not one of them!

17. How precious are your intentions for me!
Transcendent God,
how mighty is the sum total of them!

18. Should I reckon them up,
they are more than the sand!
I awake and I am still with you.

(No hiding place: God all holy, all searching)[37]

19. Oh that you would slay, God, the wicked! –
blood-guilty men, go away from me!

18 All the verbs associated with Yahweh in verses 1–5 are perfect tense – expressing unvaried, fixed habit.

19 One authority finds here a word meaning 'spring encampment' (also in Numbers 23:10, NKJV 'one fourth'). The 'path' is the general course of life, the spring encampment is the occasional halt.

20 i.e. before it is spoken aloud, still 'in' the tongue. The forming thought. Something I was still preparing to say.

21 Lit. 'besiege', here 'shut me in', inescapably, a very vigorous statement of security.

22 Lit. the 'palm' of the hand, the hand 'cupped' over me. All my movements are within his protective 'grip' (John 10:28–29) – behind, ahead and over.

23 Yahweh's knowledge is in turn beyond my range, beyond my reach, and beyond my power. Inherently it transcends. In fact there is no way I could ascend to it; and even if I could I would not be able to grasp it.

24 'Spirit' is Yahweh's active presence; 'face' his personal presence.

25 The 'where … where' of verse 7 is explored in verses 8–12 – the supernatural (8), spatial (9–10), temporal (11–12). The 'where?' invites exploration of a delightful impossibility.

26 The idiom of comprehensiveness by contrast runs through these verses: 'heaven/Sheol; dawn/west; darkness/light.

27 Here, the underworld.

28 Compare Ezekiel 1:24; 'lowered' wings signifies rest. To lift up the wings means to fly off.

20. Who keep speaking against you deviously
each pledged[38] to falsehood,
those who rouse themselves against you.

21. Is it not that those who really hate you, Yahweh, I hate?
And those who rise against you I loathe?

22. With complete hatred I hate them.
They have become enemies of mine.

23. Search me,[39] transcendent God,
and know my heart.
Test me, and know my wandering thoughts,[40]

24. and see if there is a way of distress[41] in me,
and lead me in the way everlasting.

29 So, literally. The same verb as Genesis 3:15. If we are not to resort to altering the text, an additional thought arises here: 'darkness' used as symbolic of threat – but Yahweh is the solution. This may be unexpected but it is not intrusive. Just as no place or dimension of experience excludes his protective presence, neither do the even crushing dangers inherent in this life.

30 Just as our expression 'like father, like son' does not mean total identity but identity in some significant way, so darkness and light are not totally identical. But they are identical in this way that each is filled with Yahweh's active, protective, securing presence.

---

31 This section traces individual life from conception (embryo) to resurrection (awake).

32 Or 'Indeed'.

33 *qanah,* to possess, gain possession of. Often, by purchase (e.g. Genesis 25:10; Exodus 15:16; Psalm 78:54); of 'possession', Proverbs 8:22; 16:16.

34 Or 'wove me together'.

35 The hidden life in the womb, emotional capacity (the kidneys, e.g. Psalm 16:7; 73:21), the physical frame, and a plan for the whole life ahead – all this the divine eye sees in the embryo. The personal life before it emerged from the womb, the public life before it happened.

36 A genitive of apposition, 'the lower places, namely, the earth.' Earth as lower than heaven.

37 Moves in the opposite direction from the embryo to resurrection movement of verses 13–18. Here, from coming judgment to present examination. The whole of the preceding psalm is preparatory for this prayer. The wonderful world sketched in verses 1–18 is blighted by wicked people opposed to Yahweh. The prayer is full of a proper and righteous anger at what sin and sinners have done to Yahweh's world. Psalm 139 is like all the imprecatory psalms in two main ways: first, it gives evidence of such a high and covetable spirituality that the imprecations cannot be dismissed as evidence of a low moral awareness (or as many say 'Old testament values!'). Secondly, wickedness is dealt with by prayer – no thought of personal action, nor any allowable implication of a vengeful mind. What we find here is not spite but zeal for Yahweh. To consider such prayers astray from Jesus is to forget verses like Matthew 7:23; 25:41, 46a; Revelation 6:15ff. – the whole biblical dimension of the wrath of the Lamb. If we could match the spirituality of verses 1–18, we would be in a better position to judge the morality of verses 19–24. To side with Yahweh is to identify with the totality of his ways.

38 Lit. a singular – individualizing – participle, 'lifted up to'.

39 Note the 'inclusion' with verses 1–2. This binds the whole psalms together

40 The word pictures a branch forking in different directions. Used, therefore, of thought flitting this way and that, during which our thoughts can so easily arrive at forbidden pastures.

41 Genesis 3:16–17.

Pause for Thought

The three very different psalms in today's group can each contribute a leading thought to a unified picture of living in this world. The heart-wrenching sadness of Psalm 137, living in the aftermath of a day of defeat; the simplicity of worship in Psalm 138, reacting to a recent victory; and the call of Psalm 139 to side with Yahweh against the sin and sinners that despoil his world. It all amounts to the (old-fashioned sounding) summons to be separate. We find it easy to identify with those ill at ease in the alien world of exile in Babylon, but do we *feel* it in our world where we are 'immigrants and resident aliens' (1 Peter 2:11)? We are as much in exile as ever they were but we fit so snugly into our world that no one is aware that our citizenship is elsewhere (Philippians 3:20). In Psalm 138 the kings of the earth are there to be defeated, not lauded or welcomed. They are the strongholds to be won, for in Psalm 139 we can easily test ourselves: would we dare to pray the prayer, and make the affirmations of verses 19–22? Do we not rather find such confrontation distasteful? We don't hate sin like that, do we, or regard with horror the blemishes with which sin and sinners scar the fair world Yahweh has given us? The Bible is outraged by sins of speech (look it up if you don't believe me); we allow the name of Jesus to be blasphemed without turning off our televisions. Where is the proper radicalism of Psalm 139? Back in the 1940s 'separation from the world' was taught and practised in every church that claimed to love the Word of God and the gospel of Christ. It was, of course, a merely reactive separation – if people did it, we don't! And it cut us off from many perfectly allowable avenues of life, good gifts of God in their way. What we need is the distinctiveness of obedience, life shaped by biblical commands, standards, precepts and examples, being like Jesus.

Day 71 Read Psalms 140–143[1]

Psalm 140.
Crafty Foes, Hidden Snares

Belonging to the worship-leader. A song of David.

Prayer (for protection)

1. Set me free, Yahweh, from evil humankind;[2]
   from the man of indiscriminate violence preserve me.
2. People who at heart ponder every sort of evil:
   all day they foment war.
3. They sharpen their tongue like a snake,
   the venom of a viper is under their lip. (*Selah*)
4. Keep me, Yahweh, from the hands of the wicked,
   from the man of indiscriminate violence do preserve me –
   those who ponder to trip my steps up!
5. The arrogant have hidden a trap for me,
   and with cords they have spread a net;
   beside the path they have placed snares for me. (*Selah*)

Confidence (arising from the past)

6. I have said to Yahweh:
   'You are my transcendent God.
   Open your ear, Yahweh, to the voice of my plea for grace.
7. Yahweh, Sovereign One,
   strength of my salvation,
   you have screened my head in the day of armed threat.[3]

Prayer (for disaster)

8. 'Do not grant, Yahweh, the longings of the wicked!
   Do not promote his ploy –

1. Psalms 140–145 form a linked Davidic group, with common themes: the tongue (140:2; 141:2–4); snares (140:55–56; 141:9–10; 142:3); 'I said' (140:6; 142:5; compare 143:10); the righteous (140:13; 142:7; compare 143:10); hiding place (140:7; 143:9); the 'boomerang' of sin (140:9; 141:10); overwhelmed (142:3; 143:4). The heading to Psalm 142 specifies the period when David was in deadly danger from Saul and his court, and the whole group can be seen in this light. Psalms 140–143 take up different aspects of the danger: Psalm 144, reminiscent of Psalm 18, while still praying for deliverance, gives a sense of diminishing threat and of hope for the future; Psalm 145 ends the series with an 'A to Z' of sustained praise.

2. 'Humankind … man' is the frequent contrast between *'adham* and *'ish*, which is interpreted in different ways by different commentators. It seems best to understand the words respectively as the general followed by the particular, 'humankind' and the human individual. The following verses give a very comprehensive vision of enmity: heart (2), tongue (3), hands (4), temperament (5). All true of David's experience in the days of Saul's descent into paranoia.

3. Lit. 'in the day of equipment', a noun from the verb *nashaq*, to be equipped with, e.g. Psalm 78:9. In Job 39:21, NKJV translates *nesheq*, 'clash of arms.'

4. An abruptly expressed reason why their desire should not be granted: they would get above themselves. It would encourage them in their wickedness and arrogance.

they would be uplifted!'[4] (*Selah*)

9. As for the head of those who surround me,
   may the trouble of their lips cover them!

10. Let live coals come tumbling on them!
    May someone make them fall into fire!
    Into flood waters so that they do not rise!

11. A slanderer – do not let him be established on earth!
    A man of violence is evil:
    let it hunt him down[5] diligently!

Confidence (for the future)[6]

12. I know that Yahweh will take up the case of the
    downtrodden,
    the judgment of the vulnerable!

13. Yes indeed, the righteous will give thanks to your name;
    the upright will live in your presence.

Psalm 141.
Incessant Threat, Ceaseless Safety[7]

A song of David's.

Silence

1. Yahweh, I have called you!
   Come to me quickly!
   Turn your ear to my voice when I call to you.

2. May my prayer be as securely before you[8] as incense,
   the raising up of my hands as the evening offering!

3. Set, Yahweh, a guard on my mouth,
   a preservation order[9] on the door of my lips!

Reactions

4. Do not incline my heart[10] to a word[11] of evil,
   to indulge myself in practices involving evil,

5 Compare verse 9. The 'boomerang' quality of sin. It returns to hurt the sinner.

6 The world is ordered with moral providence. Yahweh sides with the threatened and vulnerable; victory will rest with the righteous.

7 The psalm is couched in personal terms except for verse 6, where we must ask who these 'judges' are. Simplicity suggests that we are dealing with the days when David had become *persona non grata* at the court of Saul. It would be natural for the whole court, including the judiciary, to side with the king. David ponders throughout the psalm how to act and react while the stress lasts, how to respond when it is over, and where his safety rests in the meantime.

8 Lit. 'Establish my prayer before you like …' He desires Yahweh to find in his prayers all the divinely-willed authority, power and acceptability of Yahweh's own appointed ordinances.

9 Lit. 'Preserve the door …' But here 'the door' is an indirect object with the preposition *'al*, 'over, upon'. Rather than ignore this, I offer the slightly developed translation, 'a preservation order on …'

10 Not that Yahweh is responsible for the decisions we make, but he is responsible for the decisions we face. In the long run the progression of voice, hands, mouth, lips end with the heart. Cf. Proverbs 4:23; Psalm 119:36.

11 The literal translation 'word of …' suits the emphasis in context on speech. We could, of course, translate 'evil thing'.

in company with individuals[12] who are trouble-makers,
and let me not eat of their tit-bits.[13]

5. Let the righteous[14] hammer me –
faithful love![15]
Let him reprove me –
oil for the head!
Let not my head render it useless!
Indeed, while it continues,[16] my prayer is against their
evils.

6. When their judges are dropped over the side of a cliff
they will hear my words, for they are pleasant.[17]

Security

7. As when one breaks up and harrows the ground
our bones have been scattered at the mouth of Sheol

8. because[18] to you, Yahweh, Sovereign One, are our eyes.
In you I have taken refuge.
Do not pour out my soul!

9. Keep me from being taken by the snare they have baited
for me,
and from the traps of the trouble-makers.

10. Let them fall, each[19] into his own nets
at the same time as[20] I myself continually pass by.

Psalm 142.
Man-forsaken, not God-forsaken

A Maskil[21] of David's when he was in the cave.[22]
A prayer.[23]

Prayer, an overwhelmed spirit, a caring God

1. With my voice[24] to Yahweh I shout out,[25]
with my voice to Yahweh I appeal for grace.[26]

2. I pour out before him my musing;[27]

12 The plural of *'iysh*, (individual) man,
is here the rare *'iyshiym*, Isaiah 53:3;
Proverbs 8:4. Were it not for this
unusual feature *'iyshiym po'aley 'awen*
would simply be the stylish way of
saying 'trouble-makers', compare
Joshua 2:1, 'men, spies'.

13 Does this counsel against table-
fellowship or is it a metaphorical way
of warning against being allured by
what the 'trouble-makers' delight in –
the attractions with which sin adorns
itself?

14 The total self-submission which the
godly life requires – not only to avoid
the enticements of an alternative life-
style and its practitioners (4) but to
accept the admonitions of those who
are right with God (5). Proverbs 27:6a.

15 i.e. 'it is to be viewed as an act of
faithful love … as anointing on the
head.' Expressed with true poetical,
abrupt allusiveness.

16 A possible translation (a construction
found also in Hosea 1:4), reverting
to the situation in verse 4. Prayer as a
counter to their wickedness. David's
response to his opponents was silence
(1–3), but he was able to maintain it
by talking much with Yahweh.

17 When the stresses and strains are over,
then will be the time to speak. Not
gloatingly or in a triumphalist fashion,
but soothing words that make for
peace. Review this psalm as a comment
on Ecclesiastes 3:7b.

18 i.e. because David had determined on
no immediate personal counter-action
but silent waiting on and for Yahweh
to act. Compare Psalm 123:1–2.
The eye is the organ of desire and
expectation.

19 The suffix with 'nets' is singular,
individualizing/distributing the plural
of the verb.

my adversity before him I declare.

3. When my spirit faints on[28] me,
   you are the One who knows[29] my pathway.

The isolated individual and his safe-keeping; providing God

In the path[30] where I walk around,
they have hidden a trap for me.

4. Look to the right[31] and see:
   no one is concerned about me.
   A place to flee[32] to has perished from me;
   no one seeks my soul's welfare.

5. I shout out[33] to you, Yahweh.
   I say:
   'You are my refuge,[34]
   my portion in the land of the living.'

David without resource; mighty enemies; his God never failing to deal fully with the need

6. Pay attention[35] to my outcry,
   because I am exceedingly poor.[36]
   Deliver me from my pursuers,
   because they are mightier than I am.

7. Bring out my soul from confinement,
   to give thanks to your name.
   It is me the righteous will encircle,[37]
   because you will deal fully with me.

Psalm 143.

A song of David.

The righteous Yahweh[38]

1. Yahweh, hear my prayer,
   give ear to my appeal for grace.

20 Or 'as I myself continually *and entirely* pass …'

21 See Psalm 32, heading.

22 1 Samuel 22:1–27:1; Psalm 57, heading, note 23.

23 Well entitled 'a prayer', Psalm 142 is in fact a threefold prayer (verses 1–3a, 3b–5, 6–7), each specifying a distinct aspect of need and a distinct understanding of Yahweh.

24 In both lines 'my voice' is emphatic, stressing how in his personal individuality David can approach God, and (as always) stressing the importance of putting prayer into words. 'Voice' means not loudness (compare NIV) but verbalization.

25 *za'aq,* to scream, a verb used to emphasise urgency. Also verse 5.

26 'Scream' is what David feels, 'grace' is what he seeks. 'Scream' indicates human need; 'grace' divine response. 'Scream' is where prayer starts; 'grace' where it reaches.

27 A very general word: 'murmur, speak, consider, be concerned with'. Often translated contextually 'complaint'. Here it represents the subjective experience of trouble, just as 'adversity' is its objective reality.

28 Meaning 'to my sorrow, disadvantage'. The 'fainting spirit' is the keynote of this opening section; David has reached the end of vitality, buoyancy and resilience. But he still uses the vigorous term 'pour out' of his practice of prayer. It speaks of energy, commitment, effusiveness.

29 'To know' is used of the intimate relationship of a married couple, in love, care and delight. It is not a euphemism but a definition. It is what the marriage-relationship is. Compare 'know', Psalm 1:6; as here, to exercise a relationship of informed care.

In your truth, answer me;
in your righteousness.

2. And do not come to your servant in judgment,[39]
because no living being whatever[40] is righteous before you,

The fainting spirit

3. because an enemy has pursued[41] my soul;[42]
he has crushed my life to the ground;
he has made me live in dark places like the long dead.[43]

4. And my spirit has fainted away on me.
My heart within me reacts with horror.

The waiting soul

5. I remember[44] previous days.
I meditate on all your activities.
On the works of your hands I muse.

6. I spread out my hands[45] to you.
Like ground my soul is faint[46] for you. (*Selah*)

The uplifted soul

7. Answer me quickly, Yahweh.
My spirit is finished.
Do not hide your face from me,
nor let me be like people going down to the pit.[47]

8. Make me hear your committed love[48] in the morning,[49]
because in you I have put my trust.
Make me know the way where I should walk about,
Because to you I have lifted up[50] my soul.

The good spirit

9. Deliver me from my enemies, Yahweh.[51]
In you I have taken cover.[52]

10. Teach me to do what pleases you,

30 A word ('*orach*) synonymous with 'pathway' (*nathiybh*), verse 3a. '*arach* is used of travellers, passers-by (2 Samuel 12:14; Jeremiah 9:1; etc.), and is more like our word 'route', or 'course'.

31 'To the right', i.e. where a 'right hand man' should be – and there is no one.

32 If the cave is Adullam (1 Samuel 22:1) David has already tried escaping to his home (1 Samuel 19:11), to Samuel (1 Samuel 19:18), to Nob (1 Samuel 21:1) and to Gath (1 Samuel 21:10), without success. Adullam marked the low ebb in his fortunes, but also (1 Samuel 22:2) a real turning point in his pathway.

33 See verse 1.

34 'Refuge', a trustworthy place of safety; 'portion' always looks back to the land-allocation in Joshua where each tribe had territory according to its size – i.e. sufficient to provide for its needs in an agricultural economy. For the tribe of Levi, no land was allocated. Yahweh was their 'portion' (Numbers 18:20; Joshua 13:14, 33; 18:7; compare Psalm 16:5).

35 The 'other end' of the prayer-transaction. It began with David's voice, scream, outcry, outpouring; it reaches the open attentive ear.

36 Here not in the sense of finances but of resources for the time and need.

37 David envisaging the day when his present loneliness is over, and he is the centre of a nation and of those 'right with God'. The verb 'encircle' could possibly here mean 'put a crown on me'.

because you are my God.

Let your good Spirit[53] guide me in a land of uprightness.

The righteous Yahweh[54]

11. For the sake of your name, Yahweh, give me life.

    In your righteousness do bring my soul out of adversity.

12. And in your committed love strike down my enemies,

    and destroy all those who are adversaries of my soul,

    for I am your servant.

38 The seriousness of the situation is indicated in verse 2. Above all else is the dread reality of rejection by God. Hence, the three key words in verse 1. 'Grace' is the basic need: the goodness of God irrespective of deserving or merit. 'Truth' is, basically, all that God has revealed, but it includes his fidelity to his truth and his promises; and 'righteousness' is God's inflexible steadfastness in doing what is right, acting according to his character, fulfilling his righteous purposes and promises.

39 We can only assume that this prolonged period of hostility and pressure has begun to make David ask if things are right between himself and Yahweh. Is the hostility of man possibly a reflection of the wrath of God?

40 I introduce the emphasis of 'whatever' here to reflect the fact that the Hebrew at this point uses the more all-inclusive idiom, 'every living being is not righteous'.

41 The picture of the hunt: the chase ('pursued'), the quarry cornered ('crushed'), consequent terror and despair ('fainted').

42 David expresses his sense of being at the end of his tether by referring to 'soul' (*nephesh*), 'spirit' (*ruach*) and 'heart' (*lebh*). *nephesh* comprises all that we mean by person and personality (not in the derived sense of 'star quality' but the basic sense of all that makes one 'person' distinct from another). *ruach* is conscious energy, vitality, resilience, 'gusto', the ability to face life and rise to its demands. *lebh* is used for all a person's mental, spiritual and emotional faculties, the power of thought, the exercise of imagination, the working of conscience.

43 The finality of being 'dead and buried'.

44 In verse 3 there were three verbs of mounting disaster; verse 5 uses three verbs of reassurance, arising from the consolations of memory, the tonic of God's past activities. What he has done is a revelation of what he is.

45 Psalm 123:1 teaches that the uplifted eye is itself a mute appeal; here the same is implied of the outspread hand. Each rests on the assumption of an ever-watching God to whom the need of his people is itself a prayer.

46 The Hebrew does not spell out the simile. The allusiveness of poetry is often more forceful by being left in all its allusiveness! On 'fainting land', Isaiah 32:2.

47 'Pit' is a general synonym for Sheol, the abode of the dead, but sometimes it seems to stress its more objectionable aspects (e.g. Isaiah 14:15, 19; Ezekiel 32:23). Were David's troubles to bring him to the grave at this point, he fears lest he die under the displeasure of Yahweh.

48 It is significant that the prayer of verse 8 precedes that of verse 9. Before asking for a change of circumstances by deliverance, David seeks a renewal of a true relationship to a loving Yahweh. The end of any vestige of divine hostility come before the cessation of man's opposition. The longing for God himself precedes longing for the end of earthly trouble.

49 Compare Psalm 30:5; 49:14.

50 i.e. swearing an oath of personal loyalty and commitment.

51 Note how firmly the single prayer for deliverance (9a) is embraced by vows of commitment (8, 9b–10).

52 For this reflexive use of *kasah* (*piel*), compare Genesis 38:14; Deuteronomy 22:12.

53 Nehemiah 9:20.

54 The fact that we would gladly pray verse 11 but baulk at verse 12 indicates our lack of realism in prayer. There are situations where there can be no deliverance of one party without the destruction of another. To pray for the one is implicitly to pray for the other. David was realistic enough to put the latter into words, leaving the whole situation in the hands of God – as the narrative of his relationship with Saul in 1 Samuel clearly shows. e.g. 1 Samuel 24:4–6; 26:8–11.

Pause for Thought

The structure of a psalm – the way its various sections belong together, match each other, or follow in sequence – is itself as much the message of the psalm as any individual verses. Psalm 143 is a good case in point. The psalm is concerned with a particularly troubled period in David's life, but it is bracketed round by the righteousness of Yahweh (143:1–2, 11–12). His righteousness, before which we sinners stand condemned and helpless, is here the ground of our safety and salvation – because it guarantees that he will always act in fidelity to his nature as the God of grace (1), and he will never abandon his own in trouble (11). In this sense his 'righteousness' points not only to his holy character, but to his utter changelessness. The next circle of meaning in the psalm is verses 3–4 and 9–10 which are linked by the contrast between 'my spirit' and 'your Spirit' (4, 10). Prolonged trouble causes an erosion of human resilience, a loss of vitality to face another day, but there is always a second factor in every circumstance, however wearying: the good Spirit of God, seen here as at hand to take the initiative to bring about a new situation, a land where things are as they ought to be. The end of *our* tether is but the beginning of *his*! The description 'a land of uprightness' is designedly vague. It is not for us to specify how the Holy Spirit will change our circumstances; it is part of the way of faith to leave that to him, knowing that he can only do what is good. He always leads in 'paths of righteousness' (Ps. 23:3) – paths that make sense to him. The psalm contains fifteen petitions (four in each of the opening and closing sections; seven in verses 7–10) – a true lesson in how to face life and deal with difficulty. But the centre ground is the waiting soul (5) – no petitions here (remembering, meditating, musing, the mute appeal of the outspread hands) – and the committed soul (6). This is the attitude expressed by 'until' in Psalm 123:2, a place of stillness in the middle of the storm.

Day 72   Read Psalms 144–145[1]

Psalm 144.
Knowing God … Facing Life …
Taking Aim

David's.

The blessed Yahweh: his ten glories[2]

1. Blessed be Yahweh, my Rock[3]
    who teaches my hands[4] for war,[5]
    my fingers for the battle,
2. my committed love[6] and my fortress,
    my top-security and my rescuer – mine! –
    my shield and the One in whom I take refuge,
    who beats down[7] my people[8] under me.
3. Yahweh, what is humankind[9] that you know him,
    the son of mere man that you think about him?
4. Like a vapour is mankind,
    his days like a shadow passing by.

A present crisis: Yahweh's intervention[10]

(Divine sovereign power)
5. Yahweh, bend the heavens[11] and come down.
    Touch the mountains and they smoke!
6. Flash lightning flashes and scatter them;
    send your arrows and discomfort them.
7. Reach out your hands from on high.
    Set me free[12] and deliver me
    from abundant waters,
    from the hand of the sons of a foreigner,
8. whose mouth speaks falsehood,

1   The 'royal' set of psalms (90–104)
    and the Songs of Ascent (120–134)
    both ended with two psalms of praise
    (105–106, 135–136), and the pattern
    is repeated here in Psalms 144–145.
    Psalm 144 has much of the 'feeling' of
    Psalm 18, which tells us it was written
    to celebrate the end of the troubles
    with Saul. Compare Psalm 144:1b
    with Psalm 18:34; verse 2 with 18:2;
    verse 2c with 18:47; verse 5 with 18:9;
    verse 6 with 18:14; etc. Psalm 145
    is a sustained 'alphabet' of praise: as
    well as concluding Psalms 140–145,
    it prepares for the sustained praise of
    Psalms 146–150.

2   This section falls into three parts:
    (a) what Yahweh is (1a), followed by
    a relative clause ('who' [2bc], what
    Yahweh has done for David by way
    of ability); (b) what Yahweh is (2abc),
    followed by a relative clause (2d), the
    success Yahweh has given David; (c)
    Yahweh's tenth glory, condescension
    (3–4).

3   The metaphor of rock always includes
    the smitten rock of Exodus 17:6.

4   'Hands … fingers', respectively the
    agency and the skills of the individual
    warrior.

5   From *sagabh*, 'to be high': the meaning
    here is to put one on high out of harm's
    way.

6   A striking shorthand for 'the One
    who loves me with a committed love'.
    Compare Jonah 2:8, 'forsake their
    committed love' ('the One who loves
    them with what is love indeed').

and whose right hand is a right hand of lying.

(Commitment and intercession)

9. O God, a new song I will indeed sing to you.[13]
    On a ten-string harp I will indeed make music to you –

10. the One who gives salvation to the true King,[14]
    who sets David his servant free from the evil sword.

11. Set me free,[15] and deliver me
    from the hand of the sons of a foreigner,
    whose mouth speaks falsehood,
    and whose right hand is a right hand of lying.

The blessed people: seven elements of happiness under Yahweh

12. But as for[16] our sons, like plants, grown great[17] in their youth;
    our daughters strong corner pillars,
    decorated, in the manner of a palace;

13. our stores full[18] with supplies,
    every kind without exception;
    our sheep producing in thousands,
    multiplied by ten thousand in our out-of-doors;

14. our oxen loaded up;
    no breaking in and no one going out,[19]
    and no wailing[20] in our open places. –

15. Blessed[21] are the people for whom it is so!
    Blessed are the people whose God is Yahweh!

Psalm 145.
An Alphabet of Glory[22]

Praise. David's.

1. I will exalt you, my God, O King, (*Aleph*)
    and I will bless your name for ever and ever.

2. Every day I will bless you, (*Beth*)

7   Even though Yahweh equips his warrior with ability and skill, the battle is still Yahweh's. David may have in mind here how Yahweh took charge of the two battles in the Philistine War in 2 Samuel 5:17–25.

8   Psalm 18 reviews the past: David's career on the way to the throne. Psalm 144 depicts him as now king, hence 'my people'. Compare with verse 7 below.

9   'Humankind' is *'adham*, the 'general' word; 'mere man' is *'enosh*, man in his weakness.

10 The 'chorus-like' similarity of verses 7 and 11 marks this section off and reveals its balance. On the one hand it is reminiscent of Psalm 18, on the other hand David's foes are now foreigners (7, 11), and, according to my rendering of verse 10, David speaks as king. The Philistine Wars of 2 Samuel 5 present a possible situation.

11 See Psalm 18:9.

12 A possible but disputed translation.

13 As so often the psalms encourage us to use situations of stress and difficulty as opportunities to reach out for new commitments to Yahweh.

14 The parallelism of the verse makes a reference to David suitable here in the first line, and there is no reason why the plural 'to kings' should not be a plural of majesty.

15 The same disputed translation as in verse 7.

16 Verses 12–15 are somewhat imprecisely attached to the foregoing by the relative pronoun, 'Which/Who …'. (*'asher*). This is very flexible in use, with a possible fundamental meaning like 'the fact that'. In the present instance it introduces a list of descriptions which anticipate 'for whom it is so' in verse 15.

and I will praise your name for ever and ever.

3. Great is Yahweh, and exceedingly worthy to be praised; (*Gimel*)

   and there is no fathoming[23] of his greatness.

4. Generation after generation will acclaim your works, (*Daleth*)

   and your mightinesses they will declare.

5. On the splendour of the glory of your majesty, (*He*)

   and on the words[24] of your wonders I will muse.

6. And of the strength of your awesome deeds they will speak, (*Waw*)

   and your greatness I will recount.

7. The remembrance of that abundant thing,[25] your goodness, (*Zayin*)

   they will pour out,

   and shout aloud of your righteousness.[26]

8. Gracious and compassionate is Yahweh, (*Cheth*)

   slow to anger, and great in committed love.[27]

9. Yahweh is good to all, (*Teth*)

   and his compassion is over all his works.

10. All your works will praise you, Yahweh, (*Yodh*)

    and your beloved ones will bless you.

11. Of the glory of your kingliness they keep speaking, (*Kaph*)

    and of your mightiness they keep talking.

12. To make known to the sons of mankind his mightinesses, (*Lamedh*)

    and the glory of the majesty of his kingliness.

13. Your kingliness is a kingliness for all eternity (*Mem*)

    and your realm[28] for all generations.[29]

14. Yahweh supports all who are falling, (*Samech*)

    and raises up all who are bowed down.

15. Everyone's eyes are hoping[30] for you, (*Ayin*)

    and you give to them their food at its right time,

16. opening your hand,[31] (*Pe*)

    and with good will[32] satisfying every living being.

17 The picture is of a plant properly supported and tended during early, formative days, culminating in a sturdy specimen.

18 Lit. 'from (one) sort to (another) sort', i.e. comprising every sort.

19 It is speculative what this line is intended to mean. The words are sometimes interpreted as referring to miscarriages but there is no supporting evidence. The contrast seems to be between a 'breaking in' of robbers or of attacking forces, and a 'going out' of residents being taken into captivity.

20 Compare Isaiah 24:11; Jeremiah 46:12.

21 A different word from 'blessed' in verse 1. In verse 1 it is *barak* (see Psalm 26:12) – suitably introducing a list of Yahweh's glories. Here the word is *'ashrey*; compare Psalm 1:1. All its three possible senses would suit Psalm 144:15: under divine blessing; enjoying happiness and fulfilment; and being in the right – 'How blessed … how happy … how right …'!

17. Righteous is Yahweh in all[33] his ways. (*Tsadhe*)
    And changelessly loving[34] in all his works.

18. Yahweh is near[35] all who call him, (*Qoph*)
    all who call him in truth.

19. With good will he keeps acting for those who fear him:
    (*Resh*)
    he keeps hearing their cry for help and saves them.

20. Yahweh keeps all those who love him, (*Shin*)
    and all the wicked he destroys.[36]

21. The praise of Yahweh my mouth will speak, (*Tau*)
    and all flesh will bless the name of his holiness.

22. Psalm 145 is an 'alphabetic acrostic'. The successive verses take in turn the letters of the Hebrew alphabet. The letter *nun* is absent. Most would say that it has been lost in transmission and must be supplied from available sources (see NIV, ESV). It is equally possible to substantiate from the Psalms that there was a distinct literary form which we may call 'the broken acrostic', in which, for whatever reason, the poet felt that completeness could not or should not be attempted. One can well imagine David in Psalm 145 concluding that the praises of God are illimitable, running beyond human scope to itemize. If ever a psalm can be called an 'outpouring' it is Psalm 145, a river in spate of the attributes of Yahweh. It is best read like that. In a very general sense verses 1–2 are balanced by verse 21 – broad statements of the intent to praise; verse 3 (Yahweh's greatness) leads into verses 4-7 (Yahweh's mighty acts and greatness). Verses 8–9 lead into verses 10–13 ('works … works … mightinesses'); verses 14–16 prepare for verses 17–20 (the expectant eye of desire [verse 15], and the fulfilled desire of verse 19). But it is far best to let the psalm flow. Yahweh's glorious attributes are many and varied but they all belong together in the unity and harmony of the divine nature, and combine together in a picture that is glory indeed.

23 Lit. 'no search/exploration', but the thought is not that the search is impermissible but that it can never reach an end.

24 This is a literal translation, meaning 'the words (which recount) …', i.e. 'the record of/account of …' Compare Joshua 2:10–11.

25 This is an instance of the Hebrew idiom of the appositional adjective, which throws weighty emphasis on the adjective, more than simply saying 'your abundant goodness'. Compare Isaiah 53:11, which should read 'that righteous one, my servant', or Psalm 93:4, 'those mighty ones, the waves …'

26 Verses 6–7 well illustrate what is true of this whole psalm: how the divine attributes (here greatness, goodness and righteousness) all belong together and live together in harmony in the divine nature. 'Righteousness' is God's undeviating faithfulness to what he is and what he has said.

27 What Yahweh is in himself (8) is spelled out – what he is to all (9), to his people (10–11).

28 'Kingliness' is the idea in itself; 'realm' is the expression of kingliness in practice and 'place'.

29 'For all eternity' expresses the fact of duration; 'all generations' is continuance in human experience.

30 'Are hoping' is imperfect tense, the habitual, repeated attitude of expectation; 'give' is perfect tense, the unvaried, fixed response.

31 On 'eyes' and 'hand' see Psalm 123:2

32 *ratson* is mainly used of that which is pleasing, favourable, acceptable to God. The present case is imprecise but it seems best to follow the majority use. Otherwise as NKJV.

33 'All' in verse 17 picks up 'all' and 'everyone' in verses 14–16. The LORD's goodness is not an automatic benevolence to all alike. It is a righteous benevolence, i.e. exercised with moral discernment. The qualities Yahweh looks for are sketched in verses 18–20: sincerity of approach (18), reverence (19), love (20a). To the wicked he is hostile (20b).

34 The only place where the singular *chasiydh* is used of Yahweh. As a passive noun it strictly means 'beloved' (and as such is frequently used in the plural of Yahweh's 'beloved ones'). But, following the 'clue' that the plural also allows the meaning those who 'manifest love', the contextually required meaning must be allowed here.

35 *qarobh*, used of the Go'el or 'kinsman-redeemer', the one who, as next of kin, had the right to accept his kinsman's burdens, debts, needs as though they were his own and undertake to discharge them. e.g. Leviticus 25:25; Ruth 2:20; 3:12; Job 19:14. Of Yahweh's 'nearness', Deuteronomy 4:7; Psalm 34:18; Isaiah 50:8; 55:6.

36 'Keeps' is a participle, an unvarying attitude, state of affairs; 'destroys' is imperfect tense, signifying as and when needed.

Pause for Thought

There is a glorious individualism about Biblical religion. Think of 'my', nine times in the opening of Psalm 18, and its use of the first person pronoun, 'I love ... I take refuge ... I call'. Becoming and being a Christian is not just 'running with the pack', is it? Conversion is an individual experience. The great question used to be, 'Have you received the Lord Jesus Christ into your heart as your own personal Saviour?' You and him; your heart, his home. But there are other dimensions as well as the individual, and the Psalms rarely let us forget. Psalm 144 is a good example. The first eleven verses are wholly individual: there is personal trouble to be met, prayer to be made, deliverance sought, but verse 12 abruptly brings us into the bosom of the family, and verse 15 widens the scope to Yahweh's people and their corporate blessedness. We are saved into the whole company and family of the redeemed. We do not get converted and then set about thinking of church membership; as soon as we are saved we are family members. Indeed Ephesians 2:4–6 opens a thrilling vista: in the mind and estimation of God, salvation already sits us with Christ and his redeemed in heavenly places – a situation anticipated when Psalm 23:6 talks about living in Yahweh's house for ever. Psalm 145 takes us to the final step. It starts, 'I will extol' (145:1) and ends 'All flesh will bless (21). What a vision!

> From earth's wide bounds, from ocean's farthest coast,
> Through gates of pearl streams in the countless host,
> Singing to Father, Son, and Holy Ghost—

It is a visionary hope which will one day certainly be fulfilled; it is also a present task to which we are called to set our hands. We are born again into the church; we are called and commissioned to win the world. The balance between Old and New Testaments at this point is interesting – a balance, not an exclusive approach. In the New Testament, the summons is to go out (Matt. 28:19); in the Old Testament the task is to attract in, to be the magnetic people of Deuteronomy 4:5–8. If your church and mine is not worth belonging to why should anyone want to join?

Day 73 Read Psalms 146–150[1]

Psalm 146.
Merited Praise

A.1. Life-long praise

1. Praise Yah![2]
    My soul,[3] praise Yahweh!
2. Oh I will praise Yahweh while I live!
    I will make music to my God while I continue!

B.1. Why not man?

3. Do not trust in nobles,[4]
    in a son of man,
    who has no salvation.
4. His spirit goes out,
    he returns to his ground.[5]
    In that day his thoughts[6] have perished.

B.2. Why Yahweh?

5. Blessed is he whose help[7] is the transcendent God of
    Jacob.[8]
    Whose hope[9] is on Yahweh his God.
6. Making heaven and earth, the sea,
    and everything in them;
    who keeps[10] truth for ever,
7. acting with judgment[11] for the oppressed,
    giving bread to the hungry:
    Yahweh[12] loosing the bound.
8. Yahweh opens the eyes of the blind;
    Yahweh lifts up those who are bowed down;
    Yahweh loves the righteous;

1   Psalms 146–150 are a sustained
    'Hallelujah' – no intercession, no cry
    for help in time of trouble, no personal
    needs, no historical conundrums as
    to time or place. A sustained paean of
    praise, starting with 'my soul' (146:1)
    and ending with 'everything' (150:6),
    five unattributed psalms revelling in
    the praiseworthiness of the LORD God
    Almighty.

2   This call to praise has become familiar
    in English as 'Hallelu-yah' – imperative
    (*piel*) plus the abbreviated 'Yah', a
    term of endearment – throughout this
    group of psalms (146:1, 10; 147:1, 20;
    148:1, 14; 149:1, 9; 150:1, 6). The
    abbreviation, 'Yah', comes thirty-seven
    times in Psalms, e.g. 68:4, 19; 118:14;
    compare Exodus 15:2; Isaiah 12:2.

3   The 'soul' (*nephesh*) is the inner
    reality that makes a person distinctive
    in individuality. The whole 'being'
    is caught up in praise. 'Live' is the
    concrete actuality of daily life: praise
    in every situation. 'Continue', praise
    covering a whole life-time.

4   A general term for the top echelons of
    society, political leaders, those socially
    prominent. However praiseworthy
    they may seem, what are they but
    'sons of mankind'? 'Son of', is the
    idiom describing the condition which
    defines a person. No speciality (3b), no
    capacity to effect permanent change
    (3bc), no continuance (4ab), no
    control of the future (4c).

5   Genesis 3:19.

6   If Jonah 1:6 defines the verb behind
    this noun, the reference is to kindly
    plans for the relief of others.

9. Yahweh keeps the refugees;
   orphan and widow he supports;[13]
   and the way of the wicked he contorts.

A.2. Endless praise

10. Yahweh will reign for ever;
    your God, Zion, for generation after generation.
    Praise Yah!

Psalm 147.
Jerusalem Praise[14]

Care[15]

1. Praise Yah!
   Because[16] it is good to make music to our God.
   Because he[17] is lovely, praise is beautiful.
2. He builds Jerusalem, does Yahweh!
   The dispersed ones[18] of Israel he gathers.
3. He it is who heals the broken-hearted,
   and bandages up their hurts;
4. he measures the number of the stars;[19]
   all of them he calls by names.[20]
5. Great is our Sovereign,
   and abundant in strength;
   to his discernment there is no number.
6. He maintains[21] the downtrodden, does Yahweh!
   He brings down the wicked to the ground.

Productivity[22]

7. Sing to Yahweh with thanksgiving;
   make music to our God on the harp.
8. It is he covers the heavens with clouds,[23]
   who sets up rain for the earth;
   who makes grass grow on the mountains;
9. he gives to the beasts their bread,
   to the ravens[24] that keep crying out.

7 The noun 'help' here is expressed by the idiom known as 'beth essentiae', a specially emphatic way of implying 'every help that could possibly be needed'.

8 If God in his transcendent power and glory helped such as Jacob, then kindly help to the needy must surely be part of his definition, part of what he is.

9 All the Hebrew words for 'hope' are synonymous (here *shebber*) – bringing together expectation, patience and certainty.

10 In verses 6–9a there are nine participles (an unvarying state of affairs; this is how things are). Only 'keeps' (6c) is prefaced by the definite article ('who'), indicating that Yahweh's faithfulness to his truth (his revealed truth, his personal reliability, the certainty of his promises) is something deserving special emphasis.

11 i.e. making those authoritative decisions which put everything to rights.

12 The five-fold 'Yahweh' (7c–9a) could well be a 'credal hymn' sewn into the flow of the Psalm, preceded by three participles, followed by three imperfect tenses. Note the way it blends Yahweh's judgment and righteousness with his acts of mercy.

13 'Supports … contorts' are imperfect tense; what Yahweh customarily does as and when required. 'Supports' is a slightly conjectural translation.

14 Psalm 147 falls into three sections, marked out by the three calls to praise (1, 7, 12). Each section introduces some aspect of God the Creator, and shows how this works out in the way he deals with his people. Psalm 147 is more deliberately Jerusalem-centred than any other psalm in this group (2–3, 12–13).

10. It is not in the sheer strength[25] of a horse that he delights,[26]
    nor in a person's legs does he take pleasure.
11. Yahweh takes real[27] pleasure in those who fear him,
    those who wait in hope[28] for his committed love.

Transformation[29]

12. Acclaim Yahweh, Jerusalem!
    Praise your God, Zion!
13. Because he has strengthened the bars of your gates;
    he has blessed your sons within you.
14. It is he who makes your border[30] peace;[31]
    with the richest[32] of wheat keeps satisfying you.
15. It is he who sends his word to the earth;[33]
    at top speed his word runs.
16. It is he who gives snow like wool;
    hoar frost like ashes he scatters.
17. He throws out his ice like morsels;[34]
    before his cold who can stand?
18. He sends his word and melts them:
    he makes his wind blow;[35]
    waters trickle.
19. He declares his word[36] to Jacob,
    his statutes[37] and his judgments[38] to Israel.
20. He has not done so to any nation –
    as for his judgments, they do not know them!
    Praise Yah![39]

Psalm 148.
'Heaven and earth with
loud hosanna ...'[40]

Heavenly praise

1. Praise Yah!
   Praise Yahweh from the heavens![41]
   Praise him in the heights!

15 The Creator exercises his mighty power in detailed care of the individual items of his creation. He knows and oversees each star. Likewise he knows how his people are placed (2), is tender to the needy (3) and exercises detailed moral discrimination (6).

16 Or 'How!' – if we treat 'Praise Yah!' as a free-standing call to praise.

17 Or 'it'; or, 'How beautiful to offer fitting praise!'

18 This reference cannot be used to date the psalm. There must have been very few occasions during the monarchic period when there were not some Jerusalemites forcibly taken from their homes.

19 This detailed knowledge and direction of the creation first of all embroiders the thought (3) of detailed awareness of the state and ills of his people, and then, secondly, prepares for the discerning moral awareness of verse 6.

20 Meaning either he gives them their names, or he calls them to take up the position he has assigned to them (or both). Compare Isaiah 40:26–27. 'Numbering' suggests that each is important as part of the whole; 'naming' is direct knowledge of each individual as a distinct individual.

21 Or restores.

22 The particular aspect of the Creator's work for his creation is the gift of fertilising rain, making the earth productive and therefore able to sustain its creatures.

23 He determines climatic conditions.

24 Lit. 'to the sons of the raven': either 'young ravens' or 'those who are ravens'.

2. Praise him all his angels!
   Praise him all his host![42]
3. Praise him, sun and moon!
   Praise him, all stars of light!
4. Praise him, heavens of heavens,[43]
   and waters which are above the heavens![44]
5. Let them praise Yahweh's name,

(Originating)
   because it is he who commanded,
   and they were created.

(Maintaining)
6. And he made them stand for ever and ever –
   a statute he gave and it will not pass away.[45]

Earthly praise

7. Praise Yahweh from the earth!

(Mythological 'forces')
   Sea monsters[46] and all ocean depths![47]

(Natural 'forces')
8. Fire and hail, snow and smoke,
   tempestuous wind doing his word!

(The natural world, inanimate and growing)
9. Mountains and all hills,
   fruit trees and all cedars,

(Life on earth)
10. living things – all cattle,
    reptiles and winged birds,[48]
11. kings of the earth[49] and all states,
    princes and all judges of the earth,
12. young men and girls[50] too,
    old men along with youths.

25 *gebhurah*, used, e.g. of the trained 'prowess' of a warrior. Are we possibly to understand 'horse' as the cavalry division of an armed force and 'legs' as indicating the infantry? That is not what excites divine admiration. Luke 16:15b.

26 Turning from the animal creation to people, the psalm guards against possible misapplication. Yahweh adjusts the climate and earth's productivity to the production of healthy animal life. What then does he desire from his people? Not physical fitness (10) but reverence and trust (11).

27 'Real' is my addition. The verb 'take pleasure' is given the emphatic position in this line.

28 Another of Hebrew's verbs of 'hope'; trustful, patient certainty that Yahweh will act.

29 The creational aspect of this third section is that Yahweh rules creation by his word, and in particular his word is a transforming agent: think how a frozen landscape (16–17) can quickly thaw (18). It is all due to Yahweh's directive, effective word. The application of this truth is left open. How are his people to explain an experience of security, peace and plenty (13–14)? What transformed people should we be since we are the only ones who possess his word (19–20). The word of God is our distinctiveness.

30 Or 'your territory', the area enclosed within a 'border'.

31 Or 'he makes peace within your territory'. But I prefer to treat 'border' and 'peace' as nouns in apposition: such a peace that you would think Peace itself was standing at guard.

32 Lit. 'the fat of wheat'.

33 Isaiah 55:10–11.

13. Let them praise Yahweh's name,

(Uniquely exalted Yahweh)

>   because only[51] his name is lifted up to the highest,
>   his splendour above earth and heaven.

(Uniquely exalted people)

14. And he has exalted the horn of his people,[52]
>   the praise proper for all his[53] beloved ones,
>   for the sons of Israel,
>   the people near him.
>   Praise Yah!

Psalm 149.
Pillows and Swords[54]

Prologue: the new song of the beloved ones

1. Praise Yah!
>   Sing to Yahweh a new song,
>   his praise in the assembly of his beloved ones![55]

Joy is a God of salvation[56]

2. Let Israel praise his Maker![57]
>   Let the sons of Zion exult in their King!
3. Let them praise his name in dance!
>   With timbrel and lyre let them make music to him!
4. For Yahweh accepts his people with favour,
>   he beatifies the downtrodden with salvation.[58]

Joy in world-dominion

5. Let the beloved ones celebrate in glory;
>   let them shout aloud on their beds[59] –
6. the extolling of the transcendent God in their throat,[60]
>   and a totally effective[61] sword in their hand,[62]

34 Presumably a reference to hail – ice broken into small pieces like crumbled bread.

35 Compare Isaiah 40:7 where the divine outbreathing brings death. The wind/Spirit of God governs all aspects and stages of life.

36 Psalm 119:9.

37 Psalm 119:5.

38 Psalm 119:7.

39 Not – of course – praise him because they do not know, but because we do! It is our distinctiveness, privilege and honour.

40 '… with loud hosanna/Worship You the Lamb Who died …', Bourne's great hymn 'Lord, enthroned in heavenly splendour'. Not that Psalm 148 is directed openly to the Lamb of God, but it surely anticipates the worship indicated in Philippians 2:9–11.

41 The order of praise in verses 1–6 is downward; in verses 7–14 upward.

42 Parallelism suggests that the 'host' here is the angels (compare 1 Kings 22:19), not the starry host (compare Deuteronomy 4:19).

43 Compare Deuteronomy 10:14; 1 Kings 8:27; Nehemiah 9:6; Psalm 68:33. Just as 'holy of holies' means 'holiest of all/supremely holy', 'heavens of heavens' means 'the very heaven itself'.

44 The sphere of the rain clouds.

45 Or 'and none can transgress it'. This is more suited to the use of the verb 'to stand'.

46 Compare Genesis 1:21; Exodus 7:9, 10, 12; Job 7:12; Isaiah 27:1.

7. to exact vengeance[63] on the nations,
   reproof on states,[64]
8. to bind their kings with chains,
   and their eminent ones with iron fetters,
9. to perform on them the judgment written.[65]

The importance of the beloved ones

This[66] is the importance belonging to all his beloved ones.
Praise Yah!

Psalm 150.
All Praise

Praise commensurate with God himself

1. Praise Yah!
   Praise the transcendent God in his holiness![67]
   Praise him in the expanse[68] of his might!
2. Praise him in his mightinesses![69]
   Praise him according to the abundance of his greatness!

Praise commensurate with all humankind

3. Praise him with the blast of the trumpet!
   Praise him with lyre and harp!
4. Praise him with timbrel and dance!
   Praise him with strings and flutes!
5. Praise him with clear-sounding[70] cymbals!
   Praise him with commanding[71] cymbals!
6. Everything that has breath, let it praise Yah!
   Praise Yah!

47 In mythology the depths were the home of the monstrous Tiamat, the restless seas typifying ceaseless hostility to the creator god. The psalm includes 'them' as part of the earthly creation!

48 Just as mute things (mountains) 'praise Yahweh' by being what they are, occupying the place in creation that they do – his subjects, where he has put them – so animals, wild and domestic.

49 Humanity is categorized by status, function, sex and age.

50 The word is *bethulah* – for which the claim is made in the study of Isaiah 7:14 that it is Hebrew's technical term for *virgo intacta*. Its use as parallel with 'young men' (*bachuriym*) is part of the evidence that it means 'girls' – and we have no ground for claims that they are unmarried than for claiming that the young men were bachelors.

51 The word 'all' has come eight times in the foregoing list. Against this background the word 'only' has peculiar force.

52 With 'people … beloved ones … near him' we have concentric circles of increasing nearness. His people are the objects of his choice; his beloved are the objects of his love and grace; his nearness belongs to his next-of-kin (compare Leviticus 21:2–3; 25:25; Ruth 2:20; 3:12; also Deuteronomy 4:17; Isaiah 50:8).

53 See verse 2. Only the first and last items in the list are described specifically as 'his'.

54 Psalm 149 completes what is omitted in Psalm 148. There the whole earth was called to praise Yahweh – but why? Why should all the earth acknowledge the God of one people? Psalm 149 replies, poetically, because Israel has been given the responsibility of bringing all the nations under Yahweh's sway and into the blessings Israel enjoys. The psalm does this by using the metaphor of conquest, i.e. using the imagery that lay closest to hand. Earthly kingdoms extended their sway by conquering. The reality behind this picture (compare Isaiah 45:14–25; 60:1–22) is that to come to Israel's God the nations must come to Israel, forswearing their own allegiances and giving their allegiance to Israel and Yahweh. It is in this sense that the New Testament adopts military images (Ephesians 6:10–17; Revelation 1:16; etc.). The otherwise curious linking of pillow and sword (5–6) makes clear that the military language is consciously metaphorical.

55 Three titles: 'loved … Israel … Zion …'. Our standing in the heart of God, the work of God in choice, and care, and the constitution of life under the promises made to David.

56 In turn the God who is to be praised (2); the vehicles of praise (3); the reasons for praise (4).

57 Compare Psalm 95:6; 100:3; Isaiah 44:2 – the acts of God making Israel special.

58 'Salvation' is the opposite of adversity, divine and human.

59 The disparity between 'bed' and 'sword' is intentional, to indicate that it is the motif of warfare and not the actuality that is intended. Zion did not pursue a policy of conquest after the time of David. Passages like Isaiah 9:8; 11:16 show that the motif of warfare was part of Israel's messianic stock in trade. Compare Psalm 110.

60 Standing for 'voice' as in Isaiah 58:1.

61 A sword 'of multiple mouths'. The word *piypiyoth* found only in Isaiah 41:15, where it refers to a multiplicity of sharp edges. Compare 'the mouth of the sword' e.g. Genesis 34:26, and the sword 'devouring', Isaiah 1:20. The thought is not 'two-edged' but 'devouring', 'deadly'.

62 Belonging to Yahweh as his beloved ones hold together the restfulness of praise (on their beds), and the warfare of praise (sword), elaborated in verses 7–9a: vengeance (7), dominion (8) and obedience to what is written (9a).

63 'Vengeance' points to the adverse side of 'judgment'. There are enemies to be dealt with. The willing subordination of the nations (Isaiah 45:14ff.; 49:17, 23; 60 – compare Psalm 2; Isaiah 11) for the messianic work of 'subjugation'.

64 *le'ummiym* means 'peoples'. 'States', organized groupings, is the best I can think of to give the word a separate translation. Compare Psalms 44:14; 57:9; 108:3.

65 Isaiah 4:3. This is the Lord's Book of Destiny.

66 Not the exacting of vengeance but the performance of what is written, fidelity to God's written word.

67 'His holiness', *qodsho*, could mean his 'sanctuary' (earthly or heavenly), where he dwells in holiness. I prefer to think of the items listed here in descending order: God in his essential nature (holiness), in his heavenly, created realm, in the earthly scene of his mighty acts, and, as a summary statement, 'his abundant greatness'.

68 The word (*raqiy'a*) means something outspread, an expanse; it is used seventeen times in the Old Testament, of which nine are in Genesis 1. The space spread out above the earth. In Ezekiel 1:22–26, the 'platform' above the head of the cherubim, above which was the throne of God. Here the heavenly God, transcendent over all the earth.

69 *Gebhurah* is chiefly military strength, prowess. It speaks therefore of conquering might, God victorious.

70 Lit. 'cymbals of hearing', making themselves heard. Possibly 'resounding cymbals'.

71 'Cymbals of loud shout/warcry', unmistakeable, incapable of being ignored.

Pause for Thought

It is easy – and right – to get caught up in the excitement of Psalm 150 as its rises to its climax with the words, 'Everything that has breath, let it praise Yah!', and to let the excitement cloud the fact that the words express an unrealized vision, a 'would that it were so!' To realize this is more than a damper on the glory which we feel ought to mark the end of this glorious book of the Bible. A wish, at present a non-event on a large scale. Also a solemn question: what do you propose to do about it? Psalm 106, where the paean of praise starts, is addressed to 'my soul'. A call to personal praise. Right, we can do something about that, making sure Yahweh ever receives from me the praise due to his name. Psalm 107 addresses Jerusalem, a call to the church to praise, and we can do something about that, making sure our gatherings cater fervently for the corporate duty of praise. Psalm 148 deals with cosmic praise and looks after itself.

> The voice of prayer is never silent
> Nor dies the strain of praise away.

Psalm 149 presents us with the crunch moment – the psalm of evangelistic praise. We are pretty good, are we not, about 'shouting aloud in our beds' (149:5) – enjoying to the full the restful security of our salvation with all its accompanying joy? But, so to speak, all too often we have left the sword – the evangelistic thrust of the gospel – downstairs, still in its scabbard. We have every right to lay our heads on this wonderful pillow. God forbid that we should ever cease to nourish and refresh ourselves with all our delights and privileges in Jesus, but Psalm 149:6 sees the two as bound together, the head and the hand, the mouth of praise and the well-sharpened sword – 'the sword of the Spirit, which is the word of God' (Eph. 6:17, ESV). That's it, then. Praise without the sword is spiritual self-indulgence; the sword without praise is joyless duty. Together, they are the balanced Christian life. They are also the way forward to the day when everything that has breath will praise Yahweh.

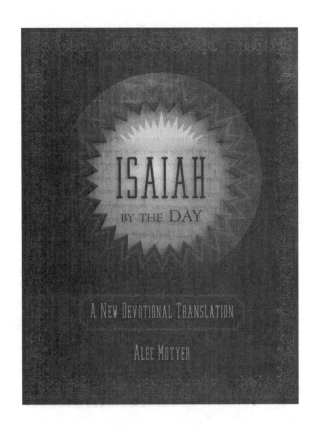

Isaiah by the Day
A New Devotional Translation
by Alec Motyer

These daily devotionals are birthed from a lifetime of study on the prophecy of Isaiah. Day by day you will be provided with passages from Isaiah and an opportunity to explore the passage further. Take time to acquaint yourself with these passages from God's Word and treasure them in your heart.

ISBN: 978-1-84550-654-4

Christian Focus Publications

Our mission statement –

STAYING FAITHFUL
In dependence upon God we seek to impact the world through literature faithful to His infallible Word, the Bible. Our aim is to ensure that the Lord Jesus Christ is presented as the only hope to obtain forgiveness of sin, live a useful life and look forward to heaven with Him.

Our Books are published in four imprints:

CHRISTIAN FOCUS

popular works including biographies, commentaries, basic doctrine and Christian living.

CHRISTIAN HERITAGE

books representing some of the best material from the rich heritage of the church.

MENTOR

books written at a level suitable for Bible College and seminary students, pastors, and other serious readers. The imprint includes commentaries, doctrinal studies, examination of current issues and church history.

CF4•K

children's books for quality Bible teaching and for all age groups: Sunday school curriculum, puzzle and activity books; personal and family devotional titles, biographies and inspirational stories – because you are never too young to know Jesus!

Christian Focus Publications Ltd,
Geanies House, Fearn, Ross-shire,
IV20 1TW, Scotland, United Kingdom.
www.christianfocus.com